# PITTSBURGH THEOLOGICAL MONOGRAPH SERIES

*General Editor*
DIKRAN Y. HADIDIAN

D1287449

34

# SCRIPTURE IN CONTEXT
Essays on the Comparative Method

# OTHER BOOKS IN THIS SERIES . . .

*Rhetorical Criticism; essays in honor of James Muilenburg.* Edited by Jared J. Jackson and Martin Kessler.

*Structural Analysis and Biblical Exegesis;* interpretational essays by R. Barthes, F. Bovan, F. J. Leenhardt, R. Martin-Achard, J. Starobinski. Translated by Alfred M. Johnson, Jr.

*The Tale of the Tell;* archaeological studies by Paul W. Lapp, Edited by Nancy Lapp.

*When Man Becomes God;* humanism and hybris in the Old Testament. By Donald E. Gowan.

*Informal Groups in the Church;* papers of the Second Cerdic Colloquium, Strasbourg. May 13-15, 1971. Edited by René Metz and Jean Schlick. Translated by Matthew J. O'Connell.

*Semiology and Parables; exploration of the possibilities offered by structuralism for exegesis.* Papers of the Vanderbilt University conference, May 15-17, 1975. Edited by Daniel Patte.

*The New Testament and Structuralism;* a collection of essays edited and translated by Alfred M. Johnson, Jr.

*Bridge Between the Testaments; reappraisal of Judaism from Exile to the birth of Christianity.* By Donald E. Gowan.

*Scripture in History and Theology; essays in honor of J. Coert Rylaarsdam.* Edited by Arthur L. Merrill and Thomas W. Overholt.

*The Hellenistic Mystery-Religions* by Richard Reitzenstein. Translated by John E. Steely.

*Jesus Christ and the Faith; a collection of studies by Philippe H. Menoud, 1905-1973.* With an appreciation of Jean-Louis Leuba and a preface by Oscar Cullmann. Translated by Eunice M. Paul.

*Exegesis; problems of method and exercises in reading (Genesis 22 and Luke 15).* Studies published under the direction of François Bovon and Grégoire Rouiller. Translated by Donald G. Miller.

*Signs and Parables: Semiotics and Gospels Text,* with a study by Jacques Geninasca and postface by Algirdas Julien Greimas. Translated by Gary Phillips.

*Candid Questions Concerning Gospel Form Criticism; a methodological sketch of fundamental problematics of form and redaction criticism.* By Erhardt Güttgemanns. Translated by William G. Doty.

*From Faith to Faith; essays in honor of Donald G. Miller on his seventieth birthday.* Edited by Dikran Y. Hadidian.

# SCRIPTURE IN CONTEXT

## *Essays on the Comparative Method*

*Edited by*

Carl D. Evans
William W. Hallo
John B. White

The Pickwick Press
Pittsburgh, Pennsylvania

1980

**Library of Congress Cataloging in Publication Data**

Main entry under title:

Scripture in context.

(Pittsburgh theological monograph series ; no. 34)
Originally presented at a seminar held at Yale
University, summer of 1978.
Contains bibliographical references and indexes.
CONTENTS: Hallo, W. W.  Biblical history in its
Near Eastern setting.--Millar, W. R.  Oral poetry and
Dumuzi's Dream.--Andreasen, N. E. A.  Genesis 14 in its
Near Eastern contex. [etc.]
    1.  Bible. O.T.--Criticism, interpretation, etc.
--Addresses, essays, lectures.  2.  Bible.  O.T.--
Comparative studies--Addresses, essays, lectures.

**Library of Congress Cataloging in Publication Data**

3.  Near East--Religion--Addresses, essays, lectures.
I.  Evans, Carl D.  II.  Hallo, William W.  III.  White,
John Bradley, 1947-    IV.  Series.
BS1171.2.S35        221.6        80-10211
ISBN 0-915138-43-3   .

# TABLE OF CONTENTS

v

PREFACE

This collection of essays had its origins in a Summer Seminar sponsored by the National Endowment for the Humanities during the summer of 1978. The seminar was conducted at Yale University under the direction of William W. Hallo who had selected the topic "Biblical History in its Near Eastern Setting" for the summer's study.

The purpose of the seminar was to study the history of Israel in the light of literary traditions preserved in the Bible and in ancient Near Eastern sources. The structure of the seminar was provided by the major phases of Near Eastern history and Israel's place in each phase (see Hallo's chart on the comparative chronology of the ancient Near East, below, p. 13). The director's presentations covered each of the phases in chronological order, focusing on the biblical and comparative literary reflexes for each phase. Special care was taken to emphasize the validity of the literary traditions in which each of the major cultures rendered account to itself of the past. The methodological issues related to this approach to historiography are discussed in Hallo's introductory essay, written expressly for this volume.

The other essays were originally read as seminar papers. The topics they address were selected to fill some of the gaps left by the director's choice of topics for his own presentations. These essays reflect, in varying degrees, the director's general concerns and interests for the seminar. Collectively they provide comprehensive summaries of recent research on many topics of interest to comparativists and many of them provide new impulses in biblical study as well.

The unity of the volume centers around the comparative or contextual approach to the study of biblical history, culture, or literature. Such a method attempts to analyze the Bible against the background of the larger Near Eastern scene. Yet, the volume also reflects the diversity of each participant's own training and area of expertise. The volume, therefore, is by no means inclusive of all issues or even all the important interfaces between biblical literature and its Near

Eastern setting. It is hoped, however, that these essays
will serve to illustrate a method which is helpful in illu-
minating the Bible's contextual sphere.

On behalf of the entire seminar, the editors offer
special thanks to the National Endowment for the Humanities
for the grant and stipends that funded both the seminar's
work at Yale and the subsequent activity in preparing this
volume for publication. Additional expressions of gratitude
are owed to the following: Dikran Y. Hadidian, general editor of this series, and Pickwick Press for their interest
and helpfulness in preparing the manuscript for publication;
Diane Pendleton and Ulla Kasten at Yale for their cordial
and efficient administrative assistance; and Karen Starr
and Mitchell Ormond, students at the University of South
Carolina, who assisted in the preparation of the indexes.

                                        CDE
                                        WWH
                                        JBW

# CONTRIBUTORS

Niels-Erik A. Andreasen, Ph.D. (Vanderbilt University),
Associate Professor of Old Testament, Loma Linda University, Riverside, California

Jean M. Davison, Ph.D. (Yale University), Roberts Professor
of Classical Languages and Literature, University of
Vermont, Burlington, Vermont

Carl D. Evans, Ph.D. (University of Chicago), Associate
Professor of Religious Studies, University of South
Carolina, Columbia, South Carolina

William W. Hallo, Ph.D. (University of Chicago), Laffan
Professor of Assyriology and Babylonian Literature,
Curator of the Babylonian Collection, and Chairman
of the Department of Near Eastern Languages and Literatures, Yale University, New Haven, Connecticut

Bruce William Jones, Ph.D. (Graduate Theological Union),
Associate Professor of Religion, California State
College, Bakersfield, California

William R. Millar, Ph.D. (Harvard University), Associate
Professor of Religion, Colby-Sawyer College, New
London, New Hampshire

Max E. Polley, Ph.D. (Duke University), Professor of Religion, Davidson College, Davidson, North Carolina

George E. Saint-Laurent, S.T.D. (Catholic University of
America), Lecturer in Religious Studies, California
State University, Fullerton, California

Mary Savage, Ph.D. (Catholic University of America), Associate Professor of English, Albertus Magnus College,
New Haven, Connecticut

John J. Schmitt, Ph.D. (University of Chicago), Chairman of the Department of Theology and Assistant Professor of Theology, St. Bonaventure University, St. Bonaventure, New York

Carl Schultz, Ph.D. (Brandeis University), Chairman of the Division of Religion and Philosophy and Professor of Religion, Houghton College, Houghton, New York

J. Douglas Thomas, Ph.D. (Baylor University), Assistant Professor of Religion, Missouri Baptist College, Creve Coeur, Missouri

John B. White, Ph.D. (Duke University), Assistant Professor of Philosophy and Religion, De Pauw University, Greencastle, Indiana

# ABBREVIATIONS

| | |
|---|---|
| AB | Anchor Bible |
| *AcOr* | *Acta Orientalia* |
| *AfO* | *Archiv für Orientforschung* |
| *AJA* | *American Journal of Archaeology* |
| *AJSL* | *American Journal of Semitic Languages and Literature* |
| *ANEH* | W. W. Hallo and W. K. Simpson, *The Ancient Near East: A History* |
| *ANET* | J. B. Pritchard (ed.), *Ancient Near Eastern Texts* |
| AnOr | Analecta Orientalia |
| AOAT | Alter Orient und Altes Testament |
| ARM | Archives Royales de Mari |
| *AUSS* | *Andrews University Seminary Studies* |
| *BA* | *Biblical Archaeologist* |
| *BAR* | *Biblical Archaeologist Reader* |
| *BASOR* | *Bulletin of the American Schools of Oriental Research* |
| *Bib* | *Biblica* |
| *BJRL* | *Bulletin of the John Rylands University Library of Manchester* |
| BKAT | Biblischer Kommentar: Altes Testament |

| | |
|---|---|
| *BO* | *Bibliotheca Orientalis* |
| BWANT | Beiträge zur Wissenschaft vom Alten und Neuen Testament |
| BZAW | Beihefte zur *ZAW* |
| *CAD* | *The Assyrian Dictionary of the Oriental Institute of the University of Chicago* |
| *CAH* | *Cambridge Ancient History* |
| *CBQ* | *Catholic Biblical Quarterly* |
| *CRRAI* | *Compte Rendu de la ... Recontre Assyriologique Internationale* |
| EA | Tell El-Amarna Letters |
| *HR* | *History of Religions* |
| HSS | Harvard Semitic Series |
| *HTR* | *Harvard Theological Review* |
| *HUCA* | *Hebrew Union College Annual* |
| *IDB* | G. A. Buttrick (ed.), *Interpreter's Dictionary of the Bible* |
| *IDBSup* | Supplementary volume to *IDB* |
| *IEJ* | *Israel Exploration Journal* |
| *Int* | *Interpretation* |
| *JANES* | *Journal of the Ancient Near Eastern Society of Columbia University* |
| *JAOS* | *Journal of the American Oriental Society* |
| *JBL* | *Journal of Biblical Literature* |
| *JCS* | *Journal of Cuneiform Studies* |
| *JNES* | *Journal of Near Eastern Studies* |
| *JPOS* | *Journal of the Palestine Oriental Society* |

| | |
|---|---|
| JQR | *Jewish Quarterly Review* |
| JSJ | *Journal for the Study of Judaism in the Persian, Hellenistic and Roman Period* |
| JSOR | *Journal of the Society of Oriental Research* |
| JSS | *Journal of Semitic Studies* |
| JTC | *Journal for Theology and the Church* |
| JTS | *Journal of Theological Studies* |
| MVAG | Mitteilungen der vorderasiatisch-ägyptischen Gesellschaft |
| Or | *Orientalia* |
| OTS | *Oudtestamentische Studiën* |
| PEQ | *Palestine Exploration Quarterly* |
| RA | *Revue d'assyriologie et d'archéologie orientale* |
| RB | *Revue biblique* |
| RevExp | *Review and Expositor* |
| RSO | *Revista degli studi orientali* |
| SBLMS | SBL Monograph Series |
| SBT | Studies in Biblical Theology |
| SJT | *Scottish Journal of Theology* |
| SR | *Studies in Religion/Sciences religieuses* |
| ST | *Studia theologica* |
| TDNT | G. Kittel and G. Friedrich (eds.), *Theological Dictionary of the New Testament* |
| TLZ | *Theologische Literaturzeitung* |
| UF | *Ugaritische Forschungen* |
| VT | *Vetus Testamentum* |

| | |
|---|---|
| VTSup | Vetus Testamentum, Supplements |
| ZA | *Zeitschrift für Assyriologie* |
| ZAW | *Zeitschrift für die alttestamentliche Wissenschaft* |
| ZDPV | *Zeitschrift des deutschen Palästina-Vereins* |
| ZRGG | *Zeitschrift für Religions- und Geistesgeschichte* |

# BIBLICAL HISTORY IN ITS NEAR EASTERN SETTING:
## THE CONTEXTUAL APPROACH*

William W. Hallo
Yale University

I

"The Reverend Ebenezer Brewer, in his *Dictionary of Phrase and Fable*, tells of a little old seventeenth-century lady who used to say to her pastor that she 'had found great support in that blessed word Mesopotamia.'" True or not, this tale reads well. It serves as title and peroration of a speech originally delivered in 1956 by Henry Allen Moe, and published in a posthumous collection of essays by the late president of the Guggenheim Memorial foundation.[1]

The acoustical powers of "that blessed word" continued undiminished into the next century, to judge by a brief bio-graphical sketch of the eighteenth century evangelist George Whitefield, which avers: "His voice had the range of an organ and with it he could reduce grown men to tears by the mere pronunciation of the word 'Mesopotamia.'"[2]

Presumably the word finally lost some of its magic in the nineteenth century with the successful decipherment of the cuneiform scripts, first of Persia and then of Mesopotamia itself. Now fantastic and baseless speculations about the Mesopotamian past gradually gave way to more sober assessments grounded in the cuneiform texts. Even earlier, the decipher-ment of Egyptian hieroglyphics had begun to discredit the naive and often mystical interpretations long attached to the surviving monuments in the valley of the Nile. Subsequent

---

*This paper was first presented to the Institute for Advanced Studies, Hebrew University, Jerusalem, May 10, 1979. I am in-debted to my colleagues at the Institute and to other scholars in Israel for many fruitful discussions.

discoveries have added many more scripts, languages and bodies of texts to the arsenal of the ancient historian, and the pace of discovery shows no sign of abating.[3]

The discipline of biblical history has inevitably responded to these intellectual developments. True, the mere mention of Mesopotamia no longer reverberates with the elusive echo of an enigma. But it, and indeed the entire ancient Near East, is still a concept to conjure with--only now in a scholarly sense. The day is long past when the history of Israel could be written solely or largely on the basis of the biblical text; now one must take into account the evidence, particularly the written documentary testimony, of the civilizations rediscovered throughout the surrounding Near East.

On this dictum there is today fairly universal scholarly agreement. But when it comes to applying the dictum, the consensus quickly breaks down. The remarks that follow will therefore address some of the considerations involved in the attempt to study biblical history in its ancient Near Eastern matrix, to see "scripture in context."[4] The intention is not to repudiate the comparative approach, but to define it, refine it and broaden it, notably by wedding it to the "contrastive approach."[5] The resulting blend can perhaps avoid both of these somewhat controversial labels and qualify instead as a "contextual approach." The allusion here is not to the "sociological context ... visible behind the [literary] material" as in Hanson's "contextual-typological" method,[6] but rather to the literary context itself, broadly interpreted as including the entire Near Eastern literary milieu to the extent that it can be argued to have had any conceivable impact on the biblical formulation.

## II

"The Use of Ancient Near Eastern Materials in the Study of Early Hebrew History" was the subject of a session of the Society of Biblical Literature some four years ago.[7] S. Dean McBride covered the question at length, and I agreed to respond to him.[8] Then as now, however, the topic hardly lent itself to true debate. This is clear if one changes just one word in the chosen title: let us suppose for a moment that the subject was "The Use of Ancient Near Eastern Materials in the Study of Early Mesopotamian History." Would anyone care to debate the validity, not to say the legitimacy, of such an enterprise? I heartily doubt it. Then why should the use of ancient Near Eastern materials still be a debatable enterprise in the study of early Hebrew (or I would say early Israelite) history? Why is it facing a frontal assault from such authorities as Morton Smith, John Van Seters, and Thomas L. Thompson? And why is it that after passing in quick review all the different narratives deriving Israel variously from Egypt, Sinai, Transjordan, Syria, Mesopotamia or Canaan, Thompson can conclude: "Of these narratives as well as all of the narratives of the pentateuch, the historical problem is not so much that they are historically unverifiable, and especially not that they are untrue historically, but that they are radically irrelevant as sources of Israel's early history"?[9]

This rather skeptical view of matters is not universally shared. Among biblical historians, for example, Abraham Malamat has been a conspicuous advocate of the judicious use of comparative data, notably from Mari, to illuminate the origins and formative stages of Israel--and vice versa.[10] On the Egyptological side, a rather ringing rebuttal to the views of Van Seters, Thompson and, for good measure, Donald B. Redford, has recently been offered by K. A. Kitchen[11] who had earlier expressed himself in sympathy with those who, like myself, "are sceptical of traditional literary-critical methods ... preferring objective comparative data to unverifiable hypotheses."[12]

As an Assyriologist, I indeed feel disposed to approach these questions from an admittedly comparativist position without, however, conceding that the critics are *not* comparativists. In fact, some of their strongest arguments are based on the comparison of biblical data with neo-Assyrian and neo-Babylonian or even with classical Greek and Roman sources. What they rule out is only the comparison with older Near Eastern materials. Therefore, let us avoid such labels as orthodox (or pseud-orthodox) and nihilist, comparativist and anti-comparativist, or Albrightian and Alt-Nothian.[13] If we must resort to labels at all, let it be the fairly innocuous maximalist and minimalist;[14] no doubt most of us can then happily place ourselves somewhere in the golden middle. And let us return for a moment to the relatively non-controversial ground of early Mesopotamian history.

The materials for that history obviously consist (apart from such relative constants as physical geography) of artifactual remains and textual discoveries. The latter, in turn, can best be divided into three broad categories, namely what I like to call monuments, archives and canons.[15] All of these

classes of evidence must be invoked in any historical reconstruction worthy of the name. If we had only canonical texts
such as the Sumerian King List, the epics, and the royal
hymns, our picture of Sumerian history would today be sadly
distorted. We would have little or no basis for establishing
a firm chronology, none at all for tracing the evolution of
social and economic institutions, and whole areas of the
Sumerian experience such as the rise and fall of Lagash or
Umma would be left largely out of account. How does this
compare with the biblical situation?

In textual terms, we deal here almost exclusively with
a canon in the sense in which that term is sometimes applied
on the cuneiform side, i.e., with the final literary formulation of a record which is itself later, sometimes later by
far, than the documents on which it may have been based, documents which in turn must often have been later than the events
which they presume to record. Generally these documents are
themselves held to have been literary in character; their reconstruction is the subject of the "documentary hypothesis"
which, as its very name implies, is doomed to remain hypothe-
tical--that is to say, beyond demonstrable proof.

On rare occasions, the "documents" may be hypothetically
described as monumental (e.g., the Psalm of Hezekiah)[16] or
archival (e.g., Numbers 7)[17] but the form in which they have
reached us is nevertheless canonical or literary. Of course,
archaeology supplies a second component here too: an occasional monument, inscribed as in the case of the bulla of
Berachyahu (=Baruch?) ben Neriyahu[18] or uninscribed as in the
case of the alleged Assyrian royal standard newly unearthed
at Tell-es-Shari'ah (ancient Ziqlag);[19] more rarely still, a
precious archival scrap like the "letter-prayer" from Meṣad
Hashavyahu,[20] or the ostraca from Samaria, Lachish and Arad.[21]
Such finds as these are universally admitted as relevant for
Israelite history, but only because they date from the Iron
Age. When it comes to "early Hebrew history," i.e., the
Bronze Age, the opinions diverge. To quote Noth: "The material remains of historical life, together with the innumerable
inscriptions (Schriftdenkmäler) recovered from the ancient
Near East, have created for the history of Israel such a lucid
background that our knowledge of Israel's history and its
integration into ancient Near Eastern history as a whole appears to be assured at least in its basic outlines. And this
is in fact the case for the later and latest history of Is-
rael--not, however, for the early history."[22]

It is only the maximalist position which holds that *all*
the monuments, archives and canons of the Bronze Age Near East

are potential building blocks in the reconstruction of early
Israelite history. In this respect, the maximalist position
is in agreement with the Bible itself which, in incorporating
so many ancient Near Eastern motifs, obviously regarded it as
legitimate to draw on all the available sources (whether written or oral). That in itself does not justify the position.
And indeed the minimalist would counter that, even when some
kind of correlation can be established between an ancient
Near Eastern source and the biblical appropriation of it,
what it amounts to is some kind of misappropriation. For him,
the history of Israel begins with the Conquest, the Iron Age,
if you like, with Pharaoh Merneptah ca. 1220 B.C.E.


III


        Between these extreme positions, where can the historian
of Egypt or Mesopotamia take his stand? Speaking as an Egyp-
tologist, Kitchen has stated "that principles found to be
valid in dealing with ancient Oriental history and literature
will in all likelihood prove to be directly applicable to Old
Testament history and literature and conversely, that methods
or principles which are demonstrably false when applied to
first-hand ancient Near Eastern data should not be imposed
upon Old Testament data either."[23] I myself phrased matters
from the Assyriologist's point of view thus: "We should neither exempt biblical literature from the standards applied to
other ancient Near Eastern literatures, nor subject it to
standards demanded nowhere else. On this basis, Israelite
traditions about its own Bronze Age, though these traditions
were written down in the Iron Age, have to be given as much
credence as Middle and neo-Assyrian notions about the Old
Assyrian past."[24]

        As much--and no more. For the very point of the analogy
is that many of these notions, as enshrined in canonical texts
like the Assyrian King List, must be sifted critically in the
light of the monuments, archives and older canons. When this
is done, it will be seen that Assyrian historiography provides
an instructive parallel to biblical historiography. In order
to stress the antiquity and continuity of Assyrian institutions, Assyrian king lists and royal inscriptions appropriated
the legendary past of the Sumerians as a common heritage;
viewed Sargonic overlords as predecessors; claimed ethnic af-
filiation to the Amorite tribes of all of Mesopotamia; raised
subservient governors to royal status; and incorporated into
Assyrian royal genealogies those foreign overlords whose memory they could not suppress.[25]

Egyptian historiography is said to have pursued directly opposite means, but to an essentially identical end. It illustrates the principle that the "collective historical memory of the nation (accepts) an acclimatized foreigner who adopts the culture of the natives and tries to become one of them (while) a foreign war-lord who reduces the country through war and rules it, not on the strength of traditional practice, but on the strength of his army, is never accepted as a native, but is forever after remembered as an alien."[26] In other words, interludes of subservience to foreign domination are not glossed over, but simply denied legitimacy except on native terms.

What these examples suggest is that historiography is a subjective enterprise in which each culture ultimately defines the ethnic parameters of its own past for itself. Or, as it has been said in a pregnant definition: "History is the intellectual form in which a civilization renders account to itself of its past."[27] I would like to put the emphasis in Huizinga's definition on the two words "to itself." I would, in fact, argue that *each* civilization or ethnic entity is entitled to render account of the past *to itself* by appropriating *to itself* that portion of the past which it chooses *for itself*. I would submit further that such appropriation can, by this very definition of history, never be misappropriation. A few examples may illustrate the point.

The Quranic view of the pre-Islamic past, for instance, includes both reasonably authentic memories of the Arabian peninsula in the early centuries of the Christian era, and thoroughly garbled "appropriations" of biblical traditions, both from the New Testament and from the Old, the latter often filtered through the aggadic versions preserved among the Jewish communities of Arabia. Both the pagan Arabian past and the Judaeo-Christian traditions are linked to the Islamic present by various means, including genealogies, and we are often in a position to evaluate these links. But we are not free to invalidate the claims based on them. Rather, we are bound to admit the reality of Islamic claims to kinship, in one form or another, with a variety of pre-Islamic ethnic entities as these claims are conceived and formulated within Islam.[28]

Again, the Roman view of the Roman past as formulated particularly under the Principate differs considerably from that of the modern historian. We would not regard the Aeneid as an unimpeachable source for the history of the Sea Peoples or of the colonization of Italy. Yet we have adopted one of its major tenets (which it shares with Livy and Roman historians generally), i.e., that the focus of Roman history is the

city of Rome and not, say, the province of Latium, the Latin-
speaking area, or the Italian peninsula.[29]  Indeed we speak
in terms of Roman history, not Latin or Italian history, when
we deal with the Western Mediterranean in classical times.
At least equal respect, then, should be accorded to Roman
claims for its Trojan ancestry, even if that does not imply
uncritical acceptance of Dido and every other episode preserved in this connection.[30]

To shift the analogy once more, American civilization can
choose (and usually does choose) to appropriate much of English
history or European history in pre-revolutionary or pre-colonial
times.  Black Americans may prefer to do likewise with African
history, while Native Americans can with equal justice relate
to the Western hemisphere in pre-Columbian times.  But by and
large, the "canonical" view of American history conceives of
the United States as a nation of immigrants from Europe, per-
petuating in cultural, legal and political institutions and
above all in language the heritage of Europe in general and of
England in particular.  And if the English tradition, including
that of America's English colonists, happened to regard itself
as indebted to classical and biblical models, then the American
tradition may claim the same derivation by right of inheritance.
Of course, we must draw the line somewhere:  the further notion
of the "British Israelites" that Britons are lineally descended
from one of the Ten Lost Tribes can be dismissed as a minority
view.[31]  But who is to deny those claims which rest on the collective judgment of the civilization as a whole?  And who is to
deny the validity, the legitimacy of the biblical claim to certain ancient Near Eastern traditions?[32]

In this light, the issue can no longer be phrased in terms
of "historicity."  The historicity of the Chaldeans, the Arame-
ans, the Habiru, the Amorites and (at least until recently)[33]
even the Sumerians is not in question, and every new piece of
evidence permits us to be more certain and more precise about
them.  And the biblical claim to some of the traditions of all
of these peoples is likewise not open to question on the factual
level--i.e., no one can deny that the biblical texts make the
claim.  Sometimes the claim is phrased in genealogical terms,
sometimes in geographical ones, sometimes simply in terms of
literary affinities as when Ezekiel invites his listeners to
consider Noah, Daniel and Job as three ancient worthies of
their own (Ezek 14:14, 20), though the first is clearly drawn
from Babylonian traditions and the second from "Canaanite"
ones.[34]  Nor are we, I submit, free to question the claim on
the level of its legitimacy, given Huizinga's definition of
history.

But once the claim is granted, the significance of the Bronze Age evidence assumes a new light, and can be assessed more dispassionately. We can then begin to argue, for example, that the primeval history of Genesis 1-11 was appropriated virtually in its entirety from external sources, or the casuistic legislation of Exodus and Deuteronomy selectively. We can ponder specific clues like the case of the goring ox which includes in the biblical formulation at least one law buried in Tell Harmal since Old Babylonian times;[35] or the possibility that the "Road to Emar" has "passed into the patriarchal narrative of the defeat of Amora."[36] And we may have to conclude that when the biblical authors appropriated Bronze Age sources for early Israelite history, they did so intelligently, purposefully and selectively. The surviving traditions were sifted and weighed. Their reflexes in biblical literature are neither free creations *de novo*, nor uncritical imitations of everything available.

The case for the use of ancient Near Eastern materials is thus the same whether we are studying early Hebrew history or early Mesopotamian or Egyptian history; it serves to tell us whether the form in which those civilizations rendered account of their past to themselves accords with the form in which we would do so for them. The seminar which generated the papers published in the present volume studied the history of Israel on the basis of these considerations, that is, in the light of literary traditions preserved in the Bible and in the ancient Near Eastern texts.[37] Defenders of the comparative approach were read and evaluated alongside its critics. Emphasis was put on the major phases of ancient Near Eastern history; on Israel's place in each phase; and on the validity of the literary traditions enshrining these phases in each of the major cultures. The seminar papers published herewith reflect some of these same concerns, and fill in a few of the numerous lacunae left by my own presentations. These ranged widely but selectively over three millenia of biblical history and its Near Eastern setting, and it would be futile to attempt to summarize them here. But it may be appropriate to consider the more general epistemological problems of the comparative approach, and the challenges raised against it.

IV

The challenges against the comparative approach to biblical literature in general, and to biblical historiography
in particular, have in recent years escalated to the level of
a frontal assault. A useful summary of the indictment has
just appeared from the pen of J. Alberto Soggin, and may serve
as point of departure for the discussion. Soggin entitles his
essay "The History of Ancient Israel: A Study in Some Questions of Method."[38] As the subtitle indicates, he is at pains
to find a proper methodology for the evaluation of biblical
historiography. His own prescription is to determine a "datum
point" for Israelite history, that is to say a *starting-point*,
or perhaps we should say a *turning-point* from legend to more
or less "objective" historiography. In early Mesopotamian
historiography, such a transition can be observed in the Sumerian King List at the point where impossibly long reigns give
way to more nearly plausible ones.[39] It would seem to have
an obvious parallel in Genesis where the life span progres-
sively diminishes from the incredible longevity of the ante-
diluvians to the standard or ideal figure of 110 or 120 years,
more or less, among the postdiluvians.[40] But Soggin does not
cite this parallel, which he would find irrelevant for his
purpose. For he considers the comparative approach altogether
inadequate from the point of view of methodology: it operates
with parallels that antedate his starting-point, and indeed
has hitherto neglected to determine a starting-point in the
first place. The only previous scholar who at least recognized the importance of such a determination is said to be
Noth, though even he was too generous in his evaluation of
early Israelite historiography when he began his history of
Israel with the Iron Age and the Conquest.[41]

Soggin himself lowers the starting-point to the reign of
David, or at the earliest Saul. It is far from clear what
motivates his choice. The apodictic statement is made that
"this new datum point has the advantage of offering a succession of events whose historicity is accepted beyond doubt,"[42]
and again: "With the foundation of a united kingdom under
David, the history of Israel leaves the realm of pre-history,
of cultic and popular tradition and enters the arena of history
proper. The kingdom under David and Solomon constitutes a
datum point from which the investigation of Israel's history
can safely be begun."[43] But it is not averred that we have
explicit archaeological or epigraphic testimony to this "succession of events," or allusions to them in extra-Israelite

sources. On the contrary, as Soggin himself admits, "archaeological evidence for the Davidic and Solomonic period is fragmentary and, on the whole, disappointingly scarce."[44] Where Jerusalem is concerned, there are still no discoveries "which can be dated with any certainty to the time of David and Solomon."[45] Whether the current excavations of the "City of David" will change this picture, remains to be seen. Outside Jerusalem, the assignment of important strata at Arad and Beer Sheva to David and at Gezer, Megiddo, Hazor and possibly Lachish to Solomon has been widely but not universally accepted.

What then is Soggin's criterion for making these reigns his "datum point"? From his other writings, it is clearly the emergence of a true historiography. "Israel achieved mature historiography at the beginning of the period of the monarchy."[46] Or again: "From the time of David and Solomon onwards, we see that in court circles there are not only traces of remarkably developed annals (we only have notes of them, the texts have been lost), but organic history-writings are beginning to take shape."[47] But the argument is circular: history begins where historiography begins, and historiography begins--or becomes "mature" or "organic"--where history is said to have its datum point. I prefer to maintain the proposition that history begins where writing begins[48] and see no reason to exempt Israel from this working hypothesis.

Admittedly, then, the comparative approach is open to criticism, but critique must go beyond fault-finding. To be constructive it must pose alternatives, and the alternatives are themselves vulnerable--notoriously so. As if to dramatize the arbitrariness of Soggin's starting-point, we may note that in the very same volume Morton Smith proposes what amounts to an even later one when he uses "East Mediterranean Law Codes of the Early Iron Age"[49] to date most of the pentateuch to the period ca. 750-450 B.C.E., or what he somewhat impishly (albeit on good "classical" authority) refers to as the "archaic period."[50] John Van Seters, though approaching the biblical material from the opposite geographical direction, similarly dates most of the patriarchal legal precedents by analogy to neo-Assyrian and especially neo-Babylonian parallels.[51] Interestingly enough, Thomas L. Thompson, who joins Van Seters in so much of his critique of established positions,[52] parts company with him precisely over these and other suggested alternatives.[53]

The basic weakness of all these proposals, it can be argued, is their discriminatory character. Call them ad hoc, ad hominem or ad corpus, they single out biblical historiography in a manner inconsistent with the principle enunciated above (p. 5). Soggin's starting-point, for example, is not applied to the history of any other people, nor is it claimed as a methodological standard for any other historiographic corpus. But a standard worthy of the name must be widely if not universally applicable and applied. Such a standard is, in my opinion, available. The history of a given entity, national or otherwise, as reconstructed by the modern historian from "external" evidence, can be confronted with the formulations as preserved by that entity itself. Most often, these formulations take the form of literary traditions. It is thus possible to take full account of ancient historiography when reconstructing the history of ancient literate societies. More, it is impossible to ignore literature in the enterprise, or to divide it hermetically from "objective history." The modern historian should aspire to write a history that is at the same time "a commentary on ancient history and historiography."[54] This is true whether his subject is ancient Mesopotamia and Egypt or ancient Israel.


V


"History as reconstructed confronted with the (native) formulations as preserved" is, then, the common standard proposed here. But confrontation does not, of course, imply uncritical equation; on the contrary, the term is chosen deliberately to stress the need for critical evaluation of the two terms of the equation. What is important, and to some extent even novel, is the choice of the terms. For hitherto the comparative method has generally implied a different sort of confrontation, namely between the biblical text and the external data, the "objective" facts recovered by archaeology from the excavations of the surrounding Near East. This was, however, a confrontation between unequals, an attempted equation between two essentially incommensurable quantities. It inevitably aroused skepticism. One need only cite the Nuzi texts in this connection. A whole generation of biblical scholars employed these texts to explain and even to date the patriarchal narratives on the basis of common juridical practices allegedly found in both. American scholars such as E. A. Speiser and C. H. Gordon led the way since American expeditions were responsible for the excavations at Nuzi. But a second generation of biblical scholars, disciples of the first prominent among them, has demolished the putative parallels one by one.[55]

Does that discredit the entire attempt to evaluate patriarchal law by Bronze Age parallels? Hardly, *pace* Van Seters

and Thompson.  Rather, it invites a reconsideration of the
terms of the comparison.  The biblical canon should be
weighed, *not* against the archival data excavated from a distant corner of the Mitanni empire, but rather, on the one
hand, against the occasional scrap of archival evidence recovered from the soil of Palestine itself[56] and, on the other
and far more important, against the literary formulations of
the surrounding Near East.  Only then will one be comparing
commensurate quantities, and only then will one be operating
with a standard equally. applicable to the other cultures of
the ancient Near East.  The entire historiographic spectrum
lends itself to this treatment, but it cannot be traversed
even in a cursory fashion here.  The relevant bibliography
is enormous; the mere sampling provided in the present volume
is drawn in part from a syllabus for the seminar, which also
included a working chronology.  The latter may serve as the
basis for a broad overview of the methodological problems at
issue (Fig. 1).[57]

     The context of biblical literature is at once spatial
and temporal.  In spatial terms, the biblical authors all
shared with the land of Israel its central location.  That
is to say, they were potentially exposed to the surrounding
Near East in the same high degree as was their native soil;
some of them, indeed, lived and wrote in the lands of the
Dispersion.  A map of the Near East should therefore be kept
in mind in what follows.  Some might wish to include the
Aegean world in such a map, but all would agree on its broad
outlines.  No comparable degree of agreement however, characterizes the temporal context, not even its outer limits.  As
is clear from the chart, that context is here regarded as
spanning three millennia (ca. 3100-100 B.C.E.).  This long
epoch is more or less co-terminous with the life-spans of the
cuneiform and hieroglyphic systems of writing in Mesopotamia
and Egypt.  It may be treated as some sort of continuum if
one accepts the central importance of written documentation
in the reconstruction--indeed in the very definition--of
history, a view of matters not universally shared.[58]

     The thirty centuries involved (col. 1) can be grouped
in various ways, to begin with by major archaeological periods
(col. 7).  The names and dates of these periods have been gradually arrived at in connection with excavations in the Levant
and the Aegean; their extension to Mesopotamia and (to a lesser
extent) Egypt[59] rests on the observation that fundamental technological developments quickly spread from one end of the ancient Near East to another, and that they therefore provide a
significant basis for synchronizing the material finds from
widely scattered excavations.[60]  Thus the terms "Stone Age,"

# Figure 1

## Comparative Chronology of the Ancient Near East

| (1) | (2) | (3) | (4) | (5) | (6) | (7) |
|---|---|---|---|---|---|---|
| 3100 B.C.E. | | | | | | |
| 3000 " | | Jemdet Nasr | Ante-diluvians | Dyn. I | Early Dynastic | |
| 2900 " | | | | | | |
| 2800 " | | Early Dynastic I | "Flood" etc. | Dyn. II | | |
| 2700 " | | Early Dynastic II | Confusion of Tongues | Dyn. III-IV | | Early Bronze |
| 2600 " | | | | | | |
| 2500 " | | Early Dynastic III | Line of Shem | Dyn. V | Old Kingdom | |
| 2400 " | Old Sumerian | | | | | |
| 2300 " | | | | | | |
| 2200 " | | Sargonic | ? | Dyn. VI-VIII | | |
| 2100 " | Neo-Sumerian | Ur III | | Dyn. IX-XI | 1st Int.P. | |
| 2000 " | | | | | | |
| 1900 " | | Early Old Babylonian | Patri-archs? | Dyn. XII | Middle Kingdom | Middle Bronze |
| 1800 " | Old Babylonian | | | | | |
| 1700 " | | Late Old Babylonian | | Dyn. XIII (+ XIV) | | |
| 1600 " | | | | | | |
| 1500 " | Middle Babylonian | | Slavery? | Dyn. XV-XVIII | 2nd Int.P. | |
| 1400, " | | Kassite | | | | Late Bronze |
| 1300 " | | | Exodus and Wanderings | Dyn. XIX-XX | New Kingdom | |
| 1200 " | Middle Assyrian | | Conquest and Judges | | | |
| 1100 " | | Post-Kassite | | | | |
| 1000 " | | | | | | |
| 900 " | Neo-Assyrian | | First Common-wealth | Dyn. XXI-XXV | 3rd Int.P. | (Early) Iron |
| 800 " | | Neo-Assyrian | | | | |
| 700 " | | | | | | |
| 600 " | Neo-Babylonian | Neo-Babylonian | Exile | Dyn. XXVI | Saïte | |
| 500 " | | | | | | |
| 400 " | | Achaemenid | Second Common-wealth | Achaemenids etc. | Late Dynastic | Graeco-Persian |
| 300 " | Late Babylonian | | | | | |
| 200 " | | Seleucid | | Ptolemies | | |
| 100 " | | | | | | |

"Bronze Age" and "Iron Age" are more than merely designations
of convenience: they actually serve to define the periods in
which these materials were the principal mediums for tools and
weapons throughout the Near East.[61] The subdivisions of these
Ages similarly are based in the first instance on technological innovations whose impact was swift and widespread, such as
the large-scale introduction of the horse both as a mount and
for drawing chariots at the beginning of the Late Bronze Age,[62]
or the official adoption of the "alphabetic" (Aramaic) script
by the Achaemenids and their (in part perhaps resultant) unification of the Near East in the Late Iron Age (here the "Grae-
co-Persian Age").

A partially co-terminous but finer breakdown of the continuum is provided by "cultural" periods. In the case of
Egypt (col. 6), the resort is to the conventional periodization; for Mesopotamia (col. 2), it is to a scheme advanced and
defended in greater detail elsewhere.[63] It is based on a succession of 300-year periods which, though schematic to the
point of appearing mechanical, nevertheless dates and identifies the "dominant cultural factor" in each period (except
possibly the neo-Assyrian one) in fairly remarkable agreement
with assessments arrived at by more traditional means. The
lacuna at the beginning of this column again reflects the importance attached to written sources and the consequent difficulty in labelling periods for which these sources are scarce
or impenetrable.

Political considerations provide a still more detailed
periodization. For Egypt (col. 5), the native system of dynasties furnishes the obvious scale; for Mesopotamia (col. 3),
modern historical reconstructions must serve. In all cases,
dates are necessarily approximate and in some debatable.[64]
But the approximations serve as the "contextual frame" for
locating the grand subdivisions of biblical history (col. 4;
no attempt is made there to differentiate between subdivisions
arrived at primarily on literary grounds from those suggested
by political history). At the same time, they show at a glance
the extent of the overlap between chronological boundaries arrived at primarily on technological, literary and political
grounds, i.e., if one prefers, between archaeological, cultural and "historical" periods.

This overlap is most conspicuous in the precise center
of the continuum: in or about 1600 B.C.E. we may date the
capture first of Memphis by Salitis and the Hyksos and then
of Babylon by Mursilis and the Hittites.[65] These "escapades"
were presumably paralleled by "many of the ruling houses in
Levantine states during the Late Bronze Age (who) traced their

descent from a Middle Bronze founder," including Ugarit,
Tunip, Alalakh, Qatna, Mitanni, Hanigalbat and possibly
Aleppo; they represent a kind of "knight-errantry" on the
analogy of William the Conqueror and differ markedly from
the *Völkerwanderungen* at the end of the Late Bronze Age.[66]
But they were equally effective in bringing about the virtually simultaneous conclusion of the Middle Kingdom in
Egypt, the Old Babylonian Dynasty in Mesopotamia, and the
Middle Bronze Age in the intervening areas of the Levant.
The chronological conjunction in question may thus be said
to embrace the entire geographical extent of the Near Eastern
setting, and one is entitled to ask whether biblical historiography recognized an equally decisive temporal watershed and
a comparable spatial sweep.

Phrased thus, the question suggests its own answer:  the
Book of Genesis involves the entire area, moving in succession
over Mesopotamia (chs. 1-11), Syria-Palestine (chs. 12-36) and
Egypt (chs. 37-end).[67] And it embraces the entire time span
here equated with the Early and Middle Bronze Periods.  It is
the only biblical book to paint history in such broad strokes;
the others focus instead much more narrowly on a restricted
theater of action over a century or two in time.  In Genesis,
it has been argued, the creation myth "serves merely as background, furnishing the physical context within which Israel's
religion originated."[68] One may extend this idea to suggest
that all of the first chronological half of ancient Near
Eastern history was drawn on by biblical historiography to
provide the geographical context for the subsequent unfolding
of Israelite history within its Near Eastern setting.


VI


"This (i.e., biblical) idea of history represents a true
historiography, for it traces the events of Israel's experience
from a distinct beginning point, follows them down through a
progression in time, and looks to a future unfolding of that
history."[69] This characterization is meant to distinguish "the
prophetic idea of history" from other schools of biblical historiography, and even more emphatically from the rest of ancient Near Eastern historiography.  But the idea of the starting-point is inherent in all of them.  For prophetic historiography it is the call of Abraham, for priestly historiography
it may have been Creation, for others the Exodus from Egypt.[70]
Thus Soggin's methodological desideratum is worth returning
to.  The concept of a starting-point is grounded in biblical

historiography, not imposed on it by modern scholarship.  But nowhere, not even in the "royal theology" as preserved particularly in the "royal psalms,"[71] does the Bible itself date the beginnings of national identity to the introduction of monarchy.  On the contrary, that event occurred relatively speaking very late in the evolution of Israel's national consciousness, well after the constitutive events--attributed to the deity--which shaped that consciousness:  the deliverance from slavery, the giving of the law, and the conquest of the land.[72]  A starting-point for Israel's history, for its awareness of a "group identity," should indeed be sought, but it should be selected from among those offered by the text itself, i.e., by one of the schools of biblical historiography.

One proposal that meets this criterion is that of Malamat who argues persuasively that Israelite history begins once the tribes demonstrably occupy the areas consistently assigned to them as their final area of settlement in all historiographical traditions.  The tribe of Asher and especially Dan is a case in point.[73]  Since their tales unfold in the Book of Judges, this theory implies that Israelite historiography began there, and that the hexateuch preserves, rather, what may be called the proto-history of Israel.[74]

The proposal here set forth is that Israelite history begins with the Egyptian oppression when the consciousness of a collective destiny first dawned on an aggregate of discrete and, in origin, perhaps diverse groups.  Israelite historiography, as distinguished, say, from the royal historiography of the Davidic court or the universal historiography of the priesthood, begins, by the test of a collective focus, with the Book of Exodus which formulates the emergence of that consciousness.  Certain corollaries which it is impossible to pursue here follow from this postulate.  In literary terms, it implies a questioning of conventional groupings of the textual material into tetrateuch (Genesis-Numbers), pentateuch (Genesis-Deuteronomy) or hexateuch (Genesis-Joshua) in favor of a more qualitative caesura after Genesis and a new beginning in Exodus--perhaps of a triteuch[75] that ran from Exodus 1:8 through Numbers and originally included the death of Moses in Deuteronomy 34.[76]  In historical terms, it implies the essential historicity of the Egyptian oppression, as well as its sequel throughout the premonarchic period as related and sequentially ordered in the historical books of the Bible:  the exodus, wanderings, conquest and period of the judges.[77]  It does not imply that all that preceded the oppressions is utterly devoid of historicity, let alone "radically irrelevant as source(s) of Israel's early history" (above, p. 3), only that it has a different character: a broader geographical and temporal scope, a liberal acceptance

or appropriation of universal or non-Israelite traditions as
the background for the emergence of a discrete Israelite ethnic consciousness, and a deliberate *Tendenz* to narrow the
focus of the selected traditions, funnelling them to the putative bearers of that consciousness. Given these characteristics, the comparative approach is as relevant for the traditions preserved in Genesis as it is for the priestly historian of Exodus-Numbers, the Deuteronomist, the "prophetic
historian" or the Chronicler.

On this view of matters, the primeval histories of Gen
1-11 illustrate the widespread "practice of beginning an
ethnic history in primordial times ... a practice extending
from the Sumerian King List to Berossos and Manetho," and as
such bear comparison with numerous other "ethnic histories"
both early and late. [78] And on the other side of the patriarchal traditions, a special new significance attaches to the
cycle of Joseph stories which concludes Genesis. The cycle
has long proved troublesome to all interpretations of Israelite historiography because (with the exception of some
intrusive elements [79] such as the story of Judah and Tamar in
Gen 38) [80] it resists facile literary analysis into separate
strands which would link it to those identified by one means
or another elsewhere in Genesis or the tetrateuch. [81] On the
contrary, it contains late technical terms--neo-Assyrian [82]
or Saite [83]--and late literary motifs [84] which call into question its ostensible early Egyptian coloring and literary
models. [85] It seems then, to constitute a discrete literary
unit best described as a novella [86] which was only slightly
modified in order to be ingeniously inserted into the seam
between the (primeval and patriarchal) traditions of Genesis
and the more vivid memories of the oppression. [87] It thus
initiates the subtle transformation of the personal biographies of the patriarchs into the ethnic histories of the
several tribes, a process in which the twelve eponymous sons
of Jacob became the one collective entity known to the Bible
as the Children of Israel and to Merneptah simply as Israel.
This process was carried further in the record of the wanderings, particularly in Numbers, and consummated in the
purely tribal account of the conquest and settlement, notably
in Judges. [88]

The stories of Joseph, so difficult to justify on other
grounds, thus achieve a lucid purpose as the turning-point
from tradition to history. Their smooth integration between
two bodies of text so disparate in character and so dispro-
portionate in size constitutes a literary achievement of
considerable magnitude. Mesopotamian historiography failed
to match it when confronted by a corresponding problem, for

at the turning-point from primordial legend to a real if remote antiquity, its principal document offered no such help to the reader. The biographies of the early kings are barely alluded to in the Sumerian King List even when they are known to have existed in separate literary traditions.[89] Here as elsewhere, comparison and contrast are alike legitimate tools in providing the essential context of biblical historiography; they are the twin components in a contextual approach to biblical literature.

## NOTES

1. Henry Allen Moe, *The Power of Freedom in Human Affairs* (Philadelphia: American Philosophical Society, 1977), 97-112: "That Blessed Word Mesopotamia: A Lawyer's Reflections." For the quotation in question, see pp. 111-112.

2. Peter J. Gomes, "Vita: George Whitefield, Flamboyant Revivalist: 1714-1770," *Harvard Magazine* 79/7 (May-June 1977), 36.

3. Maurice Pope, *The Story of Decipherment: From Egyptian Hieroglyphic to Linear B* (London: Thames and Hudson, 1975). Cf. also M. S. Dandamaev, *Persien unter den ersten Achämeniden (6. Jahrhundert v. Chr.)*, translated by H.-D. Pohl (=Beiträge zur Iranistik 8, 1976), ch. 1: "Aus der Geschichte der Erforschung der Behistun-Inschrift," 1-22.

4. I owe this title to John B. White, co-editor of this volume. Meantime I have become aware of K. A. Kitchen's *Old Testament in its Context* (1973), but have not seen the book.

5. William W. Hallo, "New Moons and Sabbaths: A Case-Study in the Contrastive Approach," *HUCA* 78 (1977; appeared 1979), 1-17.

6. Paul D. Hanson, "Jewish Apocalyptic Against its Near Eastern Environment," *RB* 78 (1971), 33.

7. Hudson-Delaware Section, Philadelphia, May 4, 1975, Jeffrey H. Tigay presiding.

8. This and the next section represent a revised version of my remarks at that time.

9. "The Narratives about the Origin of Israel" in John H. Hayes and J. Maxwell Miller, eds., *Israelite and Judeaean History* (Philadelphia: Westminster, 1977), 210-212. This book with its exhaustive and critical survey of the secondary literature provides an excellent introduction to the subject, and served as textbook for the seminar (below, note 37). Cf. the perceptive review by Robert North, *Bib* 59 (1978), 423-426.

10. See most recently his "Origins and the Formative Period," in H. H. Ben-Sasson, ed., *A History of the Jewish People* (Cambridge: Harvard University, 1976), Part I (pp. 1-87).

11. *The Bible in its World: The Bible and Archaeology Today* (Exeter: Paternoster, 1977), ch. 4: "Founding Fathers in Canaan and Egypt." Cf. also below, n. 87.

12. Kitchen, *Ancient Orient and Old Testament* (London: Tyndale, 1966), 125, n. 52.

13. "Pseud-orthodox" was coined by Morton Smith in his opening salvo, "The Present State of Old Testament Studies," *JBL* 88 (1969), 19-35. The charge of "nihilism" was first levelled against Martin Noth by W. F. Albright, echoed repeatedly by John Bright, and escalated to Nihilimismus by J. Hempel, as pointed out by Noth, "Der Beitrag der Archäologie zur Geschichte Israels," VTSup 7 (1960), 262-282 [=Aufsätze 1 (1971), 34-51]; see especially p. 263.

14. I find that W. G. Dever (i.a.) uses the same terms in the same sense in Hayes and Miller, *Israelite and Judean History*, p. 77. Dever's survey of the issues in the debate (*ibid.*, pp. 70-79) is instructive.

15. William W. Hallo and William K. Simpson, *The Ancient Near East: A History* (New York: Harcourt Brace Jovanovich, 1971), 154-156. Hereafter: *ANEH*.

16. William W. Hallo, "The Royal Correspondence of Larsa: I. A Sumerian Prototype for the Prayer of Hezekiah?" *Kramer Anniversary Volume* (=AOAT 25, ed. B. L. Eichler; Neukirchen-Vluyn: Neukirchener Verlag, 1976), 209-224.

17. B. A. Levine, "The Descriptive Tabernacle Texts of the Pentateuch," *JAOS* 85 (1965), 307-318. Cf., however, A. F. Rainey, "The Order of Sacrifices in OT Ritual Texts," *Bib* 51 (1970), 485-498.

18.   Nahman Avigad, "Baruch the Scribe and Jerahmeel the King's Son," *IEJ* 28 (1978), 52-56 and pl. 15; *BA* 42 (1979), 114-118.

19.   E. D. Oren, "Esh-Shari'a, Tell (Tel Sera')" in Michael Avi-Yonah and Ephraim Stern, eds., *Encyclopedia of Archaeological Excavations in the Holy Land* 4 (London: Oxford University, 1978), 1059-1069.  See p. 1062 for a description and p. 1069 for a photograph of the "socketed, crescent-shaped bronze (Assyrian) standard ... found on the brick-lined floor of the northern basement" of the Assyrian citadel dating from the seventh century B.C.E.

20.   Dennis Pardee, "The Judicial Plea from Meṣad Hashav-yahu (Yavneh-Yam):  A New Philological Study," *Maarov* 1/1 (1978), 33-66, with previous literature.

21.   André Lemaire, *Inscriptions Hebraïques I:  Les Ostraca* (=Littératures Anciennes du Proche-Orient 9, 1977).

22.   "Beitrag der Archäologie," p. 262.   (Translation mine.)

23.   *Ancient Orient,* p. 28.   Cf. *ibid.,* pp. 115 and 169-170.

24.   William W. Hallo, "Problems in Sumerian Hermeneutics," in *Perspectives in Jewish Learning* 5 (ed. B. L. Sherwin; Chicago, 1973), 4.   Cf. *idem,* "Assyrian Historiography Revisited," in *H. L. Ginsberg Volume* (=Eretz-Israel 14, 1978), Hebrew summary, p. 191.

25.   Hallo, "Assyrian Historiography Revisited," pp. 1*-7*.

26.   Donald B. Redford, "The Hyksos Invasion in History and Tradition," *Or* 39 (1970), 1-51, esp. pp. 9-10.   Cf. also Gun Björkman, "Egyptology and Historical Method," *Orientalia Suecana* 13 (1964), 9-33, who argues that literary evidence can be used for historical reconstruction only with the greatest caution.

27.   J. Huizinga, "A Definition of the Concept of History," in Raymond Klibansky and H. J. Paton, eds., *Philosophy and History:  Essays Presented to Ernst Cassirer* (Oxford, 1936), 1-10, esp. p. 9, quoted by J. J. Finkelstein, "Mesopotamian Historiography," *Proceedings of the American Philosophical Society* 107 (1963), 462 and n. 4.   (Note that Finkelstein wrote:  "of the past.")

28. In this connection I have noted but not studied the following: Abraham I. Katsch, *Judaism in Islam: Biblical and Talmudic Backgrounds of the Koran and its Commentaries, Suras II and III* (New York: New York University, 1954); Tor Andrae, *Der Ursprung des Islams und das Christentum* (Uppsala: Almqvist & Wiksell, 1926; French trans. Jules Roche, Paris: Adrien-Maisonneuve, 1955); Richard Bell, *The Origin of Islam in its Christian Environment* (London: Macmillan, 1926).

29. Cf. Michael C. J. Putnam, "Italian Vergil and the Idea of Rome," in Louis L. Orlin, ed., *Janus: Essays in Ancient and Modern Studies* (Ann Arbor: University of Michigan, 1975), 169-199.

30. Moshe Weinfeld calls my attention to *Iliad* 20:306-307: "and now verily the mighty Aeneas will rule over the Trojans, and his sons' sons that are hereafter to be born" where some traditions substitute "all" (*pántessin*) for "Trojans" (*Trôessin*) according to Strabo, *Geography* 13:1:53 (608); cf. Ludolf Malten, "Aineias," *Archiv für Religionswissenschaft* 29 (1931), 33-59, esp. p. 53.

31. Cecil Roth, *The Nephew of the Almighty: An Experimental Account of the Life and Aftermath of Richard Brothers, R.N.* (London: Edward Golston, 1933); *idem, Magna Bibliotheca Anglo-Judaica: A Bibliographical Guide to Anglo-Jewish History* (2nd ed.; London: Jewish Historical Society of England, 1937), B. 17: "British Israel and Lost Ten Tribes," 379-389. Note that this entry no longer appears in the newer editions of this work by Ruth P. Lehman (1961, 1973).

32. For an analogy between American and biblical historiography that has become a classic of its kind, see John Bright, "The School of Alt and Noth: A Critical Evaluation," in his *Early Israel in Recent History Writing* (=SBT 19; London: SCM, 1956), 79-110; reprinted in Samuel Sandmel, ed., *Old Testament Issues* (New York: Harper & Row, 1968), 159-195. For a response see Noth, "Beitrag der Archäologie," esp. pp. 280-282.

33. F. R. Kraus, *Sumerer und Akkader: ein Problem der altmesopotamischen Geschichte* (Amsterdam: Koninklijke Akademie der Wetenschapen, 1970); J. S. Cooper, "Sumerian and Akkadian in Sumer and Akkad," *Or* 42 (1973), 239-246.

34. S. Spiegel, "Noah, Daniel and Job, Touching on Canaanite Relics in the Legends of the Jews," *Louis Ginzberg Jubilee Volume* I (1945), 305-355; M. Noth, "Noah, Daniel and Hiob in Ezechiel XIV," *VT* 1 (1951), 251-260.

35.  J. J. Finkelstein, "The Goring Ox," *Temple Law Quarterly* 46 (1973), 169-290; B. S. Jackson, "The Goring Ox Again," *Journal of Juristic Papyrology* 18 (1974), 55-93, reprinted in *Essays in Jewish and Comparative Legal History* (Leiden:  E. J. Brill, 1975), 108-152.

36.  William W. Hallo, "The Road to Emar," *JCS* 18 (1964), 86.  See in greater detail the paper by N.-E. A. Andreasen below, 59-77.

37.  "Biblical History in its Near Eastern Setting," Summer Seminar for College Teachers sponsored by the National Endowment for the Humanities, Yale University, June 19-August 11, 1978.

38.  *H. L. Ginsberg Volume*, pp. 44*-51*.

39.  Note that a strictly historical figure like Mebaragesi still rules for 900 years!  For the Egyptian parallel, see W. K. Simpson, *ANEH*, p. 193.

40.  Cf. Gen 6:3; 50:22; Deut 34:7.  Later texts lower the optimal figures to 100 (Isa 65:20) or less (Ps 90:10). For Egyptian analogies to a 110-year life-span and other explanations of some of these figures, see Stanley Gevirtz, "The Life Spans of Joseph and Enoch ...," *JBL* 96 (1977), 570-571.  For the Mesopotamian view of the "ages of man" and a 90-year life-span, see J. Nougayrol, *RA* 62 (1968), 96 *ad* STT 400; cf. Hallo, *Assur* 1/4 (1975), 1.

41.  *H. L. Ginsberg Volume*, pp. 45*-46*.

42.  *Ibid.*, p. 51*.

43.  Soggin, "The Davidic-Solomonic Kingdom," in Hayes and Miller, eds., *Israelite and Judean History*, ch. vi, p. 332.

44.  *Ibid.*, p. 340.

45.  *Ibid.*, quoting G. E. Wright; cf. North, *Bib* 59 (1978), 425.

46.  Soggin, *Introduction to the Old Testament*, trans. John Bowden (London:  SCM, 1976), 50.

47.  *Ibid.*, p. 51.

48.  Below, n. 58.

49. *H. L. Ginsberg Volume*, pp. 38*-43*.

50. *Ibid.*, p. 43*.

51. *Abraham in History and Tradition* (New Haven: Yale University, 1975); *idem*, "The Childless Wife in Assyria and the Stories of Genesis," *Or* 44 (1975), 485-486 (with A. K. Grayson).

52. *The Historicity of the Patriarchal Narratives* (=BZAW 133; Berlin: de Gruyter, 1974).

53. "A New Attempt to Date the Patriarchal Narratives," *JAOS* 98 (1978), 76-84.

54. Hallo, *ANEH*, p. vi. Differently Björkman, "Egyptology and Historical Method."

55. For a partial list, see Kitchen, *The Bible in its World*, pp. 68-71 and 144-145, esp. nn. 64-66.

56. William W. Hallo and Hayim Tadmor, "A Lawsuit from Hazor," *IEJ* 27 (1977), 1-11 and pl. 1.

57. See also Hayes and Miller, eds., *Israelite and Judean History*, for extensive bibliography.

58. *ANEH*, pp. 4-5. For a critique of this position, see Ray L. Cleveland, review of *ANEH*, in *JNES* 32 (1973), 252-253.

59. Systematically first in *ANEH*; cf. also Hallo, "Mesopotamia, History," *Encyclopedia Judaica* 16 (Jerusalem: Keter Publishing House, 1971), cols. 1483-1505.

60. James D. Muhly, *Copper and Tin: The Distribution of Mineral Resources and the Nature of the Metals Trade in the Bronze Age* (Connecticut Academy of Arts and Sciences Transactions 43, 1973 and 46 [*Supplement*], 1976). Although the author himself is extremely cautious about drawing the above conclusion, it can in my judgment be inferred from the massive data he has assembled.

61. *ANEH*, pp. 6-7, 29-33, 123.

62. Cf. e.g., J. A. H. Potratz, *Die Pferdetrensen des Alten Orient* (=AnOr 41, 1966), ch. 1: "Das domestizierte Pferd." Potratz (p. 4) credits the Mitanni kingdom with this innovation.

63. William W. Hallo, "Toward a History of Sumerian Literature," in S. J. Lieberman, ed., *Sumerological Studies in Honor of Thorkild Jacobsen* (=Assyriological Studies 20, 1976), 181-203, esp. pp. 196-201.

64. See *ANEH* for details.

65. Redford, "The Hyksos Invasion," pp. 2-3 and 23 associates the fall of Memphis with the founding of the 15th (Hyksos) Dynasty which he dates between 1660 and 1649 B.C.E.

66. *Ibid.*, pp. 16-17.

67. See in somewhat greater detail: William W. Hallo, "Genesis and Ancient Near Eastern Literature," in W. Gunther Plaut, ed., *The Torah: A Modern Commentary*, vol. 1: *Genesis* (New York: Union of American Hebrew Congregations, 1974), xxix-xxxiv.

68. Hanson, "Jewish Apocalyptic," p. 41.

69. *Ibid.*, p. 40.

70. *Ibid.*, and n. 23, citing H. Ringgren.

71. *Ibid.*, pp. 43-44.

72. *Ibid.*, p. 42.

73. Malamat, "The Canite Migration and the pan-Israelite Exodus-Conquest: A Biblical Narrative Pattern," *Bib* 51 (1970), 1-16.

74. I am grateful to Professor Malamat for showing me the manuscript of his Haskell Lectures (1979) which deal with many of these questions.

75. The term is borrowed from Athanasius' Letter to Marcellinus (*Patrologia Graeca* 27, 1887, col. 12) who applied it to the sequence Joshua-Judges-Ruth, as is clear from his Festal Epistle 39, for which see most recently Sid Z. Leiman, *The Canonization of Hebrew Scripture* (Connecticut Academy of Arts and Sciences Transactions 47, 1976), 157, note 207. It is entered in older editions of Liddell and Scott, *Greek-English Lexicon*, but not in the newer ones nor in Guido Miller, *Lexicon Athanasianum* (Berlin: de Gruyter, 1952).

76. Martin Noth, *Überlieferungsgeschichtliche Studien I: Die Sammelnden und Bearbeitenden Geschichtswerke im Alten Testament* (Halle: M. Niemeyer, 1943), 39-40 *et passim*. Sigmund Mowinckel, *Tetrateuch-Pentateuch-Hexateuch: Die Berichte ueber die Landnahme in den drei altisraelitischen Geschichtswerken* (=BZAW 90, 1964).

77. Insistence on the biblical sequence might seem superfluous but for a new theory calling it in question: Seán Warner, "The Period of the Judges Within the Structure of Early Israel," *HUCA* 47 (1976), 57-79; *idem*, "The Dating of the Period of the Judges," *VT* 28 (1978), 455-463. Warner would date the Judges before the Wanderings and Conquest. Cf. also Yohanan Aharoni, "Nothing Early and Nothing Late: Rewriting Israel's Conquest," *BA* 39 (1976), 55-76. Contrast Kitchen, *The Bible in its World*, p. 87 and nn. 44-47.

78. Paul D. Hanson, "Rebellion in Heaven, Azazel, and Euhemeristic Heroes in 1 Enoch 6-11," *JBL* 96 (1977), 196 and n. 4.

79. Herbert Donner, *Die literarische Gestalt der alttestamentlichen Josephsgeschichte* (=Sitzungsberichte der Heidelberger Akademie der Wissenschaften, ph.-hist. Kl., 1976/2), esp. pp. 24-35. For Genesis 49, cf. B. Vawter, "The Canaanite Background of Genesis 49," *CBQ* 17 (1955), 1-18; differently Donald B. Redford, *A Study of the Biblical Story of Joseph (Genesis 37-50)* (=VTSup 20; Leiden: E. J. Brill, 1970), esp. p. 234.

80. M. C. Astour, "Tamar the Hierodule," *JBL* 85 (1966), 185-196; differently Umberto Cassuto, "The Story of Tamar and Judah," in *Biblical and Oriental Studies* 1 (Jerusalem: Magnes, 1973), 29-40.

81. Redford, *Biblical Story of Joseph*, esp. ch. 1. (Redford thinks that all of Gen 37:2-46:7 is an interpolation in the *tōlᵉdôt Yaʿᵃqōb*.) Differently Otto Eissfeldt, *The Old Testament: An Introduction*, trans. P. R. Ackroyd (New York: Harper and Row, 1965), 186.

82. J. S. Croatto, "'*Abrek* 'Intendant' dans Gen. XLI 41, 43," *VT* 16 (1966), 113-115.

83. Redford, *Biblical Story of Joseph*, ch. 9.

84. A. Meinhold, "Die Gattung der Josephgeschichte und des Estherbuches: Diasporanovelle," *ZAW* 87 (1975), 306-324;

88 (1976), 72-93; S. Niditch and R. Doran, "The Success
Story of the Wise Courtier: A Formal Approach," *JBL* 96
(1977), 179-193. Cf. also W. L. Humphreys, "A Life-Style
for Diaspora: A Study of the Tales of Esther and Daniel,"
*JBL* 92 (1973), 211-223.

85. J. Vergote, *Joseph en Égypte: Génèse ch. 37-50
à la lumière des études égyptologiques récentes* (Louvain:
Publications Universitaires, 1959). Cf. J. Janssen, "Egyptological Remarks on the Story of Joseph," *Jaarboek Ex Ori-
ente Lux* 14 (1956), 63-72; S. Morenz, "Joseph in Ägypten,"
*TLZ* 84 (1959), 401-416.

86. Redford, *Biblical Story of Joseph,* ch. 4, calls
it a "novelette." For the corresponding genre in cuneiform,
see for now Hallo, "Toward a History of Sumerian Literature,"
p. 196, with nn. 102-103.

87. For a different view, see Kitchen, review of
Redford, *Biblical Story of Joseph,* in *Oriens Antiquus* 12
(1973), 233-242.

88. See in somewhat greater detail my "Numbers and
Ancient Near Eastern Literature," in Plaut, ed., *The Torah*
vol. 4: *Numbers* (in press).

89. For the Egyptian situation, see Redford, "The
Hyksos Invasion," pp. 28-29.

# ORAL POETRY AND *DUMUZI'S DREAM*

William R. Millar
Colby-Sawyer College

James Wellard, in an article entitled, "My ... Hurts Me,"[1] voiced a frustration frequently felt by "enthusiastic but non-specialized students of the Sumerians" when confronted with some translations of this ancient literature. Dots, non-translated words, or italicized conjectures frequently appear in the text which occasionally derail all efforts on the part of the reader to grasp meaning. Among his many illustrations was the following:

> Uttu with joyful heart opened the door of the
>   house
> Enki to Uttu, the fair lady,
> Gives the cucumbers in their ...
> Gives the apples in their ...
> Gives the grapes in their ...
> Uttu, the fair lady, ...s for him, ...s for him,
> Enki took his joy of Uttu
> He embraced her, lay in her lap,
> ...s the buttocks, touches the ...[2]

This problem voiced by Wellard is shared in a different sense even among seasoned cuneiformists. Landsberger prefaced some recent remarks with this statement:

> My remarks today fall into the genre of "pro-
> grammatical essay" ..., for there is no other
> escape from being completely lost in details.
> A superficial, even distorted, position is
> better than no position; the latter is chaos,
> the former at least begs correction and im-
> provement.[3]

To begin one's study of a field so vast and complex as that represented by the literature of Sumer requires that one

catch hold somewhere and then offer his thoughts in the
spirit that a "superficial, even distorted, position is
better than no position" because it "at least begs correction and improvement." Such is the spirit of this essay.


The place I have chosen to catch hold is with the topic
of oral poetry and *Dumuzi's Dream*. Bendt Alster has brought
these two subjects together in his recent treatment of *Dumuzi's
Dream*.[4] It is this writer's feeling, however, that perhaps a
bit more can be said on this interesting, though admittedly
elusive, topic.

I have been struck in my reading of scholarly studies of
Sumerian literature by the frequently less than enthusiastic,
if not negative, assessments of the ancient poets' artistic
ability. The following observation by Kramer is a case in
point:

> Sumerian narrative poetry--the myths and epic
> tales, for example--abounds in static epithets,
> lengthy repetitions, recurrent formulas, lei-
> surely detailed description, and long speeches.
> By and large, the Sumerian writers show little
> feeling for closely knit plot structure; their
> narratives tend to ramble rather disconnectedly
> and monotonously, with but little variation in
> emphasis and tone. Above all, the Sumerian
> poets seem to lack a sense of climax. The
> myths and epic tales show little intensifica-
> tion of emotion and suspense as the story pro-
> gresses, and often the last episode is no more
> moving or stirring than the first. Nor is there
> any attempt at characterization and psychological
> delineation; the gods and heroes of the Sumerian
> narratives tend to be broad types rather than
> recognizable flesh-and-blood individuals.[5]

This suggests to me that perhaps the problems in translation of Sumerian literature alluded to by Wellard may rest a
little deeper. Could the literature itself have been produced
under circumstances with which the modern reader is largely un-
familiar?[6] More specifically, could the literature--at least
some of it--have been created to be heard rather than read?
Kramer allows for this in his discussion of Sumerian poetry,[7]
as do others,[8] but the implications for the product do not seem
to be sufficiently addressed. Oppenheim refers to Dumuzi's
call of Geštinanna as "long-winded repetitions."[9] Lambert and
Millard, though not dealing with Sumerian, assess *Atra-hasīs*

with the comment, "the ancient author nowhere shows any real
poetic spirit...."10

On the biblical side, Bernhard Anderson11 has noted three
contemporary interests which are having an impact on biblical
studies.  Each is arguing for a more synchronic reading of
texts as opposed to the dominant diachronic approach of recent
scholarship.  These interests include contemporary studies in
oral literature, structuralism and rhetorical criticism.  Each,
to use the happy phrase of Mary Savage, is attempting to "render the text opaque rather than transparent."12  Or as Muilenburg has recently argued, in addition to our form critical
studies, we must also work to come to terms with the text at
hand.13

This essay proposes to focus on the first of these interests, oral literature, more precisely, oral poetry.  The question being raised is, does contemporary oral theory provide us
with an avenue of approach to Sumerian literature that may
give an explanation for what frequently looks to us like "narratives tending to ramble rather disconnectedly and monotonously."

Since we will be discussing *Dumuzi's Dream* in particular,
a word first about recent discussion concerning the Dumuzi materials.

## I.  Dumuzi in Recent Criticism

Among the issues raised by recent discussion concerning
the Dumuzi materials have been the following: A) the historical origins of the cult; B) new materials for our understanding of the myth; C) the nature of the god Dumuzi; and D) the
literary composition of *Dumuzi's Dream*.

A) Falkenstein,14 after studying the occurrences of the
name Dumuzi in the texts, has argued that rather than being
a god whose nature was differentiated into separate local
cults, Dumuzi was an historical figure who has been mythologized into religious tradition.  He suggested that a king
named Amaushumgal of Badtibira, a name applied to Dumuzi, may
have started the process of a king participating in rites to
insure fertility, which was ultimately to center on Dumuzi,
a king of the first dynasty of Uruk.  Once Dumuzi was deified,
the pattern spread by identification to other localities and
deities.

B) Kramer[15] has reopened discussion concerning the Dumuzi myths themselves by publishing additional texts dealing with the Descent of Inanna into the Underworld. They have revealed that Inanna did not go to release Dumuzi from the nether regions, rather it was her judgment that sent him there in the first place. This, coupled with the fact that *Dumuzi's Dream* ends with Dumuzi dead at the hands of the *galla*-demons, has raised the suggestion that perhaps this is the end of the story. Perhaps Dumuzi did not return from the netherworld at all.

The obscure reference to Tammuz at the end of the later and shorter Akkadian version of the Sumerian myth, Ishtar's Descent into the Underworld,[16] has led earlier commentators to suggest that the reason for Ishtar's, hence Inanna's, descent into the lower regions was to release Tammuz/Dumuzi. The additional materials published by Kramer, however, argue against this conclusion.

According to the texts, Inanna, dressed in all the finery of her queenly status, chose to abandon heaven and earth for the Great Below, presumably[17] to extend her domain into the reaches of the netherworld. Recognizing the danger involved in such a journey, Inanna called Ninshubur, her attendant, before she left and instructed her on what she should do if her return were delayed. She was to approach, successively, the gods Enlil, Nanna and Enki entreating them to help in securing her release from the domain of the dead.

She then made her way to the gate of the underworld. When questioned by the gatekeeper of the Land of No Return as to the purpose of her visit, Inanna answered that she wished to witness the funeral rites of Ereshkigal's dead husband, Ereshkigal being queen of the nether regions and enemy of Inanna. Ereshkigal perceived Inanna's visit as a threat, admitted her, but insisted that as she traversed through the seven gates, Inanna's queenly finery be removed so that she might appear appropriately naked before the queen of the dead. Thus appearing before Ereshkigal, seven Anunnaki gods pronounced judgment on Inanna. She was killed; her body became a decaying corpse hung on a nail.

After a time, Ninshubur, concerned about Inanna's delay, approached the gods as instructed. Enlil and Nanna refused to help, citing their disapproval of Inanna's desire to extend her rule to the underworld. Enki, however, agreed to help. He created two creatures from the dirt under his fingernails, and charged them to trick Ereshkigal[18] into giving them the corpse of Inanna. Once acquired, they were to sprinkle the food and water of life on the body, thereby reviving Inanna.

They succeeded in their task.  But before Inanna could
leave the underworld, the Anunnaki reminded her that no one
returned to the land of the living unless a substitute were
provided for their domain.  Inanna agreed and was accompanied
by demons from below, to the land of the living to insure
that she would fulfill her part of the bargain.

Inanna and the demons encountered first Ninshubur and
later two of her sons, Shara and Latarak, all of whom appropriately grieved the absence of Inanna.  She, therefore, dis-
couraged the demons from taking any of them as the substitute.
Upon seeing Dumuzi, however, they discovered he was not griev-
ing at all, indeed, he seemed to be having a good time.  He
was dressed in regal garments and seated on his throne.  En-
raged, Inanna turned Dumuzi over to the demons.[19]

Dumuzi attempted to flee the clutches of the demons by
appealing to his brother-in-law, the sun god Utu, for help.
Utu agreed to help, changed him into a snake, and Dumuzi fled
to the home of Geštinanna, his sister.  Not to be let off so
easily, the demons pursued him to the house of Geštinanna. She
did not betray Dumuzi's whereabouts in spite of their insistent questioning.  They pursued him further to his holy stall
in the steppe and there he was captured.  In one last gesture
to save her brother, Geštinanna offered herself to go to the
underworld in Dumuzi's place, a gesture which Inanna acknowledged, with her judgment that Geštinanna would spend half the
year in the underworld, Dumuzi the other half.

C)  Jacobsen[20] has offered a suggestion which takes into
account the complexities of a possible multiple origin of the
Dumuzi materials.  As these materials have come together, we
now face cycles of tradition which have different emphases.
Attempts to determine the nature of the god Dumuzi have thereby run into difficulties.[21]

Jacobsen attempts to resolve many of these difficulties
by appealing to regional economies.  Depending on the particular economy involved, certain themes within the Dumuzi tradition were stressed.  Later as the culture became more complex,
these economies began to intersect, and so, too, the stories.
According to Jacobsen, Dumuzi was basically the intransitive
power for new life, encountered in milk, lambing and calving
by the shepherd; encountered in grain by the farmer; encountered in the rising sap in trees and in the date palm by
orchardmen.

With this linkage to the various economies of Mesopotamia, one can organize certain of the traditions associated with Dumuzi. The sacred marriage rite, a cult which focused on the joy and lightness of courtship and marriage is to be associated with Dumuzi Amaushumgalanna. Since the date was relatively preservable, the theme of death and dying was not central to this cult. The production of milk and the slaughter of animals for meat were economies which brought one into the frequent experience of food going sour, or the necessity of slaying animal life to survive. Stories about Dumuzi the Shepherd, therefore, incorporated more centrally into its tradition the slipping away of the power for new life and the grief and lamentation it precipitated. Similarly, as grain was cut and transformed in the process of making beer, death and restoration became the experienced theme. The rising sap experienced by the orchardman was anthropomorphized into the image of a young boy and a mother's and sister's love for their boy. This theme became central to the Damu cult.

Using this insight, Jacobsen interpreted Inanna's sending of Dumuzi to the underworld as her substitute and the subsequent giving of Geštinanna of herself to spend one-half year in his place as follows:

Inanna embodied the power of the storehouse. Her move toward taking over the realm of the dead was experienced as the storehouse gradually being emptied, toward the end of winter. Her queenly finery, the provisions in the storehouse, was removed piece by piece until the storehouse stood bare, perhaps down to one side of decaying meat. This condition was represented mythopoeically as Inanna, naked before Ereshkigal, was condemned to death, and was turned into a decaying piece of meat on a peg.

The restoration began with the waters of Enki, as spring began to take hold. Refilling the storehouses, however, was achieved at the expense of Dumuzi, the Shepherd, who embodied the power of newborn animals, now to be slaughtered to provide fresh meat. In the myth, this was expressed in the form of Inanna's decision to turn Dumuzi over to the underworld as a substitute to bring about her release to reassert the power of her being.

Jacobsen suggested the episode about Geštinanna and Dumuzi spending each one-half year in the nether regions was a separate myth and can be understood when linked to the grain economy. The grain was cut and brewed and allowed to ferment, accounting for Dumuzi's death and stay in the underworld, later to be released as the life-giving substance in beer.

Geŝtinanna was the power of the grape to produce wine. It, too, must ferment for a time. Grain was harvested in the spring, vineyards in the fall, hence the alternative times for the sojourn of Geŝtinanna and Dumuzi in the underworld.

Allowing for a return from the dead, Jacobsen pointed out, however, that Dumuzi's return was not a victorious conquering of the forces of evil and death. It was, rather, a return to the intransitiveness of being, after having embodied the intransitiveness of absence. Dumuzi returned to the beginning and the cycle repeated itself.[22]

D) Alster labels Jacobsen's methodology as an "emotional approach" resulting in the fact that the "evidence of the different sources is not treated systematically."[23] On the contrary, I find that Jacobsen's identification of Dumuzi as the power to new life, encountered in the experience of ancient man, is an insight which does integrate a number of separate traditions. The resulting interpretation of what otherwise often appear as rather fanciful stories, takes on new and profound meanings.

Alster, on the positive side, has suggested that the variant traditions concerning Dumuzi--for instance, the manner of his death in *Inanna's Descent* and in *Dumuzi's Dream*--could be traced to different themes in an orally created literature. "The character of Dumuzi cannot be defined by a simple adding up of the available information, and thereby straightforwardly drawing a conclusion."[24] But, could not this insight into the mode of creation be harmonized with the insights of Jacobsen? Certain stories could have circulated orally in regions where certain economies were dominant. Alster's appeal to the structuralism of Lévi-Strauss, who described the function of myth as overcoming contradiction, in this instance is too general.[25] Alster argued that Dumuzi would embody the tension between man-god, death-life and desert-city. But the same could be said of many ancient Near Eastern myths. In this regard, it would seem that Jacobsen has moved us closer to an understanding of the Dumuzi texts at hand.

The contribution that Alster has made to the discussion of *Dumuzi's Dream* was his invoking of oral theory to aid in our understanding of the nature of the text. To that subject we now turn.

## II.  Oral Theory in Recent Criticism

The ingredients important for a proper understanding of
oral poetry are as follows.[26]  1) The definition should allow
for oral composition.  This is not simply the act of composing
a poem in one's head, working through various possibilities,
and perhaps later writing it down.  Oral composition presupposes the poet working within a stream of tradition.  Within
that tradition is what could be described as an oral lexicon,
containing what some have called formulae, formulaic expressions, word-pairs, the concept of parallelism, and the like.
Included in this oral lexicon would be themes and thematic
patterns of well known stories in the tradition.  The act of
oral composition would be the act, at that moment, when the
poet draws upon the lexicon within the parameters of a rhythm
supplied by music or dance.  It is that moment when the poet
fills the space of the metric pattern with formulae, formulaic
expressions, bicola, tricola, catalogues, rhyme, chiasm, alliteration, assonance.

2)  A second ingredient that should be allowed for in a
definition of oral poetry is oral transmission.  Simply memo-
rizing a piece that has been created and then passed on does
not capture its force.  It is the artist's recreation of a traditional song that is the act of transmission.  It is to be
expected that any two creations of a song, even by the same
poet, would not be precisely the same, since the technique is
not simply memorization but pulling the pieces of a tradition
together to meet the occasion of the moment.  Therefore, poetry
that is orally created would show variants.  There is no original that is being passed on.  One could reconstruct an "original" of a text that had been put in writing and after having
been written was subject to modification in scribal transmission; but there would be no original oral text.

3)  A third ingredient that should be allowed for in a
definition of oral poetry is the performance.  It is the performance before an audience that provides the occasion of the
creation.  The artist responds to the interests and moods of
his audience.  In developing a theme, the artist would lengthen
or shorten the number of formulae, or formulaic expressions or
other items from his oral lexicon to suit the pressures of the
moment.  The creativity of the artist is not in coming up with
a new story.  It would be expected that the audience knew already the skeleton outline.  It would be for the poet to flesh

out the skeleton. The joy and interest in the song would depend on how well the artist juxtaposed and manipulated the patterns at his disposal.

Oral poetry, then, is what happens at that moment when the artist simultaneously creates from tradition, transmits a portion of that tradition, all in a performance before a living audience. Oral poetry is alive only in that moment. When the performance is over, that creation dies and recedes into memory, the various parts fall back, as it were, into the oral lexicon of the tradition.

As is evident, the above description is strongly influenced by the work of Albert B. Lord,[27] who in turn has continued the work of Milman Parry.[28] They derived their model for oral creation from field studies in Yugoslavia and applied their findings to the study of Homeric verse.

To explain the method of oral creation, Lord drew an analogy from the way we acquire and use general language. The process of speaking is essentially one of "substitution in the framework of grammar."[29] One learning a foreign language may observe its structure by studying such items as verbal paradigms, nominal declensions, case systems, or the like, as they are drawn out in a grammar. But one learns the structure of one's native language as it emerges from habitual use.

It is by this latter method that an oral poet learns his craft. By listening to other singers, one absorbs the "grammar of the poetry, a grammar superimposed, as it were, on the grammar of the language concerned."[30] Listening to the formula creation of other singers gradually implants in the mind of the singer-apprentice the mold of ideas wedded to words in a metrical framework. "I believe that the really significant element in the process is ... setting up of various patterns that make adjustment of phrases and creation of phrases by analogy possible."[31]

As a singer becomes accomplished and certain phrases begin to be used regularly in his professional singing, then one may say a formula is born. It is the formula-producing skill that characterizes a singer's ability. At any given moment in time, there will be some formulae firmly fixed in a singer's repertory, some relatively fixed and other phrases newly created which would not yet give evidence of extended usage.

Therefore, in studying the formulae of orally produced poetry, identifying identical usage of phrases in more than

one context is a beginning.  But from there one must discern
a system or pattern into which substitutions can be made that
give evidence of the singer's skill to develop themes within
the tradition.  It is this focus on formulaic systems that led
to a definition of a phrase called "formulaic."  "They follow
the basic pattern of rhythm and syntax and have at least one
word in the same position in the line in common with other
lines or half-lines."[32]

Robert C. Culley[33] has made some valuable methodological
observations when it comes to the application of the results
of contemporary oral theory to ancient texts.  For clarity, he
divided the research being done into those who are refining
principles from field studies and those who are applying the
principles to the study of ancient and medieval texts.  Since
there are no longer opportunities to observe firsthand the
oral composition techniques of ancient societies, one must
always treat the results of textual studies secondarily when
developing principles of oral theory.

As well, adjustments need to be made when applying the
principles to a particular body of literature.  Many of Parry
and Lord's generalizations about oral theory were worked out
in their application to Homeric verse.  The emphasis, for
instance, on strict metrical symmetry and the principle of
thrift do have applicability in the Homeric context, but need
to be modified or at least re-evaluated when approaching other
literatures.

In Culley's approach to the Hebrew Psalms, he first established the nature of Hebrew poetic structure which would influence the shape of formulae in that context.  This was consistent with Lord's approach because Lord has insisted that it
was the poetic-grammar system that produced the formulae.  The
system was more basic than the individual formulae alone, even
though the latter were the initial clues one worked with to arrive at the sense of that system.  Culley argued, in the Hebrew
context, strict syllabic symmetry was not as essential as in
the Greek.[34]  The framework was determined more by the parallel
structure of cola.  The basic units with which the Hebrew poet
worked were the lines, made up, normally, of two or three cola.
An individual colon could be broken down into smaller units,
though Culley preferred to label this "free substitution" within the framework rather than postulate a number of formulae of
that length, available to the poet.  Cola could be of varying
length but, characteristic of oral composition, run-on lines
would be unusual.

In presenting the data from the Psalms, Culley identified

formulae[35] and from the identification, analyzed the formulaic system behind the group of words, which then opened up
the possibility of identifying similar groups of words that
had been created through substitution of parallel lexical
elements within that system. He subsequently applied those
results to an analysis of individual psalms.

One of the devices used by the poet in constructing
parallel cola may have been the use of fixed-pairs of words.
Gevirtz[36] and Whallon[37] have discussed the relationship between word-pairs and oral creation. They have suggested
that within the framework of a formulaic system available to
the poet was a catalogue of fixed word-pairs useful as a
mnemonic device in the construction of poetic lines that assumed parallel structure.

In Alster's applications of the principles of oral theory
to his study of *Dumuzi's Dream*, he, similarly, made adjustments
for the poetry at hand. It is interesting that what he saw in
the structure of Sumerian poetry shows similarities to what
had been found for Hebrew poetry. There was the use of parallelism as a recurrent pattern and the lack of a rigid metrical
symmetry. Alster noted, too, the existence of word-pairs.

Alster recognized some problems with the approach of formula identification in Sumerian. First, the Sumerian corpus
is comparatively small and therefore, what may be a formula
could not be identified because of the lack of sufficient material. Second, the structure of the Sumerian language itself
may lead to the over-identification of formulaic expressions.
"Sumerian syntax favors constructions in fixed patterns, with
the result that a given expression may look formulaic, although
it is so general that it had better not be classified as such."[38]
A third problem is that parallelism may produce what looks like
formulaic expressions. He argued, however, that parallelism
itself is bound to traditionally fixed patterns, and the formulae to some extent are formed so as to fit these patterns,
as the formulae in the Homeric epics are formed to fit a metric
system.[39]

In spite of these difficulties, it would appear to this
writer that Alster has discovered a possible explanation for
what Kramer has described as "static epithets, lengthy repetitions, recurrent formulas, leisurely detailed description, and
long speeches ... narratives [that] tend to ramble rather disconnectedly and monotonously ... gods and heroes [that] tend
to be broad types."[40] Are not these marks of a literature that
was created to be heard rather than read? The function and
usefulness of repetition or redundancy was to lay bare the

structure of the story for a listening audience. The use of parallelism and word-pairs and traditional themes was useful to the story teller under the pressure of oral performance as composition techniques.

Since Alster has already gathered parallel passages and made suggestions concerning what in *Dumuzi's Dream* are formulae, formulaic expressions, themes and the like, for the remainder of this essay I propose to focus on the system into which the substitutions were made--to use Lord's terminology, to focus on the poetic grammar, "superimposed, as it were, on the grammar of the language concerned." Are there stylistic devices in evidence in the text of *Dumuzi's Dream* that would be particularly useful to a poet creating orally and to an audience that was listening, rather than reading?

## III. Oral Stylistic Devices in *Dumuzi's Dream*

### A. *Call to Lament*

Lines 1-14[41] form the introductory unit to *Dumuzi's Dream*. Lines 1-3 introduce Dumuzi. Lines 5-6 contain his call for a lament. Lines 8b-11 assert that his mother will call. Lines 4, 7-8a and 12-14 function as transitions between each of these units.

Using definitions worked out for formulae and formulaic expressions discussed above, Alster identifies the formulae used in this first section as, edin-šè ba-ra-è, i-lu mu-un-di₆ (DU)-di₆, and edin i-lu gar-ù. i-lu gar-ù is a formulaic expression. Word-pairs in parallel position are al-lub/bí-za-za, ama-ugu-mu/ning-bàn-da-mu and the number iá/u.

The technique employed by the poet seems to be that he established the general framework of a line or stanza with his opening colon. This colon was then expanded at the front or internally with information he wanted to highlight for the hearer. The opening colon of the first unit is šà-ga-né ír im-si; the opening colon for the second unit is i-lu gar-ù i-lu gar-ù; and the opening colon of the third unit is ama-mu gù hé-em-me. Each of these cola becomes the frame for further development.

1) šà-ga-né ír im-si

| | |
|---|---|
| šà-ga-né ír im-si | edin-šè ba-ra-è |
| *guruš* šà-ga-né ír im-si | edin-šè ba-ra-è |
| ᵈ*dumu-zi* šà-ga-né ír im-si | edin-šè ba-ra-è |

His heart was filled with tears, he went out to the plain,

*The lad*--his heart was filled
   with tears,                     he went out to the plain,

*Dumuzi*--his heart was filled
   with tears,                     he went out to the plain.

The expansion occurs at the beginning of the line and
moves from zero to general to specific. This pattern of
"particularizing," as Jacobsen calls it, is so widely documented in Sumerian literature, that one may call the pattern
formulaic. Note the internal rhyme of šà-ga-né, edin-šè and
ba-ra-è.

2) i-lu gar-ù i-lu gar-ù

The pattern of this unit and that which opens line 15
is precisely the same. A phrase is repeated, expanded at the
head, the expansion is repeated, followed by parallelism
closing with the same verb.

| | |
|---|---|
| i-lu gar-ù i-lu gar-ù | ul-e ba-ná ul-e ba-ná |
| edin i-lu gar-ù | sipa ul-e ba-ná |
| edin i-lu gar-ù | sipa ul-e ba-ná-gim |
| ambar gù gar-ù | ma-mú-dè ba-ná |

Set up a lament, set up         He lay down to rest,
   a lament,                       he lay down to rest

| | |
|---|---|
| O Plain, set up a lament, | The shepherd lay down to rest |
| O Plain, set up a lament, | When the shepherd lay down to rest |
| O Swamp, set up a cry! | He lay down to dream |

The vocabulary used in line 4 appears to link lines 1-3 with 5-6. gú-na, "his shoulder," recalls šà-ga-né, "his heart," and i-lu looks forward to the formulaic expression i-lu gar-ù of line 5.

The stable element of the parallelism in 7-8 is i₇-da. The word-pair al-lub/bí-za-za was employed to open the lines. i-lu gar-ù is paralleled by gù gar-ù making the latter formulaic, or perhaps better, free substitution within a formulaic system.

3) ama-mu gù hé-em-me

In this case the framework is established by the opening colon and expansion occurs internally.

ama-mu gù hé-em-me

ama-mu $^d dur_*(BU)$-tur-mu gù hé-em-me

ama-mu ninda-iá-am gù hé-em-me

ama-mu ninda-u-àm gù hé-em-me

My mother will call,

My mother, my Duttur, will call,

My mother, for the five breads, will call,

My mother, for the ten breads, will call!

Again, the reference to mother moves from general to specific, she being named in the second colon. Alster lists some interesting parallels to this passage, amply illustrating the word-pair nature of the numbers iá/u.[42]

Lines 12-13 function as a transition to the opening of
the dream section at line 15. Of interest is the stability
of the suffix pronoun mu located at about the center of each
line. Note the *inclusio* of ír in line 14 connecting this conclusion of the introductory section with the opening line.
The reference to mother and plain links this unit to what
precedes. The reference to sister looks forward to what is
to follow. ama-ugu-mu and nin₉-bàn-da-mu are a word-pair.


## B. *The Dream and its Interpretation*

The next major section develops the theme of the dream
and its interpretation. Lines 15-16 describe Dumuzi's lying
down to rest. Lines 19-24 introduce Geštinanna. Lines 27-40
contain the dream; lines 44-69, the interpretation. Lines
17-18, 25-26, 41-43 are transitions between these major sections.


### 1. Lying down to rest

As indicated above, the pattern in lines 15-16, which
open this section, is precisely the same as that used in lines
5-6.

| | |
|---|---|
| ul-e ba-ná ul-e ba-ná | i-lu gar-ù i-lu gar-ù |
| sipa ul-e ba-ná | edin i-lu gar-ù |
| sipa ul-e ba-ná-gim | edin i-lu gar-ù |
| ma-mú-dè ba-ná | ambar gù gar-ù |
| He lay down to rest, he lay down to rest | Set up a lament, set up a lament |
| The shepherd lay down to rest | O Plain, set up a lament, |
| When the shepherd lay down to rest | O Plain, set up a lament, |
| He lay down to dream | O Swamp, set up a cry! |

## 2. Waking from the dream

Lines 17-18 are formulae.  In this context, they function as a transition to the introduction of Geštinanna.

## 3. The call for Geštinanna

Line 19 establishes the framework and then develops the motif of calling for Geštinanna.

> túm-mu-un-zé-en túm-mu-un-zé-en
>
> ninɔ-mu túm-mu-un-zé-en
>
> Bring, bring
>
> My sister, bring!

The repetition of ninɔ-mu túm-mu-un-zé-en after each of the cola containing an epithet of Geštinanna reminds one of the opening unit of the song where one finds the repetition of edin-šè bar-ra-è after lines introducing Dumuzi.

The first túm-mu-un-zé-en of the opening colon was replaced one by one with an epithet from a catalogue of epithets describing Geštinanna.  In this case, Geštinanna was named first, the epithets following:  dub-sar-im-zu-mu, nar-èn-du-zu-mu, lú-bàn-da-šà-inim-ma-zu-mu, um-ma-šà-ma-mú-da-zu-mu, each enclosed by the pronominal suffix mu.

> My tablet knowing scribe
>
> My song knowing singer,
>
> My skillful girl, who knows the meaning of words,
>
> My wise woman, who knows the portent of dreams.

Alster lists the occurrences of these epithets elsewhere.[43] Such a device would be useful for both composer and listening audience.

Lines 25-26 are a transition unit building on the word
for dream, ma-mú-da, setting the stage for Dumuzi's recounting
of his dream.


4.  Dumuzi's Dream


Lines 27-30 and 31-34 are related.  Both employ *inclusio*,
ma-ra-zi-zi in the first instance and mu-da-an-dé in the second.  Within the stanzas there is a chiastic use of verbs.

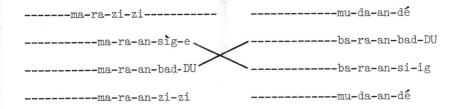

In line 27, note the alliteration of ma-ra-zi-zi and
ma-ra-mú-mú.  Note also the internal rhyme of verbs beginning
with ma-ra-an... and ba-ra-an....  gi-dili/gi-didli form a
word pair and lines 28-29 form part of a formulaic system.
After the utensils in lines 31-32 note the rhyme of -kù-gá,
-kù-mu and -mu.  Compare lines 253, 255 and 257 at the end
of the poem, which link the dream with its fulfillment by
referring to these utensils.  Note the formulaic nature of
the closing lines of the dream.

<sup>dug</sup>sakir₃ *i-dúr-dúr* ga nu-un-dé

an-za-am *i-dúr-dúr* <sup>d</sup>dumu-zi nu-ti

The churns were lying (on their side), no milk
   was poured,

The drinking cups were lying (on their side),
   Dumuzi was dead.

## 5. The Interpretation

Line 41 is a rubric. There is a transitional line formed in a pattern much like lines 2-3 at the opening of the poem.

šeš-*mu* ma-mú-zu nu ša₆-ša₆

nam-ma-an-búr-e

$^d$*dumu-zi* ma-mú-zu nu-ša₆-ša₆

nam-ma-an-búr-e


*guruš* šà-ga-né ír im-si

edin-šè ba-ra-è

$^d$*dumu-zi* šà-ga-né ír im-si

edin-šè ba-ra-è


*My brother,* your dream is not favorable,

It is very clear to me!

*Dumuzi,* your dream is not favorable,

It is very clear to me!


*The lad,* his heart was filled with tears,

He went out to the plain,

*Dumuzi,* his heart was filled with tears,

He went out to the plain.


The interpretation is a line by line interpolation of material between each line of the original narration of the dream. In the first three lines, the interpretation picks up on a verb in the original line to expand on the meaning of the dream. The structure of the dream itself, as has already been noted, is equipped with devices for the poet to draw on key phrases. Alster has gathered some parallel materials relevant to the lines of interpretation.[44]

### C. Avoiding the Demons

1. "Sister, go up the hill"

After the rubric in line 70, a new section opens, reminiscent of the pattern of internal repetition which opened the sections at lines 5 and 15.

$nin_9$ $du_6$-da $e_{11}$-bí $nin_9$ $du_6$-da $e_{11}$-bí

$nin_9$ $du_6$-da $e_{11}$-da-zu-dè

Sister, go up upon the hill, sister, go up
   upon the hill

Sister, when you go up upon the hill

There is a tricolon which compares with lines 69 and 242-244. Then the opening phrases repeat.

$nin_9$ $du_6$-da $e_{11}$-bí $nin_9$ $du_6$-da $e_{11}$-za-dè

2. Hiding from the Demons

Lines 79-88 are obscure. Line 89 opens a unit that established a key phrase which was built upon to develop the theme of avoiding the demons. The pattern of particularizing has been encountered before.

šeš-mu $gal_5$-lá-zu im-ši-$re_7$-eš

sag ú-a šub-ù

$^d$dumu-zi gal$_5$-lá-zu im-ši-re$_7$-eš

*sag ú-a šub-ù*

My brother!  It is your demons coming against you!

*Duck down (your) head in the grass!*

Dumuzi!  It is your demons coming against you!

*Duck down (your) head in the grass!*

Then, internal expansion:

nin$_9$-mu *sag ú-a ga-an-šub*

ki-mu na-ab-pà-dè

sag *ú-di$_4$-di$_4$-lá* ga-an-šub

ki-mu na-ab-pà-dè

sag *ú-gal-gal-la* ga-an-šub

ki-mu na-ab-pà-dè

*e-a-ra-li-ka* ga-an-šub

ki-mu na-ab-pà-dè

My sister!  *I will duck down (my) head in the grass!*

Show (them) not my place!

(My) head, *in the small plants,* I will duck down

Show (them) not my place!

(My) head, *in the big plants,* I will duck down

Show (them) not my place!

*In the ditches of Arali* I will duck down

Show (them) not my place!

Note the alliteration of ú-di₄-di₄-lá and ú-gal-gal-la.
This unit is duplicated at line 103.


### 3. The Dog

There follows a catalogue building on the motif of the
dog.

> ur-zu hu-mu-kú-e
>
> ur-gi₆ ur-nam-sipa-da-zu
>
> ur-gi₇ ur-nam-en-na-zu
>
> ur-zu hu-mu-kú-e
>
> May your dog devour me!
>
> The black dog, your dog of shepherdship,
>
> The noble dog, your dog of lordship,
>
> May your dog devour me!

Note the *inclusio* of hu-mu-kú-e and the parallelism and
internal rhyme of the epithets describing the dog. This unit
is duplicated at line 107.


### 4. Those who would go against the king

Lines 98-102 are obscure. Lines 103-109 form a duplicate already discussed. Line 110 opens a catalogue describing
those who would move against the king. The opening line established the framework.

> lugal-ra lú mu-<ši>-re₇-eš-àm
>
> lú-he-he-a-me-eš

> Those who moved against the king
>
> Were a mixed group of men.

The latter colon is developed first.

ú *nu-zu-me-eš*                                a *nu-zu-me-eš*

zì dub-dub-ba                                 *nu*-kú-*me-eš*

a-bal-bal-a                                   *nu*-nag-nag-*me-eš*

kadra nì-du$_{10}$-ga šu *nu-gíd-i-me-eš*

úr-dam nì-du$_{10}$-ge-eš                     *nu*-si-ge-*me-eš*

dumu nì-ku$_7$-ku$_7$-da ne *nu*-su-ub-ba-*me-eš*

sum$^{sar}$ nì-šeš-àm zú *nu*-gub-bu-*me-eš*

lú ku$_6$ *nu-kú-me-eš*                        lú ga-ras$^{sar}$ *nu-kú-me-eš*

Who know not food,                            know not drink,

Eat no sprinkled flour,

Drink no poured out water,

Accept no pleasant gifts,

Enjoy no spouse in embrace,

Kiss not the very sweet children

Taste not the bitter garlic

They eat no fish,                             they eat no leek.


Internal parallelism opens and closes the catalogue. The verbs are enclosed with the negative nu and -me-eš.

The first colon of the initial line is brought to bear as the catalogue now moves from the general to the specific with internal expansion and interpolation between the members of the catalogue.

lugal-ra lú mu-<ši>-re$_7$-eš-àm

$^{119}$lugal-ra *dumu-adab*$^{ki}$*-a min-àm* mu-un-ši-re$_7$-eš

$^{122}$lugal-ra *dumu-akšak*$^{ki}$ *min-àm* mu-un-ši-re$_7$-eš

$^{124}$lugal-ra *dumu-unu*$^{ki}$*-ga min-àm* mu-un-ši-re$_7$-eš

$^{126}$lugal-ra *dumu-uri*$^{ki}$*-ma min-àm* mu-un-ši-re$_7$-eš

$^{128}$lugal-ra *dumu-nibru*$^{ki}$ *min-àm* mu-un-ši-re$_7$-eš

$^{119}$The two sons from Adab moved against the king.

$^{122}$The two sons from Akšak moved against the king.

$^{124}$The two sons from Uruk moved against the king.

$^{126}$The two sons from Ur moved against the king.

$^{128}$The two sons from Nippur moved against the king.

The re-use of the verb mu-un-ši-re$_7$-eš in line 129 makes the transition from the catalogue to the next unit involving Geštinanna.


5.  Bribes and Capture


Geštinanna's response to the bribe offered by the demons is formulaic (131-132). In addition to noting the parallel passages of the demons talking amongst themselves[45] is to be noted the onomatopoeia of the words used. The many g's and l's sound like frustrated demons in conference faced by the refusal of Geštinanna to cooperate. Such a device would delight an audience listening to the narrative.

At line 142, the bribe is offered to the friend who accepts. The search for Dumuzi is described in the same manner introduced at line 89, reaching its climax when Dumuzi is caught at line 151.

> e-a-ra-li-ka hé-en-šub ki-ni ba-ra-zu
>
> $^d$dumu-zi-dè e-a-ra-li-ka mu-ni-in-dab$_5$-bé-ne
>
> He has fallen down in the ditches of Arali,
> but I do not know his place.
>
> Dumuzi they caught in the ditches of Arali.

Line 152 is a formula functioning here as a rubric marking the transition to a new section. Alster writes of lines 154-155, "The use of positive statements, introduced by hé-, followed by a negative statement, introduced by na-, is comparable to proverbs...."[46] Note the internal expansion and rhyme of lines 157-159. Alster lists the parallels to lines 164-182 where Dumuzi appeals to Utu for help.[47] It includes a catalogue of his good deeds.

There are then rehearsed a series of scenes. Utu agreed to help; Dumuzi escaped; he was found and captured again by the demons; Dumuzi appealed to Utu; Utu agreed to help; Dumuzi escaped; he was found and captured again by the demons. This continued until he went to the sheepfold and stall of Geštinanna. There he was captured. The demons entered. Lines from the dream were repeated and described as fulfilled. Dumuzi died.

## IV.  Conclusion

The oral poet is faced by two fundamental challenges in any given performance. The framework of the poem must be sufficiently simple and clear to avoid confusion. The movement of the poem must be sufficiently active to avoid boredom. *Dumuzi's Dream* employed techniques that would meet both challenges. For the former, the poet used repetition; for the latter, the poet used substitution and expansion.

## A. Repetition

To establish the framework of a particular unit, the unit opened with a colon. This colon would be repeated throughout the unit, becoming the base from which to vary the order or to introduce new material. The opening colon itself could contain within it internal repetition. Compare i-lu gar-ù i-lu gar-ù (5), ul-e ba-ná ul-e ba-ná (15), túm-mu-un-zé-en túm-mu-un-zé-en (19), $\text{nin}_9$ $\text{du}_6$-da $\text{e}_{11}$-bí $\text{nin}_9$ $\text{du}_6$-da $\text{e}_{11}$-bí (71). A variation on this pattern could be $^u$numun ma-ra-zi-zi $^u$numun ma-ra-mú-mú (27) and ú nu-zu-me-eš a nu-zu-me-eš (111). This latter device could close a catalogue, lú $\text{ku}_6$ nu-kú-me-eš lú ga-ras$^{sar}$ nu-kú-me-eš (118).

Such a technique could be expanded to the repetition of an entire colon. Again, the purpose was to aid a listening audience in keeping in touch with the framework. edin-šé bara-è is repeated in lines 1-3; $\text{nin}_9$-mu túm-mu-un-zé-en in lines 19-24; ki-mu na-ab-pà-dè in lines 91-94; ki-nu ba-ra-zu in lines 144-150.

In addition to the widespread practice of particularization, note also the re-use of a pattern that encompassed two lines.

| | |
|---|---|
| i-lu gar-ù i-lu gar-ù | ul-e ba-ná ul-e ba-ná |
| edin i-lu gar-ù | sipa ul-e ba-ná |
| edin i-lu gar-ù | sipa ul-e ba-ná-gim |
| ambar gù gar-ù | ma-mú-dè ba-ná |

## B. Substitution and Expansion

To highlight the movement of the poem, the poet would use substitution or expansion. Frequently, the substitution or expansion employed established word-pairs for use in parallel lines or drew on material from well-known catalogues. Expansion could occur at the head of a line or internally. Sometimes an internal element remained stable with the variation at either end. In the following example, al-lub/bí-za-za was a word-pair, and i-lu gar-ù a formulaic expression.

al-lub i₇da-<<ka>>i-lu gar-ù

bi-za-za i₇-da gù gar-ù

O Crabs, in the river, set up a lament.

O Frogs, in the river, set up a cry.


A frequent device to insert movement into the poem was the use of the catalogue. Note the epithets of Geštinanna (21-24), the description of those who would attack the king (111-118), the attributes of the dog (95-97), Dumuzi's recital of his good deeds before Utu (165-169), the list of cities against Dumuzi (119-128). Since most of the material in these catalogues had parallels elsewhere, it was new in the sense of new to this narration of traditional lore.

More elaborate devices were employed with Geštinanna's interpretation of Dumuzi's Dream. But, again, the poet was careful not to lose his audience. The dream was interpreted line by line, not as one solid unit. The closing of the poem treated each demon, one at a time, making the connection to specific lines in the original dream.

The episodes of Dumuzi hiding from the demons reflect the heightened excitement of the poem, but again note the frequent repetition of key lines so the listener was not lost. The escapes and recaptures built the suspense, but within the measured steps of an appeal to Utu, escape, recapture, appeal to Utu, escape and recapture until Dumuzi's final demise at the end. Even with this complex section, there is sufficient use of repetition, familiar catalogues and predictable motifs, within the larger theme development, to argue that it continues to show the marks of a composition designed less to be read and more to be heard.

With the model of oral composition in mind,[48] the contemporary reader approaches the texts a little differently. Rather than being turned off by the nature of the received text, leading us to render evaluations of inferiority to the material, one begins to enter the space between the lines, as it were, as the structure of the story begins to take shape around one in the way the story would have taken shape as the sound of the lines surrounded the listener in ancient times. Literature designed for the ear is to be appreciated differently than literature designed for the eye.

# NOTES

1. J. Wellard, "My ... Hurts Me," *Encounter* 36/5 (1971), 16-21.

2. *Ibid.*, 17. From S. N. Kramer, *Lamentations Over the Destruction of Ur* (=Assyriological Studies 12), 352-354.

3. C. H. Kraeling, ed., *City Invincible* (Chicago: University of Chicago, 1960), 95.

4. B. Alster, *Dumuzi's Dream: Aspects of Oral Poetry in a Sumerian Myth* (=Mesopotamia 1, 1972).

5. S. N. Kramer, *The Sumerians: Their History, Culture and Character* (Chicago: University of Chicago, 1963), 170-171.

6. See the comment of H. Sauren in "Zur poetischen Struktur der sumerischen Literatur," *UF* 3 (1971), 332: "Diese Wiederholungen mögen für unser Stilempfinden fremd sein, und man ist geneigt, darin einen Mangel an schöpferischer Gestaltung zu sehen. Für die Antike war dies keineswegs so. Die Wiederholung ist ein konstruktives Element der epischen Werke."

7. S. N. Kramer, *The Sacred Marriage Rite* (Bloomington: Indiana University, 1969), 23, 141, nn. 1, 2.

8. See, for instance, J. Laessøe, "Literacy and Oral Tradition in Ancient Mesopotamia," *Studia Orientalia Ioanni Pedersen ... Dicata* (Copenhagen, 1953), 210.

9. A. L. Oppenheim, *The Interpretation of Dreams in the Ancient Near East* (Philadelphia: The American Philosophical Society, 1956), 213.

10. W. G. Lambert and A. R. Millard, *Atra-Ḫasīs, The Babylonian Story of the Flood* (Oxford: Clarendon Press, 1969), 13.

11. B. W. Anderson, "From Analysis to Synthesis," *JBL* 97 (1978), 23-29.

12. See Mary Savage, "Literary Criticism and Biblical Studies: A Rhetorical Analysis of the Joseph Narrative," below, pp. 79-100.

13. J. Muilenburg, "Form Criticism and Beyond," *JBL* 88 (1969), 1-18.

14. A. Falkenstein, "Tammuz," *CRRAI* 3 (1954), 41-65.

15. See S. N. Kramer, "Inanna's Descent to the Nether World. Continued and Revised," *JCS* 5 (1951), 1-17, *The Sacred Marriage Rite*, chap. 6 and note 19 below.

16. E. A. Speiser, "Descent of Ishtar to the Nether World," *ANET*[3] (Princeton: Princeton University, 1969), 109, n. 28.

17. For a discussion, see S. N. Kramer, *The Sacred Marriage Rite*, 154, n. 4.

18. A. D. Kilmer, "How Was Queen Ereshkigal Tricked?" *UF* 3 (1971), 299-309. T. Jacobsen, *The Treasures of Darkness* (New Haven: Yale University, 1976), 246, n. 38.

19. For some recent commentators, this was the end of the story. O. R. Gurney, "Tammuz Reconsidered: Some Recent Developments," *JSS* 7 (1962), 159: "Tammuz ... was a shepherd, condemned to reside in the Underworld by an angry goddess whose lover he had been." E. M. Yamauchi, "Tammuz and the Bible," *JBL* 84 (1965), 28: "He died and had to remain dead as Inanna's substitute in the underworld." Kramer, too, held such an opinion until a suggestion by Falkenstein led him to revise his judgment. See Falkenstein's review of C. J. Gadd and S. N. Kramer, *Ur Excavations Texts VI* in *BO* 22 (1965), 281, and S. N. Kramer, "Dumuzi's Annual Resurrection: An Important Correction to 'Inanna's Descent,'" *BASOR* 183 (1966), 31.

Falkenstein proposed that a key line be read, "You (Dumuzi), half the year! Your sister (Geštinanna), half the year." This would mean that rather than being dead forever, Dumuzi would return from the underworld for a period of six months annually at which time Geštinanna took his place for the other half.

W. W. Hallo's (unpublished) suggestion interpreting the Descent of Inanna into the underworld is that it reflects a "dim memory of pre-historic 'transhumance,' with Sumerian *kur* a double-entendre for netherworld and mountain. A myth originally relating Dumuzi's semi-annual ascent to the hilly flanks of the Zagros became in time a story of his descent to the netherworld which equals death, both occurring during the summer."

20. T. Jacobsen, "Toward the Image of Tammuz," *HR* 1 (1961), 189-213. Reprinted in William Moran, ed., *Toward the Image of Tammuz* (Cambridge: Harvard University, 1970), 73-103. See also T. Jacobsen, *Treasures of Darkness,* chap. 2.

21. O. R. Gurney, in his article, "Tammuz Reconsidered," has an excellent summary tracing the gradual dissolution of the synthesis proposed by Frazer early in this century, who suggested that Tammuz was a god of the dying and rising type to be equated with Osiris, Adonis, and Attis. Gurney demonstrates that the data is not as unified as it was once thought to be.

22. T. Jacobsen, "Toward the Image of Tammuz," 97.

23. B. Alster, *Dumuzi's Dream,* 12.

24. *Ibid.,* 14.

25. *Ibid.*

26. See the excellent discussion of definitions by R. Finnegan, *Oral Poetry: Its Nature, Significance and Social Context* (Cambridge: Cambridge University, 1977), 1-87.

27. The literature on oral poetry is now quite extensive. The key work for our purposes is A. B. Lord, *The Singer of Tales* (Cambridge: Harvard University, 1964), 3-138. An excellent critique of Lord is to be found in R. Finnegan, *Oral Poetry,* 1-87, 272-275. See also C. M. Bowra, *Heroic Poetry* (London: MacMillan and Co. Ltd., 1952), esp. chaps. 5, 7, 8; and R. C. Culley, *Oral Formulaic Language in the Biblical Psalms* (Toronto: University of Toronto, 1967), 3-27. *Semeia* 5 (1976) edited by R. C. Culley is devoted to the subject of *Oral Tradition and Old Testament Studies,* and contains many valuable articles on the subject. A full and up-to-date bibliography compiled by Culley may be found on pp. 24-33.

28. See most recently M. Parry, *The Making of Homeric Verse, The Collected Papers of Milman Parry,* ed. by Adam Parry (Oxford: Clarendon Press, 1971).

29. A. B. Lord, *Singer of Tales,* 36.

30. *Ibid.*

31. *Ibid.,* 37.

32. *Ibid.,* 47.

33. See, in addition to his work on the Psalms cited in note 27, R. C. Culley, "An Approach to the Problem of Oral Tradition," *VT* 13 (1963), 113-135, and "Oral Tradition and the OT: Some Recent Discussion," *Semeia* 5 (1976), 1-33.

34. F. M. Cross, drawing from his work in early Hebrew and Ugaritic poetry, is more inclined to apply a strict sense of metrical symmetry to Hebrew poetry. For a recent discussion applied to Ugaritic texts, see his "Prose and Poetry in the Mythic and Epic Texts from Ugarit," *HTR* (1974), 1-15. For a critique of that study, see B. O. Long, "Recent Field Studies in Oral Literature and Their Bearing on Old Testament Criticism," *VT* 26 (1976), 187-198.

35. Culley modified Parry's definition of a formula to make it applicable to the Hebrew context: "Repeated groups of words the length of which corresponds to one of the divisions in the poetic structure," (R. C. Culley, *Oral Formulaic Language in the Biblical Psalms*, 10).

36. S. Gevirtz, *Patterns in the Early Poetry of Israel* (=Studies in Ancient Oriental Civilization 32; Chicago: University of Chicago, 1963). See also P. B. Yoder, "A-B Pairs and Oral Composition in Hebrew Poetry," *VT* 21 (1971), 470-489. While not postulating oral theory, M. Held has studied fixed word-pairs in Ugaritic and biblical Hebrew; see *JBL* 84 (1965), 272-282.

37. W. Whallon, *Formula, Character and Context* (Cambridge: Harvard University, 1969), 139-172.

38. B. Alster, *Dumuzi's Dream*, 24. For an excellent discussion of the bound nature of the Sumerian verb, see Thorkild Jacobsen, "About the Sumerian Verb," reprinted in W. Moran, ed., *Toward the Image of Tammuz*, 245-270, 430-466. For the nominal part of the sentence and the strict sense of rank to be found there, see A. Falkenstein, *Grammatik der Sprache Gudeas von Lagaš II: Syntax* (=AnOr 29, 1950), 1-5.

39. For a sense of the structure of Sumerian poetry, see H. Sauren, "Zur poetischen Struktur der sumerischen Literatur," 327-334; S. N. Kramer, *The Sacred Marriage Rite*, 23-48; and T. Jacobsen, "The Myth of Inanna and Bilulu," the latter reprinted in W. Moran, ed., *Toward the Image of Tammuz*, 334, n. 5.

40. See above, p. 28.

41. The line numbers refer to Alster's edition of the text, chap. 6. I have used his transliterations and translation uncritically. While there may be debates over particular items in Alster's text, it should not affect, to a great extent, the argument presented here.

42. B. Alster, *Dumuzi's Dream,* 86-87.

43. *Ibid.,* 89-90.

44. *Ibid.,* 91-98.

45. *Ibid.,* 109-110.

46. *Ibid.,* 111.

47. *Ibid.,* 114-117.

48. Because of the considerable evidence that Mesopotamia was a relatively literate culture, Professor Hallo is more inclined to account for the items isolated above as part of the text, or "libretto," for a musical performance. This would account for such things as repetition and alliteration and obviate the need for a theory of oral composition. See Hallo's review of B. Alster, *The Instructions of Suruppak: A Sumerian Proverb Collection,* in *JNES* 37 (1978), 269-273.

# GENESIS 14 IN ITS NEAR EASTERN CONTEXT

Niels-Erik A. Andreasen
Loma Linda University

The story of Abram and the four kings in Gen 14 has been characterized as "most difficult,"[1] "most unusual," yet "most perplexing,"[2] "most controversial,"[3] and "most puzzling"[4] by some of its recent investigators. The problem centers in the Near Eastern setting of our story. In this story alone Abram is thrust into what appears to be an incident of international proportions with the tantalizing prospect of enabling us to relate the biblical story of his life to Near Eastern history in a precise way. Can Gen 14 be said in any way to represent an identifiable historical event in the ancient Near East?[5]

Essentially two answers to this question emerge from the history of the study of this chapter, and they appear to be live options today as much as they were a century ago.[6]

According to one view (representing probably a majority opinion), Gen 14 retains a genuine historical memory concerning an expedition into Palestine of four foreign kings, or at least foreign royal representatives, with an ensuing battle. Some proponents of this view posit the existence of an original Akkadian account of the event upon which the biblical narrative is based. Their conclusion is drawn from a consideration of certain awkward syntactical constructions in the chapter supposedly carried over from Akkadian into the Hebrew text.[7] W. F. Albright, on the other hand, in a series of writings on the subject beginning in 1921, followed by a major essay in 1926, and continuing until 1968, argued that the chapter is based upon an old Hebrew poem, remnants of which can still be detected in the present narrative.[8] Without taking sides in this particular issue, a considerable number of recent interpreters have accepted the essential historicity of Gen 14 and placed it in the first half of the second millennium B.C.E.[9]

According to a second view, Gen 14 is a late (first millennium) midrash with no discernible historical veracity. Older proponents of this view (before the recent explosion of our knowledge of the ancient Near East) generally found the chapter to be a pure fabrication,[10] while more recently others have conceded the historicity of certain elements of the story, but not of the event itself.[11]

## I. *Traditional Evidences for the Historicity of Gen 14*

An attempt at reassessing these two divergent views regarding the historical context of Gen 14 may best begin with a brief review of the types of evidence traditionally advanced in support of its setting in the early second millennium. They include: identification of the foreign kings, identification of the Palestinian kings, description of the population patterns in early second millennium Palestine, characterization of Abram the Hebrew, and identification of Melchizedek of Salem.

(a) *The foreign kings:* Amraphel, king of Shinar, once identified with Hammurabi of Babylon,[12] is now generally considered to be a (royal) bearer of a typical west Semitic name[13] coming from Babylon (Shinar) between the fall of Ur III and the rise of the Old Babylonian kingdom of Hammurabi, i.e., during the 20th-19th centuries B.C.E. In his later writings Albright proposed a relationship between Amraphel and Emutbal, a province between Elam and Babylon whose rulers enjoyed prominence in the same general period.[14]

Arioch of Elassar is now commonly identified with the name *Arriyuk* which is known from both Mari and Nuzi.[15] Elassar, however, has proved difficult, though some have related it to Larsa.[16]

Chedorlaomer of Elam bears a recognized Elamite name beginning with the element "Kudur" and used by several Elamite kings.[17] Albright who once hoped to identify an Elamite king Kudur-laomer/lagamer among the Elamite rulers between 2100-1100 B.C.E.[18] later abandoned that hope and identified Chedorlaomer simply as Kudur-X.[19]

Tidal, king of Goim (nations), is generally identified with a Hittite king Tudhalias. Tudhalias I is dated in the 18th-17th centuries B.C.E., but the name continued in use into the 12th century B.C.E.

(b) *The kings of Palestine:* General agreement exists
that at least some of these royal names are pejorative epithets selected in accordance with the reputed sinfulness of
the cities with which they are associated. Thus Bera may
mean "in evil," Birsha "in wickedness," and the city Bela
"destroyed."[20] These names also appear to form allitera-
tions, e.g., Bera-Birsha, Shinab-Shemeber.[21] It has thus
been suggested that the names (one is actually left out)
are not essential to the narrator, but that a reference to
the presumed evil character of their respective cities is.
Needless to say, the bearers of these names and their cities
have not yet been identified elsewhere in ancient sources,[22]
but preliminary reports now have it that the names of the
five cities appear on a tablet from ancient Ebla in the same
order as in Gen 14:2 (Sodom, Gomorrah, Admah, Zeboiim, Bela).[23]

(c) *The population patterns in early second millennium
Palestine:* The peoples subdued by the foreign invaders, the
Rephaim (Deut 2:11), the Zuzim (perhaps the Zamzummim, Deut
2:20), the Emim (Deut 2:10), the Horites (Deut 2:12), the
Amalekites (Exod 17:8-16; 1 Sam 15), and the Amorites (Num
21:26), are all traditional enemies of Israel that figure
prominently in the conquest traditions. Consequently it has
been observed by literary analysis of Gen 14 that these represent secondary additions to the basic story, perhaps inserted to defend Israel's right to the land.[24] But they also
indicate a setting in the distant past (presettlement) for
this episode.

It has been pointed out, correctly, that in confronting
these peoples the invading force followed the King's Highway
east of the Jordan from Ashteroth-karnaim in Bashan, past the
Dead Sea, south to El-paran (perhaps Elath), back to Enmish-
pat (Kadesh-barnea), then east to Hazazon-tamar (perhaps
Engedi, 2 Chr 20:2), until a determined opposition forced a
pitched battle in the valley of Siddim (west or south-west
of the Dead Sea?).[25]

Nelson Glueck's conclusions regarding sedentary occupation in southern Trans-Jordan,[26] which were followed by Albright,[27] were that from the 18th-13th centuries B.C.E. none
existed. Consequently he reasoned that the foreign invasion
must have preceded this period and, moreover, that it was
responsible for the sudden subsequent disappearance of settled occupation in the region.[28] Glueck's findings and conclusions have recently been seriously questioned.[29]

(d) *Abram the Hebrew:* Two different arguments for the

historicity of our story have been derived from this characterization of Abram.  First, that "Hebrew" is a biblical designation of an Israelite used by foreigners (e.g., Gen 39:14), or used by an Israelite to identify himself to foreigners (e.g., Gen 40:15;  Jonah 1:9).  This might suggest a foreign source of the story,[30] or at least a non-Israelite setting for it.  Second, it has been suggested that Abram is here identified with the *Habiru* who are well known from the beginning to nearly the end of the second millennium B.C.E.[31] This identification was developed in the hands of Albright into his so-called caravan hypothesis[32] which may deserve mention if for no other reason than that it has met with so much opposition.[33]  Pertinent to our discussion is Albright's contention that Gen 14 describes a conflict over trade routes. The trade in question would involve Egypt of the 12th dynasty (20th-18th centuries B.C.E.) and Palestinian donkey caravaneers, to whom Abram is assigned, of the MB I period whose dates Albright lowered to the 20th-19th centuries B.C.E.  It is on the matter of this chronology that Albright's views are meeting with such stern criticism, but notice has also been given that he has misrepresented the biblical portrayal of the life of the patriarchs, making it nomadic rather than pastoral.[34]

(e)  *Melchizedek of Salem:*  The name Melchizedek is recognized as having parallels in west-Semitic literature of the 20th-18th centuries B.C.E., at least,[35] and general agreement exists that Melchizedek was king (and priest) of Jerusalem (Salem).[36]

Taken together, these traditional evidences suggest very strongly that in Gen 14 we are at least confronting a form of historiography.  The narrator is telling us about something that happened in his past.  Whether the story can also claim historicity depends upon whether or not it can also be said to have happened in our past.  To establish that fact we need as far as possible to locate the historiographical data of the narrator's past within the historical reconstruction that we call our past, and that has proved extraordinarily difficult, as T. L. Thompson has argued.[37]

## II.  *The Spartoli Tablets*

One attempt at tacking down into known history the four foreign kings of Gen 14 can be illustrated by reference to the Spartoli tablets, so named after the dealer from whom

they were acquired for the British Museum. They were first
studied by Th. G. Pinches in 1894 and promptly dubbed the
"Chedorlaomer texts" because of certain similarities between
some names mentioned in them and in Gen 14.[38] After several
attempts at restoring the text of the fragmentary tablets, a
workable translation was produced by A. Jeremias in 1917,[39]
and it was followed by Albright in his basic study of Gen 14
in 1926.[40] The texts speak of "evil, sinful kings" (*šarrāni
limnūtu, bēlē arni*) descending upon Babylon and Esagila, apparently as a punishment from the gods for some cultic ne-
glect.[41]

The kings in question are first, *DUR.MAH.DINGIR.ME*, the
ideograms of which Albright read as Tukulti-Belit-ilani. He
bears the patronymic Arad-Eaku (servant of Eaku) which suggested the name Arioch of Gen 14. Second, Tudhula, son of
Gazza (a Hittite) suggested a relationship to Tidal of Genesis 14. Third, Kutirnahute, king of Elam, was thought to be
related to Chedorlaomer, also of Elam. According to the
Spartoli tablets, these kings executed their destruction
upon Babylon by plunder and with inundation by water, where-
upon they were killed by their own sons (perhaps in divine
retribution). According to Albright they likely describe
the unrest surrounding Babylon in the 19th-18th centuries
B.C.E.[42]

The existing tablets are dated towards the end of the
first millennium, but their source is recognized as being
much earlier.[43] Were the narrator of Gen 14 acquainted
with this source, he could be said at least not to have cut
his story out of whole cloth. Hence the relationship between
the royal names in the two texts, Albright suggested long
ago (and others before him), endows Gen 14 with historical
probability.[44] Nevertheless, the four foreign kings of
Gen 14 were not yet identified precisely in history.

To this unfinished task M. C. Astour turned after an
interval of some 40 years by means of a reassessment of the
Spartoli tablets. At first he undertook an ingenious, but
in places forced, linguistic analysis of the royal names on
the tablets.[45] Its technical aspects cannot be discussed
here for lack of both space and linguistic ability, and moreover, some evaluation has already been offered elsewhere,[46]
but the basic conclusions can at least be provided. According
to Astour, Tukulti-Belit-ilani is a reference to Tukulti-
Ninurta I of Assyria (13th century B.C.E.), but thereby the
patronymic Arad-Eaku does not fit without strained linguistic
arguments. Tudhula becomes Mursilis I, a Hittite king (17th
century B.C.E.), but again the patronymic Gazza does not

immediately seem to fit. Kutirnahute becomes Kutir-Nahhunte III of Elam (12th century B.C.E.), an identification which is least strained of all. These three kings are known from other witnesses to have invaded Babylon, but did not use water (a flood) to destroy it. To meet that discrepancy, Astour proposed a transferral of the flood theme from Sennacherib to Tukulti-Ninurta I (both of Assyria), caused by another motif suffered by both these kings, namely parricide. Subsequently, one may presume, these two themes, parricide and flooding, were attached to all three kings. A last fourth king Ibil-Tutu is mentioned in the tablets as a southern king who did not destroy Babylon but usurped its throne. He is identified by Astour as Marduk-apal-iddina (Merodach-Baladan) of the 8th century B.C.E.

These four kings, concluded Astour, represent the same four regions from which also the four kings of Gen 14 came: Akkad (south), Subartu (north), Amurru (west), and Elam (east). Hereby a certain cosmic symbolism is introduced into the Spartoli texts, and according to Astour, it is further elaborated in Gen 14.[47] It tells of four kings, historical enemies of Babylon, representing the world, who at different times visited divine punishment upon that city. The Spartoli texts thereby advance a moral philosophy of history, namely that sin will be followed by divine punishment, here executed by the representatives of the "whole world" who employed a deluge to execute their work.[48] Such an understanding of history was shared by the deuteronomistic historian who in the 6th century B.C.E., according to Astour, borrowed the names of the four punishing kings, made them contemporaries, and applied their destructive activities to the evil cities of the plain.

How are we to respond to such a tour de force? The reader finds himself saying alternately "yes" and "no" to Astour's proposal. Some etymological reconstructions seem ingenious and probable, while others strain the author's credibility and the reader's imagination. Moreover, some functional shifts are rather large, for example, from a destruction by water to one by fire. Astour suggests a "fiery rain" (p. 103), but even that is not associated with Gen 14. Thirdly, Astour's proposals require that the narrators of both the Spartoli texts and of Gen 14 somehow obscured the historical data before them in order to strengthen their theology of history.[49] Though this could happen, it is an unhappy requirement to have to ask of a successful interpretation of a literary work.

However, having said this, the Spartoli texts (as

opposed to the late Spartoli tablets) do suggest the possibility that the narrator of Gen 14 was informed about the story of kings representing the four corners of the world, executing divine punishment upon a city, and their subsequent fate. This cosmic motif has some merit in a consideration of Gen 14 although the late date of the existing tablets, their poor state of preservation, and the single copy known so far, all weaken the case for finding a relationship between them and Gen 14.[50] Moreover, according to some recent studies of the Spartoli texts, they may belong to a different literary genre (unsuccessful temple robbery) and have little to do with exacting divine punishment by military means.[51]

Still Astour's proposal, if we take it seriously, would identify the four kings of Gen 14 in ancient Near Eastern history and would provide a specific context for the composition of the chapter. But the event itself would of course be deprived of any historical setting in the "patriarchal age." Very much the same conclusion is reached by J. Van Seters in his more recent analysis of the problem, though he bases it upon internal evidence without the benefit of any Near Eastern parallels.[52]

### III. Ancient Itineraries and Gen 14

A last, and to my knowledge new, attempt at finding a Near Eastern context for Gen 14 is based upon the well documented inter-city diplomatic and commercial traveling practices between locations in Mesopotamia and in Syria-Palestine during the 18th century B.C.E. Of course, already the earlier Kültepe texts reveal extensive trade relations between northern Mesopotamia (Assur) and Kanish in Anatolia to the north-west.[53] However, according to the 18th century Mari archives, such extensive trade continued between that city and the cities and provinces in Syria to the west,[54] and from some commercial documents involving the export of tin we learn that the trade routes also turned southward and included the Palestinian cities of Hazor and Laish (Dan).[55] The tin, used to manufacture bronze, apparently was exported from Mari to the cities of the west, including Hazor and Laish.[56] Perhaps a part in that same trade relationship was played by the unfortunate man from Hazor who while traveling to Mari with silver, gold, and valuable stones was robbed of his merchandise on the way to Emar.[57] At any rate the Mari correspondence as well as cuneiform inscriptions found at Hazor suggest a lively relationship between these two distant cities.[58] The same Mari archives that report on this trade relationship also describe the then current procedures employed to maintain it, namely a highly developed system of diplomatic visits and traveling envoys between cities.

According to the summary of the evidence provided by Munn-Rankin,[59] inter-city affairs, whether of a business, military, or diplomatic sort, were conducted by traveling diplomats who apparently functioned much like secretaries of state with very broad powers. To that end they could negotiate independently of their king when changed circumstances would recommend this. They enjoyed immunity when on duty, but could be detained or ignored by their hosts, even though this was considered inappropriate. They generally received clothing and were boarded at or near the palace upon their arrival with a diplomatic message, though that privilege could also be revoked. For protection they often traveled in sizable parties consisting of diplomats whose ultimate destinations varied widely.[60] To provide additional security a party of soldiers, in one instance numbering as many as 200, would escort the diplomats.[61] Furthermore, it was customary that a returning diplomat as a matter of courtesy would be given a native traveling escort for company and support.[62]

Such diplomatic missions established direct lines of communication between, for example, Mari and Hazor,[63] a distance of some 700 km. by direct route, but increasing to about 900 km. if a more circuitous way via Emar and Aleppo was taken, perhaps to avoid the dangers of hostile or uncivilized territory.[64] Along these routes diplomats and agents from various Mesopotamian cities (among others Babylon, Ekallatum, Eshnunna) passed through Mari on their way to their respective destinations, including Hazor.[65] Their objectives, we may presume from the texts, were to establish or facilitate trade, exchange gifts, gather information, and arrange for military endeavors.[66]

To this pattern of activity can perhaps be added the itinerary described on the Urbana tablets,[67] of which another copy was discovered at Yale.[68] It may in fact portray such a diplomatic mission, albeit a momentous one.[69] The journey from Larsa in southern Mesopotamia to Emar in Syria and back lasted six months, fourteen days, may have employed both ships and chariots, was able to cover 25-30 airline km. per day (on the outbound trip), and with relatively few exceptions was interrupted only by overnight halts. There are indications that the travelers (or at least some of them) were armed,[70] but no hint is given that they took time out for battle.[71] Even more remarkable is the fact that the party of travelers

stayed only one night (or at the most three) at their destination Emar.[72] However, that an important mission had been
accomplished is suggested by the fact that they returned home
almost immediately, but at a much more leisurely pace (107
days vs. 87 days on the outbound trip).[73] Is it possible
that the itinerary describes an important, escorted, diplomatic mission of the type portrayed in the Mari archives?
It is in fact dated in the time of Zimri-Lim (18th century
B.C.E.),[74] and may well represent an urgent mission from
Larsa in the south to Emar in the west which out of fear or
in the interest of secrecy followed the longer route along
the Tigris (to avoid Mari!). Possibly a new route to the
west was being opened up in the face of a hostile Mari on
the Euphrates,[75] and the Old Babylonian itinerary recorded
the event.

Two suggestions regarding the Near Eastern setting of
Gen 14 have been made on the basis of these various cuneiform
texts. A. Malamat has suggested that the commercial/diplo-
matic texts from Mari may provide a model for understanding
the context of the four invading kings in Gen 14.[76] W. W.
Hallo has suggested that the Old Babylonian itinerary itself
in the form in which it is preserved represents a historical
record on the way to becoming a piece of "canonical" literature, and that echoes of this literature may have passed into
Gen 14.[77] How are we to evaluate these suggestions? They
do in fact seem to answer some issues frequently raised in
connection with the problem of finding a Near Eastern historical context for our story.

(a) The itineraries under discussion fit chronologi-
cally into the period generally assigned to the patriarchs,
namely the Palestinian MB II period, or the 19th-18th centuries B.C.E.[78]

(b) A frequent objection to the historicity of Gen 14
has been that a grand military alliance of four major Mesopotamian kings directed against rather small Palestinian
towns as indicated in Gen 14 seems "ludicrous."[79] The itineraries, on the other hand, suggest the possibility of a
small operation, perhaps a trade or political mission with
military escort, possibly involving only a few hundred persons. Such a limited mission might well include the interests
of several foreign kings (some perhaps joining the mission
along the way) due to a common destination or mutual interests.

(c) A second objection has it that a cuneiform source
could not possibly be concerned with matters so far afield
as Trans-Jordan, presumably because major Mesopotamian centers

could have no business or interest there.[80] That view
may be misleading and is certainly weakened by the Old
Babylonian itinerary which appears to be preserving not
simply a historical record but perhaps a near "canonical"
account of a journey lasting over six months and covering
some 2500 km. It is further suggested that this itinerary
may have been part of a larger historical account of wider
scope, as is also the case with the itinerary of Gen 14.[81]

(d) A third incongruity has been noted between Abram's
fear before the petty king of Gerar (Gen 20) and his courage
before the four Mesopotamian kings.[82] But that too falls
away if the latter constituted a small mission of royal envoys with a military escort. That Abram's rescue team is
said to have overtaken the invaders at Dan (Laish) supports
the fact that the foreign mission is reported as having returned the way it came and as having moved swiftly.

(e) According to one reconstruction of the Palestinian
itinerary,[83] the foreign invaders moved south from Bashan,
along the King's Highway, passed the Dead Sea to the east,
as far south as El-paran (Elath), before they returned to
Kadesh-barnea, Hazazon-tamar and north to Dan (Laish). The
expedition is understood to have moved swiftly, as in the
case of our known itineraries, and it stopped only momen-
tarily to confront an opposing coalition force that had
hastily gathered at the valley of Siddim, presumably to cut
off its return.

In short, the picture of a swift, small force following
a set itinerary whose essential objectives are lost to us,
and at which we can only guess,[84] offers a possible model for
the account in Gen 14 and may help to place it in a feasible
ancient Near Eastern context. That major journeys of this
kind should be recorded, as illustrated by the Old Babylonian
itinerary, and perhaps eventually added to the "canonical"
literature further enhances the possibility that the account
of such happenings could be recalled in Palestine.

Naturally this does not explain the appearance of Gen 14
in its present form in the Bible, but only the event or source
which may have instructed it, or part of it.[85] If, however,
an ancient itinerary of an expeditionary force provides the
Near Eastern context for the story of Gen 14, the report of
it has been seriously enlarged and reinterpreted by the theological mind of the narrator. The limited expedition is seen
as a major military campaign against Israel's traditional
enemies, particularly the kings in the rich valley of Siddim
whose urban immorality will be contrasted to the bucolic

idealism attributed to Abram (Gen 18-19). The story whose inclusion here may be triggered by the Lot cycle serves to establish that Abram (and subsequent Israelite leaders, like David) is the sole sovereign and protector, according to the promise, of a land already occupied.[86] That this sovereignty should be compatible with certain indigenous elements, including a cult center in Jerusalem, as becomes obvious in the time of David and Solomon, is verified by the Melchizedek incident in the same story.[87]

# NOTES

1. G. von Rad, *Genesis* (rev. ed.; Philadelphia: Westminster, 1972), p. 175; S. Hermann, *A History of Israel in Old Testament Times* (Philadelphia: Fortress, 1975), p. 49.

2. N. M. Sarna, *Understanding Genesis* (New York: McGraw-Hill, 1966), p. 110.

3. B. Vawter, *On Genesis: A New Reading* (Garden City: Doubleday, 1977), p. 185.

4. W. F. Albright, "The Historical Background of Genesis XIV," *JSOR* 10 (1926), 231.

5. Nelson Glueck was so confident of this that he spoke of "the age of Abraham in the Negev," *Rivers in the Desert* (New York: Farrar, Straus and Cudahy, 1959), pp. 68-84.

6. For a full treatment of the study of Gen 14, see J. A. Emerton, "Some False Clues in the Study of Genesis XIV," *VT* 21 (1971), 24-47; W. Schatz, *Genesis 14: Eine Untersuchung* (Frankfurt: Peter Lang, 1972), pp. 13-61.

7. First proposed by A. Jirku, "Neues keilinschriftliches Material zum Alten Testament: Zu Gen 14," *ZAW* 39 (1921), 152-156. Recently E. A. Speiser, *Genesis* (AB 1; Garden City: Doubleday, 1964), pp. 101, 108. One problem concerns the syntax of Gen 14:1-2.

8. See especially "A Revision of Early Hebrew Chronology," *JPOS* 1 (1921), 49-79; "Shinar-Šangar and its Monarch Amraphel," *AJSL* 40 (1923), 125-133; "The Jordan Valley in the Bronze Age," *Annual ASOR* 6 (1924-25), 13-74; "The Historical

Background of Genesis XIV," *JSOR* 10 (1926), 231-269; "A
Third Revision of the Early Chronology of Western Asia,"
*BASOR* 99 (1942), 28-36; "Abram the Hebrew," *BASOR* 163
(1961), 36-54; *Yahweh and the Gods of Canaan* (Garden City:
Doubleday, 1968), pp. 53-109.

9.  See J. Bright, *A History of Israel* (2nd ed.;
Philadelphia: Westminster, 1972), p. 83; Sarna, *Genesis*,
pp. 110-119; Vawter, *Genesis*, pp. 185-203; *et al.*

10.  See Schatz, *Genesis 14*, p. 46.

11.  Thus M. Noth, *The History of Israel* (2nd ed.;
New York: Harper and Row, 1960), p. 124; J. Van Seters,
*Abraham in History and Tradition* (New Haven: Yale, 1975),
p. 120; T. L. Thompson, *The Historicity of the Patriarchal
Narratives* (BZAW 133; Berlin: de Gruyter, 1974), p. 190;
Hermann, *A History of Israel in Old Testament Times*, p. 50;
M. C. Astour, "Political and Cosmic Symbolism in Genesis 14
and in Its Babylonian Sources," *Biblical Motifs* (ed. A. Alt-
mann; Cambridge: Harvard, 1966), pp. 65-112. R. de Vaux
who had earlier affirmed the historicity of the chapter
turned from this position in his latest writings. See *The
Early History of Israel* (Philadelphia: Westminster, 1978),
pp. 216-220.

12.  This identification is all but abandoned. See,
however, F. Cornelius, "Genesis 14," *ZAW* 72 (1960), 1-7.
See also Schatz, *Genesis 14*, pp. 84-85.

13.  Most recently Vawter, *Genesis*, p. 188. The following etymology is suggested: Amraphel=amar-pi-el=the mouth of
god has spoken.

14.  "Abram the Hebrew," pp. 49-50; *Yahweh and the Gods
of Canaan*, pp. 68-69.

15.  This identification was first made by F. M. Th.
Böhl, "Brieven uit het archief van Mari (Tell Hariri),"
*BO* 2 (1945), 66. See also J.-R. Kupper, *Les nomades en Méso-
potamie au temps des rois de Mari* (Paris: Université de
Liège, 1957), p. 232. For a contrary view see M. Noth,
"Arioch-Arriwuk," *VT* 1 (1951), 136-140; P. Grelot, "Ariok,"
*VT* 25 (1975), 711-719.

16.  Recently Vawter, *Genesis*, p. 188. However, this
identification is problematic. See Schatz, *Genesis 14*, p. 87.

17.  See *CAD*[3] I, 2, 640; II, 1, 266-267.

18. "The Historical Background," p. 233; "A Third Revision," pp. 33-34.

19. "Abram the Hebrew," p. 49.

20. Shinab is more difficult and has been variously interpreted as "*sin* (the moon) is a father," or following the Samaritan Pentateuch, *Shem-abad* "the name is lost." For this proposal and a suggestion regarding Shemeber, see Astour, "Genesis 14," pp. 74-75.

21. Thus Albright, "Abram the Hebrew," pp. 51-52.

22. For an older discussion of the lost cities of the plain, see J. Penrose Harland, "Sodom and Gomorrah," *BAR* I, 41-75.

23. Thus M. Dahood, "Ebla, Ugarit and the Old Testament," *The Month*, 2nd New Ser. 11, No. 8 (1978), 275. However, see now D. N. Freedman, "The Real Story of the Ebla Tablets: Ebla and the Cities of the Plain," *BA* 41 (1978), 143-164.

24. Recently Vawter, *Genesis*, p. 192.

25. Y. Aharoni, *The Land of the Bible* (London: Burns and Oates, 1967), pp. 127-129. An association of Hazazon (Gen 14:7) with the otherwise unknown town Hazazar of the Mari tin text is possible but cannot be demonstrated. See G. Dossin, "La route de l'étain en Mésopotamie au temps de Zimri-Lim," *RA* 64 (1970), 98:23; A. Malamat, "Syro-Palestinian Destinations in a Mari Tin Inventory," *IEJ* 21 (1971), 37. In another Mari text (ARM VI, 23:19-24), the name of a city, presumably south of Hazor, is broken off. A. Malamat, "Hazor, 'The Head of All Those Kingdoms,'" *JBL* 79 (1960), 15.

26. "The Negev," *BA* 22 (1959), 82-97; *Rivers in the Desert*, pp. 11, 68-84.

27. "Abram the Hebrew," p. 36.

28. Nelson Glueck, "Transjordan," *Archaeology and Old Testament Study* (ed. D. Winton Thomas; Oxford: University Press, 1967), p. 445. Cf. William G. Dever in J. H. Hayes and J. M. Miller, eds., *Israelite and Judean History* (Philadelphia: Westminster, 1977), pp. 93-96.

29. Dever in Hayes and Miller, eds., *Israelite and Judean History*, p. 90; Thompson, *Historicity of the Patriarchal Narratives*, pp. 192-194.

30. Speiser, *Genesis*, p. 103.

31. *SA.GAZ* meaning "rob," "plunder," or the like already occurs in the third millennium B.C.E. See J. Bottero, "Habiru," *Reallexikon der Assyriologie und vorderasiatischen Archäologie*, IV, 14-27. Cf. Albright, *Yahweh and the Gods of Canaan*, pp. 75-89.

32. "Abram the Hebrew," pp. 36-54; *Yahweh and the Gods of Canaan*, pp. 53-109.

33. Recently Thompson, *Historicity of the Patriarchal Narratives*, pp. 172-186.

34. Dever in Hayes and Miller, eds., *Israelite and Judean History*, pp. 99-102, 118.

35. Thus Albright, "Abram the Hebrew," p. 52; F. M. Cross, *Canaanite Myth and Hebrew Epic* (Cambridge: Harvard, 1972), p. 209. Cf. W. Zimmerli, "Abraham und Melchisedek," *Das Ferne und Nahe Wort* (ed. F. Maass; BZAW 105; Berlin: de Gruyter, 1967), pp. 225-264.

36. See, however, Albright's emendation of the text: *u-Malkiṣedeq, melek šelomoh*, "and Melchizedek, a king allied to him" ("Abram the Hebrew," p. 52).

37. *Historicity of the Patriarchal Narratives*, pp. 187-195. Thompson here follows the distinction between historiography and history made by H. Cancik in his 1970 Tübingen dissertation, now published as *Grundzüge der hethitischen und alttestamentlichen Geschichtsschreibung* (Wiesbaden: Otto Harrassowitz, 1976). However, he draws a different conclusion than Cancik regarding the historiographic character of Gen 14. "The study of the archaeology and the history of the early Second Millennium has nothing to offer directly to the interpretation of the traditions about Abraham, Isaac, and Jacob, though it has much to offer to an understanding of the culture of the ancient Near East, of which the Bible and the patriarchal narratives form a part" (p. 195). This conclusion was of course anticipated by de Vaux in his later writings (*The Early History of Israel*, p. 219, published originally in French in 1971).

38. "Certain Inscriptions and Records Referring to Babylonia and Elam and their Rulers, and Other Matters," *Journal of the Transactions of the Victoria Institute* 29 (1897), 43-89.

39. "Die sogenannten Kedorlaomer-Texte," MVAG (1917), 69-97.

40. "The Historical Background," pp. 237-239.

41. Especially in tablet III, 2 in Jeremias' sequence, the correctness of which is not assured. "Die sogenannten Kedorlaomer-Texte," pp. 93-95.

42. Albright's dating of Gen 14 changed over the years as new evidence was introduced into the case. Thus, " A Revision of Early Hebrew Chronology," pp. 68-78; "Shinar-Šangar," p. 133 (1675 B.C.E.); "The Jordan Valley in the Bronze Age," pp. 65-66 (1775 B.C.E.); "The Historical Background," pp. 238-241 (19th-18th centuries B.C.E.); "A Third Revision," p. 36 (1700-1550 B.C.E.); "Abram the Hebrew," p. 50; *Yahweh and the Gods of Canaan,* p. 69 (19th century B.C.E.).

43. Though the matter is uncertain, a second millennium date is considered probable. See Albright, "The Historical Background," p. 236.

44. "The Historical Background," p. 259.

45. "Genesis 14," pp. 81-100.

46. See Emerton, "Some False Clues," pp. 38-46.

47. For example, the water (flood) may be related to the sea of Gen 14:3. The twelve years service (Gen 14:4) has been related to the zodiac signs. Abram's 318 servants have been associated with certain lunar or astral calculations, but it is all very speculative. See now S. Gevirtz, "Abram's 318," *IEJ* 19 (1969), 110-113.

48. This theme is familiar in the cuneiform literature. See A. K. Grayson, *Assyrian and Babylonian Chronicles* (Texts from Cuneiform Sources 5; Locust Valley, NY: J. J. Augustin, 1975), pp. 145-150; J. J. M. Roberts, "Nebuchadnezzar I's Elamite Crisis in Theological Perspective," *Essays on the Ancient Near East in Memory of Jacob Joel Finkelstein* (ed. M. de Jong Ellis; Connecticut Academy of Arts and Sciences; Hamden, Conn.: Archon, 1977), pp. 183-187.

49. For example, it assumes that the author of the Spartoli texts purposely chose a pseudonym for Mursilis I, while the narrator of Gen 14 unwittingly made the four kings contemporaries and transferred their activities from Babylon to Palestine (Astour, "Genesis 14," pp. 89, 100).

50. For a discussion of this and related problems see W. W. Hallo, "Problems in Sumerian Hermeneutics," *Perspectives in Jewish Learning*, vol. 5 (ed. B. L. Sherwin; Chicago: Spertus College of Judaica, 1973), pp. 1-12.

51. See J. A. Brinkman, *A Political History of Post-Kassite Babylonia, 1158-722 B.C.* (AnOr 43; Rome: Pontifical Biblical Institute, 1968), pp. 18, 33; N. Stockholm, "Zur Überlieferung von Heliodor, Kuturnahhunte und anderen missglückten Tempelräubern," *ST* 22 (1968), 1-28. Stockholm, however, treats only the second (largest) tablet, leaving the other two with the specific royal references out of consideration.

52. *Abraham in History and Tradition*, pp. 112-120.

53. See M. T. Larsen, *Old Assyrian Caravan Procedures* (Istanbul: Nederlands Historisch-Archaeologisch Instituut, 1967); K. R. Veenhof, *Aspects of Old Assyrian Trade and Its Terminology* (Leiden: Brill, 1972).

54. ARM VII. See W. F. Leemans, *Foreign Trade in the Old Babylonian Period* (Studia et Documenta 6; Leiden: Brill, 1960).

55. ARM VII, 236. See A. Malamat, "Hazor, 'The Head of All Those Kingdoms,'" pp. 12-19; "Northern Canaan and the Mari Texts," *Near Eastern Archaeology in the Twentieth Century* (ed. J. A. Sanders; Garden City: Doubleday, 1970), pp. 164-177; "Syro-Palestinian Destinations in a Mari Tin Inventory," pp. 31-38; Dossin, "La route de l'étain en Mésopotamie au temps de Zimri-Lim," 97-106; J. A. Sasson, "Mari Notes," *RA* 65 (1971), 172; *CAH*[3] II, 1, 12-13. According to some preliminary reports relationships existed between Ebla (of Syria) and various Palestinian cities, presumably at an even earlier time. G. Pettinato, "The Royal Archives of Tell Mardikh-Ebla," *BA* 39 (1976), 46.

56. J. D. Muhly, *Copper and Tin* (Transactions of the Connecticut Academy of Arts and Sciences 43; New Haven: Conn. Academy of Arts and Sciences, 1973), pp. 288-335.

57. M. Birot, "Nouvelles découvertes épigraphiques au palais de Mari (salle 115)," *Syria* 50 (1973), 10-11.

58. ARM VI, 23, 78: VII, 236; XII, 747. See above, note 54. G. Dossin, "Kengen, pays de Canaan," *RSO* 32 (1957), 37-38; Y. Yadin, *et al.*, *Hazor II* (Jerusalem: Magnes, 1960), pp. 115-116; B. Landsberger and H. Tadmor, "Fragments of Clay Liver Models from Hazor," *IEJ* 14 (1964), 201-218; W. W. Hallo and H. Tadmor, "A Lawsuit from Hazor," *IEJ* 27 (1977), 1-11; H. Tadmor, "A Lexicographical Text from Hazor," *IEJ* 27 (1977), 98-102.

59. "Diplomacy in Western Asia in the Early Second Millennium B.C.," *Iraq* 18 (1956), 99-109.

60. *Ibid.*, p. 107.

61. *Ibid.*, p. 106. The provisions for such a mission would be considerable. In one case they included 30 sheep, 30 qa of oil, etc. (p. 105).

62. *Ibid.*, p. 106. Such a companion, lit. *ālik idi*, is a "person assigned to escort diplomats, foreigners, and persons in need of surveillance—a helper, protector, partner," *(CAD A/1, 343)*.

63. Beyond the commercial texts this may also be concluded from the names in the so-called dream-land itineraries. See A. L. Oppenheim, *The Interpretation of Dreams in the Ancient Near East* (Transactions of the American Philosophical Society 46; Philadelphia: American Philosophical Society, 1956), pp. 260, 268, 312-313.

64. Thus Malamat, "Northern Canaan," p. 166, n. 15. See also W. W. Hallo, "The Road to Emar," *JCS* 18 (1964), 86.

65. ARM VI, 23; Malamat, "Northern Canaan," p. 164; A. L. Oppenheim, "The Archives of the Palace of Mari II," *JNES* 13 (1954), 147; *CAH*3 II, 1, 13.

66. Munn-Rankin, "Diplomacy," pp. 104-109.

67. Identified by A. Goetze in the University of Illinois Urbana collection and published as "An Old Babylonian Itinerary," *JCS* 7 (1953), 51-72.

68. W. W. Hallo, "The Road to Emar," *JCS* 18 (1964), 57-88. D. O. Edzard has questioned that the two texts are duplicates ("Itinerare," *Reallexikon der Assyriologie und vorderasiatischen Archäologie* V, 217-218).

69. See Hallo ("Road to Emar," p. 85) for the suggestion
that it was a military expedition. A possible parallel may
be found in the "Epic of the King of Battle," translated and
discussed by Albright, *JSOR* 7 (1923), 1-20. See also "Abram
the Hebrew," p. 53, n. 76. For the suggestion that trade was
involved, see W. F. Leemans, "Old Babylonian Letters and Economic History," *JESHO* 11 (1968), 211.

70. At Dur-Apilsin (north of Sippar) "they girded themselves." At Sugagu (south of Assur) "the troops rested for
two days." At the last stop before reaching the destination,
Emar, "the chariots had to be repaired." Hallo, "Road to
Emar," pp. 67, 70, 80.

71. An armed conflict would certainly have called for a
marginal notation like the ones noted above (note 70).

72. Hallo, "Road to Emar," p. 81. On the difficult
topography of the north-west sector of the itinerary, see now
Barry J. Beitzel, "From Harran to Imar Along the Old Babylonian
Itinerary: The Evidence from the Archives Royales de Mari,"
in *Biblical and Near Eastern Studies* (ed. G. A. Tuttle; Grand
Rapids, MI: Eerdmans, 1978), pp. 209-219.

73. Hallo, "Road to Emar," p. 84.

74. *Ibid.*, p. 86.

75. *Ibid.* See, however, M. Stol, *Studies in Old Babylonian History* (Istanbul: Nederlands Historisch-Archaeologisch Instituut, 1976), pp. 40-41.

76. "Northern Canaan," p. 172.

77. "Road to Emar," p. 86. A suggested possibility of
a confusion of Emar and *'amora* (Gomorrah) is not likely and
would be invalidated by the reported references to the cities
of the plain in the Ebla texts, above, note 23.

78. Dever in Hayes and Miller, *Israelite and Judean
History*, pp. 84-89, 95-96.

79. Most recently, Van Seters, *Abraham in History and
Tradition*, p. 115.

80. *Ibid.*, p. 116.

81. Hallo, "Road to Emar," p. 84.

82. Recently, Van Seters, *Abraham in History and Tradition*, p. 115.

83. See above, note 25.

84. The rebellion of the five kings mentioned in Gen 14: 4 offers only a partial (stock in trade?) explanation that does not account for the references to the other peoples who were subdued along the way (vv. 5-7), nor does it explain the continuation of the journey, perhaps as far south as Elath, and back north along a slightly different route.

85. For the problem of the literary composition of Gen 14, see J. A. Emerton, "The Riddle of Genesis XIV," *VT* 21 (1971), 403-439; Van Seters, *Abraham in History and Tradition*, pp. 296-308.

86. Emerton, "The Riddle of Genesis," pp. 422-423; B. Mazar, "The Historical Background of the Book of Genesis," *JNES* 28 (1969), 74.

87. Emerton, "The Riddle of Genesis," pp. 421-422; Mazar, "The Historical Background," p. 74.

# LITERARY CRITICISM AND BIBLICAL STUDIES:
## A RHETORICAL ANALYSIS OF THE JOSEPH NARRATIVE

Mary Savage
Albertus Magnus College

## I.  Literary Criticism and Biblical Studies

The critic who discusses literature in an inter-disci-
plinary context is often reminded of a scene C. S. Lewis
creates for *The Discarded Image*.  In Lewis' vision, Chaucer,
when asked why he does not write brand-new stories, replies
'Surely we are not yet reduced to that?'[1]  Nevertheless, the
disciplines have much to learn from each other.  For its
part, literary criticism can learn from history, anthropology,
and religion as criticism itself moves beyond a narrow for-
malism to admit that literature does not exist in a vacuum,
that it is related to the culture which produced it.  Conversely, literary criticism can contribute to history, anthropology, and religion a more thorough understanding of the
literary artifacts which are so often the objects studied by
these disciplines.

The shift which Bernhard Anderson notes in biblical
studies from the diachronic to the synchronic investigation
of texts[2] is perhaps creating a ground where students of
literature can meet students of the Bible, although at first
glance it may seem the disciplines have no room in which to
stand together.  In general, for the literary critic a text
is opaque, something to be seen in and of itself.  For the
student of history, religion, or anthropology, however, a
text is transparent--or at least something to be gotten
beyond, or behind, or over to the real object of investigation.  Nevertheless, the movement toward synchronic investigation provides a common ground for the disciplines because
it suggests that the effort to get *beyond* the text might
better be an effort to get *through* the text.  This latter
effort is especially productive for the study of biblical

narrative since narrative is obviously synchronic in nature.
No matter where an episode may have originated in the process
of composition, in the received text episodes bear synchronic
relations to each other as they are told by the narrator.
Moreover, episodes frequently bear synchronic relations to
one another along a time line which informs the events of a
tale. A scholar, literary or biblical, who deals with narrative necessarily encounters synchronic phenomena.

The study of biblical narrative has been inhibited, it
seems to me, by inattention to the synchronic aspects of
texts and by a general failure to recognize the principle that
some literary theory (or at least a theoretical stance) is always implicit in a description of a literary text.[3] Critics
working out of a theoretical framework--a particular understanding of the nature of narrative, for example--are aware of
the model or models they use for analysis and are less likely
to impose those expectations on a particular text. In effect,
possession of a literary theory renders texts more opaque. On
the other hand, a theory, or theoretical stance, which works
unconsciously is likely to distort a text. Such a situation
exists in the study of biblical narrative. Because contemporary biblical scholarship generally--and unconsciously--re-
flects the stance taken toward narrative literature by the
Jamesian tradition, it frequently imposes norms for narrative
which are quite alien to biblical narrative itself.

The following presentation is an attempt to enter the
common ground between literary criticism and biblical studies
by treating the Joseph Narrative opaquely, that is, by discussing it from the framework of the particular literary theory
implicit in rhetorical criticism. First, however, I will explore some of the configurations of the ground by (1) discussing synchronic and diachronic study, (2) describing the
Jamesian tradition which has influenced the way most of us
think about narrative, (3) suggesting two other models (structuralism and rhetorical criticism) which may be more useful
for biblical studies.

Anderson's observation that recent scholarship is hospi-
table to the synchronic study of received texts is certainly
born out by the work of this volume. There is increasing
respect for and careful attention being paid to the texts in
other scholarly literature. Wilson's work, for example,
stresses the interrelationship of form and function in genealogy.[4] Van Seters, in his investigation of the Abraham material, states that structural analysis precedes source division
and functions as a control for it.[5] Coats goes further in
*From Canaan into Egypt* to state that the principle that the

received text should be the point of departure is "perhaps
too painfully obvious to be worthy of explicit mention."[6]
A more theoretical statement about the nature and value of
synchronic study is made by Fokkelman in the first section
of his *Narrative Art in Genesis*.  Relying on Wellek and
Warren's *Theory of Literature*, Fokkelman argues that the
received text has an ontological status of its own, that is,
a mode of existence which is linguistic and literary.[7]

Anderson suggests that the trend toward synchronic study
can be assisted by three kinds of literary study:  (1) studies
in oral literature, (2) stylistic and rhetorical criticism,
(3) structuralism.[8]  Since William Millar has provided an example of the usefulness of oral studies (above, pp. 27-57), I
will focus on the usefulness of structuralism and rhetorical
criticism.

First, however, I wish to preface my discussion of these
methods with an account of the theoretical orientation of diachronic study.  Meyer Abrams offers as a device for comparing
theories of art the following schematic representation of the
total situation in a work of art.

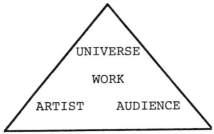

At the center of the diagram is the work itself.  The angles
of the triangle represent the work's maker, its audience (to
whom it is addressed or made available), and its subject matter (what is is about).  Although any adequate literary theory
"takes some account of all four elements, almost all theories
exhibit a discernable orientation toward one only.  That is,
a critic tends to derive from one of these terms his principal
categories for defining, classifying, and analyzing a work of
art, as well as the major criteria by which he judges its
value."[9]  One may classify a literary theory according to its
orientation toward one of these four elements.  A theory oriented (as classical literary theory is, for example) toward
the universe, Abrams classifies as a mimetic theory.  Theories
oriented toward the audience (like much neo-classical criticism) are pragmatic; those oriented (like many Romantic theories) toward the artist are expressive; those oriented toward
the work itself are objective (or, we would probably say,
formalist).

Literary criticism in this century has been characterized by some form of the objective orientation. (Note the
way Abrams, almost instinctively, places the work itself at
the center of his scheme.) In biblical studies, on the other
hand, the emphasis on diachronic phenomena has tended to lead
the scholar away from the received text—a tendency which Fokkelman suggests is based on the "tacit presupposition that
the text is not to be interpreted in itself because it is
stratified or composite and that to understand it we must
first reconstruct its genesis and its process of growth."[10]
In its emphasis on origins and processes of composition, form-
criticism seems to me to possess a theoretical orientation
which is primarily expressive, that is, form criticism looks
in the direction of the producing artist—whether the producer
is an individual singer, author, editor; or a sequence of pro-
ducers; or even the spirit of a whole people—to discover the
intentions, thoughts and feelings which the producer expresses.
From this orientation, the value of a text is tied to its ex-
pressiveness: the truer, the more authentic the expression,
the more valuable the text. There is also an assumption—at
least in Gunkel's work—that the earlier periods of the tradition are the most authentic ones. *The Legends of Genesis*
is filled with a kind of nostalgia for scenes like the one
depicted in Josh 4:6 in which storytellers are trained to hand
on the authentic tradition.[11] As Anderson says in his introduction to Noth's *History of the Pentateuchal Traditions*,
Gunkel's concern was "to find a way of studying the material
which would enable the scholar to go beyond literary dissec-
tion to enter esthetically into the interior experience of the
people, into their real history."[12]

## II. The Jamesian Tradition

Like many disciplines, the study of narrative (narratology) is subject to fads. Frye's *Anatomy of Criticism*, for example, which classifies narrative genres according to the
archetypal images which lurk behind them, gave birth to diverse progeny, the most famous of which is Scholes and Kel-
logg's *The Nature of Narrative*. Since the mid-fifties, however, the clear direction of narratology has been a movement
beyond the Jamesian tradition. In the first part of this
century, the influence of Henry James and of his followers,
like Percy Lubbock whose *Craft of Fiction* popularized the
term *point of view*, resulted in the canonization of the
realistic novel as the paradigm for all narrative literature.[13]
This Jamesian tradition of criticism imposed the following

prescriptions on all narrative:

1. Character is action. That is, stories are about individuals and their psychological motivations and developments.

2. Plots follow consistent patterns of causality which may be charted as rising and falling action.

3. The conventions of narrating are based on what Ian Watt has called "formal realism." Akin to philosophical realism, "formal realism" rests on the assumption that an authentic account is an objective account, an account based on empirical observations and expressed in descriptive and denotative language.[14]

In the Jamesian tradition, "formal realism" has meant concern for a point of view from which action is seen, for the objectivity of the narrator, for enmeshing character and action in a fabric of detailed times and places, that is, for setting character and action in a circumstantial context.

The Jamesian tradition has been reinforced by the general popularity of New Criticism, an objective theory of literature which views the literary work as separate from its creator. New Criticism affirmed the notion that narrators should be objective.

The Jamesian tradition is the one in which most of us were formed. Unless we consciously construct another model for narrative, we read texts as if they were realistic novels. We expect motivation, rising and falling action. It is exactly the Jamesian model which influences the work of Van Seters, Coats, Anderson, and Redford. Their collective work indicates, I think, that we cannot make biblical narrative opaque by using this model.

Narratology began to move beyond the Jamesian tradition as it encountered stories which did not fit the prescriptions of the model: ancient stories in which character is not action, that is, stories which do not focus on psychological motivation; modern stories in which actions do not follow a pattern of rise and fall (the Borges story in which a character faced with two alternatives selects both, or Calvino's _T-Zero_ in which a character faced with a multiplicity of alternatives selects none of them and remains frozen in time);

medieval stories in which the conventions of narrating dis-
rupt "formal realism." The impulse of critics to move beyond
the Jamesian tradition is also part of a revolt against New
Criticism. Critics recognized that, to use Abrams' term,
pragmatic concerns were not wholly lacking in narrative, that
stories were not objective accounts, that, indeed, they did
convey values. The clarion call for this position is Wayne
Booth's *Rhetoric of Fiction*.


## III. Models Beyond the Jamesian Tradition


Structuralism and rhetorical criticism, two models of
literary study mentioned by Anderson, make narrative more
opaque than their Jamesian counterpart. Because structuralism
is both subjective and self-conscious, there are almost as
many structuralisms as there are structuralists.[15] Instead
of defining structuralism, here I wish to describe the analogy
to modern linguistics which provides the impetus for structuralism and to investigate three structuralist concepts, two
of which render texts more opaque and one of which makes them
more transparent.

We may begin with Roland Barthes' description of structuralism. Structuralism, he writes, is a "mode of analysis of
cultural artifacts which originates in the methods of contemporary linguistics."[16] The linguistic concept on which structural analysis is based is Saussure's distinction between
*langue* ("a system, an institution, a set of interpersonal
rules and norms") and *parole* ("Actual manifestations of this
system").[17] *Langue* is the language, as in the phrase, *the
English language; parole* is an individual utterance. *Langue*
permits the production and interpretation of *parole*. For example, *langue* permits us to understand *Park the car in Harvard
Yard* when spoken by a Bostonian and a New Yorker as essentially
the same sentence in spite of obvious difference in pronunciation (in the *parole*).

Structuralism views individual artifacts as members of a
system and believes that all elements of a system are related
in a law-like way which is discernable.[18] In other words,
just as the grammar of the language permits the production
and interpretation of individual utterances, the institution
of literature (whose laws are discernable) permits the production and interpretation of poems.

Lévi-Strauss has applied the concept of *langue* to myth

in a way which reduces stories to their lowest common (in this case, conceptual) denominator. According to Lévi-Strauss, an individual myth *(parole)* is a message in code.[19] "A code is a set of objects or categories drawn from a single area of experience and related to one another in ways which make them useful logical tools for expressing other relations."[20] Thus empirical categories such as 'raw' and 'cooked' serve as tools for abstract notions like nature and culture. The task of analysis is to explain the myth by identifying the code and by showing what it expresses. The method of analysis is to discover a set of binary opposites (e.g., life and death) which are resolved by the myth. (The theoretical assumption here is that the binary opposition characteristic of language is also characteristic of the human mind.)

The weakness of Lévi-Strauss' model, especially for comparative study, is its emphasis on paradigmatic relationships. In linguistics, paradigmatic relations "determine the possibility of substitution," while syntagmatic relations "bear on the possibility of combination."[21] For example, in the sentence "_____ kicked the door," paradigmatic relations obtain among all the nouns which could fill the subject slot, while syntagmatic relations obtain between the subject and its predicate. Although Lévi-Strauss does attend somewhat to the resolution of polar opposites (a syntagmatic relationship), the emphasis of his method is on the paradigmatic qualities of the code. This approach reduces distinctions among stories; it renders them more transparent. As Leach says in his structural analysis of Genesis, "instead of taking each myth as a thing in itself with a 'meaning' peculiar to itself it is assumed, from the start, that every myth is one of a complex and that any pattern which occurs in one myth will recur."[22]

Two other structuralist concepts are more useful for comparative study: Barthes' concept of codes and Todorov's concept of discourse. Barthes' *S/Z* is an exercise in the structuralist reading of narrative. In this two hundred page reading of a thirty page short story, Barthes describes various systems of meanings (codes) which render stories more opaque than Lévi-Strauss' categories. Barthes' code (or code of actions) is composed of actions and their logical relations. The *hermeneutic code* (or code of puzzles) is composed of elements which raise questions, e.g., to create suspense. The *connative code* and the *symbolic code* are systems creating what has been called character and theme respectively. Consistent use of these codes facilitates the description and comparison of narratives without, however, reducing story to concept. Moreover, the final code, the *cultural code,* may be useful to biblical students interested in *Sitz im Leben.*

Distinct from (but related to) other cultural systems, the
cultural code, the system of knowledge and value evoked by
the text,[23] may provide a means for exploring the interface
between a setting in life and (as Koch maintains) the "particular linguistic forms" to which it gives rise.[24]

Todorov is perhaps the most readable of the French structuralists. The concept of discourse which he presents in his
essay on "Language and Literature" renders narrative opaque
by making us conscious that stories are not events, that they
do not tell themselves. Narratives are related by narrators
and addressed to audiences. Drawing on Benveniste, Todorov
distinguishes between two levels of the speech-act: the *level
of story* presenting phenomena "which occurred at a certain
moment of time without any intervention on the part of the
speaker in the story" and the *level of discourse* presenting
a "speech-act supposing a speaker and a listener."[25] Using
this distinction to analyze a verse from the Joseph Narrative
("When the report was heard in Pharaoh's house"), it is possible to separate the level of story (hearing the report) from
the level of discourse (in which the narrator tells about the
report's being heard). The implication of the concept of discourse for comparative study is the requirement that compari-
sons be made at both levels of the speech-act.

Of the two models discussed thus far, structuralism is
more useful for biblical studies in that unlike the Jamesian
model, it does not canonize a single narrative genre as the
paradigm for all others. The weakness of structuralism is
perhaps its central analogy to linguistics. In taking linguistics as its model, structuralism not only asserts that
literature is a system, but that the system is to be analyzed
primarily in grammatical terminology.[26] Because the structuralist model is one based on reading, on decoding a text,
it tends to be both subjective and self-conscious in method.

In contrast to the structuralist model, one may offer
a model based on rhetoric and communication. This model,
offered by classical rhetorical theory, should first be distinguished from that school of biblical scholarship initiated
by Muilenburg in the presidential address he delivered to the
Society of Biblical Literature in 1968. In this address,
Muilenburg called for a criticism which would define the
scope of the literary unit and illuminate the structure of
its parts.[27] Kikawada has described rhetorical criticism
more recently as "a system of describing the organizational
scheme of a composition."[28] As practiced by Kikawada in
his article on Genesis and in the Muilenburg memorial volume,
however, rhetorical criticism generally divides a text into

units which are then analyzed stylistically.

The scope of classical rhetorical theory is broader.
In addition to the division of a text into its parts (*disposition*) and an account of style (patterns in the *lexis*),
classical rhetoric considers the *dianoia* or thought which
a speaker composes. This last aspect of composition (called
*Invention*) is the cornerstone of Aristotle's *Rhetoric*. According to Aristotle, the end of most speech is in a hearer--
in convincing, moving, or communicating with an audience.
In order to enter this social process, in order to address
an audience, a speaker must craft certain elements of the
general speech situation to fit the given speech-act. The
general speech situation offers a speaker three kinds of
materials, three models of persuasion: "The first kind depends on the personal character of the speaker (ethos); the
second on putting the audience in a certain frame of mind
(pathos); the third on the proof, or apparent proof, provided by the speech itself (logos)."[29]

Most people who write or speak for a public audience
are quite conscious of *logos*, of building a careful argument,
of selecting examples known to an audience. But a speaker
also fashions *ethos* and *pathos*, even if not quite so consciously. The personal character which one chooses at a
gathering of colleagues, for example, is generally related
to, but different from, the *ethos* which is adopted for
classroom teaching. In fact, it is often the careful craft-
ing of *ethos*, of personal character, rather than the invention
of *logos* which assures the success of a teacher or a politi-
cian.

The usefulness of the concept of *Invention* for literary
analysis has been developed by James Craig LaDriere in his
articles on "Voice and Address" and "Rhetoric and 'Merely
Verbal' Art."[30] The rhetorical model makes texts opaque by
reminding us, much like Todorov's level of discourse, that
texts are crafted artifacts. For LaDriere, all those elements of tone, attitude, emotional appeal, which constitute
the relationship between speaker and addressee are formali-
ties implicit in the work itself. Indeed the relationship
between speaker and addressee frames all other elements of
meaning. Biblical scholars, for example, understand that
the materials of each of the synoptic gospels are influenced
both by the character of the author(s) and by the nature of
the audience. For LaDriere, these influences permeate the
work itself as part of (and frame for) its meanings and,
consequently, these elements are available for analysis.

Perhaps the essential differences between the structuralist and rhetorical models are differences of emphasis and orientation.  Structuralism emphasizes a *STRUCTURE of meaning* and is oriented toward the process of reading, while rhetorical criticism emphasizes a *structure of MEANING* and is oriented toward the whole speech-act.  Because structuralism draws its model from the grammar of language and from the analogy between *langue* and other symbolic systems, its emphasis is finally on structural relations rather than on the meanings structured.  Rhetorical criticism, on the other hand, while recognizing grammatical conventions at work in a text, views these as subsumed into rhetorical norms and, consequently, draws its categories for analysis from these.  Thus where structuralism tends to describe a text in terms of the aspect of its verbs or of its codes of meaning, rhetorical criticism draws its methodology from the larger processes of human communication which, in addition to the level of *lexis* (at which grammar operates), also includes *dianoia* or thought.  Moreover, while rhetorical criticism assumes the art of rhetoric is somewhat systematic (and consequently subject to description), it does not assume that rhetorical thought is rigorously systematic.  As a result, rhetorical criticism tends to emphasize meanings rather than the system which structures them.

A second essential difference is the orientation of each model.  Given structuralism's reliance on the concept of *langue*, what its model finally makes opaque is the process of reading itself.  Barthes' *S/Z* is as much (or more) a record of reading as it is an account of the meanings of the text.  Rhetorical criticism, on the other hand, is oriented toward the whole speech-act as a function of its persuasiveness and looks to relations in the text itself, rather than to the process of decoding the text.  Thus rhetorical criticism finally renders the text opaque.

Now we turn to the Joseph Narrative to discover whether an analysis of its *Invention* will allow us to solve the problems raised by reading the narrative from within the Jamesian tradition.

## IV.  Rhetorical Analysis of the Joseph Narrative

Throughout this presentation, I have asserted that one's model influences one's analysis and that biblical scholars dealing with synchronic relations in narrative unconsciously adopt some form of the Jamesian model. Criticism of the Joseph Narrative bears out this generalization. Redford, because he is looking for the genre of a young man's rise to greatness, sees that pattern controlling the Joseph Narrative and, consequently, rejects episodes which do not fit this pattern.[31] Moreover, although he is looking for an ancient genre, he actually reads the text according to the Jamesian model and so is troubled by meanings foreign to this model. Coats is more overt in his use of the Jamesian model. In his reading of the narrative, Coats looks for character and plot as these are described in the Jamesian tradition and, consequently, finds a family tragedy reconciled by means of recognition and reversal. In order to make the Joseph Narrative fit this pattern of rising and falling action, Coats is forced to treat the Egyptian materials as a digression.[32]

The following analysis of the *Invention* of the Joseph Narrative proceeds in three steps:  (1) indication that there is a level of discourse in the narrative; (2) identification of the *ethos* and *pathos* of the tale; (3) demonstration of rhetoric at work in the narrative structure.

(1)  Like much traditional narrative, the Joseph Narrative seems to proceed by mere chronology, but there is a level of discourse in the tale, although not a self-conscious or an elaborate one. The story does not tell itself. It is told by a narrator whose process of speech frames the story and controls its telling. The narrator sets up situations, manipulates the duration of events, narrates sequentially events which are simultaneous (see "meanwhile"[33] in 37:36). Verse 37:5 is a useful illustration of the narrator at work. Here the narrator disrupts simple chronology (Joseph tells his dream; his brothers respond) to narrate the scene twice (once in direct and once in indirect discourse), thus emphasizing the brothers' hatred for Joseph.

(2)  Given the fact that there is a level of discourse, that the meanings of the tale are framed by a voice and address relationship, what is the character of the speaker (his *ethos*) and what kind of appeal does he make to his audience (*pathos*)? The character of the speaker is that of

a traditional narrator, a rather transparent, yet authoritative, personality defined almost solely in terms of his function in telling the tale. His style is characteristically
brief and understated and his voice frequently gives way to
those of his characters. Although capable of flashes of
realism, the narrating is not based on the "formal realism"
of the novel and the narrator does explain and interpret
events. The brief and understated style is frequently ironic
(for example, in the three mentions of Joseph's coat in chapter 37, in the narrator's preface to Joseph's interpretation
of the baker's dream: "When the chief baker saw that the
interpretation was favorable, he said to Joseph, 'I also had
a dream' [40:16]"). This capacity for irony distances us
from the characters and affects the tone of the story.

The *pathos* of the tale is based on three related appeals
which the narrator makes to the audience:

1. A narrative appeal (the pleasure of the
   story as story). This has two bases:
   (a) the mimetic, vivid, or life-like elaboration of action in order to display
   customs; (b) the construction of the story
   so that the audience knows what is going
   to happen but not when or how. Redford's
   description of the use of pace and repetition explains something of this latter
   aspect of the appeal.[34]

2. The second constituent of the *pathos* is
   a pathos of affectivity. Its base is
   the display of strong emotions, e.g.,
   Jacob's lament for Joseph.

3. Finally, there is the pathos of providence
   and prosperity: "The Lord was with Joseph
   and he became a successful man."

Modern readers are attracted to the tale by the first two
constituents of the *pathos*. The Joseph Narrative is justly
famous for its artistic construction, its flashes of realism,
the poignancy of its pictures of grief and remorse. However,
it is the final constituent, the pathos of providence, which
determines the structure of the tale. This structure is controlled by what I have chosen to call a central rhetoric of
revelation. All elements of the tale--the authority of the
narrator, the progress of the story, the emotions of the
characters--work to reveal the constancy of God's favor to
Joseph and his provision for the family of Jacob.

The rhetoric of revelation, central as it is to the tale, cannot be illuminated by the Jamesian model.

(3) Using the rhetorical model, however, it is possible to demonstrate that the Joseph Narrative turns on the revelation of God's providence in the seventh episode of the tale. For purposes of analysis the tale may be divided as follows:

1. Joseph sold into Egypt (37:1-37:36)

2. Judah and Tamar (38:1-38:30)

3. Joseph in Potiphar's household (39:1-39:23)

4. Joseph in prison (40:1-40:23)

5. Joseph set over Egypt (41:1-41:57)

6. Joseph's brothers secure grain in Egypt (42:1-42:38)

7. Joseph reveals God's providence (43:1-45:28)

8. Jacob's theophany (46:1-46:27)

9. Jacob settles in Egypt (46:38-47:12)

10. Joseph deals with the Egyptians (47:13-47:26)

11. Death and departing (47:29-50:26)

EPISODE 1 is an overture which establishes all three constituents of the *pathos:* the narrative appeal, the pathos of affectivity, the pathos of providence. It is on affectivity, however, that emphasis is placed. The pathos of providence is present only in an implicit and ironic form. Vv. 37:2-4 present two explanations for the brothers' hatred of Joseph. Vv. 5-11 contain Joseph's accounts of his dreams. These verses establish narrative expectations that the dreams will be fulfilled, but, as we saw earlier, the emphasis of this section is on the brothers' hatred. Vv. 12-17 are a small, rather realistic, interlude. Vv. 18-28 chronicle the decision to put Joseph into the pit. This section is the narrative core of the episode: actions are located in the perceptions of agents; a consistent chronology is used; hostilities intensify; the pace increases. The discussion of the brothers about what to do with Joseph is the first of several episodes centered on negotiation and dealing and the results of dealing are here rather ironic. The result of the brothers' hatred, of their discussion, of the suggestions of Reuben and Judah is that the

Midianites take Joseph to Egypt. All their dealing comes to
naught. (The irony remains whether the stories arise from a
mixture of sources or not.)

It is at first surprising that the audience is so detached from this scene. The focus of the unit is on the
brothers' dealing, rather than on the person of Joseph, and
the ironic resolution of the scene creates an emotional distance.

The affective pathos reasserts itself in vv. 29-39.
Reuben's cry breaks out of the cognitive, understated tone
of the narrative. The brothers' attempt to deal with their
father over Joseph's alleged death climaxes in Jacob's lament.
The final verse of the episode, however, reintroduces the
understated, implicit pathos of providence: "Meanwhile the
Midianites had sold him in Egypt."

*EPISODE 2.* The Judah and Tamar episode has little syntagmatic relationship, except for sequence, to the rest of
the tale, but it does have a number of paradigmatic relationships: as a seduction, as a failure to recognize a family
member, as a revelation of identity.

*EPISODES 3-5* compose a series of paradigmatic units in
which Joseph is given charge over Potiphar's household, the
prison, and the whole of Egypt. This section which depends
on the genre of the wise courtier[35] includes a great deal of
narrative appeal. The audience anticipates the death of the
baker, enjoys Pharaoh's retelling of his dream, wants to suggest Pharaoh's call for Joseph. There is also pleasure in the
social mimesis: in Joseph's making himself presentable after
he leaves prison, in the ceremony of his appointment.

The pathos of providence becomes explicit in this section
of the tale. In chapter 39, there is a conspiracy to recognize that things prosper under Joseph's management because God
is with him. The narrator recognizes this; Potiphar recognizes
it; Joseph recognizes it. The pathos of providence is also at
work in that, unlike a usual paradigmatic pattern in which the
hero's fortunes increase steadily from episode to episode,
there are syntagmatic relations at work here. As a result of
episode 3, Joseph is thrown into prison where it is God who
brings good out of evil.

The fifth episode is a proclamation of the pathos of
providence. Because everyone recognizes that God is with

Joseph, he is set over the whole of Egypt. The recognition which the Egyptians accord Joseph contrasts sharply with the brothers' hatred. The pathos of providence has become much more overt in these episodes, but it is still quite separate from Joseph's family.

*EPISODES 6-7* are the focal points of the narrative. Here, especially in episode seven, we can see how the rhetoric of revelation controls the structure of the tale. Both episodes are filled with dealing. The brothers negotiate with Joseph for grain, with their father for the return to Egypt, with Joseph's servants over the money and the cup, with Joseph for the life of Benjamin. Throughout the episodes, the famine and Joseph conspire to place the brothers in exactly the position required by Joseph's dreams. But there are also larger patterns at work. The brothers begin to get the point in 42:26 when they ask what God is doing to them.

The heart of the tale is the negotiation between Joseph and Judah over the life of Benjamin (44:14-45:15), a negotiation in which Joseph reveals that God has sent him to Egypt to provide for his family. Yet both Coats and Redford have great difficulty with this moment of the tale, because it does not fit the Jamesian model implicit in their analyses.

Redford writes:

> The supreme irony of the narrative, and one which seems debilitating to the plot, lies in Joseph's revelation of the underlying divine plan. God had brought about the entire affair as part of a preconceived design, and it was he who had contrived to turn the evil the brothers had intended. With the knowledge that God was the real source of the action, the motivation of the actors themselves appears trivial. To what purpose the cries of Joseph, the grief of Jacob, the earnest persuasion of the brothers, or the concern over Benjamin? ... God had manipulated the principles of the drama like so many marionettes.[36]

Redford assumes that character is action, that motivation should end in results, that displays of emotion should be intimately connected to the plot. In the Joseph Narrative, however, the action is the action of God's providence and human agency (with its motivations and expressions of emotion)

is secondary. Moreover, it is just this separation of affectivity and action which is a major technique of the tale.
The brothers' hatred and their fear are subordinate to God's
providence. Since the tale supports the pathos of providence
and since the audience remains detached from the brothers, the
audience is pleased, even perhaps a little triumphal, about
the brothers' position before Joseph. After all, is this not
the scene for which the audience has waited from the opening
section of the tale?

The pathos of affectivity is only connected to action
when Joseph responds to his brothers and draws them into the
providence and prosperity which he represents. In the second
part of the tale, the pathos of affectivity and prosperity
draw closer together.

If Redford relies on the postulate that character is action, Coats relies on the postulate that action can be charted
in a rising and falling pattern. Of the Joseph-Judah scene,
he says:

> A change occurs in this scene, compassion
> for Benjamin and Jacob replaces hostility
> and deceit. But the change occurs as if
> in response to a call for the future, not
> as an uncovering of character already ef-
> fective in the past. The change is thus
> not the work of any one figure in the
> scene. To the contrary, the change trans-
> cends the people who thought they controlled
> the crucial event. Joseph's contribution
> to the change (45:1-13) follows Judah's of-
> fer with a reversal of the entire plot of
> the story.[37]

Coats reads this scene in terms of reversal and recognition.
Reversal of the fortunes of Jacob's family *is* implicit in the
scene. However, this has been a story about Joseph and God's
providence and from this perspective there is no sudden change
in fortune. God is constantly with Joseph. Joseph always
prospers. There is irony, of course, in the changed position
of the brothers, but there is not reversal in the classical
sense of that term.

Nor, in the classical sense of the term, is there a
recognition. Recognition is not a matter of psychological
realization and especially not of changes or developments in
character. In Greek drama, recognition is a realization of
the way the world runs and of one's earlier mistake (one's

earlier missing of the mark) in this regard. In the scene
between Judah and Joseph, Joseph has no need of recognition.
It has always been apparent that God is with him. It is
significant, moreover, that the narrator pays such little
attention to the brothers' response when this reality is
revealed.

If there is no recognition or reversal here, no pattern
of rising and falling action; if character is not action,
what is the function of this scene? The rhetoric of revelation is at work. Consider the speeches of Judah and Joseph.
The audience knows that Judah's speech, for all its display
of emotion, will not influence the way things turn out in
this tale. What is its function? The speech recapitulates
the negotiations between Joseph and his brothers and sets
these in the context of Jacob's age and his love for his sons.
In effect, the speech changes the audience's view of the earlier scenes of the brothers before Joseph. The audience's
detached, triumphal enjoyment of the picture is replaced by
their being drawn, finally, into the affectivity displayed
by Jacob's family. The audience cares what happens to them.
Joseph's speech serves a similar function. It explains the
pathos of providence at work in Joseph's past, in the present
situation, and in the future of the family. Addressed as it
is to Jacob and tender as it is, the speech joins the pathos
of affectivity to the pathos of providence.

What happens in this scene is revelation. Action is not
character; action is providence. Moreover, the revelation of
providence is not directed at characters in the story. It is
directed at the audience. Redford is right. Judah's earnest
persuasion will not alter the outcome of events. Thus the
speech is not so much action as it is a display of affectivity
intended to make the pathos of providence more appealing to
the audience. If there is a recognition to this scene, the
audience has it.

*EPISODES 8-11* open the tale out to connect its pathos
with that of the patriarchal narratives and with Exodus. In
these episodes, the context of revelation broadens to the
scope of 37:1-2: "Jacob dwelt in the land of his father's
sojournings, in the land of Canaan. This is the history of
the family of Jacob." As the scope of the revelation broadens,
a great deal of affectivity surrounds it. In other words, in
this section of the tale, we see the frequent joining of the
pathos of providence to the pathos of affectivity.

Episode 8, Jacob's theophany, confirms the move into

Egypt. Joseph has said the move is a good idea; Pharaoh has
said so. Now God says so. The theophany also joins this
story to others in Genesis where the paradigm is used.

Episode 9, one of the last deals in the tale, is the
first time Joseph deals with the Egyptians on behalf of the
Hebrews. In episode 10, the audience sees Joseph the pro-
vider dealing with the Egyptians as they come for food. The
prosperity of the Hebrews contrasts sharply with the abject
submission of the Egyptians and reverses the audience's
feelings about the comparative position of the two groups.

With the exception of 50:15, episode 11 replaces dealing
with ceremonial language. The episode continues the opening
out of the pathos. There is a great deal of gathering here:
of the family, of the generations, of the tribe, of the promise. The opening out is accompanied by a thrust into the future and is imbued with a sense of telos.

## Conclusion

Rhetorical analysis makes the workings of this tale
opaque. Analysis demonstrates that a central rhetoric of
revelation controls the structure of the Joseph Narrative.
The tale opens with the brothers' hatred directed against
Joseph whose dreams hold such promise. In this first part
of the tale, the pathos of providence is only implicit and
is subordinate to the pathos of affectivity. In the Egyptian
sequence, the pathos of providence becomes more overt. Both
aspects of the pathos are joined in the seventh episode so
that the audience rejoices in the providence shown to Joseph.
In the remainder of the tale, both appeals are opened out to
encompass the affectivity associated with God's providence
in the patriarchal narratives and to join the Joseph Narrative
to the telos implicit in Exodus. Moreover, analysis has shown
that the central rhetoric of revelation is exercised for the
sake of the audience.

The use of the rhetorical model for analysis of the
Joseph Narrative may have several wider implications.

1. No matter what the diachronic situation of
   the Joseph Narrative may be, rhetorical analysis (a synchronic approach) has demonstrated
   that the episodes of the received text (with
   the possible exception of the Tamar episode)

are integral to the narrative structure
of the tale.

2. Rhetorical analysis broadens the bases on
which the Joseph Narrative can be compared
with other narratives in Genesis. I suggest,
for example, that rhetorical analysis may
show that the patriarchal narratives share
a fundamental *pathos* (the rhetoric of revelation I describe here), but that the Joseph
Narrative differs from these in its use of
social realism and in its detachment from
the main characters of the story.

3. The rhetorical model suggests that the comparative study of texts include the study of
the level of discourse and that definitions
of genre include descriptions of the *ethos*
and *pathos* common to the literary type.

4. The model further suggests that attempts to
relate biblical texts to the time of their
composition take account of *ethos* and *pathos*
as well as of the level of story.

5. Finally, in the study of texts, especially
of ancient texts, the rhetorical model suggests that the description of *ethos* and
*pathos* be interdisciplinary. Questions
about the assumptions, emotions, values
which a text evokes necessarily create an
interface among various disciplines.

## NOTES

1. C. S. Lewis, *The Discarded Image* (Cambridge: Cambridge University Press, 1964; rpt., 1970), 211.

2. Bernhard W. Anderson, "From Analysis to Synthesis:
The Interpretation of Genesis 1-11," *JBL* 91 (1978), 23.

3. On this topic, see chapter IV of Rene Wellek and
Austin Warren's *Theory of Literature* (New York: Harcourt,
Brace and Co., 1956).

4. R. R. Wilson, "The Old Testament Genealogies in Recent Research," *JBL* 94 (1975), 189.

5. J. Van Seters, *Abraham in History and Tradition* (New Haven: Yale University Press, 1975), 312.

6. George W. Coats, *From Canaan into Egypt: Structural and Theological Context for the Joseph Story* (CBQMS 4; Washington, D.C.: The Catholic Biblical Association of America, 1976), 58.

7. J. P. Fokkelman, *Narrative Art in Genesis: Specimens of Stylistic and Structural Analysis* (Amsterdam: Van Gorcum, 1975), 12.

8. Anderson, "From Analysis to Synthesis," p. 25.

9. Meyer Abrams, *The Mirror and the Lamp: Romantic Theory and the Critical Tradition* (New York: Oxford University Press, 1953), 6.

10. Fokkelman, *Narrative Art,* p. 4.

11. Hermann Gunkel, *The Legends of Genesis* (New York: Schocken Books, 1964).

12. Anderson, in M. Noth, *A History of the Pentateuchal Traditions* (Englewood Cliffs: Prentice Hall, 1972), xviii.

13. Henry James, *The Art of Fiction and Other Essays,* ed., Morris Robert (New York, 1948); *The Art of the Novel,* ed., R. P. Blackmur (New York, 1937); Percy Lubbock, *The Craft of Fiction* (New York, 1955).

14. Ian Watt, *The Rise of the Novel* (Berkeley: University of California, 1967), 29.

15. For the subjective nature of structuralism, see Robert Polzin, *Biblical Structuralism: Method and Subjectivity in the Study of Ancient Texts* (Philadelphia: Fortress, 1977).

16. Barthes as quoted in Jonathan Culler, *Structuralist Poetics* (Ithaca: Cornell University, 1975), 97.

17. *Ibid.,* p. 8.

18. Polzin, *Biblical Structuralism,* p. 2.

19. Robert Scholes, *Structuralism in Literature* (New Haven: Yale University, 1974), 6.

20. Culler, *Structuralist Poetics*, p. 43.

21. *Ibid.*, p. 13.

22. Edmund Leach, "Genesis as Myth," *Genesis as Myth and Other Essays* (London: Jonathan Cape, 1969), 17.

23. Roland Barthes, *S/Z: An Essay*, trans., Richard Miller (New York: Hill and Wang, 1974).

24. K. Koch, *The Growth of the Biblical Tradition* (New York: Charles Scribner's Sons, 1969), 28.

25. Tzvetan Todorov, *The Poetics of Prose*, trans., Richard Howard (Ithaca: Cornell University, 1977), 25.

26. *Ibid.*, "The Grammar of Narrative," pp. 108-119.

27. James Muilenburg, "Form Criticism and Beyond," *JBL* 88 (1969), 1-18.

28. Issac Kikawada, "The Unity in Genesis 12:1-9," *Proceedings of the 6th World Congress of Jewish Studies* (Jerusalem, 1977), 229-230; *Rhetorical Criticism: Essays in Honor of James Muilenburg* (Pittsburgh: Pickwick, 1974).

29. Aristotle, *The Rhetoric*, trans., W. Rhys Roberts (New York: Modern Library, 1954), I, 2.

30. James Craig LaDriere, "Voice and Address," *Dictionary of World Literature*, ed., Joseph Shipley (Totowa: Littlefield, Adams, 1953), 441-444; "Rhetoric and 'Merely Verbal' Art," *English Institute Essays: 1948*, ed., D. A. Robertson, Jr. (New York: Columbia University, 1949).

31. D. B. Redford, *A Study of the Biblical Story of Joseph* (VTSup 20; Leiden: E. J. Brill, 1970), 17.

32. Coats, *From Canaan into Egypt*, p. 9.

33. *The New Oxford Annotated Bible* (New York: Oxford University, 1973). All quotations are taken from this edition.

34. Redford, *Biblical Story of Joseph*, p. 76.

35.  S. Niditch and R. Doran, "The Success Story of the Wise Courtier:  A Formal Approach," *JBL* 96 (1977), 179-193.

36.  Redford, *Biblical Story of Joseph,* p. 74.

37.  Coats, *From Canaan into Egypt,* pp. 42-43.

# PRE-ISRAELITE JERUSALEM

John J. Schmitt
St. Bonaventure University

Because humankind depends on water, it is not surprising that a fresh-water spring is the probable reason for Jerusalem growing where it did. The general area around the site of Jerusalem gives evidence of human activity in the Paleolithic and the Mesolithic Ages. Flints were found around the location of later Jerusalem.[1] Pottery from the beginning of the Early Bronze Age suggests a settlement ca. 3000 B.C.E. on the site which was later to become Jerusalem.[2] Conclusive evidence of settlement in the third millennium are the tombs from that period.[3] The presence of water furnished by the spring (called, since biblical times, Gihon) is but one element that invited settlement there.

A second element which invited settlement is the terrain of the site, for the first settlement occurred on a spur of a double-ridged hill, the spur of the eastern ridge having steep drops on three sides. Such a condition would allow for easy defense against attackers from the valleys to the east and west and south. A settlement which wanted to become walled could incorporate the steep slopes in all directions except to the north as part of a defense system.

The spring, however, the only one near the hill, lay lower than the walls that were built by early settlers. The inhabitants demonstrated their ingenuity by the creation of several shafts and tunnels which would make the water of the spring outside the walls of the town accessible from inside the walls of the town, so that the population could make use of the spring's water even during a siege.[4] There were a number of unsuccessful starts for these tunnels, but the technology involved in their conception and completion is impressive. Archaeology shows that Jerusalem was not unique in accomplishing this kind of engineering feat: such tunnels and shafts have been discovered at Gezer, Megiddo and Lachish.[5]

It is not clear that the settlement on the hill was continuous beginning with the earliest pottery finds of the Stone Age, but additional pottery is represented from the Early and Middle Bronze Ages.[6] Whether the size of the settlement increased rapidly at any one time is not known. One can estimate, however, that the spring, if its water supply remained constant over the centuries, could furnish in total output enough water for 10,000 people, allowing each person two buckets (20 liters) a day. Normal means of utilizing the yield would serve at least 2,500 persons.[7] The area of pre-Israelite Jerusalem, analyzed from the perspective of population density, suggests a population of about 2,000 at David's time.[8]

An additional technological accomplishment of the inhabitants of pre-Israelite Jerusalem is the construction of the terraces on the eastern slope of the hill. These fourteenth or fifteenth century terraces were made apparently to increase the area on the hilltop on which to build structures for various purposes.[9] Dame Kathleen Kenyon says that for pre-Israelite Jerusalem there is a skeleton but very little flesh.[10] Perhaps one can say that the skeleton needed the addition of more bones to carry the weight of the activity in Jerusalem even before the Israelites set foot in the city.

Before a discussion of the comparative, extrabiblical materials, it is appropriate to review those passages of the Bible where the consciousness of the biblical authors is observable with respect to Jerusalem before it becomes Israelite.

Jerusalem is first named in the Bible in Joshua 10. If the narrative of the coalition of the five kings against Gibeon reflects some historical consciousness and even some historical event, one can deduce from the account that Jerusalem, at least in the person of its king Adonizedek, played a significant role of leadership over a fairly large area of southern Canaan before it belonged to Israel. The initiative of Adonizedek, king of Jerusalem,[11] successfully brought other cities to arms.[12]

The king of Jerusalem, unnamed, occurs in the list of kings defeated by Joshua in Josh 12:10. If this list were independent of other materials, it would be another piece of evidence for kingship and all that goes with it in Jerusalem before David. Martin Noth thinks that the king of Jerusalem

occurs in this list only because he was added to the tradition in chapter 10.[13] However, Alberto Soggin thinks that
this list in Joshua 12, because it disagrees with the accounts
of chapters 1-11, is independent of all other traditions about
the conquest which have survived. He says its origin is unknown, and he claims that it is certainly very ancient.[14]

Jerusalem next appears in Josh 15:8 as situated within
the boundaries laid out for the tribe of Judah. Here it is
called "the shoulder of the Jebusite."[15] However, the final
verse of the chapter, v. 63, after the city lists of Judah,
admits that "the people of Judah could not drive out the Jebusites, the inhabitants of Jerusalem; so the Jebusites dwell
with the people of Judah at Jerusalem to this day." This
verse intends to claim that the city of Jerusalem is part of
the holdings of the tribe of Judah. It also points out that
the fate which befell many other cities of Canaan according
to the traditions of Israel's conquest of the land, viz.,
bloodshed, annihilation of the male population, destruction
of buildings, did not befall Jerusalem.

The remaining mention of Jerusalem in the book of Joshua
is in Josh 18:28. The verse declares that the city is within
the sphere of the Benjaminites. Such a declaration is witness
to this tribe's claim to the important city. The statement
would seem to be a counter claim against that of the tribe of
Judah. It should not surprise one that there were different
tribal claims to the same site.[16] And these texts would simply be another, albeit small, example of literature or literary traditions as politics in the ancient Near East.[17]

The first chapter of Judges gives two contrasting and
seemingly contradictory views of Jerusalem in its pre-Israelite existence. Jerusalem, after being the site of the death
of Adonibezek, v. 7, is conquered by the "men of Judah," "who
took it," "smote it with the edge of the sword," and "set the
city on fire," v. 8. This depiction likens Israel's treatment
of Jerusalem to that meted out to the other Canaanite cities.[18]

However, in the same chapter, v. 21 states: "The people
of Benjamin did not drive out the Jebusites who dwelt in Jerusalem; so the Jebusites have dwelt with the people of Benjamin
to this day." This description of the situation repeats the
ideas expressed in Josh 18:28, viz., that the city was not
captured, but that the inhabitants live on there "to this day."
The variation is simply that it is the Benjaminites here, instead of the Judahites as in Josh 18:28, who would have taken
the city.

These contrasting views of Jerusalem in the pre-Israelite times from within the biblical traditions serve to point out the variety of traditions that might attach themselves to an important site.[19] They also show that one tradition, the impossibility of capture, can be used by various groups for the same purpose, namely, to claim ultimately a specific city for itself. From a different perspective, one can note here again that for later Israelites, Jerusalem was something that one was forced to reflect upon. There seem to have been reasons for Israel to do so in the premonarchic period as well.

The last mention of Jerusalem in the book of Judges is the curious tale in chapter 19. Certainly Jerusalem does not play an essential role in this story, even though that city might have saved the life of the concubine of the Levite from Ephraim. Jerusalem here, however, does have a distinctive aura: it is seen as a hostile, enemy city. And it ill behooves an Israelite to "turn aside into the city of foreigners who do not belong to the people of Israel." The story is told more as an explanation of an intertribal war than as glorification of the people of Israel. Regardless of the period from which the narrative in reality dates,[20] it reflects the memory of the time when Jerusalem was an unfriendly city with which Israel was uncomfortable.

The major extrabiblical texts which refer to Jerusalem before David's time come from Egypt. These are two groups of documents: the execration texts and the tablets from El Amarna.

The discovery of the execration texts and the history of their interpretation and their continued reinterpretation as a basis for tracing the history of Palestine from about 2000-1800 B.C.E. is well sketched by Thomas L. Thompson.[21] The texts themselves are inscriptions in Egyptian on bowls and figurines with the names of rulers of various cities in Nubia and Palestine. The bowl fragments were published in 1926.[22] The inscriptions on figurines saw publication in 1940.[23] And a third group, comprising both bowls and statuettes, was discovered 1962-1963.[24] From these texts one learns that certain cities and their rulers were important enough for the Egyptian authorities to employ a symbolic shattering of these selected people. It is not clear whether the places and persons listed in these texts were feared because they offered a real and direct threat against Egypt or whether they simply were a possible obstacle in Egypt's trade through this area.[25] Regardless of the specific causes of the execrations, Jerusalem does appear among these sources of worry as a place whose people had to be reckoned with.

The city of Jerusalem is one of those cities in south
Palestine that has more than one ruler named in the bowl texts.
William F. Albright took this as an indication that Jerusalem
was ruled at that time by a tribal form of government based on
several rulers, while the coastal towns had a more traditional
city-monarchy form of government. He saw this as a breakdown
of traditional government in the cities of southern Palestine,
and he regarded this political breakdown as the evidence one
needs to place the patriarchs in this period of Amorite occupation.[26] Since the figurine texts often give a more monarchi-
cal form of government, even in some southern cities, they
were read as an apparent return to the normal one-chief kind
of rule in the town.[27]

The judgment of Thompson, on the other hand, is that no
real chronology can be set up among the different sets of execration texts. The finding of bowls and figurines in the same
group suggests that there is no important difference in time.
Thompson would date them all to ca. 1810-1770 B.C.E.[28] The
conclusion that one can draw from these reflections on the
execration texts is that Jerusalem was a significant and for-
midable enough city from the viewpoint of Egypt, that the city
had to be counted among those places which needed to be controlled by various kinds of sympathetic magical devices by the
Egyptian officials.

One final comment on the execration texts which mention
the leaders of Jerusalem is this:  the names of the rulers are
good West-Semitic, Amorite names, Yaqir-'ammu and Shayzanu.[29]
The first is a sentence name which may well include reference
to a divinity. The sentence type name is frequent in the Bible
and the ancient Near East.

The next group of texts from Egypt which mention Jerusalem before David is the Amarna letters. These come from the
reigns of Amunhotpe III and Amunhotpe IV (Akhenaten), 1402-
1347 B.C.E.[30] These tablets are famous for at least two reasons:  they are written in Akkadian and they mention rather
frequently the presence of the Ḫabiru in the area of Palestine.
The Ḫabiru were a social feature that had to be dealt with--a
social class which either could be the cause of suffering for
the cities which they attacked, or could be a real asset for
the ruler who needed mercenaries to help him in his competi-
tion with other rulers for the same area.

The letters from Jerusalem show that its king 'Abdiḫepa
had serious troubles on many fronts. The guards that the
Egyptians garrisoned in Jerusalem, perhaps because they were
underpaid by the Pharaoh,[31] broke into the palace, raided the

king's house and almost killed him.[32] Jerusalem, as a strate-
gic site, was among those city-states against whom certain
other rulers of the city-states had made major advances. 'Abdiḫepa is careful to point out how much the Pharaoh is losing
with each loss that his man in Jerusalem suffers. A recurrent
threat, and a persistently troublesome one in Palestine and
Syria, were the attacks by the Ḫabiru and those who had become
Ḫabiru.[33] 'Abdiḫepa asks for special archers to help defend
the Pharaoh's interests in Jerusalem.

Jerusalem is not the most powerful city in central or
southern Palestine in the letters. The most powerful city is
Shechem with its unpleasant and aggressive king Lab'ayu.
Jerusalem, however, does play a role large enough that its
ruler wrote letters with some degree of self-confidence and
with the awareness that Jerusalem was of importance for the
ultimate security of the Egyptian realm. 'Abdiḫepa speaks of
his own importance, and at least one other ruler of the time
points out that the king of Jerusalem had an aggressive attitude and warns the Pharaoh about the ambitions of the ruler
of Jerusalem.[34]

It is significant that the city of Jerusalem in the fourteenth century is politically and culturally advanced enough
to carry on correspondence directly with the royal court. The
style of these letters from Jerusalem has been studied on several occasions. Most recently William Moran has done a thorough examination of all the special characteristics of the
scribe of Jerusalem.[35] From a study of the mechanics of his
writing (paleography, syllabary, orthography, punctuation)
and of the peculiarities of his language (Assyrianisms in the
use of demonstratives, the choice of nouns, verbs and other
words, and the making of a postscript), the scribe appears as
a man imported from the north, in Syria "somewhere along the
border between 'Reichsakkadisch' and 'Canaanite-Akkadian.'"[36]
Moran ventures further to suggest that this scribe did not
find his way to Jerusalem on his own, but that he was brought
there by 'Abdiḫepa himself who came to the throne of Jerusalem
which had at some earlier time belonged to his family. 'Abdiḫepa continually insists that the Pharaoh is responsible for
'Abdiḫepa's occupation of the Jerusalemite throne.

Moran's analysis of the scribal traits of 'Abdiḫepa's
writer and of his origin is convincing. Moran's suggestion,
however, of the circumstances under which the Syrian scribe
came to Jerusalem is not the only possibility. Syria seems
simply to have had better scribal schools, so that the more
ambitious and adventuresome of the rulers of the city-states
of Palestine may well have desired to acquire their scribes

from Syria.[37] The scribe of Jerusalem could have been brought there to add stature, dignity, grace, and eloquence to the court in Jerusalem.[38]

Whether 'Abdiḫepa owes his rulership completely to the Pharaoh can be questioned. He does point out three times in his six or seven letters that he rules not by his mother and father but by the favor and strong arm of the king.[39] It is nevertheless the house of his father into which he has entered.[40] This insistent claim that he does not rule without the support of the Pharaoh could be part of the general fawning attitude of 'Abdiḫepa's letters because of his need to win the attention and sympathy of the reader in the court of Egypt. It is not certain that all the letters to the court reached the Pharaoh's ears.[41] Special flattery for the king could be a ploy to gain a good reception and a winning presentation before the Pharaoh. Hence the view that 'Abdiḫepa brought the scribe with him as he moved to Jerusalem to regain the family throne loses some of its force. 'Abdiḫepa is a figure of stability rather than discontinuity in Jerusalem.

One should mention that the ruler in these letters bears a name which contains the name of a principal deity of the Hittite state religion, Hebat. It is unexpected that this non-Semitic element appears in this city which was earlier ruled by persons with Semitic names. One could suppose that some non-Semitic immigrants or invaders from the north had attained the throne in Jerusalem.[42] Or one might agree with Benjamin Mazar in thinking that it is simply a stylish use of a Hittite substitute for the Semitic Šulamit, the consort of Šalim.[43] At any rate, there are currently no means to judge whether the thought or practice of Jerusalem underwent any Hittite influence at this time.

In summary, the Amarna tablets show that pre-Israelite Jerusalem was an important and flourishing center of political activity in the Amarna Age.[44] And one can assume that such a political center would be some kind of center of religious concerns.[45]

None of the texts which survive give much information about what kind of religion was established in this ancient city which finally became Israel's capital. Any proposal that there was some continuity of religious traditions and persistence of religious ideas over the many centuries from long before David's time right through the early monarchy even into the last days of the kingdom of Judah must seek evidence or at least some basis for probability.

Some hints of continuity would be the names which appear before and during David's time. The obvious start is the name of the city, Jerusalem. In biblical Hebrew, the first element would seem to be a formation of the Semitic root *yarah*, to throw, cast, or lay (of foundations).[46] The earliest attestations of the name, however, are in Egyptian and in cuneiform. The cuneiform orthography rendered the name as [URU]sa-lim and once as ú-ru-sa-lim.[47] Thus, the scribe writing cuneiform understood the first element to be "city." The Egyptian is probably to be read Rushalimum.[48] The second element is probably a divine name, Šalim, a Semitic god known from early times.[49] The divine name is part of the city's name when it first appears in any texts. Perhaps the name by itself might suffice to identify the city.[50] The Masoretic tradition of pointing the consonantal writing of the city's name can be interpreted as a deliberate attempt to disguise this divine name by a different pronunication.[51] It is this divine name that David used in the names he gave his sons Solomon and Absalom. In the Hebrew Bible there are many people who bear names with this divine element. Meshullam seems to be the name of twenty-one different persons.

Another persistent Semitic root in names connected with Jerusalem is ZDK.[52] It appears in the name Melkizedek, the king of Salem, Gen 14:18, generally taken as a reference to Jerusalem. The root occurs again in the name of the king of Jerusalem in Joshua 10, Adonizedek. And in the time of David, Zadok is the name of the priest in Jerusalem when David takes over the city.[53]

Other factors of probability of a continuity between pre-Davidic and Davidic Jerusalem would include the biblical account of the taking of Jerusalem. When David "takes" the city, there is no bloodshed, no executions, no driving out, no real overthrow of a previous system.[54] Further, David, who grew up in Bethlehem just four miles south of Jerusalem, would have been familiar with any establishment in Jerusalem.[55] If he could simply move into it, without destroying it, that would be an advantage for him. And that seems to have been his tactic. David did keep his previous officials that he had before he entered Jerusalem, but he also acquired Nathan the prophet, Zadok the priest, and Benaiah the captain of the royal guard. These are those who later support Solomon, the Jerusalem-born, as successor to David. They appear to be parts of a Jerusalem establishment. Finally, the Masoretic text suggests that David and Araunah dealt with each other as if they were both kings in the transaction by which Jerusalem's threshing floor came under the ownership of David, 2 Sam 24:23.[56]

The weight of probability seems to lie with those who would maintain some kind of cultural and religious continuity between pre-Israelite Jerusalem and Israelite Jerusalem. Of course, the Bible itself does not speak of this continuity or the shape and content that it had. Scholars are forced to reconstruct the kinds of religious continuity that existed. Three different ways of attempting to reconstruct what pre-Israelite Jerusalem traditions might have been are discussed below. These three were chosen for their contrasting methodologies. The contrasts are exaggerated for the sake of discussion. All three have used extrabiblical materials to some extent.

Julius Lewy based a proposal for a kind of reconstruction on a phrase in one of the Amarna texts.[57] The text names Jerusalem and then calls it *bît* $^d$*NIN.IB*.[58] $^d$*NIN.IB* is usually read Ninurta. Lewy relied on another text which equated Ninurta and Šulmanu.[59] He concluded that at the time of the text Jerusalem was known also as *bît Šulmani* (or in Hebrew, one might say Beth Shulman, or even Beth Shalem).[60] In other words, the city was called after the temple of the god of the city. Lewy was struck by the fact that this name for the city did not persist. The city reverted to its previous designation: Yeru Shalem instead of Beth Shalem. Lewy reasoned that the temple and the name connected with it must have disappeared before the next appearance of the name of Jerusalem in history.

The position of Lewy has indefensible weaknesses.[61] The equation of Ninurta with Šulmanu must be called into question. Not only is the reading of Šulmanu in the text questionable,[62] but the text itself can hardly be used for the purpose to which Lewy put it. The equating occurs in a list from neo-Assyrian times in which syncretistic speculation was popular and lively.[63] Even though the name of Ninurta occurs in the West later,[64] the name in the text at issue occurs with a Mesopotamian name which has no immediate reference to Palestine.[65] Even though it is probable that the god of a city would have a shrine in its honor, this text can no longer be used to reconstruct the pre-Israelite worship in Jerusalem.[66]

A different attempt to reconstruct the religious establishment of Jerusalem before David is that of the Scandinavian school of Old Testament interpretation which is related to the Myth and Ritual School. The Myth and Ritual School saw a pattern in the whole ancient Near East by which the king, who represented the god in the cult, underwent a ritual humiliation and death and final resurrection.[67] This ritual suffering and victory is enacted in the New Year Festival where it has an internal connection with the annual creation/recreation of order

out of chaos.[68] This is a general picture of all religions
in the ancient Near East in the broad theory of this approach.
There are extremely significant variations among the various
adaptations of this structure, but the structure is there to
find beneath each people's religion.

Jerusalem shared in this general picture. Themes of
death and resurrection, of victory over chaos can be found
in the Old Testament, and these were identified as the religious substratum over which the Israelite experience imposed
its own configurations and modifications. There is some disagreement within this approach on the religion of Jerusalem.
G. W. Ahlström disagrees with Geo Widengren who proposes that
Yahweh himself died and rose:[69] Ahlström denies Yahweh's death
and resurrection, but he sees Yahweh's son, the god Dod, who
did die and rise.[70]

This approach is a clear example of the comparative
method of studying the Bible. This approach, however, has
been criticized for haste in generalization. Most scholars
in the school currently pursue additional lines of research.
The approach has brought to light various things in the text
that had previously not been seen. But the critique remains
that the texts were not always seen in isolation first.

A third attempt to reconstruct the cult of Jerusalem
tries to work closely with the uniqueness of some biblical
texts. The city of Jerusalem is often singled out as God's
chosen spot, the invincible city which he will always cherish
and guard. This city of God was founded by God to be a place
of refuge against the attacks of hostile enemies. Nations
may rush against her, but Zion, the dwelling of God, rests
secure above the confusion.[71]

Herbert Schmid singled out this theme of the city of
God as one of the cult traditions that existed in pre-Israelite Jerusalem and which continued to thrive in Jerusalem under
David and his successors.[72] Edzard Rohland singled out the
election of the city and its dynasty as another element in
the religious complex of pre-Israelite Jerusalem which David
was only too happy to agree with and use.[73] Various German
Old Testament scholars accepted this view.[74]

Fritz Stolz has recently written extensively on the pre-
Israelite Jerusalem traditions.[75] He tries to set the tradi-
tions of the city in the broader ancient Near Eastern setting.
His work has six parts: (1) the battle against chaos, (2) the
battle against the nations, (3) the distant God--An, Enlil,
El, (4) El of Jerusalem, with aspects of closeness: creation

and judgment, (5) other gods in the Jerusalem pantheon, especially Salem, (6) Israel's creative adaptation of these themes.

The comparative method of studying the Bible offers an interesting, previously unnoticed analogy to the inviolability of Jerusalem, if one understands "inviolable" in a broader sense than security during attack. Nippur was the sacred city of Mesopotamia for centuries, and it was never taken by military force. This center of religious life was patronized and supported by the various cities and districts of Mesopotamia.[76] During the late dynasties of Isin and Larsa, Nippur seemed to recognize successively one then the other of the two cities as the dominant political power in relation to itself (or to its scribes) by naming the years according to the kings of one then the other city.[77] Although one cannot exclude the possibility that the city was not taken because of the astuteness of political factions in the city or because of an impressive defense system,[78] it is easy to conceive that the inhabitants of the city may have attributed this special state of never being attacked to divine protection. Nippur thus furnishes some parallel for the experience of the Jerusalemites who knew the tradition of inviolability by divine election.

Stolz's book was the occasion for J. J. M. Roberts' assessment of the origin of the Zion Tradition.[79] He claims that the idea of the inviolability of the city is best understood as emerging from the historical experience of David's time. David conquered many peoples, and these would have been tempted to rebel against David.[80] David's defeat of these rebels created the tradition of attack and salvation. Roberts would agree with the idea that historical events have sometimes become myths.[81] John Bright is also convinced of the historical origins of the idea of inviolability. He posits two campaigns of Sennacherib against Jerusalem, the first one ending in the capitulation of the city, the second one, years later, in its deliverance. Only by a historical miraculous deliverance of Jerusalem could the myth of the inviolability of the city come into existence.[82]

This writer judges the tradition of the invincibility of the city by virtue of divine foundation to be of such antiquity in Jerusalem that the origin of the tradition should be placed in the pre-Israelite times. The first person in the Bible to be called as a spokesman of Jerusalem, one might say, is the prophet Isaiah in the eighth century. And from the lips of Isaiah one does not hear the story of Israel: no patriarchs, no Moses and Exodus, no Sinai.[83] The recurrent themes of Isaiah, who grew up in Jerusalem are different: the city of

God, its attack by nations (often Zion remains unconquered,
but sometimes Zion is chastened by means of the enemy), and
the dynasty of the great king (if one accepts those passages
as from Isaiah).[84]

This survey of studies of pre-Israelite Jerusalem was
attempted from a comparative method. The artifacts and the
documents from outside the Bible help somewhat to see this
period of the history of the ancient city in a dim light.
Some texts are ambiguous enough to have led scholars astray.
A cautious judgment, in this writer's view, would be that no
document or unwritten material has been found to solve the
mysteries of pre-Israelite Jerusalem. As of now any evidence
on the religious element of Jerusalem before David seems sus-
ceptible to various interpretations. It seems to this writer,
however, that some of the religious atmosphere of pre-Israelite Jerusalem is to be found in parts of Isaiah and in some
of the biblical psalms.[85]

# NOTES

1. George Adam Smith, *Jerusalem: The Topography,
Economics and History from the Earliest Times to A.D.70* (2
vols; New York: A. C. Armstrong, 1908), 2.284-285.

2. Benjamin Mazar, *The Mountain of the Lord* (Garden
City: Doubleday, 1975), 42.

3. Kathleen Kenyon, *Digging Up Jerusalem* (London:
Ernest Bean, 1974), 79.

4. *Ibid.*, 84-89.

5. R. J. Forbes, *Studies in Ancient Technology* I (2d
ed.; Leiden: E. J. Brill, 1964), 155-156. Forbes refers to
these shafts as *ṣinnôr*. It is not clear that this is the
appropriate term for such projects. The word comes from the
Hebrew of the narrative of David's taking of Jerusalem, 2 Sam
5:8. The translation, however, is problematic. See note 54
below.

6. Kenyon, *Digging*, 80-81.

7. John Wilkinson, "Ancient Jerusalem: Its Water Supply
and Population," *PEQ* 106 (1974), 33.

113

8. Magen Broshi, "La population de l'ancienne Jérusalem," *RB* 82 (1975), 13.

9. Kenyon, *Digging*, 94-96.

10. *Ibid.*, 96.

11. It is striking that Adonizedek is the only person in the Hebrew Bible who receives the unqualified designation "king of Jerusalem."

12. It is noteworthy that the LXX reads Adonibezek for Adonizedek in Joshua 10. Martin Noth judges that the king of Jerusalem in this passage is secondary, and that the original name was Adonibezek, the same person as in Judg 1:5-7. See Noth, "Jerusalem and the Israelite Tradition," in his *The Laws in the Pentateuch and Other Studies* (Philadelphia: Fortress, 1966), 132. See in more detail his *Das Buch Josua* (2d ed.; Tübingen: J.C.B. Mohr, 1952), 63.

13. Noth, "Jerusalem," 132, n. 1.

14. J. Alberto Soggin, *Joshua: A Commentary* (Philadelphia: Westminster, 1972), *ad loc.*

15. The Jebusites are a significant problem in one's view of pre-Israelite Jerusalem. In the Bible the word functions as a gentilic of Jebus. Georg Fohrer, however, sees Jebus as a backformation from the name of the group of people called the Jesubites with the result that the city was never called Jebus, "Zion-Jerusalem im Alten Testament," in his *Studien zur Alttestamentliche Theologie und Geschichte (1949-1966)* (BZAW 115; Berlin: de Gruyter, 1969), 204 (also published in *TDNT* 8.300). However, cf. J. Maxwell Miller who would place Jebus to the north of Jerusalem ("Jebus and Jerusalem: A Case of Mistaken Identity," *ZDPV* 90 [1974], 115-127). Some of the difficulty of finding some historical ethnic identity to the names used by the biblical authors for the previous inhabitants of Canaan is discussed in John Van Seters, "The Terms 'Amorite' and 'Hittite' in the Old Testament," *VT* 22 (1972), 64-81 and Robert North, "The Hivites," *Bib* 54 (1973), 43-62.

16. Yehezkel Kaufmann, *The Biblical Account of the Conquest of Palestine* (Jerusalem: Magnes Press, 1953), 24-25, simply avers the Benjaminite claim to be more ancient, originating in the period of the conquest, while the Judahite attribution is due to the historical fact that David, the conqueror of Jerusalem, was of Judah.

17. A study of literature as politics on a much larger scale is that of Peter Machinist, "Literature as Politics: the Tukulti-Ninurta Epic and the Bible," *CBQ* 38 (1976), 455-482.

18. See, e.g., the smiting and burning of Ai, Josh 8: 19-22.

19. The contrast between the capture and non-capture of Jerusalem in the book of Judges was seen already by Josephus. His solution was to see two Jerusalems, the lower taken in Judg 1:8, the upper taken by David; see John H. Hayes and J. Maxwell Miller, eds., *Israelite and Judean History* (Philadelphia: Westminster, 1977), 12.

20. The passage well reflects a pre-monarchic period, but its incorporation into the Deuteronomic History seems to be exilic; cf. Robert G. Boling, *Judges* (AB 6A; Garden City: Doubleday, 1975), 278.

21. Thomas L. Thompson, *The Historicity of the Patriarchal Narratives: The Quest for the Historical Abraham* (BZAW 133; Berlin: de Gruyter, 1974), 98-106.

22. K. Sethe, *Die Ächtung feindlicher Fürsten, Völker und Dinge auf altägyptischen Tongefassscherben des mittlern Reiches* (Berlin: Preussische Akademie der Wissenschaften, 1926).

23. G. Posener, *Princes et pays d'Asie et de Nubie: textes hiératiques sur des figurines d'envoûtement du Moyen Empire* (Brussels, 1940).

24. Some of these texts are translated into French by Posener, "Les textes d'envoûtement de Mirgissa," *Syria* 43 (1966), 277-287.

25. The latter seems the more plausible to James M. Weinstein, "Egyptian Relations with Palestine in the Middle Kingdom," *BASOR* 217 (1975), 13.

26. W. F. Albright, "Palestine in the Earliest Historical Period," *JPOS* 15 (1935), 217-219.

27. Albright, "New Egyptian Data on Palestine in the Patriarchal Period," *BASOR* 81 (1941), 19.

28. Thompson, *Historicity*, 113.

29. John Gray, *A History of Jerusalem* (London: Hale, 1969), 65, interprets the names "The Uncle, or Patron-god of the Tribe, is Noble" and "Cleaver."

30. J. A. Knudtzon, *Die El-Amarna Tafeln* (2 vols.; Leipzig: J. C. Heinrichs, 1910 and 1915) and Anson F. Rainey, *El-Amarna Tablets 359-379: Supplement to J. A. Knudtzon, Die El-Amarna Tafeln* (AOAT 8; Neukirchen Vluyn: Butzon & Bercker Kevelaer, 1970).

31. This is the suggestion of Mazar, *Mountain,* p. 48.

32. EA 287 (*ANET*, p. 488).

33. See Giorgio Buccellati, "'*Apiru* and *Munnabtūtu*-- The Stateless of the First Cosmopolitan Age," *JNES* 36 (1977), 145-147, esp. n. 6 on "becoming a ḫabiru."

34. EA 280 (*ANET*, p. 487), but ʿAbdiḫepa must also be meant in EA 279.

35. William L. Moran, "The Syrian Scribe of the Jerusalem Amarna Letters," in *Unity and Diversity: Essays in the History, Literature, and Religion of the Ancient Near East* (eds. Hans Goedicke and J. J. M. Roberts; Baltimore: Johns Hopkins, 1975), 146-166.

36. *Ibid.,* 156.

37. See the literary ability of the scribe of the Tyre letters analyzed by Stanley Gevirtz, "On Canaanite Rhetoric: The Evidence of the Amarna Letters from Tyre," *Or* N.S. 42 (1973), 162-177.

38. Cf. ʿAbdiḫepa's (or his scribe's) request to the Egyptian official to "tell it to the king in good (i.e., eloquent) words," in EA 289:49, also 286:62-63, 287:67-68 and 288:64-65 (all in *ANET*, pp. 488-489). See Gevirtz, "Canaanite Rhetoric," 164, n. 10.

39. EA 286:13, 287:25-28, 288:13-15.

40. *bīt* $^{amēlu}$ *a-bi-ia* in EA 286:13, *bīt* $^{amēlu}$ *a[b]i* in EA 288:15. "To enter his father's house" may indeed be "a long-established expression for accession to the throne" (Moran, "Syrian Scribe," 156), but it need not imply coming from a distance. Cf. C. J. Mullo Weir, "The phrase indicates that Abdiḫepa was a hereditary ruler, confirmed in his position by the Pharaoh," in *Documents from Old Testament Times*

(ed. D. Winton Thomas; New York: Harper Torchbooks, 1961),
44, and John Gray, *A History of Jerusalem*, 69.

41. See A. Leo Oppenheim, "A Note on the Scribes in
Mesopotamia," in *Studies in Honor of Benno Landsberger* (Assyriological Studies 16; Chicago: University of Chicago,
1965), 253-256.

42. Some see this Hittite connection as the basis for
the prophet's charge against Jerusalem, "Your father was an
Amorite and your mother was a Hittite," Ezek 16:3, e.g.,
Gerhard von Rad, *Old Testament Theology* (2 vols.; New York:
Harper & Row, 1962, 1965), 2.221. However, Van Seters ("The
Terms 'Amorite' and 'Hittite'") points out that both terms
are generally used as rhetorical pejoratives. There is no
clue in the passage that the prophet is attempting to be an
historian, but simply to reprimand the ingratitude and infi-
delity he sees in some people.

43. B. Maisler (Mazar), "Das vordavidische Jerusalem,"
*JPOS* 10 (1930), 189.

44. Jerusalem seems to have been the major city in the
southern hill country, functioning as Shechem did in central
Palestine and Hazor in the north. See Zechariah Kallai and
Hayim Tadmor, "Bīt Ninurta=Beth Horon: On the History of the
Kingdom of Jerusalem in the Amarna Period," *Eretz Israel* 9
(1969), 138-147 (in Hebrew with an English summary). A study
to which I have not had access is A. Malamat, "The Dawn of
Jerusalem: On the Portrait of a Canaanite City State," in
*Selected Studies of the Bible Circle in Memory of Yishei Ron*
(Tel Aviv, 1973), 139-149 (in Hebrew), previously published
in *And For Jerusalem* (ed. G. Elgoshi, *et al.*, 1968), also
in Hebrew.

45. On the importance of religion in the development
of cities, cf. Lewis Mumford, *The City in History* (New York:
Harcourt, Brace & World, 1961), 3-54. On the erection of
monumental buildings as an essential ingredient of urbanization, see Hallo in William W. Hallo and William K. Simpson,
*The Ancient Near East: A History* (New York: Harcourt Brace
Jovanovich, 1971), 33.

46. See, e.g., Fohrer, "Zion-Jerusalem," 202 (*TDNT* 8.
298) who takes the first element, $y^eru$, as a noun in the construct state. Albright, on the other hand ("Palestine," 218-
219, n. 78) prefers a verbal form "let Šalim found."

47. EA 290.

48. So, e.g., B. Mazar, in *Jerusalem Revealed: Archaeology in the Holy City 1968-1974* (ed. Y. Yadin, *et al.*; Jerusalem: Israel Exploration Society, 1975), 1. However, the letters are most easily read 'Awshlmm' according to Alexis Mallon, "Jérusalem et les documents égyptiens," *JPOS* (1927), 1-6.

49. Ps 122:6 gives a word pláy on the sound of the word "peace" by trying to echo it in the second half of the name of the city (along with at least one other word play); see also Jer 15:5. Heb 7:2 is perhaps the first attempt to give "peace" as a part of the etymology of the city's name; cf. George Wesley Buchanan, *To the Hebrews* (AB 36; Garden City: Doubleday, 1972), 118. By comparison with other ancient place names, the second element is most probably a divine name. The earliest appearance of the divine name Salim is from Sargonic times; see J. J. M. Roberts, *The Earliest Semitic Pantheon: A Study in the Semitic Deities Attested in Mesopotamia before Ur III* (Baltimore: Johns Hopkins, 1974), 51.

50. This might be the case in Gen 14:18. There is also the report that Salim appears in the Ebla tablets; Giovanni Pettinato, "The Royal Archives of Tell-Mardikh-Ebla," *BA* 39 (1976), 46, n. 7 says the name appears "repeatedly."

51. This seems the more probable explanation of the *qere perpetuum* of ירושלים as *yerushalayim*. The original pronunciation, to judge from the appearance of the name in other languages, ended in *-salem*. Biblical Aramaic has the form *yᵉrûshᵉlem* in Daniel and Ezra. Cf. Fohrer, "Zion-Jerusalem," 200-201 (*TDNT* 8.296-297). How the tradition of a second pronunciation arose is unclear. Grammatically, the form appears to be dual. There are other biblical place names which bear this same dual appearance, e.g., Ephrayim, Naharayim, Misrayim. Some names in this form are logically dual, e.g., Miṣrayim, Ramathayim, perhaps Naharayim. For a possible logical dual for Jerusalem, see Josephus' thoughts in n. 19 above. Kautzsch's *Gesenius' Hebrew Grammar* (trans. and adjusted to the twenty-sixth ed. by A. E. Cowley; Oxford: Clarendon, 1898), 256 explains these not as true duals but as expansions in Hebrew and Aramaic of *-am* and *-an* endings. For a possible cuneiform appropriation of such a West Semitic form at pre-Israelite Hazor, see William W. Hallo and Hayim Tadmor, "A Lawsuit from Hazor," *IEJ* 27 (1977), 8; and for parallel forms of a place name in cuneiform and in the Bible, see Hayim Tadmor, "The Campaigns of Sargon II of Assur: A Chronological-Historical

Study," *JCS* 12 (1958), 40. If in the biblical text the Maso-
retes deliberately changed the vocalization of the name Jerusalem, the change would be comparable to their change of Baal
to *bosheth* in the name of the son of Saul and to their choice
of vowels for the Moabite god's name Molek.

52. Ṣaduq(a) occurs as a divine name or epithet in
Amorite; cf. Herbert B. Huffmon, *Amorite Personal Names in
the Mari Texts: A Structural and Lexical Study* (Baltimore:
Johns Hopkins, 1965), 92-93, 98-99, 256-257.

53. For a succinct review of the studies on Zadok, see
Christian Hauer, "Who was Zadok?" *JBL* 82 (1963), 89-94.

54. The way that one scholar has turned the event into
a military action, "his big military operation," is to trans-
late the word ṣinnôr in 2 Sam 5:8 as "trident"; see Yigael
Yadin, *The Art of Warfare in Biblical Lands in the Light of
Archaeological Studies* (2 vols.; New York: McGraw-Hill, 1963),
2.267-268, basing himself on the suggestion of E. L. Sukenik.
For a full review of the various interpretations, see Hans
Joachim Stoebe, "Die Einnahme Jerusalems und der Ṣinnôr,"
*ZDPV* 73 (1957), 73-99.

55. This is a factor rarely considered by scholars in
assessing David's action. His familiarity with Jerusalem and
with the god Šalim is shown by naming one of his sons born in
Hebron Abshalom, 2 Sam 3:3.

56. Cf. G. W. Ahlström, "Der Prophet Nathan und der
Tempelbau," *VT* 11 (1961), 113-127.

57. Julius Lewy, "The Šulman Temple in Jerusalem," *JBL*
59 (1940), 519-522.

58. EA 290:14-16.

59. K.4339, text in *Cuneiform Texts from the Babylonian
Tablets in the British Museum* XXV (1909), plate 12, line 1.

60. See the acceptance of this position by Millar Bur-
rows, "Jerusalem," *IDB* 2.844.

61. Lewy's work sparked an interesting study on the
worship of Nergal, the companion of Ninurta, on the hill
across from Jerusalem, viz., John Briggs Curtis, "The Mount
of Olives in Tradition," *HUCA* 28 (1957), 137-177. He proposes this worship of Nergal in the form of Chemosh and Molek
for the reign of David, and hence the topic lies outside the
present study.

62. The full equation reads $^d$DI.MEŠ=$^d$Nin-urta in Elam. This contradicts another God-list (An=Anum ša amēli, line 2) where $^d$DI.MEŠ is explained as "Anu of women." In order to read DI.MEŠ in K.4339 as Šulmanu, one would have to read DI as *silim* and interpret the logographic marker MEŠ as reflecting the Akkadian ending *-anu* which here is not likely intended as a true plural.

63. Oral statement of Prof. Hallo.

64. The name, pronounced Inurta then, appears on an Ammonite seal in Aramaic in the seventh century B.C.E.; see N. Avigad, "Seals of the Exiles," *IEJ* 15 (1965), 222-228 and H. Tadmor, "A Note on the Seal of Mannu-ki-Inurta," *IEJ* 15 (1965), 233-234.

65. Lewy accepted the opinion of Zimmern that the appearance of "Elam" was a mistake. Lewy might have added to his argument the remarkable equation in an Assyrian God-list, $^d$Inanna uru-silim-ma=Šul-ma-ni-tu, as did Fr. Boehl ("Älteste keilinschriftliche Erwähnungen der Stadt Jerusalem und ihrer Göttin?" *AcOr* 1 [1922], 76-80) and B. Maisler (Mazar), "Das vordavidische Jerusalem," 183.

66. Other interpretations of the phrase have referred *bīt* $^d$NIN.IB to some other location, e.g., Zimmern to Beth Shemesh, Schroeder to Bethlehem. Most recently, Kallai and Tadmor, "Bīt Ninurta = Beth Horon," cited above in note 44. See also Albright, *Yahweh and the Gods of Canaan* (London: Athlone, 1968), 120, where he identifies Hauron with Ninurta.

67. See further S. H. Hooke, ed., *Myth, Ritual, and Kingship* (Oxford: Clarendon, 1958), especially for some of the reaction to the school.

68. Ivan Engnell, "New Year Festivals," in his *A Rigid Scrutiny* (trans. and ed., J. T. Willis; Nashville: Vanderbilt, 1969), 180-184.

69. Geo Widengren, *Sakrales Königtum in Alten Testament und in Judentum* (Stuttgart: Kohlhammer, 1955), 67-76.

70. G. W. Ahlström, *Psalm 89: Eine Liturgie aus dem Ritual des Leidenden Königs* (Lund: Gleerup, 1959), 163-173.

71. The attack is seen in fleeting visions in Psalms 47, 48 and 76.

72. Herbert Schmid, "Jahwe und die Kulttraditionen von Jerusalem," *ZAW* 67 (1955), 168-197.

73. Edzard Rohland, "Die Bedeutung der Erwählungstra-
ditionen für die Eschatologie der alttestamentliche Propheten"
(diss.; Heidelberg, 1956).

74. E.g., Hans-Joachim Kraus, Gerhard von Rad, Josef
Schreiner, Werner Schmidt, Hans-Martin Lutz. See the bibliography in the Roberts article in note 79 below.

75. Fritz Stolz, *Strukturen und Figuren im Kult von
Jerusalem: Studien zur altorientalischen vor- und frühis-
raelitischen Religion* (BZAW 118; Berlin: de Gruyter, 1970).

76. William W. Hallo, "A Sumerian Amphictyony," *JCS*
14 (1960), 88-114.

77. R. Marcel Sigrist, "Èš-ta-gur-ra," *RA* 71 (1977),
117-124, esp. pp. 122-123, and *idem*, "Nippur entre Isin et
Larsa de Sin-iddinam à Rim-Sin," *Or* 46 (1977), 363-374.

78. R. Marcel Sigrist in personal correspondence.

79. J. J. M. Roberts, "The Davidic Origins of the Zion
Tradition," *JBL* 92 (1973), 329-344.

80. A full assessment of Roberts' study is beyond the
scope of this paper. However, it should be pointed out that
Roberts admits that he depends ultimately on possible theories
(as do the holders of the "Jebusite hypothesis"). One major
aspect of an appraisal of David's action would seem to be
David's familiarity with and appreciation of Jerusalem during
the formative years of his life. See note 55 above.

81. Cf. the paper below on the universalizing of history
by John Bradley White.

82. John Bright, *A History of Israel* (2d ed.; Philadelphia: Westminster, 1972), 299. It should be pointed out here
that the intention is not to challenge the idea that a historical event becomes mythologized. The question is, "Whose history?" The inhabitants of Jerusalem over the centuries could
well have experienced deliverance in their strategically
placed walled city. The position that Sennacherib led only
one campaign into Judah is generally affirmed by scholars who
have weighed the matter in the light of the extrabiblical materials, e.g., W. W. Hallo, in Hallo and Simpson, *The Ancient
Near East*, 142; K. A. Kitchen, "Late Egyptian Chronology and
the Hebrew Monarchy," *JANES* 5 (1973), 225-231; and A. F.
Rainey, "Taharqa and Syntax," *Tel Aviv* 3 (1976), 38-41. See
also the paper in this volume by Carl D. Evans, esp. pp. 164-
165.

83. Note that the references to the heptateuch mentioned by Seth Erlandsson in his *The Burden of Babylon: A Study of Isaiah 13:2-14:23* (Lund: Gleerup, 1970), p. 120, esp. n. 52, are all either quite vague or appear in passages which are often denied to Isaiah of Jerusalem.

84. Cf. the treatment of Isaiah in Gerhard von Rad, *Old Testament Theology*, vol. 2, trans. D. M. G. Walker (New York: Harper & Row, 1965).

85. Five of the passages in Isaiah which allude to the attack of the nations are analyzed in my unpublished dissertation, "The Zion Drama in the Tradition of Isaiah ben Amoz," (University of Chicago, 1977), written under the direction of Professor Jay A. Wilcoxen.

# LIGHT FROM RAS SHAMRA
# ON ELIJAH'S ORDEAL UPON MOUNT CARMEL

George E. Saint-Laurent
California State University, Fullerton

If one were to ask who it is that ranks side by side
with Moses, both in the living memory of Judaism and in actual historical significance, the response would have to be:
"Elijah." In the last two verses of the Book of Malachi, the
prophet declares that Elijah will return as harbinger of the
Day of the Lord.[1] Ben Sirach ascribes the future restoration
of Israel to the ministry of that same man of God.[2] Throughout Jewish rabbinical literature, mysticism, and folklore,
we find abundant allusions to the fiery figure clothed in
haircloth, so that he seems to rival the prominence of the
Messiah himself in the consciousness of his people. One
need only think of the "Elijah-cup" prepared during the Passover feast for this special guest, who, as always, could be
expected to appear suddenly, without warning.

The ninth century prophet holds a conspicuous place in
the Christian scriptures as well. Some thought that Jesus
might be Elijah.[3] Jesus, however, says that John the Baptist
has come in the spirit of Elijah.[4] It is clear that there is
a fundamental expectation of Elijah's return before the messianic age.[5] In the transfiguration story,[6] the disciples
have a vision of Jesus conversing with Moses and Elijah.
Finally, within the Islamic tradition, Allah himself praises
Elijah in the pages of the Qur'ān:

> Elias too was one of the Envoys;
> When he said to his people, 'Will you not
> be god-fearing?
> Do you call on Baal, and abandon the best
> of creators?
> God, your Lord, and the Lord of your fathers,
> the ancients?'
> But they cried him lies; so they will be among
> the arraigned, except for God's sincere serv-
> ants; and We left for him among the later

folk 'Peace be upon Elias!'
Even so We recompense the good-doers:
  he was among Our believing servants.[7]

Surely one of Israel's most irrepressible and colorful heroes, he stamped his personality indelibly upon the whole stream of western religious tradition, and he has captured the fascination of all who have heard his story. This strange and even frightening man of God has been the very type of the solitary prophet who must embody in his own person the ultimate protestantism: No compromise, God alone! His very name means "My God is Yahweh," and it encapsulated his life's focus and vocation.

If ever there was a human being of single-hearted zeal for the rights of God, it was Elijah. We read his story in 1 Kgs 17-19; 21:1-19. He appears abruptly, without genealogy or herald. But from that point on there can be no question about his identity in terms of the consuming thrust of his life. Yahweh alone is God in Israel, and Yahweh alone is to be worshipped in Israel. Yahweh will brook no rival, he will tolerate no division of loyalties, for he is a jealous God. Israel has arrived at a critical juncture, probably the most crucial moment since the sealing of the covenant itself. The temptation is not to abandon God, but rather to humiliate him. It is not so much a matter of atheism as it is a question of syncretism. Is Yahweh to exercise sole dominion among his people or is he to be dethroned, reduced to the status of merely one god among many in a foreign pantheon?

It is the purpose of this essay to investigate the biblical account of Elijah in its Near Eastern setting, especially insofar as the Ugaritic literature from Ras Shamra can shed light upon Baalism, the Canaanite religion which it was his vocation to oppose in the name of Yahweh, the God of Israel. It will be convenient to divide the pertinent material into three sections. In the first part, we shall briefly rehearse the contemporary consensus of scholars in regard to the sources of the Elijah-cycle as traditions independent of the royal annals, the theological portrait of the prophet as "The New (or Second) Moses," and the paradoxical congeniality of the account within the Deuteronomistic account of Kings Ahab and Ahaziah in the Northern Kingdom of Israel. For this summary I am heavily dependent upon the analysis contributed by John Gray.[8]

In the second part, we shall go beyond the immediate Hebrew context of the man of God in order to investigate the religion he so vigorously combatted. Here I wish to indicate my debt to the research of Arvid Kapelrud,[9] Norman Habel,[10] and John Gray[11] for their work on the basic myths about the god Baal, as these have emerged from the Ugaritic literature available.

In the concluding section, we shall focus particularly on the story of Elijah's contest with the prophets of Baal on Mount Carmel, i.e., 1 Kgs 18:16-46, insofar as Baalistic allusions can now be identified in the light of the texts from Ras Shamra. For this inquiry I have drawn especially upon the basic study of Ugaritic literature presented by U. Cassuto[12] and the monograph of Leah Bronner[13] on the Elijah-cycle.

For all biblical citations I shall be utilizing the English translation found in *The Jerusalem Bible.*[14] For the Ugaritic texts I shall be employing the translation of G. R. Driver.[15]

# I. Literary and Theological Perspectives

The Elijah stories had an existence of their own before they were incorporated into the First Book of Kings. Albright[16] suggests that they must have already existed in written form at an early date, since they so faithfully mirror the circumstances of ninth century Israel. We must, however, distinguish carefully between two diverse genres of vastly different credibility. When we read of Elijah's decisive role in the crises of his nation, we are dealing with sober, factual accounts of genuine historical reliability. Such stories—for example, the ordeal on Mount Carmel (1 Kgs 18:16-46), the experience at Horeb setting the stage for the commission of Elisha and for the rallying of opposition to the House of Omri (1 Kgs 19), and the extortion of Naboth's vineyard (1 Kgs 21)—may be traced to the authority of Elisha himself, Elijah's contemporary and successor in the prophetic office. Nevertheless, this in no way prevents them from being exploited for apologetic and polemic purposes in the combat against Baalism which continued during the lifetime of Elisha and thereafter.

On the other hand, we may also detect legendary accretions woven about Elijah's private life, limited in significance and devoid of moral tone, which belong rather to the sphere of local hagiology or folk-lore. Such legends—for instance, Elijah being fed by the ravens (1 Kgs 17:2-6), the prophet calling down fiery death upon the messengers of Ahaziah (2 Kgs 1), and the ascent of Elijah in a blazing chariot

(2 Kgs 2:1-13)--are ascribed to the oral traditions of pro-
phetic circles which were concerned to magnify the historical
Elijah for purposes both of edification (!) and, again, anti-
Baalistic polemics.

It is most probable that the man of God was already understood and theologically portrayed as a Second Moses, whose
historical vocation was to save the divinely-established religion of Sinai when it was in grave danger of syncretism with
Canaanite religion. We are supposed to think of Moses' trial
with the magicians of Pharaoh in Egypt[17] when we read of Elijah's ordeal with the prophets of Baal on Mount Carmel. The
parallel between the Mosaic challenge to Israel after the destruction of the Golden Calf, with the subsequent slaughter
of the idolaters,[18] and the ultimatum of Elijah, with the immediate execution of the prophets of Baal, is unmistakeable.
Nor is it any accident that Elijah should make his way through
the wilderness back to Mount Horeb (Sinai), when he is pursued
by Jezebel. He must re-live the experience of Moses, and meet
Yahweh himself in the same place where Moses had first met him
in the burning bush[19] and had later encountered him for the
sealing of the covenant.[20] Once again a theophany occurs
which is accompanied by fire and earthquake, and once again
God speaks with his prophet. This time, however, a clear distinction is made between Yahweh and the signs which accompany
his self-disclosure, since Yahweh must not be confused with
the forces of nature as Baal was construed among the Canaanites.

Other, less plausible, resemblances between Moses and
Elijah may be suggested. Moses parted the Reed Sea with his
staff so that Israel could cross; Elijah traversed the Jordan
River on his mantle. Moses designated his successor, Joshua,
who then led the Israelites through the Jordan into Canaan;
Elijah appointed Elisha as his successor in the prophetic office, and Elisha then returned through the Jordan River. A
certain mystery surrounded the death of Moses, because "to
this day no one has ever found his grave"[21]; Elijah was not
buried but was taken into heaven in a chariot. As H. H. Rowley has written:

> Without Moses the religion of Yahwism as it
> figured in the Old Testament would never have
> been born. Without Elijah it would have died.
> The religion from which Judaism, Christianity
> and Islam all in varying ways stemmed would
> have succumbed to the religion of Tyre. How
> different the political history of the world
> might have been it is vain to speculate. But

it is safe to say that from the religion of
Melkart mankind would never have derived that
spiritual influence which came from Moses and
Elijah and others who followed in their train.[22]

Consequently, it is not surprising to find the Elijah-
saga included together with the Deuteronomistic account of
Kings Ahab and Ahaziah in 1 Kings. It is true that the stories betray none of the characteristic Deuteronomic language.
Elijah is not reproached for having constructed an altar to
Yahweh outside of Jerusalem and on a rather high place, and
the prophet himself fails to condemn the cult of the calf at
Bethel. The man of God meets the most fundamental criterion
of Deuteronomistic theology: he served as Yahweh's agent in
the victory over Baal. No further comment was needed.


## II. The Character of the God Baal

Although the shadowy and distant god El was father of
the gods, president of the divine assembly, and theoretical
king of all, it was his son (or grandson?) Baal who exercised
the kingship in practice, and it was certainly Baal who was
the most popular god in the Canaanite pantheon. The name
*Baal* has the generic sense of a title meaning "master" or
"lord," but it developed into a proper name for Hadad, the
god of fertility, also known as "The Son of Dagan." Favorite
epithets for Baal were *Aliyan*, meaning "mighty" or "ruler,"
and *zebūl*, meaning "prince," together with a title given to
Yahweh in Ps 68:4: "Rider of the Clouds." As "the Lord of
the Storm," his voice was the thunder and his dwelling-place
was in the clouds astride Mount Zaphon, north of Ugarit.

We should note that the gods El and Baal are both kings,
but in vastly different ways. El is the high god who is already old, receding, a mere figurehead, whose status is immutable and eternal. Baal, however, is always portrayed as
young, even adolescent, with unbridled passions and a surprising dependence upon goddesses, who, like big sisters or even
mothers, must cater to his desires. El is always a king by
right. Baal must win his kingship in combat, rising from
humiliation without any natural claim to the throne. Even
when he has won the right to rule, he must still build a
palace for himself, and go on to suffer defeat, loss of kingship, and death, only to rise again as king in the end.

Employing Cyrus Gordon's distinction between "myth" and

"epic,"[23] we may speak of three myths among the poetic literature discovered at Ras Shamra:  the myths of Aqhat, Keret, and
Baal.  It is the latter myth which is the most extensive, consisting of three episodes, preserved on seven tablets.  The
tablets have unfortunately endured some damage, so that some
of the details and the exact sequence are uncertain.  There
can be no doubt about the general outline, however, and Baal
emerges clearly as the god of fertility, growth, and life,
who preserves the creation of El.

All living things must echo the vicissitudes of Baal,
suffering sterile famine when he is vanquished, but trium-
phantly acclaiming him when he rises again:  "the victor Baal
is alive, for the prince lord of earth exists."[24]  For Baal
has two mortal adversaries:  Yam and Mot.  Yam's full name is
"Prince Sea, Ruler River," which points to his dominion over
the ocean, source of destruction and symbol of chaos.  Mot,
the god of death, properly rules over drought, desert, and
the underworld.

In the first episode, Yam challenges Baal's domain by
unleashing his power together with the monsters Leviathan and
Tannin against the vegetation of the land.  He insists that
the gods deliver Baal into his hands, but Baal rallies their
will to resist, and only El is ready to acquiesce.  Kathir-
and-Khasis, the god of arts and crafts with the compound name,
assures Baal that he will triumph, and creates two magic weapons with which, in fact, Baal proves victorious over Yam.

In the second story, Baal wants to build a temple-palace
as a concrete testimony to his kingship.  He is able to enlist
the intercessory services of the goddesses Anat and Athirat,
so that El grants his permission for the project.  It is Kathir-
and-Khasis, once again, who does the actual work, and the edi-
fice is appropriately consecrated with sacrifices and a lavish
banquet for the gods.

It is the third and final narrative which appears to be
the most important for agricultural religion, and which is the
most pertinent to our purpose.  It describes the conflict of
Baal with Mot, the god of death.  Baal is surprisingly meek
and compliant when Mot issues his threats, as though he has no
choice but to die at a certain time and descend into the nether-
world--whether seasonally, at seven-year intervals, or irregu-
larly is by no means evident.

The death of Baal is reported to the earth above.  Anat
thereupon conducts her longing search for his body, recovers
it, and buries it upon Mount Zaphon.  The god Athtar is ap-

pointed to rule in Baal's stead, but his reign proves to be ineffectual, and he resigns. At length, Anat can control her grief no longer, and she wreaks violent vengeance upon Mot, treating him in a way reminiscent of grain in its agricultural development. She splits him, winnows him, burns him, grinds him, and scatters him on the earth, where he is consumed by birds. As long as Baal remains dead, there can be neither dew nor rain, and the earth becomes a desert. But, inexplicably (so far as extant evidence is concerned) El suddenly has a dream of oil descending from the sky and streams overflowing with honey, a proof that Baal is alive again! After seven years, he fights a fierce battle with Mot (who reappears without explanation) and overcomes him, apparently once and for all. There is no indication that Baal must die and rise again repeatedly.

## III.  Ras Shamra and 1 Kgs 18:16-46

It must be conceded that Ugarit is farther north than Palestine and that it evidently flourished between 1400 and 1200 B.C.E., a much earlier period than that of King Ahab's ninth century rule. Consequently, it is impossible with the available evidence to draw apodictic conclusions regarding the Baalist religion which Elijah was combatting. In the first place, there is some dispute regarding the actual identity of the "Baal" in question. Rowley[25] and de Vaux,[26] among others, identify him with Baal Melkart of Tyre. Gray[27] agrees with Mulder[28] that he was not only the Baal Melkart of Tyre, but also a local realization of the familiar Baal of the Canaanites and of the Hebrew scriptures. At the very least we may regard the Baal of Ugarit as a *typical* Canaanite Baal, if not in fact that same Baal whom Jezebel was later to export from Tyre to Israel. In the second place, we cannot demonstrate that the myths rehearsed in the Ugaritic literature were a cultural legacy throughout Canaan and for several subsequent centuries. Nevertheless, it does seem safe to suppose at the very least that Baalism shared some common features throughout that area, even if there were some local, accidental variations, and that therefore the Ras Shamra literature constitutes an excellent monument to the *substance* of Canaanite religion. In point of fact, the stories do fit very well with what we know of Baalism from the Bible. How, then, can the Ugaritic material help us?

Professor Cassuto[29] argues effectively that Hebrew

literature was the heir to a Canaanite tradition which had developed long before Israel entered the Promised Land. The Bible, then, represents not an absolutely new beginning--as though Joshua had achieved a *total* annihilation of all that was Canaan--but rather one more step in a single, literary continuum. Biblical authors used conventional phrases and linguistic patterns that had already been utilized both in the religious sphere and in the secular life of the Canaanites. Therefore, Ugaritic literature can be of inestimable value in exegeting the biblical text. Moreover, previously obscure allusions can now be interpreted in a fuller context, made intelligible in terms of concrete historical and cultural circumstances. Most important of all for the purpose at hand, the texts from Ugarit can illuminate biblical references to Canaanite religion.

In 1 Kgs 18:16-46, we read the story of the dramatic contest between Elijah and the prophets of Baal. Professor Bronner[30] has shown that there is a deliberate and sustained polemic against Baalism to be discerned throughout this pericope. The sacred writer is forcefully demonstrating through incisive irony that it is Yahweh, not Baal, who is the only God in Israel. It is Yahweh alone who is the God of power, not the allegedly "Aliyan" Baal. It is Yahweh alone who transcendently controls the forces of nature and fertility, not the supposedly immanent Baal, the so-called "Son of Dagan" and "Prince, Lord of the Earth." Baalism, then, is being ridiculed not only by the mocking taunts of Elijah, but also by the total thrust of the story.

Ugaritic sources present Baal not only as the god of life, vegetation, and fertility, but also of fire and lightning.[31] We know that Baal was believed to have power over thunder and lightning from texts such as the following, which presents a message of Baal: "I will create lightning that the heavens may know, thunder (that) mankind may know and the multitudes of the earth understand."[32] The blazing, all-consuming fire which Yahweh sends from heaven, on the other hand, seems to be a lightning bolt which totally devours the altar and its contents. As Elijah has already declared: "the god who answers with fire, is God indeed."[33]

After a three-year drought, however, rain was wanted as well, and at this juncture it is important to appreciate the fundamental role of rain in the mind of Canaanite man. In an agricultural society, life, even minimal survival, depended upon sufficient rainfall. Without moisture at the right season of the year, there can be neither vegetation for humans nor grazing-grounds for sheep and cattle. Once again,

Baal is presented as the storm god, the "Rider on the Clouds," who lives on cloudy Mount Zaphon, the source of dew and rain; we read, for example: "Now moreover Baal will abundantly give abundance of rain, abundance of moisture with snow, and he will utter his voice in the clouds, his flashings (and) lightnings on the earth."[34] That is why he became the most important god in the pantheon. For example, when Mot kills Baal, a famine is inevitable. Thus the description of Baal's death is described:

> .... Even as Mot has
> [jaws (reaching)] to earth, lips to heaven
> [and] a tongue to the stars, Baal
> will enter his stomach (and) go down into his
>     mouth
> as the olive, the produce of the earth and the
>     fruit of the trees,
> is swallowed. Shall the victor Baal be afraid
>     of him, the rider on the clouds fear him?[35]

The meaning is that with Baal's entrance into Mot's mouth, vegetation (the scorched olive) must also die and the earth must dry up. Further on, Baal is ordered to take the various symbols of moisture with him:

> ... I will put it in a hole
> of the earth-gods; and thou, take thou
> thy clouds and thy wind, thy bucket
> (and) thy rains, with thee, thy seven
> servitors (and) thine eight boars,
> (take) Pidriya daughter of mist with thee
> (and) Taliya daughter of showers with thee.[36]

On the other hand, Elijah had told Ahab, "As Yahweh lives, the God of Israel whom I serve, there shall be neither dew nor rain these years except at my order."[37] At the end of the drought, Elijah has brought word that Yahweh is about to send down rain on the land. Despite the most extreme efforts, the prophets of Baal fail to move their god to fulfill his prerogatives according to the myth. Yahweh, however, pours forth water in abundance: "And with that the sky grew dark with cloud, and rain fell in torrents."[38]

Perhaps there is a deliberate mockery of Baalism to be discovered in later Judaism as well. Professor Gray[39] has suggested that the name *Jezebel*, which occurs throughout the story in reference to the Tyrian princess who had married King Ahab and was now persecuting Yahwism, is an obvious parody as pointed in the MT: *'Îzebel*. Perhaps the name was changed first to *'t-zebûl* ("No nobility") from an original *'î zebûl* ("Where is the Prince?"), and then corrupted still further by scribes so as to read *'i zebel* ("Where is the dung?"). *ZBL* is found as an element in the divine name Baalzebul and, in the Ras Shamra texts, as an epithet of Baal. The real name of Jezebel, then, was probably *'î zebûl*, "Where is the Prince (i.e., Baal)?" We cannot be certain about cultic questions at Ugarit as such, but it does seem that this phrase was actually a cry of those who wept over the death of Baal in the liturgy: "Where is the victor Baal, where is the prince lord of earth?"[40]

It could easily be, then, that Jezebel had been born during a season of the year--late summer--when such ceremonies had been held, to herald the resurrection of the god of fertility. In that event, the acceptance of the phrase from the LXX in 1 Kgs 19:2, "If you are Elijah, I am Jezebel," becomes all the more poignant in irony. "Yahweh is my God" (Elijah) meets "Where is the Prince?" (Jezebel) after Baal has been defeated not by the mythical Mot but by Yahweh, the God of Israel!

We find the description of a Baalistic cultic ceremony in 1 Kgs 18:26-29:

> They took the bull and prepared it, and
> from morning to midday they called on the
> name of Baal. "O Baal, answer us!" they
> cried, but there was no voice, no answer,
> as they performed their hobbling dance
> around the altar they had made. Midday
> came, and Elijah mocked them. "Call
> louder," he said, "for he is a god: he
> is preoccupied or he is busy, or he has
> gone on a journey; perhaps he is asleep
> and will wake up." So they shouted
> louder and gashed themselves, as their
> custom was, with swords and spears until
> the blood flowed down them. Midday passed,
> and they ranted on until the time the of-
> fering is presented; but there was no voice,
> no attention given to them.

In this passage the prophets of Baal are certainly made to appear ridiculous, with their pathetic hobbling dance,[41] their ludicrously anthropomorphic conception of the deity, and their desperate, frantic attempts to arouse his attention. They even obediently shout the more loudly, at Elijah's urging. The texts discovered at Ras Shamra can provide some insight into the significance of this description.

Elijah has good reason to refer to Baal being "pre-occupied" in terms of the Baal-cycle, which speaks of a very busy god indeed, concerned about a wide variety of matters, from the building of his castle, to the defeat of his rivals, to the satisfaction of his prodigious sexual appetite.

There is also a basis for the mocking suggestion that perhaps Baal is "on a journey." In the Ugaritic literature we find a passage which tells of the goddess Anat seeking Baal at his house and inquiring of his servants where he is:

> [Is Baal in his mansion],
> [El Hadad in] the midst of his palace?
> And the servitors of Baal answered:
> "Baal is not in his temple
> (nor) El Hadad in the midst of his palace.
> Lo! he did take (his) bow in his hand
> and his arrows in his right hand,
> then verily he set his face
> toward the brink of Shamak teeming with
> wild oxen."[42]

Elijah's taunt that perhaps Baal is asleep and will wake up if his prophets shout more loudly is more than scathing ridicule. The Canaanites certainly believed that the god El could sleep, because there is a reference in the Ras Shamra texts to him dreaming:

> [that the victor Baal has died],
> that the prince [lord of earth] has perished.
> And lo! the victor [Baal] is alive,
> and lo! the prince lord of [earth] exists;
> (for) in a dream of Lutpan kindly god,
> in a vision of the creator of creatures
> the heavens rained oil,
> the ravines ran with honey,
> and I knew that the victor Baal was alive,
> that the prince lord of earth existed.
> In a dream of Lutpan kindly god
> in a vision of the creator of creatures
> the heavens rained oil,
> the ravines ran with honey.[43]

Presumably, then, Baal also was subject to fatigue, just as he was subject to death itself.

The self-laceration of the prophets of Baal finds its

mythical parallels in those texts according to which the deities themselves resorted to such frenzied activity. For example, the god El is said to gash open his own flesh when he learns of the death of Baal at the hands of Mot:

> Thereupon Lutpan kindly
> god came down from (his) throne, he sat
> on a stool, and (coming down) from the stool
> he sat on the ground; he strewed straw
> of mourning on his head, dust in which a man
> wallows on his pate; he tore the clothing
> of his folded loin-cloth; he set up a bloody
> pillar on a stone, two pillars in the forest;
> he gashed his (two) cheeks and (his) chin,
> thrice harrowed the upper part of his arm,
> ploughed (his) chest like a garden, thrice
> harrowed (his) belly like a vale.[44]

When the goddess Anat discovers the dead body of Baal, she also gives herself over to bloody expressions of grief:

> Anat went to and fro and scoured every rock
> to the heart of the earth (and) every mountain
> to the heart of the fields, she arrived at the
> pleasant tracts
> of [the land of] decease, the fair tracts of the
> edge of [the strand] of death, she [arrived] where
> Baal had fallen [into] the earth;
> (and) she tore [the clothing of] (her) folded
> loin-cloth.
> She set up a bloody pillar on a stone, two pillars
> [in the forest],
> she gashed her (two cheeks) and (her) chin, thrice
> harrowed
> the upper part of her arm, ploughed (her) chest
> like a garden, thrice harrowed (her) belly like a
> vale, (she lifted up her voice and cried):
> "Baal is dead. What (will become of) the people
> of Dagon's son,
> what (of) the multitudes belonging to Baal?"[45]

In conclusion, the discovered literature from Ras Shamra has become our principal source for understanding a strangely fascinating religion which previously could speak to us only through the compositions of its archenemies, the sacred writers of Israel. Now we can understand the full thrust of anti-Baalistic polemics as well as the broad meaning of Baalism itself as a deification of the forces of nature through mythology.

This paper has been an analysis of the contest between Elijah and the prophets of Baal on Mount Carmel, insofar as that account may be illumined by the Ugaritic data. It appears evident that the biblical author has deliberately emphasized those dimensions of the story which most sharply contrast the powerful dominion of Yahweh with the impotence of Baal. Yahweh is clearly delineated as the victorious God in the very area where Baal was supposed to rule: lightning, rain, and vegetation. Baalism, on the other hand, is scathingly mocked through the mouth of Elijah in the very terms of the Baalist myth. The humiliation of Baal serves as the exaltation of Yahweh, whose holiness is vindicated by the forces of nature itself. And Elijah becomes the very type of the prophetic figure who has experienced the true God and consequently can endure not the slightest compromise of the allegiance due to him.

# NOTES

1. "Know that I am going to send you Elijah the prophet before my day comes, that great and terrible day. He shall turn the hearts of fathers toward their children and the hearts of children toward their fathers, lest I come and strike the land with a curse" (Mal 3:23-24).

2. "The prophet Elijah arose like a fire, his word flaring like a torch. It was he who brought famine on them, and who decimated them in his zeal. By the word of the Lord, he shut up the heavens, he also, three times, brought down fire. How glorious you were in your miracles, Elijah! Has anyone reason to boast as you have?--rousing a corpse from death, from Sheol by the word of the Most High; dragging kings down to destruction, and high dignitaries from their beds; hearing reproof on Sinai, and decrees of punishment on Horeb; anointing kings as avengers, and prophets to succeed you; taken up in the whirlwind of fire, in a chariot with fiery horses; designated in the prophecies of doom to allay God's wrath before the fury breaks, *to turn the hearts of fathers toward their children,* and to restore the tribes of Jacob. Happy shall they be who see you, and those who have fallen asleep in love; for we too will have life" (Sir 48: 1-12).

3. "When Jesus came to the region of Caesarea Philippi he put this question to his disciples, 'Who do people say the Son of Man is?' And they said, 'Some say he is John the Baptist, some Elijah, and others Jeremiah or one of the prophets'" (Matt 16:13-14).

4. "'Because it was toward John that all the prophecies of the prophets and the Law were leading; and he, if you will believe me, is the Elijah who was to return'" (Matt 11:13-14).

5. "This is how John appeared as a witness. When the Jews sent priests and Levites from Jerusalem to ask him, 'Who are you?' he not only declared, but he declared quite openly, 'I am not the Christ.' 'Well then,' they asked, 'are you Elijah?' 'I am not,' he said. 'Are you the Prophet?' He answered, 'No.' So they said to him, 'Who are you? We must take back an answer to those who sent us. What have you to say about yourself?' So John said, 'I am, as Isaiah prophesied: *a voice that cries in the wilderness: Make a straight way for the Lord.*' Now these men had been sent by the Pharisees, and they put this further question to him, 'Why are you baptizing if you are not the Christ, and not Elijah, and not the prophet?' John replied, 'I baptize with water; but there stands among you--unknown to you--the one who is coming after me; and I am not fit to undo his sandal strap'" (John 1:1-27).

6. "Now about eight days after this had been said, he took with him Peter and John and James and went up the mountain to pray. As he prayed, the aspect of his face was changed and his clothing became brilliant as lightning. Suddenly there were two men there talking to him; they were Moses and Elijah appearing in glory, and they were speaking of his passage which he was to accomplish in Jerusalem. Peter and his companion were heavy with sleep, but they kept awake and saw his glory and the two men standing with him. As these were leaving him, Peter said to Jesus, 'Master, it is wonderful for us to be here; so let us make three tents, one for you, one for Moses and one for Elijah.'--He did not know what he was saying. As he spoke, a cloud came and covered them with shadow; and when they went into the cloud the disciples were afraid. And a voice came from the cloud saying, 'This is my Son, the Chosen One. Listen to him'" (Luke 9:28-35).

7. Surah 37.123-130.

8. J. Gray, *I & II Kings: A Commentary* (2d ed.; London: SCM, 1970), 362-414, 432-444.

9. A. Kapelrud, *The Ras Shamra Discoveries and the Old Testament* (Norman: University of Oklahoma, 1963).

10. N. Habel, *Yahweh Versus Baal: A Conflict of Religious Cultures* (New York: Bookman, 1964).

11. J. Gray, *The Legacy of Canaan* (Leiden: E. J. Brill, 1957).

12. U. Cassuto, *The Goddess Anath* (Jerusalem: Magnes, 1971).

13. L. Bronner, *The Stories of Elijah and Elisha* (Leiden: E. J. Brill, 1968).

14. A. Jones, ed., *The Jerusalem Bible: Reader's Edition* (Garden City: Doubleday, 1966).

15. G. Driver, *Canaanite Myths and Legends* (Edinburgh: T. & T. Clark, 1956).

16. W. Albright, *From the Stone Age to Christianity: Monotheism and the Historical Process* (2d ed.; Garden City: Doubleday, 1957), 306-309.

17. Exod 7-8:19.

18. Exod 32:25-29.

19. Exod 3:1-6.

20. Exod 19-40.

21. Deut 34:6.

22. H. Rowley, "Elijah on Mount Carmel," *BJRL* 43 (1960), 219.

23. C. Gordon, *Ugarit and Minoan Crete* (New York: W. W. Norton, 1966), 40.

24. *Baal* III.iii:21-22 (Driver, *Canaanite Myths*, 113).

25. Rowley, "Elijah," 190-219.

26. R. de Vaux, "Les prophètes de Baal sur le mont Carmel," *Bulletin du Musée de Beyrouth* 5 (1941), 8-9.

138

27.  Gray, *I & II Kings*, 393.

28.  M. Mulder, *Ba'al in het Oude Testament* (The Hague: Van der Gang en Van Wageningen, 1962).

29.  Cassuto, *The Goddess*, 18-52.

30.  Bronner, *Elijah and Elisha*.

31.  There is a fascinating emphasis upon the role of fire in the construction of Baal's temple-palace in Baal II. v:22-33 (Driver, *Canaanite Myths*, 99):

> Fire was set in the mansion,
> flames in the palace.
> Lo! (one) day and a second the fire
> consumed in the temple, the flames
> in the palace, a third (and) a fourth day
> the fire consumed in the mansion,
> the flames in the palace,
> a fifth day and a sixth day the fire
> consumed [in] the temple, flames
> in the midst of the palace; but
> on the seventh day the fire was extinguished (?)
> in the mansion, the flames in the palace.

32.  *Baal* V.iii:41-43 (Driver, *Canaanite Myths*, 87).

33.  1 Kgs 18:24b.

34.  *Baal* II.v:6-9 (Driver, *Canaanite Myths*, 97).

35.  *Baal* I*.ii:1-7 (Driver, *Canaanite Myths*, 105).

36.  *Baal* I*.v:5-11 (Driver, *Canaanite Myths*, 107).

37.  1 Kgs 18:15.

38.  1 Kgs 18:45.

39.  Gray, *I & II Kings*, 368.

40.  *Baal* III.iii:20-21; Baal III.iv:15-16 (Driver, *Canaanite Myths*, 113).

41.  De Vaux, "Les prophètes de Baal," 9-11, notes that the Greek verb given for "hobble" in the LXX is *epoklázontes*, the same verb which renders the meaning of "bending the knee"

(to Baal) in 1 Kgs 19:18, and suggests that the ritual dance of the prophets may have resembled a Russian Cossack dance.

42.   *Baal* IV.ii:2-9 (Driver, *Canaanite Myths,* 117).

43.   *Baal* III.iii:1*-13 (Driver, *Canaanite Myths,* 113).

44.   *Baal* I*.vi:11-23 (Driver, *Canaanite Myths,* 109).

45.   *Baal* I*.vi:26-I.i:8 (Driver, *Canaanite Myths,* 109).

# HEBREW PROPHECY WITHIN THE COUNCIL OF YAHWEH,
# EXAMINED IN ITS ANCIENT NEAR EASTERN SETTING

Max E. Polley
Davidson College

H. Wheeler Robinson was the first scholar to explore the concept of the council of Yahweh in Hebrew thought.[1] Since that day, the council of Yahweh has been compared to the assembly of the gods in ancient Near Eastern thought[2] and has been related to the call and commission of the Hebrew prophets.[3] It is the intent of this paper to relate the two subjects by placing the council of Yahweh in its Near Eastern setting and by examing Hebrew prophecy within that same setting. Three types of prophetic materials will be related to the council: (1) the call and commission of the prophet which takes place through vision in the council meeting; (2) the messenger formula passages which state that the prophet has been sent from the council meeting to proclaim God's decisions; and (3) the lawsuit passages which are best set within the context of a court meeting of the council.

The person who has written most extensively on the assembly of the gods in Mesopotamian thought is Thorkild Jacobsen. He has demonstrated that the background for the portrayal of the divine assembly is the primitive political situation in early Mesopotamia. While the form of government employed in later times was autocratic kingship, Jacobsen believes that Sumerian myths and epics point back to an earlier political situation he designates as "primitive democracy."[4] "Since it is difficult to conceive that the original myth-makers could have depicted as settings for their stories a society quite outside their experience and unrelated to anything they or their listeners knew, and since furthermore the myths of a people usually constitute the oldest layers of its traditions, one must assume that a political setting such as occurs in these tales once existed in Mesopotamia and was later replaced by more developed forms."[5] "Primitive democracy" he defines as "... a form of government in which internal sovereignty

resides in a large proportion of the governed, namely all
free, adult, male citizens without distinction of fortune or
class."[6] These citizens meeting in assembly *(unkin)* constituted the supreme judicial authority in the state; rulers
were chosen and derived their power from the consent of these
same citizens. The assembly was called in time of crisis,
enabling the community to draw upon the available experience
and to achieve a united action. During such times of crises
the assembly would appoint a leader to serve for the duration
of the emergency. When the emergency passed, the community
would return to simpler forms of organization such as the
family, households, and villages. Because Nippur and its
chief god, Enlil, were accorded a special place as a source
of rule over Sumer, Jacobsen argues that "primitive democracy"
applied to the country as a whole. All this occurred from the
Jemdet Nasr Period through the Early Dynastic I Period (ca.
3100-2700 B.C.E.).[7] The Early Dynastic II Period (ca. 2700-
2500 B.C.E.) was a time of increased warfare which witnessed
the growing power of a leader in what Jacobsen designates
"primitive monarchy." This policy culminated in the kingdom
of Kish with its undisputed power over all Sumer, a power
which lasted to the middle of the Early Dynastic III Period
(ca. 2400 B.C.E.). Therefore, it can be said that the third
millennium, a period of increased warfare, witnessed the formation of assemblies for collective security, the creation of
great leagues which appointed temporary officers, and particularly the emergence of a new institution of kingship, government under the autocracy of one man who held a permanent position.[8]

Vestiges of this "primitive democracy" survive in the
historical records. During the reign of Naram-Sin of Akkad,
there is a tradition which claims that the assembly of most
of the Akkadian and Sumerian subordinates rebelled against
him and elected as their leader the king of Kish. "In the
'Common of Enlil,' a field belonging to Esabad, the temple of
Gula, Kish assembled and Iphurkish, a man of Kish ... they
raised to kingship."[9] But most of the examples of "primitive
democracy" were identified by Jacobsen in the myths and
epics. In the Gilgamesh Epic (Assyrian version, Tablet III,
lines 1-11) the elders meet in assembly *(puḫrum)* and advise
Gilgamesh, the king, not to trust in his own strength but
rather to accept the mighty Enkidu as a companion for his
journeys. "We, the Assembly, entrust the King to thee. Deliver thou back the King unto us."[10] In the account of Gilgamesh and Agga of Kish, the ruler does no action in peace
or war until he obtains the consent of the assembly. Internal sovereignty rests in the assembly. Agga of Kish sends
messengers to Gilgamesh of Uruk, demanding that he surrender.

Gilgamesh consults with two assemblies, first that of the elders and then that of the young arms-bearing males, before he acts. Gilgamesh advises that Uruk resist the invasion of Kish, but it is not until the two assemblies agree with him that warfare takes place.[11] The assembly appears to be the ultimate political authority. Another example from the Gilgamesh Epic concerns the sending of the flood to destroy mankind. Utnapishtim explains to Gilgamesh that the decision was made to send the flood on humanity in the assembly of the gods. "That city (Shuruppak) was ancient, (as were) the gods within it, when their hearts led the great gods to produce the flood" (Tablet XI, lines 13-14).[12]

A significant development occurs in *Enuma Elish*. The conflict with Tiamat, where both Anu and Ea are unsuccessful in defeating primordial chaos, forces the gods to confer permanent and absolute power on Marduk in return for his protection. Yet the assembly of the gods is not disbanded. The assembly becomes subordinate to Marduk and provides a means for enhancing his majesty through their praise of him. They now receive orders from him and do his bidding rather than making decisions following debate. Autocracy has replaced democracy among the gods.[13]

Not only has the assembly the power to grant kingship, but it also can remove rulers. In the "Lamentation Over the Destruction of Ur," the Third Dynasty of Ur falls because of a decision made in the assembly to destroy the city and depose the goddess of Ur, Ningal. In the fourth song (lines 134-169) Ningal pleads with Anu and Enlil to spare the city of Ur, but they refuse. In the sixth song (lines 207-250) Ur is destroyed and Ningal is forced to abandon her city.

> Its lady like a flying bird departed from
>   her city;
> Ningal like a flying bird departed from
>   her city (lines 237-238).[14]

*Enuma Elish* continues to give elaborate details about the assembly of the gods. The court is called at Ubshukkinna where the gods gather, banquet, and fix the decrees for Marduk. "They kissed one another in the Assembly. They held converse as they (sat down) to the banquet. They ate festive bread, poured (the wine), they wetted their drinking-tubes with sweet intoxicants. As they drank the strong drink, (their) bodies swelled. They became very languid as their spirits rose. For Marduk, their avenger, they fixed the decrees" (Tablet III, lines 132-138).[15]

The assembly of the gods among the Mesopotamians had two major functions: (1) it was a court of law in which divine decisions were made which affected both the gods and mankind; (2) it had the authority to grant and to remove kingship.

While the concept of the assembly of the gods also existed in Canaan, detailed information about its organization and function is lacking. The positions of both El and Baal are ambiguous in the Ugaritic texts. El is referred to as "king"; the other gods do him homage; his consent is needed for decisions to be made. Yet, the other gods challenge him, often ignoring his orders. In *Baal* III AB B, Baal is in conflict with Prince Yam and Judge Nahar. The assembly of the gods is in session with El as supreme; Baal is clearly subordinate to El. El gives Baal into Prince Yam's hand to be Yam's slave. Yet Baal resists the will of El, grows angry, and, with a cudgel in his hand, confronts the messengers of Yam and Nahar.[16]

While a divine assembly does appear in Egyptian thought, it does not play a prominent role in the mythology. The "Ennead," the "Nine Gods" of cosmic order, were created out of the original, primordial abyss (*Nun*) and the ninth of their number, the sun-god, ruled them. In the middle kingdom the account is given of a judgment taking place in the council meeting with the sun-god as judge.[17]

In Hebrew thought there existed a similar concept designated the "council of Yahweh."[18] What needs to be explored is the nature of the divine beings in the council meeting and how they are related to the sovereignty of Yahweh. One way to confront this issue is to note the terminology used for the council of Yahweh in the OT.

1. *běnê (hā)-'ělōhîm*    "sons of God" (Gen 6:2; Job 1:6; 2:1; 38:7)

2. *běnê 'ēlîm*    "sons of God" (Pss 29:1; 89:7)

3. *běnê 'ělyôn*    "sons of the Most High" (Ps 82:6)

4. *qědōšîm*    "holy ones" (Deut 33:2)

5. *sôd-qědōšîm*    "council of the holy ones" (Ps 89:8)

6. *sôd 'ělôah*    "council of God" (Job 15:8)

7. *sôd yĕhōwah*          "council of the Lord" (Jer 23: 18, 22)

8. *'ădat-'ēl*           "midst of the gods" (Ps 82:1)[19]

9. *qĕhal qĕdōšîm*       "assembly of the holy ones" (Ps 89:6)[20]

Inasmuch as this terminology is similar to that used in both Mesopotamia and Canaan for the assembly of the gods, it is highly probable that Israel borrowed the concept from her Near Eastern neighbors.[21] But what do these terms mean in Israel's faith? G. Ernest Wright states that the concept of the heavenly council was the greatest threat to the sovereignty of Yahweh ever faced by Israelite religion.[22]

There are a number of texts which have been thought to refer to the existence of a pantheon in Israel at some period in her religious development. Four of these texts are especially helpful in examining the council of Yahweh in Israel's faith. Psalm 29:1 reads:

> Ascribe to the Lord, O sons of gods *(bĕnê 'ēlîm)*, ascribe to the Lord glory and strength.

Canaanite affinities with this psalm have been pointed out in articles by Albright, Cross, Gaster, and Ginsberg.[23] Given a Canaanite background, it would appear that the text refers to a divine pantheon which is called to praise Yahweh, the God of Israel. Psalm 89:6-8 is even more startling:

> Let the heavens praise thy wonders, O Lord, thy faithfulness in the assembly of the holy ones *(biqhal qĕdōšîm)*.
>
> For who in the skies can be compared to the Lord? Who among the sons of gods *(bibnê 'ēlîm)* is like the Lord?
>
> a God feared in the council of the holy ones *(bĕsôd-qĕdōšîm)*, great and terrible above all that are round about him?

Again, the passage appears to refer to a pantheon which glorifies the chief God, Yahweh. Psalm 82 is particularly difficult to interpret:

God has taken his place in the divine council
   *(ba'ădat-'ēl)*
   in the midst of the gods *(bĕqereb 'ĕlōhîm)*
   he holds judgment:

"How long will you judge unjustly and show
   partiality to the wicked?

Give justice to the weak and fatherless;
   maintain the right of the afflicted and the
   destitute.

Rescue the weak and the needy;
   deliver them from the hand of the wicked."

They have neither knowledge nor understanding,
   they walk about in darkness;
   all the foundations of the earth are shaken.

I say, "You are gods, sons of the Most High
   *(ûbĕnê 'ĕlyôn),* all of you;
   nevertheless, you shall die like men, and
   fall like any prince."

Arise, O God, judge the earth;
   for to thee belong all the nations!

Articles by O'Callaghan and Morgenstern have pointed out the
Canaanite setting for this Psalm.[24]  God is pictured as the
judge who takes his place in the divine council in the midst
of the gods.  These gods are condemned for their moral fail-
ures--"How long will you judge unjustly and show partiality to
the wicked?"  Further, they are condemned for their ignorance
of the future (i.e., they walk about in darkness).  Hence,
though they are sons of the Most High, yet they are condemned
to death.  God alone is declared judge of the earth.  Here is
seen Hebrew monotheism in the making as the so-called divine
beings (formerly immortal) are declared to be mortal.[25]  Finally, there is Deuteronomy 32:8-12:

When the Most High gave to the nations their
      inheritance;
   when he separated the sons of men,

He fixed the bounds of the people
   according to the number of the sons of gods
      *(bĕnê 'ēlîm);*

For the Lord's portion is his people,
   Jacob his allotted heritage.

It is an election passage which refers to the time when the Most High gave the nations their inheritance.  The Most High fixed the boundaries of the people according to the number of the sons of gods--here the Greek and Qumran reading is preferred--almost assuredly the Massoretes emended the text to read "sons of Israel" (běnê yiśrā'ēl).  Then Yahweh is assigned his portion, Israel.  The identification of Elyon and Yahweh in Hebrew faith has obscured the fact that in ancient mythology it was Elyon who assigned the guardian gods to their respective nations.  Again, emerging monotheism is seen in verse 12:  "Yahweh alone did lead him (Israel), and there was no foreign god with him."  All these texts point to the tendency in Israel to borrow the ancient Near Eastern myth of the assembly of the gods, to place Yahweh as head of the pantheon, and then to reduce the status of the "gods" to spiritual beings which surround Yahweh's throne.[26]

However, there are two major differences between the council members in Hebrew thought and their Near Eastern counterparts.  First, the members of the council of Yahweh lack mythological details.  They do not have special functions nor do they participate in feasts and banquets.  Second, Yahweh is never pictured as begetting these divine beings.  In short, the divine beings in the council of Yahweh are not given as concrete a representation as they are in other Near Eastern mythologies.  Or, to use a popular term, the council members seem to be partially demythologized.[27]

It can be argued that a possible origin of the council of Yahweh in Hebrew thought is the political institution of kingship and council in Israel.  David consulted with the commanders of the thousands and the hundreds, in addition to all the assembly of Israel, before the decision was made to bring the ark of the covenant to Jerusalem (1 Chr 13:1-4).  After hearing the conflicting advice of Ahithophel and Hushai, Absalom and the whole assembly decided in favor of the counsel of Hushai (2 Sam 16:20-17:14).  Jeroboam I of Israel took counsel before he announced the decision to make two golden calves and set them up at Bethel and at Dan (1 Kgs 12:28-29).  Rehoboam of Judah counselled first with the old men, who advised him to be generous in his treatment of the north, and then with the young men, who advised oppression of the north.  He heeded the latter's advice (1 Kgs 12:6-14; 2 Chr 10:6-11).[28]  Jehoshaphat took counsel with "the people" before appointing those who were to praise God with psalms (2 Chr 20:21).  Hezekiah took counsel with his princes and all the assembly in Jerusalem to keep the passover at a different time--the plan devised was agreed upon by both the king and all the assembly (2 Chr 30:2-4).  Hezekiah planned with his officers and his mighty men to stop the flow of water outside Jerusalem in order to hinder the invasion of Sennacherib (2 Chr 32:3). These texts reveal that the royal councils of Israel differed in character and procedures. Whybray has argued that where the particle '*ēl* is used for consultation with someone, the purpose of the meeting is to communicate a royal decision; whereas when '*im* or '*ēt* is used, consultation is taking place.[29] While the council of the king may provide background for the council of Yahweh, still, given the antiquity of the divine council in the biblical passages cited earlier and the striking parallels to the assembly of the gods in ancient Near Eastern mythologies, it is more reasonable to assume that Israel borrowed the concept from her neighbors.

Further details about the council of Yahweh will become apparent in this final section of the paper which deals with Hebrew prophecy within a council of Yahweh setting. There are three types of prophetic materials that should be related to the council: (1) the call and commission of the prophets which takes place through vision in the council meeting; (2) the messenger formula passages which state that the prophets have been sent from the council meeting to proclaim God's judgment; and (3) the lawsuit passages which are best set within the context of a court meeting of the council.

The call of Isaiah of Jerusalem (Isa 6), Deutero-Isaiah (Isa 40), and the vision of Micaiah (1 Kgs 22:19-23) are the best examples of the prophets within the council meeting.[30] In all three passages members of the council speak--in 1 Kings 22 and Isaiah 40 these spiritual beings advise God on the best course of action to follow; in Isaiah 6 the seraphim glorify God with words of praise.[31] The spirits never rival God's power; rather they are there to enhance his glory by providing a court befitting his majesty. It is to these spiritual beings that God speaks in the Genesis 1-11 passages where the divine plural is used: "Let us make man in our image" (Gen 1:26); "Behold the man has become like one of us" (Gen 3:22); "Come, let us go down, and there confuse their language" (Gen 11:7).

The prophets never become members of the council; they are called into God's presence and commissioned to bear a message: "Go, and say to this people" (Isa 6:9). The heart of the prophetic credentials is to have stood within the council of Yahweh. Jeremiah says: "For who among them (false prophets) has stood in the council of the Lord to receive and to hear his word?" (Jer 23:18) "... but if they (false prophets) had stood in my council (God is speaking), then they would have proclaimed my words to my people" (Jer 23:22).

All passages in the prophets that refer to vision should be examined for possible council of Yahweh settings. Amos 1:1 combines word and vision in a curious fashion. "The *words* of Amos, who was among the shepherds of Tekoa, which he *saw* concerning Israel" (italics mine). A council meeting would provide an ideal setting for both seeing a vision of God and receiving the word to proclaim. In like manner, Amos' five visions of the locusts (7:1-3), fire (7:4-6), plumb line (7:7-9), basket of summer fruit (8:1-2), and altar (9:1) could be interpreted within the context of the council meeting. The visions of the locusts and fire are interrupted before they are completed--God turns back from the decision to condemn Israel. The visions of the plumb line and basket of summer fruit are completed--the decision of the council meeting is to condemn Israel: "I will never again pass by them" (7:8 and 8:2).[32] It has often been suggested that the use of *sôd* in Amos 3:7 is a reference to a decision made at the council meeting. "Surely the Lord God does nothing without revealing his secret (*sôdô*, i.e., his counsel) to his servants the prophets."[33] It is the secrets revealed at the council meeting that the prophet is to make known to the people.[34]

There are no parallel passages in Mesopotamian, Egyptian, or Ugaritic texts which present the prophet as called within the assembly of the gods in order to speak forth the decision of the assembly. The texts which deal with the prophetic vision of the council meeting are unique to Hebrew thought. However, parallels do exist for the "messenger formula" passages and for the "lawsuit" passages, and to these we now turn.

The messenger formula, "Thus says the Lord," provides a body of material that should be related to the council meeting. There are some sixty-one examples of this type of speech in the prophetic books. The connective link between the council meeting and the oracles proclaimed is the verb *šālah*, "to send." This verb is used in the accounts of the prophets' calls within the council meeting: "Whom shall I send, and who will go for us? Here am I, send me" (Isa 6:8). The same verb is also used as an introduction to the oracles. From Ezek 2:4, following a vision of God in the heavenly council, we read: "I send you to them; and you shall say to them, 'Thus says the Lord God'...."

In the ancient Near East, the prophets were referred to as ones who were sent to bear a message. In the Mari texts, a man has a dream in which Dagon tells him: "Now go, I send you. Thus shall you speak to Zimri-Lim, saying: 'Send me your messengers....'"[35] Another letter from Mari reads:

"Moreover, the day I sent this tablet of mine to my land (an ec)static of Dagan came and addressed me as follows: 'The god sent (me). Hurry, write to the ki(ng). ...'"[36] In the Tale of Wen-Amon, the hero is referred to as a messenger of Amon.[37] In all these cases the authority of the messenger rests back upon the authority of the one who has sent him--Dagon or Amon.

What is true of the messengers of the gods is also true of the messengers of kings. Both the Ras Shamra Tablets and the Amarna Letters abound with examples of messenger oracles.[38] In the Bible, the authority of the Assyrian envoy's speech rests upon the King of Assyria who sent him, and it is significant that the speech begins with the messenger formula, "Thus says the great king, the King of Assyria" (2 Kgs 18:19).[39] Jacob sends messengers to Esau, commanding them, "Thus you shall say to my lord Esau: 'Thus says your servant Jacob'" (Gen 32:4). The messenger speaks for Jacob.

These examples provide the proper setting for the interpretation of the Hebrew prophetic messenger formulas. The authority of the prophets rests with Yahweh and his council meeting, from which they have been sent to proclaim his decisions, prefacing these judgments with the formula, "Thus says the Lord."[40]

Finally, it can be argued that the lawsuit passages of the prophetic materials *(rîb)* are best set within the context of the council of Yahweh (see Isa 1:2-3; Mic 6:1-8; Jer 2:4-13; Deut 32:1). Here scholarly opinion divides. Because these lawsuit passages often call for the heavens and the earth, the mountains and the hills, to listen to God's case against those who have committed evil, H. B. Huffmon argues that the Hittite international treaties form the best setting for these texts.[41] In these Hittite treaties, he argues, not only do the gods witness the covenant, but also the mountains, rivers, heaven, sea, wind, and clouds. The natural forces, he continues, were not part of the assembly of the gods in Mesopotamia, nor do they appear as part of the council of Yahweh in the OT. On the other hand, Wright argues that because the assembly of the gods in Mesopotamian religion is a court where judgments are rendered, to refer to heaven and earth, mountains and hills hearing Yahweh's case is but a way the Hebrew people demythologized the council meeting.[42] In support of Wright's position is the Hebrew people's view of nature as having a psychical life of its own[43] and, therefore, being able to incorporate natural elements into the council meeting with no difficulty. Because these natural elements were never deified in Israel's faith, they could be allowed admission to the council of Yahweh without fear of challenging

his sovereignty.  There they could hear God's case against
his rebellious people; yet it was God himself who rendered
the decision, being at one time both prosecutor and judge.
The prophets were admitted to the court, saw and heard the
judgments, and announced the decisions to their people.

The council of Yahweh is rooted in the ancient Near
Eastern concept of the assembly of the gods.  The Hebrew
faith reduced these divine-assembly members to spiritual
beings and resisted the temptation to allow them to rival
God.  The messenger formulas in the prophets also have a
counterpart in the ancient Near East; the authority of the
messenger rests upon the authority of the one sending him
forth.  The Hebrew prophets are sent forth from the council
meeting to proclaim the decision made there.  The lawsuit
passages found in the prophetic books can best be seen as
set in the context of the heavenly court where God renders
the judgment.  What remains totally unique to Israel's
faith is that material which presents in vision form the
call and commission of the prophets within the council of
Yahweh.  For the prophetic consciousness, the council meeting was none other than the Holy of Holies, where God truly
dwells.[44]

NOTES

1.  See H. W. Robinson, "The Council of Yahweh," *JTS* 45
(1944), 151-157, where he argued that the council should be
interpreted realistically rather than figuratively.

2.  See R. N. Whybray, *The Heavenly Counsellor in Isaiah
xl 13-14: A Study of the Sources of the Theology of Deutero-
Isaiah* (Cambridge:  Cambridge University Press, 1971), 34-38,
64-77; R. E. Brown, "The Pre-Christian Semitic Concept of
'Mystery,'" *CBQ* 20 (1958), 418-419; G. Cooke, "The Sons of
(the) God(s)," *ZAW* 76 (1964), 22-47.

3.  E. C. Kingsbury, "Prophets and the Council of Yahweh," *JBL* 83 (1964), 279-286; F. M. Cross, Jr., "The Council
of Yahweh in Second Isaiah," *JNES* 12 (1953), 274-277.

4.  T. Jacobsen, "Primitive Democracy in Ancient Mesopotamia," *Toward the Image of Tammuz and Other Essays in Mesopotamian History and Culture* (=HSS 21, 1970), ed. W. L. Moran,
157-170, 396-407 (first published in *JNES* 2 [1943], 159-172);

"Early Political Development in Mesopotamia," *Toward the Image of Tammuz,* 132-156, 366-396 (first published in *ZA* 52 [1957], 91-140); "Third Millennium Metaphors. The Gods as Rulers: The Cosmos a Polity," *The Treasures of Darkness: A History of Mesopotamian Religion* (New Haven: Yale University, 1976), 77-91.

5.  T. Jacobsen, "Early Political Development in Mesopotamia," *Toward the Image of Tammuz,* 137.

6.  T. Jacobsen, "Primitive Democracy in Ancient Mesopotamia," *Toward the Image of Tammuz,* 157.

7.  Following the chronology in W. W. Hallo and W. K. Simpson, *The Ancient Near East: A History* (New York: Harcourt Brace Jovanovich, 1971).

8.  See T. Jacobsen, "Early Political Development in Mesopotamia," *Toward the Image of Tammuz,* 137-154.

9.  As quoted in T. Jacobsen, "Primitive Democracy in Ancient Mesopotamia," *Toward the Image of Tammuz,* 162.

10.  E. A. Speiser, "The Epic of Gilgamesh," *ANET*[3], 81.

11.  Kramer and Jacobsen differ in their interpretations of this text. According to Kramer (*ANET*[3], 45-47) the assembly of elders reject Gilgamesh's advice to resist Kish and recommend submission. It is then that Gilgamesh consults with the arms-bearing males and obtains their counsel to resist Kish. According to Jacobsen, both the elders and the arms-bearing males agree with Gilgamesh and recommend armed resistance. See T. Jacobsen, "Primitive Democracy in Ancient Mesopotamia," *Toward the Image of Tammuz,* 162-163. A. Malamat, "Kingship and Council in Israel and Sumer: A Parallel," *JNES* 22 (1963), 247-253, agrees with Kramer.

12.  E. A. Speiser, "The Epic of Gilgamesh," *ANET*[3], 93. According to the Atrahasis Epic, the assembly of the gods was disturbed by the noise of mankind, and Enlil advised the assembly to punish mankind (Tablet I). See E. A. Speiser, "Atrahasis," *ANET*[3], 104-106; J. Laessøe, "The Atrahasis Epic; A Babylonian History of Mankind," *BO* 13 (1956), 90-102; and especially W. G. Lambert and A. R. Millard, *Atra-ḫasīs: The Babylonian Story of the Flood* (Oxford: Oxford University, 1969). G. Pettinato, "Die Bestrafung des Menschengeschlechts durch die Sintflut," *Or* n.s. 37 (1968), 165-200, interprets the "noise" which disturbed the gods as "evil conduct"; T. Frymer-Kensky, "The Atrahasis Epic and Its Significance for

Our Understanding of Genesis 1-9," *BA* 50 (1977), 147-155, believes the noise is equivalent to overpopulation, a problem the gods attempted to solve through the flood.

13. E. A. Speiser, "The Creation Epic," *ANET*[3], 60-72.

14. S. N. Kramer, "Lamentation Over the Destruction of Ur," *ANET*[3], 455-463.

15. E. A. Speiser, "The Creation Epic," *ANET*[3], 65-66.

16. H. L. Ginsberg, "Poems About Baal and Anath," *ANET*[3], 130. For the assembly of gods in Canaanite thought, see W. F. Albright, *Yahweh and the Gods of Canaan: A Historical Analysis of Two Contrasting Faiths* (London: Athlone, 1968), 104-109; F. M. Cross, Jr., *Canaanite Myth and Hebrew Epic: Essays in the History of the Religion of Israel* (Cambridge: Harvard University, 1973), 13-43, 186-190; M. H. Pope, *El in the Ugaritic Texts* (=VTSup 2, 1955), 27-29, 47-54; E. T. Mullen, *The Divine Council in Canaanite and Early Hebrew Literature* (to be published by Harvard Press, 1979).

17. I am indebted for the summary of the divine assembly in Egyptian thought to G. Cooke, "The Sons of (the) God(s)," *ZAW* 76 (1964), 27. See also H. Frankfort, *et al.*, *The Intellectual Adventure of Ancient Man: An Essay on Speculative Thought in the Ancient Near East* (Chicago: University of Chicago, 1946), 50, 52, 108.

18. See Gen 1:26-27; 3:22; 6:1-4; 11:7; Deut 32:8-9; 33:2-3; 1 Kgs 22:19-23; Job 1-2; Pss 29; 58:1; 82; 89; Isa 6; 24:21; 40:1-11; Jer 23:18-22; Ezek 1:1-3:15; Zech 3; Dan 10.

19. The Jerusalem Bible translates "divine assembly."

20. R. N. Whybray, *The Heavenly Counsellor in Isaiah xl 13-14*, 40.

21. F. M. Cross, Jr. and D. N. Freedman, "The Blessing of Moses," *JBL* 67 (1948), 201, note 19.

22. G. E. Wright, *The Old Testament Against Its Environment* (London: SCM, 1950), 30-41; also see "The Faith of Israel," *The Interpreter's Bible* (New York: Abingdon, 1952), I. 360. It was probably because of the concept of the heavenly host that Manasseh was able to introduce so easily Assyrian astral worship into the Jerusalem cult.

23. W. F. Albright, "The Psalm of Habakkuk," *Studies in*

*Old Testament Prophecy: Presented to Theodore H. Robinson on His Sixty-fifth Birthday* (ed. H. H. Rowley; Edinburgh: T. & T. Clark, 1950), 1-18; F. M. Cross, Jr., "Notes on a Canaanite Psalm in the Old Testament," *BASOR* 117 (1950), 19-21; T. H. Gaster, "Psalm 29," *JQR* 37 (1946-1947), 57; H. L. Ginsberg, *The Ugaritic Texts* (Jerusalem, 1936), 129-131.

24. J. O'Callaghan, "The Canaanite Background of Psalm 82," *CBQ* 15 (1953), 311-314; J. Morgenstern, "The Mythological Background of Psalm 82," *HUCA* 14 (1939), 29-126. It is conceivable that in Psalm 82 *'elōhîm* has its secondary meaning of "judges." See Martin Buber, "Judgment of the Judges: Psalm 82," *Good and Evil* (New York: Charles Scribner's Sons, 1953), ch. III, 20-30.

25. See G. Cooke, "The Sons of (the) God(s)," *ZAW* 76 (1964), 29-35.

26. The spiritual beings are also referred to as the "host of heaven." The term "host of heaven" is used in two ways within the OT: (1) in referring to stars, especially as objects of worship. To honor the hosts of heaven in this sense is condemned; (2) in referring to spiritual beings in the council meeting (i.e., angels, messengers--*mal'āk*--although a developed angelology did not exist in the early period). Apparently the spiritual beings in the council began as gods within the pantheon and were gradually reduced in status to angelic beings assembled to praise Yahweh and convey his messages to mankind: Josh 5:13-15; 1 Kgs 22:19-23. See D. Neiman, "Council, Heavenly," *The Interpreter's Dictionary of the Bible Supplementary Volume* (New York: Abingdon, 1976), 187-188; B. W. Anderson, "Host, Host of Heaven," *The Interpreter's Dictionary of the Bible* (New York: Abingdon, 1962), II. 654-656; J. Gray, "Host of Heaven," *Hasting's Dictionary of the Bible* (second edition, eds. F. C. Grant and H. H. Rowley; New York: Scribners, 1963), 401. The term "Lord of Hosts" for Yahweh may have been originally used of Yahweh as leader of the armies of Israel, then came to refer to his authority over the celestial hosts--both the stars and the spiritual beings in his council. See B. W. Anderson, "Lord of Hosts," *The Interpreter's Dictionary of the Bible*, III. 151.

27. G. Cooke, "The Sons of (the) God(s)," *ZAW* 76 (1964), 28.

28. For Near Eastern parallels to this two-fold consultation, see A. Malamat, "Kingship and Council in Israel and Sumer: A Parallel," *JNES* 22 (1963), 247-253, and "Organs of Statecraft in the Israelite Monarchy," *The Biblical Archaeologist Reader*

(eds. E. F. Campbell, Jr. and D. N. Freedman; New York: Doubleday, 1970), III. 163-198.

29. R. N. Whybray, *The Heavenly Counsellor in Isaiah xl 13-14*, 28, 31-33.

30. E. C. Kingsbury, "The Prophets and the Council of Yahweh," *JBL* 83 (1964), 279-286; F. M. Cross, Jr., "The Council of Yahweh in Second Isaiah," *JNES* 12 (1953), 274-277; H. W. Robinson, "The Council of Yahweh," *JTS* 45 (1944), 151-157; J. Muilenberg, "Introduction and Exegesis of Isaiah 40-66," *The Interpreter's Bible* (New York: Abingdon, 1956), V. 422-434.

31. There is no evidence that the seraphim of Isaiah 6 are regular members of the council of Yahweh. Like the cherubim of Ezekiel 1, they appear to be mythological cultic figures which glorify God and do not participate in the deliberations of the council. See G. Cooke, "The Sons of (the) God(s)," *ZAW* 76 (1964), 37-38.

32. For this interpretation of the visions, see J. L. Mays, *Amos: A Commentary* (Philadelphia: Westminster, 1969).

33. H. W. Robinson, "The Council of Yahweh," *JTS* 45 (1944), 152; R. E. Brown, "The Pre-Christian Semitic Concept of 'Mystery,'" *CBQ* 20 (1958), 417-418; G. Cooke, "The Sons of (the) God(s)," *ZAW* 76 (1964), 39; Brown-Driver-Briggs and Koehler-Baumgartner dictionaries; J. F. Ross, "The Prophet as Yahweh's Messenger," *Israel's Prophetic Heritage: Essays in Honor of James Muilenberg* (eds. B. W. Anderson and W. Harrelson; New York: Harper, 1962), 102-104.

34. It has been suggested that Amos 8:14 be emended to read *dōrĕkā be'ēr-šābaʿ* (your pantheon, O Beer-sheba) rather than *derek be'ēr-šābaʿ* (the way of Beer-sheba). See F. J. Neuberg, "An Unrecognized Meaning of Hebrew *DŌR*," *JNES* 9 (1950), 215-217 where he argues that *dôr* is used for council of the clan or tribe. We reject this emendation not only on the basis of textual evidence, but because we believe Amos is a nationalistic prophet who called for worship in Jerusalem (1:2), condemning all northern shrines (4:4-5; 5:4-5, 21-24) including the pilgrimage site of Beer-sheba (the way of Beer-sheba) located in Judah but sacred in the patriarchal traditions of the north.

35. W. L. Moran, "Akkadian Letters," *ANET*[3], 623.

36. *Ibid.*, 624. See also W. L. Moran, "New Evidence

from Mari on the History of Prophecy," *Bib* 50 (1969), 15-56.

37.  J. A. Wilson, "The Journey of Wen-Amon to Phoenicia," *ANET*3, 25-29.

38.  J. F. Ross, "The Prophet as Yahweh's Messenger," *Israel's Prophetic Heritage*, 100-101.

39.  See J. S. Holladay, Jr., "Assyrian Statecraft and the Prophets of Israel," *HTR* 63 (1970), 29-51.

40.  J. F. Ross, "The Prophet as Yahweh's Messenger," *Israel's Prophetic Heritage*, 106-107, suggests that the pre-exilic writing prophets do not use the word "messenger" because it was associated in the pre-writing prophetic period with the false prophets who proclaimed "peace."  But after the exile it was used again (Isa 42:19; 44:26; Hag 1:13) until it finally became the name of a prophetic book--Malachi--my messenger (Mal 3:1).

41.  H. B. Huffmon, "The Covenant Lawsuit in the Prophets," *JBL* 78 (1959), 285-295.

42.  G. E. Wright, "The Lawsuit of God:  A Form-Critical Study of Deuteronomy 32," *Israel's Prophetic Heritage*, 26-67.

43.  H. W. Robinson, *Inspiration and Revelation in the Old Testament* (Oxford:  Clarendon, 1946), 1-16.

44.  After the preparation of this article, I became aware of another important allusion to the divine assembly in the Deir-'Alla texts.  See J. Hoftijzer, ed., *Aramaic Texts from Deir 'Alla* (Leiden:  E. J. Brill, 1976), Combination I lines 16-26.  Cf. also Hoftijzer, "The Prophet Balaam in a 6th Century Aramaic Inscription," *BA* 39 (1976), pp. 11-17.

# JUDAH'S FOREIGN POLICY FROM HEZEKIAH TO JOSIAH

Carl D. Evans
University of South Carolina

The use of comparative materials to illuminate aspects
of biblical history and literature can be enormously valuable,
as many recent studies have demonstrated. Comparative materials can supply additional data, fill in historical gaps, provide analogies, or offer an independent account of matters reflected in the Bible. Accordingly, it should not be surprising to the biblical specialist that the evidence from the comparative side can, on occasion, necessitate a reconstruction
of biblical matters that have been misinterpreted. All of
these functions, from supplementation to correction, are
served by the comparative materials that relate to the biblical period from Hezekiah to Josiah, but the last-named function
provides the point of departure for the present study.

The case in point is the matter of Judahite religion under
the Assyrians in eighth and seventh centuries B.C.E. Until the
recent studies of Cogan[1] and, to a more limited extent, McKay[2],
brought extensive evidence from the Assyrian side to bear on
the question, it was generally believed by interpreters of the
biblical data that the Assyrians required their Judahite vassal
kings to adopt Assyrian religious practices as part of their
obligation to the empire. Thus, the religious measures attributed in the Bible to the reigns of Ahaz and Manasseh--the altar
reform of Ahaz, the cult of Molech, astral worship, etc.--have
traditionally been interpreted as Assyrian imposts, whereas the
cult reforms of Hezekiah and Josiah have been interpreted as
the removal of the symbols of Assyrian imperialism and, hence,
as religio-political rebellions against the empire. But now
Cogan and McKay, in independent studies which approach the matter from opposite sides (Cogan, from the Assyrian side; McKay,
from the biblical side), have reached conclusions about the
religio-political policies of the Assyrians which substantially
invalidate the standard modern assessments of Judahite religion
in the eighth and seventh centuries B.C.E.

The main conclusions of Cogan and McKay, when summarized together, are the following: 1) The Assyrian imperial policy concerning religious matters was somewhat different in provinces, on the one hand, and vassal states, on the other. In provincial territories a certain amount of cultic imposition did occur, whereas there is no evidence that cultic practices were imposed on vassal states. 2) The evidence indicates, rather, that the Assyrians tended to incorporate the cult of subject peoples into their own cultic system, ideally carrying the cult statue of the conquered vassal back to Assyria. 3) Vassal states such as Judah, who were made politically subservient through tribute payments and other expressions of allegiance such as loyalty oaths, were nonetheless spared Assyrian interference in cultic matters. Religious autonomy for vassal states was thus granted by the empire. 4) The fluctuations in religious practices which the Bible acknowledges in the reigns of the kings from Ahaz to Josiah must be understood without reference to Judah's political stances vis-à-vis Assyria. In other words, the cultic measures of Ahaz and Manasseh, which the biblical historiographers deemed detrimental to true Yahwism, can no longer be explained simply as the religious price of Assyrian allegiance, nor can the cultic reforms of Hezekiah and Josiah be understood simply as the religious expression of a defiant anti-Assyrian political stance. Rather, the religious fluctuations must be explained in other ways. Thus, these conclusions call for a new assessment of the dynamics of religious life in Judah under the Assyrians, the task to which McKay's book is primarily devoted and to which Cogan has given more limited treatment.

The purpose of the present study is to re-examine the evidence concerning Judah's foreign policy under the Assyrians, presupposing the validity of the reconstructed view of the Assyrian religio-political ideal offered by Cogan and McKay. That such a study is needed is indicated by the fact that most conventional assessments of the subject at hand reconstruct Judah's foreign policy using evidence that the studies of Cogan and McKay would rule inadmissible. Specifically, it has been commonplace to characterize the foreign policies of Ahaz, Manasseh, and Amon as pro-Assyrian on the basis that the religious practices attributed by the biblical historiographers to these kings were, presumably, Assyrian impositions necessitated by pro-Assyrian political alignments. In a similar way, the foreign policies of Hezekiah and Josiah have conventionally been characterized as anti-Assyrian on the basis that the religious reforms of these kings were believed to have been motivated, in part at least, by religio-political rebellions against Assyria.[3] Apart from the obvious circularity of such reasoning, the complex interrelationships of religious and political policies, which are still not clearly understood, justify the present reassessment of the evidence which can be admitted into a new examination of Judah's foreign policy.

The present study will be limited to the period from Hezekiah to Josiah. A more complete study would include the reign of Ahaz, but other considerations have made the more limited scope preferable. The procedure will be to discuss each king's reign in chronological sequence, focusing on the more pertinent evidence that the comparative, archaeological, and biblical materials bring to bear on the topic of investigation. Preference of treatment will be given to the evidence which has been the subject of recent discussion. With regard to the biblical evidence, a distinction will be presupposed between religious policies that support either religious syncretism or Yahwistic exclusivism, on the one hand, and those that support either cult centralization or decentralization, on the other hand. Such a distinction seems justified in view of the political and economic consequences produced by the latter policies, whereas the former policies are more ambiguously related to political matters. In the present study, therefore, the biblical evidence from religious policies will be limited to that which is related to the various programs of cult centralization and decentralization attributed to the kings in question.

## I.  Hezekiah

For the greater part of Hezekiah's reign, Judah was in no position to challenge the superior strength of Assyria. Despite this, however, the evidence suggests that Hezekiah pursued a consistently anti-Assyrian policy throughout his reign. Whenever the opportunity seemed right, the Judahite king aligned his nation with anti-Assyrian coalitions and withheld the burdensome tribute payments, hoping to remove the Assyrian yoke once and for all. But the infrequency of such opportunities, and the success of the Assyrians in discouraging rebellions, accounts for the fact that, throughout most of his twenty-nine years as king, Hezekiah was compelled to submit to the demands of the empire.

Apart from the well-documented invasion of Sennacherib into Judah in 701 B.C.E., the Assyrian records contain only a few scattered references to Judah for the period of Hezekiah's reign. And due to a recent join of British Museum cuneiform fragments, the imbalance has been made even greater

by the probable assignment of one of those scattered references to the events of 701. It is with the recent developments that the present survey begins.

The recently joined fragments--the so-called "Azekah inscription" (BM 82-3-23, 131) and the "Azriau episode" (K 6205)--
had previously been ascribed to Sargon II[4] and Tiglath-Pileser
III,[5] respectively. But now Na'aman has sought to demonstrate
that both parts are fragments of a single tablet and that the
document is to be ascribed to neither Tiglath-Pileser III nor
Sargon II but to Sennacherib.[6]

Without going into the details which explain how two
fragments of the same tablet were separately ascribed to different Assyrian kings, neither of which turns out to be correct
in Na'aman's view, it will suffice here to say that Na'aman believes that the tablet belongs to a literary type known as
"Letters to God" which, in this case, describes the campaign
of Sennacherib to Palestine in 701 B.C.E. Probably written at
the close of the campaign, it was apparently composed "in order
to magnify and glorify the god Ashur, on the one hand, and on
the other hand, to explain and give an excuse for the events of
the campaign to Judah, which seems to have been a doubtful success as far as the Assyrians were concerned...."[7] The two parts
of the document, describing respectively Assyrian conquests of
the town of Azekah and an unnamed Philistine city which apparently had been annexed to Judah by Hezekiah, have a common literary structure and distinctive style which has several verbal
parallels in Sennacherib's annalistic account of this campaign,
suggesting the possibility of ascribing the whole document to
Sennacherib. Na'aman discusses several other factors which
strengthen this possibility and then draws some important conclusions for the purpose of this study.

By disassociating the first part of the document, the
"Azekah inscription," from the reign of Sargon II, the evidence
for Assyrian military action against Judah during the reign of
Sargon II is greatly diminished, if not removed entirely. Judah
is otherwise mentioned in Sargon's inscriptions only two times.
The first of these, occurring in the Nimrud inscription, refers
to Sargon as "the subduer of Judah which lies far away."[8] Written around 717 B.C.E., and probably referring to events in 720
when Hamath, Gaza, Samaria and perhaps also Judah participated
in an insurrection against Assyria, this inscription has bearing
on Hezekiah only if the early chronology for Hezekiah's reign is
adopted.[9] But even if the early chronology is followed, this
inscription offers little support for a whole-hearted rebellion
by Hezekiah. If the Judahite king did participate in the 720
revolt, Na'aman concludes that he was "quick to surrender to

the king of Assyria and to pay the demanded tribute so that
his country would not be harmed during the Assyrian campaign
along the Philistine coast."10  In any event, there is no
evidence that Judah suffered military action by the Assyrians
at this time.

The other reference to Judah in Sargon's inscriptions occurs in the context of the revolt of Ashdod which began in 713
B.C.E., i.e., early in Hezekiah's reign according to the late
chronology being followed here.  This inscription11 records
that the kings of Philistia, Judah, Edom, and Moab conspired
against Assyria by appealing to Egypt for assistance, sending
"evil words and unseemly speeches (with) their presents to
Pharaoh."12  Interestingly, the Assyrian sources give no indication that the campaign of 712 was directed against anyone
but the Philistines.  From this, and from the reluctance of
Pharaoh Shabako to be a party to conspiracies against Assyria,13
it is doubtful whether the conspiratorial allegiance was able
to put forth much of a threat.  Hence, "it can be assumed that
all the rulers mentioned hastened to submit to Assyria immediately upon the appearance of Assyrian troops in Philistia, and
the main sufferer in the campaign was Ashdod, whose principal
towns were conquered."14

If Na'aman's views are granted, there remains no evidence
on the comparative side that Judah ever suffered military action by Sargon II.  As long as Sargon II ruled the empire, Judah remained relatively submissive as an Assyrian vassal.  On
only one or two occasions is there evidence that Hezekiah may
have been involved in conspiratorial alliances against Assyria.
On those occasions, however, the evidence suggests that Hezekiah quickly relented and reaffirmed his allegiance to Assyria
by paying the requisite tribute.

It was not until the death of Sargon (705) and the accession of Sennacherib that Hezekiah renewed an overt anti-Assyrian stance by withholding the payment of tribute (2 Kgs 18:7).
It was a propitious time for such a revolt because Sennacherib
was confronted with simultaneous rebellions in Babylonia and
the west.  Attending first to the Babylonian revolt, it was
not until 701 that Sennacherib advanced against Hezekiah.

Due to recent developments in archaeology and the study
of comparative materials, it is now possible to identify some
aspects of the larger context in which Hezekiah's rebellion
occurred.  Very early in his reign (in the first year, according to 2 Chr 29:3), Hezekiah began to purge the Judahite cult
of its non-Yahwistic practices.  The reform measures taken
were fundamentally religious in character, i.e., they were

intended to purify the religion of Judah.  Although some
aspects of Assyrian religion may have been removed in the
purge, there was no hint of an anti-Assyrian rebellion in
the reform.[15]  The lack of Assyrian reprisals against Judah
before 701 is an indication that a revolt against the empire
was not involved in these measures.

One aspect of Hezekiah's religious program deserves
special notice, viz., the centralization of the cult.  Various attempts have been made to understand Hezekiah's rationale
for this highly innovative religious policy, offering as explanations religious, political, and economic considerations.
The alternative religious and political explanations are con-
veniently surveyed by Nicholson[16] who offers a critique of the
views discussed and adds his own religio-political interpretation.  To these must now be added the economic explanation of
Claburn.[17]  This is not the place to enter into the debate
about the underlying rationale for the cult centralization
program, but certain consequences of this program, whatever
its motivation may have been, are clearly reflected in the
biblical materials.  In the first place, offerings at the
Temple became quite bountiful.  This increase perhaps began,
as implied by the Chronicler, as the result of the religious
revival sponsored by the king from the beginning of his reign
(2 Chr 29:31-36).  But modest bounty became great abundance
once the cult centralization program was effected (2 Chr 31:
1-10).  The large quantities of tithes and offerings received
at the Temple necessitated additional measures.  Provisions
were made to store the goods offered at the Temple (2 Chr 31:
11) and officers were set up to oversee both the receiving and
distribution of goods (2 Chr 31:12-15).  The distribution was
apportioned to both the priestly personnel of the Temple and
the priests and Levites in the cities of Judah (2 Chr 31:14-
19).  The latter, presumably, had been adversely affected by
the cult centralization program, necessitating the redistribution program.

Thus the testimony of the Chronicler indicates that the
cult centralization program had the effect of placing additional resources under the king's control, enhancing the royal
treasury and providing the occasion for creating an administrative system to handle the increased contributions.  Various
considerations suggest that these measures were taken before
701 rather than after as suggested by Nicholson.[18]  In the
first place, there is the testimony of the biblical writers.
Both the Deuteronomistic historian and the Chronicler place
the reform, including the centralization of the cult, before
Sennacherib's invasion.  Secondly, it is difficult to visual-
ize the redistribution process, as described by the Chronicler,

after 701 when much of Judah was taken by Sennacherib and handed over to the Philistines. The latter is a matter to be discussed more fully in the Manasseh section below. Thirdly, the increase of royally-controlled revenue in the period before 701 accords fully with the account of the Babylonian envoys' visit with Hezekiah (2 Kgs 20:12-15), to which the discussion shall presently return. And, finally, Hezekiah would have been in a stronger position to attempt a revolt after, rather than before, the cult centralization program had brought new resources into the hands of the king. These considerations virtually assure that Hezekiah's total religious reform was effected prior to 701 and thus provide some of the background for his rebellion against Sennacherib.

The internal reorganization necessitated by the centralization of the cult may be reflected in the production and use of royal storage jars bearing the *lmlk* stamp. More than a thousand jar handles bearing the *lmlk* stamp and a seal impression have been found at a large variety of sites throughout Judah, but more have been uncovered at Lachish than any other site. It has become increasingly clear, on the basis of new stratigraphical evidence at Lachish, that the royal seal impressions of all types[19] should be dated in the reign of Hezekiah before 701. Prior to the latest excavations at Lachish, the majority opinion was that the seal impressions of all types should be assigned to Josiah's reign.[20] But this dating proved to be problematic, even before the latest work at Lachish, inasmuch as the seal impressions have been found almost exclusively at sites within the kingdom of Judah. This state of affairs prompted Lance to conclude that "much of what has been written on the Josianic 'empire' will have to be reexamined" and "the total absence of the stamps in the north can only mean that in the time of Josiah *not even trade was carried on with the territory of the former northern kingdom*" (italics his).[21] But since the new stratigraphical evidence at Lachish has raised the dating of the stamps to the period before 701,[22] the problem of the location of the stamps entirely within Judah no longer exists. Hezekiah's control over north Israelite territory was obviously limited by the boundary of the Assyrian empire, however much he may have wanted, and may have appealed to, the north Israelites to join in his cultic innovations. The archaeological evidence thus indicates that the special provisions for the collection and redistribution of the religious offerings, if indeed reflected in the use of the storage jars in this period,[23] did not extend northward beyond the boundary claimed by the Assyrian empire.

Another aspect of the background for Sennacherib's

campaign against Judah is the matter of the envoys sent by
Merodach-Baladan II to Hezekiah (2 Kgs 20:12-19 and Isa 39:
1-8; cf. 2 Chr 32:31). In an important study on Merodach-
Baladan II, Brinkman[24] has discussed the evidence for postulating that the purpose of the Babylonian embassy to Judah
was "to cement an alliance with Hezekiah" against the Assyrians. "The bestowal of gifts by Merodach-Baladan fits in well
with his known monetary benefactions to Elam to insure support. And, on the other side, Hezekiah's display of the
treasures of his house and kingdom substantiates the theory
that the ambassadors came to assess his strength."[25]

Of course, to date the Babylonian embassy to the period
before 701 (sometime between 704 and 702) it is necessary to
suppose that the narrative sequence in the biblical accounts,
all of which place the visit of the Babylonian envoys *after*
the account of Sennacherib's invasion, has been arranged by
considerations other than chronological ones.[26] This seems
entirely possible, especially in view of the fifteen years
of additional life promised to Hezekiah (2 Kgs 20:6 and Isa
38:5) on the occasion of his recovery from illness. Hezekiah's illness had provided the pretext for the visit of the
Babylonian ambassadors (2 Kgs 20:12 and Isa 39:1) and if this
occurred fifteen years before his death in 687, the date of
the embassy would, on these grounds also, be placed prior to
701.[27]

Hezekiah's prayer on the occasion of his illness has
recently been illuminated by Hallo who has published a Sumerian analogue to the prayer.[28] The superscription to Hezekiah's prayer calls it a *miktāb* (Isa 38:9), a term which refers generally to something that is written. Hallo points
out, however, that in later biblical Hebrew the term occasionally refers specifically to a form of communication, i.e.,
a letter (e.g., 2 Chr 21:12). This letter-prayer literary
type is found in the Akkadian materials and, much more extensively, in the Sumerian sources, including "a whole sub-cate-
gory of Sumerian letter-prayers addressed by ailing persons
to a healing goddess."[29] But until recently the known examples of letter-prayers inspired by illness did not include
any by an ailing king addressed to a deity. Hallo's publication of a letter-prayer by Sin-iddinam, king of Larsa from
1849 to 1843 B.C.E., now fills that gap, thus providing a
complete analogy to Hezekiah's *miktāb* prayer.[30]

Sennacherib's campaign against Judah in 701 is well-
attested in both the comparative and biblical materials. The
relatively full accounting, however, is not without considerable ambiguity, leading some interpreters to posit a second

campaign against Hezekiah sometime after 701.[31] The ambiguities arise, however, primarily because of the apparent double campaign in the biblical materials. The Assyrian materials, on the other hand, give a full accounting of Sennacherib's exploits for the years covering the balance of Hezekiah's reign. This evidence suggests there is no place to fit a second campaign against Hezekiah.

It is worth mentioning at this point that Jenkins has proposed a new solution which attempts to explain the biblical implication of two campaigns without attributing both to Sennacherib.[32] Adopting the early chronology for Hezekiah's reign, Jenkins proposes that at the time of the Ashdod revolt Hezekiah joined the rebellion and the inexplicable withdrawal of Assyrian troops from an advance on Jerusalem produced the biblical accounts of the miraculous deliverance of the city (2 Kgs 18:17-19:37 and Isa 36:2-37:38).[33] After the Sennacherib invasion of 701, Jenkins proposes, the latter event was interpreted in light of the former, resulting in the telescoping of the two events and the association of the deliverance report with the events of 701.

Whatever the merits of Jenkins' proposal, the evidence from the comparative side against a second campaign continues to mount. Recent publications by Kitchen[34] and Rainey[35] have shown that the reference to Tirhaka in 2 Kgs 19:9 and Isa 37:9 no longer provides a valid basis for arguing that Sennacherib conducted a second campaign against Judah after 701. The two-campaign theorists have argued that since Tarhaqa did not become king in Egypt until a decade or so after 701, the biblical reference to the involvement of "Tirhaka king of Cush" in the events surrounding Sennacherib's campaign must indicate the occurrence of a second campaign sometime between 690 and 681 (i.e., between Tarhaqa's accession and Sennacherib's death). Moreover, the likelihood of Tarhaqa's involvement in the events of 701 has been discounted because of the belief that he would have been only nine years of age at that time. But the new evidence indicates that Tarhaqa was at least twenty years of age in 701, certainly old enough to have led an army against the Assyrians, as the biblical accounts claim. Furthermore, the biblical reference to Tarhaqa as "king of Cush" is not out of keeping with Tarhaqa's own language about himself. On the Kawa stelae, for example, he can be found "speaking of himself as 'His Majesty' in a passage referring to his being a prince (of whom, contemporarily, the phrase would not be used)."[36]

By eliminating a second campaign of Sennacherib against Judah, as the comparative evidence seems to require, the inevitable conclusion is that after 701 Hezekiah must have reverted to his earlier submissive stance vis-à-vis Assyria. Hence, the comparative, archaeological, and biblical evidence discussed here leads to the conclusion that Hezekiah, for the greater part of his reign, submitted to the demands of the empire. However, the one or two occasions for which there is evidence of his involvement in anti-Assyrian alliances and revolts suggest that his policy throughout was anti-Assyrian, even though the vastly greater strength of the empire forced him to acquiesce, for the most part, to the political demands of Assyria.

## II.  Manasseh

It is a great understatement to say that Manasseh ascended the throne of Judah under trying circumstances. Only a few years earlier Judah had suffered a humiliating defeat at the hands of Sennacherib. According to the Assyrian annals, Sennacherib's army had besieged and conquered forty-six "strong cities" in the kingdom of Judah and, to make matters worse, had handed over the conquered towns to the kings of Ashdod, Ekron, and Gaza.[37] Moreover, with a much diminished kingdom, and the consequent loss of sources of revenue, the Bible indicates that Hezekiah, after emptying the Temple and palace treasuries, found it necessary to strip the gold from the doors and doorposts of the Temple in order to meet the tribute demands of Sennacherib (2 Kgs 18:15-16). Such circumstances hardly constitute an ideal time to inherit the throne.

In addition, Manasseh's difficulties were perhaps complicated by the conditions which necessitated a co-regency with his father Hezekiah for as many as ten years. According to the biblical historiographers, Manasseh and Hezekiah followed quite different courses during their respective reigns. One would expect, therefore, considerable discord during the co-regency period. Still, there is no evidence that indicates any foreign policy changes in the transition period and the length of the co-regency itself implies a continuation of Hezekiah's policies into the early years of Manasseh's reign. Given the diminutive stature of Judah at the time, it is difficult to imagine anything but Manasseh's early acquiescence to Assyria. He was forced, as Hezekiah had been after 701, to accede.

If the reduced stature of Judah offered little encouragement for Manasseh, he could hardly have found comfort from the

international scene. Although Sennacherib continued to be
plagued with problems in Babylonia, the accession of Esarhaddon in 680 brought a vigorous king to the Assyrian throne
who was able to advance the empire to the pinnacle of power,
settling the problems in Babylonia and extending the Assyrian
grasp as far west and south as Egypt and as far east as Elam.

In light of the strength of Assyria, and the weakness of
Judah, it is reasonable that Manasseh would have felt compelled to continue the submissive stance that had characterized the policy of Judah since 701. To have done otherwise
would have courted disaster and Judah was in no position to
suffer additional losses. The destruction and humiliation
suffered in the earlier defeat had to be avoided a second
time, if at all possible. Accordingly, it is not surprising
to find that the Assyrian records count Manasseh among the
tribute-paying vassal kings of the empire. The first such
reference to Manasseh comes from the reign of Esarhaddon.
Manasseh is named as one of twenty-two western kings who were
compelled to transport building materials to Nineveh for the
construction of a royal project in that city.[38]  And, again,
almost the identical list of twenty-two kings, including
Manasseh, appears in the Cylinder C fragment of Ashurbanipal's
first campaign against Egypt (688/687).[39]  The better preserved
account[40] doesn't list the twenty-two kings, but records that
they presented Ashurbanipal with expressions of allegiance
("brought heavy gifts [tâmartu] to me and kissed my feet,"
according to Ashurbanipal's account of the event) and that
they accompanied the Assyrian army into Egypt, augmenting the
imperial forces with their own troops.

In addition to the two references to Manasseh in the materials just discussed, another fragmentary text has prompted
speculation about a possible third reference to Manasseh.  The
text in question is an inscription of Esarhaddon[41] which apparently belongs in the context of the Assyrian king's campaign
to Egypt in 671.  During this campaign reprisals were taken
against Phoenician and Philistine cities which presumably had
conspired against Assyria with the Egyptian king Tarqu (Tarhaqa).  The inscription refers to twenty-two western kings--the
tablet is broken right at the point that the list of kings
might have been included--and seems to record that the western
kings had been subdued during the course of the campaign.  This
has suggested the possibility to various scholars that the report of Manasseh's capture and removal from Judah by the commanders of the Assyrian army, found in 2 Chr 33:11-13, belongs
in this general context, implying that Manasseh also had joined
in Tarhaqa's rebellion.[42]  The return of Manasseh to the Judahite throne, after such a revolt, would not have been without

parallel in Assyrian practice.[43]  In light of this, one of
the proponents of the view has stated:  "We can only imagine
the terms under which Esarhaddon re-installed Manasseh on
the throne; but if similar reports from the annals are any
indication, a renewed pledge of loyalty and tribute headed
the list."[44]

Regardless of the weight put on this fragmentary inscription, and the possible correlation to 2 Chr 33:11-13,
the impression is given that Manasseh had little choice but
to obey the Assyrian demands.  It is interesting to note,
however, that sometime during the seventh century the territory that Sennacherib had taken from Hezekiah and turned over
to the Philistines was returned to Judah.  No comparative or
biblical text records when, or under what circumstances, this
occurred, but it is most improbable that Manasseh could have
regained it without authorization by Assyria.  It may be assumed that it was given back to him under circumstances that
served the purposes of the Assyrian empire.

One possibility is that Ashurbanipal returned the territory to Manasseh in order to create a buffer zone between the
Egyptian and Assyrian borders.[45]  In the absence of any direct
information about the matter, however, it could also be suggested that a clue has been preserved by the Chronicler who
connects Manasseh's recall by the Assyrians with a report of
his reinstatement and fortification of Judah, including place-
ment of army commanders in the fortified cities of Judah (2
Chr 33:11-14).  On the theory that Manasseh's recall occurred
in the context of Esarhaddon's campaign against Egypt in 671,
it is plausible that Esarhaddon had Manasseh carried away in
chains to force his submission and to gain his support by offering to return the captive territory to Judah.[46]  Although
no record of such exists, Esarhaddon would have required Manasseh's pledge of loyalty so that from then on--approximately
the last half of Manasseh's reign--the Judahite king loyally
supported Assyria, as is evident in the record of Manasseh's
expressions of allegiance to Ashurbanipal.

The probability that Manasseh at some point was party to
a vassal treaty of Esarhaddon is enhanced by the remarkable
correspondence between Esarhaddon's vassal treaties[47] and
Deuteronomy which is believed to have received final shape
during Manasseh's reign.  The studies of Frankena[48] and Weinfeld[49] have cited and discussed some of the more striking of
these correspondences, especially in Deuteronomy 28, and conclude that the curses found in that chapter were adapted from
the maledictions in the vassal treaties.  Frankena proposes
that the Deuteronomists would have known about the vassal

treaty formulae in the period of Esarhaddon when Manasseh
may have been compelled to swear allegiance to support the
succession of the crown prince Ashurbanipal--the subject of
a loyalty oath taken by a well-known group of nine vassals
in 672.[50] Frankena reasons that the same oath would have
been required by other vassals as well, so he speculates
that the report of the twenty-two western kings, including
Manasseh, who delivered building materials to Nineveh, refers to the occasion of the gathering of the western kings
to swear their allegiance "to safeguard the succession of
Ashurbanipal."[51] He further speculates that a copy of the
vassal treaty was then taken by Manasseh back to Jerusalem
where it could have had its peculiar influence on the formation of Deuteronomy.

Whether one associates an Esarhaddon vassal treaty with
Manasseh on the occasion proposed by Frankena or on the occasion of Esarhaddon's politico-military maneuvers following
his 671 Egyptian campaign, as proposed above, it is clear
that Assyria reckoned Manasseh as a loyal vassal from as early
as the latter years of Esarhaddon. But since there is nothing
that indicates Manasseh's whole-hearted loyalty to Assyria before that time, the intimations of a sometimes rebellious Manasseh suggest that his allegiance to Assyria for the first
twenty or twenty-five years was given out of necessity rather
than a pro-Assyrian political alignment. The situation would
have changed, however, when the Assyrians returned to him the
captive Judahite territory, perhaps circa 671 or 670. From
that time on, Manasseh could be genuinely pro-Assyrian, for
such a policy had become, by the vicissitudes of history,
also pro-Judahite in the sense that the repossession of the
lost territory was perceived to be in the best interests of
Judah.


III. Amon


Such a policy shift during Manasseh's reign--from sup-
porting Assyria only to the extent necessary, with perhaps
one occasion of anti-Assyrian alignment and rebellion, to
whole-hearted allegiance--undoubtedly created dissension
within Judah and perhaps created competing political factions.
At any rate, pro- and anti-Assyrian factions seem to emerge
from the background after Manasseh's death. Manasseh's son
and successor, Amon, evidently continued the pro-Assyrian
foreign policy that had guided Judah for three decades. But
Amon's reign was cut short (only two years) when a group of

his own courtiers conspired together and killed him (2 Kgs 21:23; 2 Chr 33:24). Whatever their motivation might have been, the conspirators' victory was short-lived, for the "people of the land" asserted themselves by killing the conspirators and placing Josiah, the eight-year old son of Amon, on the throne (2 Kgs 21:24; 2 Chr 33:25). It is tempting to see in these bloody reversals a domestic power struggle between factions favoring, on the one hand, the earlier policy of Manasseh and, on the other hand, the later policy which had also guided Amon.

It is significant, however, that the internal power struggle did not erupt with deadly force immediately upon the accession of Amon. Two years were to pass before this occurred when the eruption was triggered by international events. According to the Assyrian sources,[52] a rather extensive rebellion against Assyria occurred in this same period, i.e., circa 640, in the region 'Eber ha-Nahar. This term refers generally to everything from the Euphrates to the Mediterranean but it is known that the rebellion included, specifically, the Arabian tribes and Acre and Ushu (mainland Tyre). Malamat has proposed[53] that the assassination of Amon was carried out by advocates of a vigorous anti-Assyrian policy who hoped that the general insurrection against Assyria would be the occasion for reversing Judah's course. This could not be done, however, with the pro-Assyrian Amon at the helm, so the conspiracy against him was planned and executed. To explain the counter-revolution by the "people of the land," Malamat reasons: "Upon the approach of the Assyrian army and its initial successes against the rebels, those forces in Judah who wished to prevent a military encounter with Assyria gained the upper hand .... It was a stitch in time, and it seems to have placated the Assyrians, for we hear of no punitive action being taken against Judah by their army."[54] An alternative suggestion, more in keeping with the typical role played by the "people of the land" in the politics of Judah, is that the "people of the land" assassinated the conspirators and placed Josiah on the throne in order to safeguard the Davidic succession. From this perspective,[55] their hasty action to eliminate the conspirators and restore the throne to the House of David had nothing to do with the westward movement of the Assyrian army. Fortunately for Judah, however, their quick action appeared to the Assyrians as a pro-Assyrian move, so Judah was spared any reprisals.

## IV.  Josiah

Although Josiah began his reign as a nominal Assyrian vassal, throughout the greater part of his reign he pursued a course bent on reviving Judah to independent status and restoring Davidic control over the north Israelite territory. The Chronicler's account of Josiah's reign, by referring to different developments in the eighth, twelfth, and eighteenth years (2 Chr 34:3a, 3b-7, and 34:8-35:19), preserves echoes of the progressive stages by which Josiah's program was implemented. Cross and Freedman[56] have attempted to relate the eighth and twelfth year developments to events marking the progressive decline of Assyria--the deaths of Ashurbanipal and Ashuretililani, respectively. These synchronisms, however, are too problematic to put much weight on them. The recent reconstruction of Assyrian chronology in the 620's by Reade[57] places the death of Ashurbanipal in 627 (Josiah's thirteenth year) and the death of Ashuretililani in 623 (Josiah's seventeenth year). This makes the direct correlation of developments in Josiah's reign with stages of Assyrian decline rather problematic, but this does not mean that Josiah was not taking full advantage of Assyria's rapid fall. The actions taken in his twelfth year, according to 2 Chr 34:3b-7, carried the Judahite king's religious and imperial program into the cities of Manasseh, Ephraim, Simeon, and Naphtali, i.e., cities within the Assyrian provinces. That his actions were not answered by the Assyrians is an indication that Assyria had already lost effective control of Judah and her neighboring provinces.

Josiah's religious and imperial program, with all its anti-Assyrian implications, continued without interruption throughout the balance of his reign. The discovery of the "book of the covenant" in his eighteenth year no doubt emboldened his efforts and undergirded his program with Mosaic religious authority. At any rate, Josiah was unrelenting to the end in the pursuit of his course. At Megiddo in 609 he met his death when he attempted to stop Pharaoh Necho's advance toward Assyria.[58] Necho was on his way to lend support to the Assyrians who were attempting to survive in a struggle against the emerging Neo-Babylonians. Thus, Josiah's anti-Assyrian policies, while allowing his nation to experience a brief period of revival, ultimately cost Judah the life of a vigorous king and cast her into the maelstrom of Egyptian and Neo-Babylonian politics[59] from which she never recovered.

## V.   Conclusions

This paper set out to re-examine the foreign policy of Judah from Hezekiah to Josiah by reassessing the data which can be admitted into such an investigation, given the strictures required by the recently reconstructed view of the Assyrian religio-political policies.  The following conclusions can now be drawn:  the anti-Assyrian policy of Hezekiah appears to have also guided the period of his co-regency with Manasseh as well as the early years of Manasseh's sole regency; for the greater part of Manasseh's reign, however, Judah pursued a pro-Assyrian course, as was the case during the brief reign of Amon; the course was changed by Josiah who pursued his reform and imperial program in the absence of effective Assyrian control over Judah and the neighboring provinces.

What emerges from this study, then, is a sequence of foreign policy positions in Judah which was shaped more by international events than the transitions of leadership within Judah.  Policy shifts seldom coincided with the transitions in leadership.  In view of this, and in light of the conclusions of Cogan and McKay on the religious side, important qualifications should be made in the traditional assessments of Hezekiah as anti-Assyrian, Manasseh and Amon as pro-Assyrian, and Josiah as anti-Assyrian.  Such broad characterizations tend to mask the many nuances discussed in this paper--nuances which diminish, to a certain extent at least, the distinctions conventionally attributed to the foreign policies of these kings.

## NOTES

1.  Morton Cogan, *Imperialism and Religion:  Assyria, Judah and Israel in the Eighth and Seventh Centuries B.C.E.* (SBL Monograph Series 19; Missoula:  Scholars Press, 1974).

2.  John McKay, *Religion in Judah under the Assyrians* (SBT Second Series 26; Naperville:  Allenson, 1973).

3.  See, e.g., John Bright, *A History of Israel* (2d ed.; Philadelphia:  Westminster, 1972), 274-323, and Siegfried Hermann, *A History of Israel in Old Testament Times* (Philadelphia:  Fortress, 1975), 255-273, for expressions of the standard view.

4. H. Tadmor, "The Campaigns of Sargon II of Assur:
A Chronological-Historical Study," *JCS* 12 (1958), 80-84,
assigned BM 82-3-23, 131 to the campaign of 712.

5. P. Rost, *Die Keilinschrifttexte Tiglat-Pilesers III*
(Leipzig, 1893), 18-20: 103-119.

6. N. Na'aman, "Sennacherib's 'Letter to God' on His
Campaign to Judah," *BASOR* 214 (1974), 25-39. The article includes a transcription and translation of the joined fragments
plus a photograph of the join.

7. *Ibid.*, p. 31. It should be noted that Tadmor had
already identified the BM 82-3-23, 131 fragment as a "Letter
to God" ("Campaigns of Sargon II," p. 82). Na'aman, however,
has now abandoned the "Letter to God" identification in "Sennacherib's Campaign to Judah and the Date of the *LMLK* Stamps,"
*VT* 29 (1979), 61-86, esp. p. 63, n. 4.

8. H. Winckler, *Die Keilschrifttexte Sargons*, I (Leipzig, 1889), 188; 28-36. Cf. Na'aman, "Sennacherib's 'Letter
to God'," p. 38, n. 146.

9. The late chronology, followed in this study, dates
Hezekiah's reign from 715. For a thorough discussion of the
chronological problems, and argumentation for the position
adopted here, see E. R. Thiele, *The Mysterious Numbers of the
Hebrew Kings* (2d ed.; Grand Rapids: Eerdmans, 1965), 118-140.
A verification of Thiele's chronology from a more strictly
Assyriological perspective is provided in William W. Hallo,
"From Qarqar to Carchemish: Assyria and Israel in the Light
of New Discoveries," *BA* 23 (1960), 33-61; updated version in
*The Biblical Archaeologist Reader*, vol. 2 (ed. E. F. Campbell,
Jr. and D. N. Freedman; Garden City: Doubleday, Anchor Books,
1964), 152-188.

10. Na'aman, "Sennacherib's 'Letter to God'," p. 32.

11. See James B. Pritchard, ed., *Ancient Near Eastern
Texts Relating to the Old Testament* (3d ed.; Princeton:
Princeton University, 1969), 287. On the victory stele
erected by Sargon II, see H. Tadmor, "Philistia Under Assyrian
Rule," *BA* 29 (1966), 86-102, esp. p. 95 and n. 36. The text
of the stele fragments has been published by Tadmor in *Eretz-
Israel* 8 (1967), 241-245.

12. Na'aman's translation, "Sennacherib's 'Letter to
God'," p. 32.

13. K. A. Kitchen, "Late-Egyptian Chronology and the Hebrew Monarchy," *JANES* 5 (1973), 229-230.

14. Na'aman, "Sennacherib's 'Letter to God'," p. 32.

15. Any Assyrian religious practices in Judah at the time were carry-overs from the reign of Ahaz or perhaps resulted from the assimilation of Assyrian religion as a part of the phenomenon of acculturation under Assyrian rule. On this see Cogan, *Imperialism and Religion,* pp. 88-96.

16. E. W. Nicholson, "The Centralization of the Cult in Deuteronomy," *VT* 13 (1963), 380-389. For a different religio-political interpretation, cf. M. Weinfeld, "Cult Centralization in Israel in the Light of a Neo-Babylonian Analogy," *JNES* 23 (1964), 202-212.

17. W. E. Claburn, "The Fiscal Basis of Josiah's Reforms," *JBL* 92 (1973), 11-22. Although Claburn's study focuses on Josiah's cult centralization program, his analysis is intended to apply to Hezekiah's program as well.

18. Nicholson argues that Sennacherib's victory in 701 probably resulted in "the customary Assyrian policy of replacing those whom he took captive by importing into Judah foreigners from other parts of the empire. At any rate ... from this time onwards all sorts of foreign cults gained a footing in Judah." Under these circumstances, Nicholson suggests, "Hezekiah was forced to abolish the high places and to concentrate worship in Jerusalem" ("Centralization," p. 385).

19. The three basic types, based on Diringer's classification (see D. Diringer, "The Royal Jar-Handle Stamps of Ancient Judah," *BA* 12 [1949], 70-86), are: I. naturalistic scarab type; II. stylized scarab type; and III. two-winged type.

20. See, e.g., F. M. Cross, "Judean Stamps," *Eretz-Israel* 9 (1969), 20-22; A. D. Tushingham ("A Royal Israelite Seal (?) and the Royal Jar Handle Stamps," *BASOR* 201 [1971], 33-35) however, suggests that the four-winged scarab, which he believes was the royal seal of Israel, was brought back into use by Josiah, along with the winged sun-disk, in an effort to lay claim to the north Israelite territory. H. D. Lance, "The Royal Stamps and the Kingdom of Judah," *HTR* 64 (1971), 315-346, concurs with Cross. Aharoni, however, had dated the stamps to Hezekiah's reign on the basis of his work at Ramat Raḥel (see Y. Aharoni, *The Land of the Bible* [Philadelphia: Westminster, 1967], 340-346). P. W. Lapp, "Late

Royal Seals from Judah," *BASOR* 158 (1960), 16-21, dates the stamped handles over a broader range, beginning probably with the reign of Manasseh (the scarabs). The two-winged impressions, he believes, were introduced during Josiah's reign.

21. Lance, "Royal Stamps," pp. 331-332.

22. See D. Ussishkin, "The Destruction of Lachish by Sennacherib and the Dating of the Royal Judean Storage Jars," *Tel Aviv* 4 (1977), 28-60. The latest excavations have demonstrated that the destruction Level III, in which all types of seal impressions have been found, can only date to 701, not 598 as held by those who date the stamps to Josiah's reign. Cf. A. F. Rainey, "The Fate of Lachish During the Campaigns of Sennacherib and Nebuchadrezzar," *Investigations at Lachish (Lachish V)* (ed. Y. Aharoni; Tel Aviv: Gateway, 1975), 47-60, who shows that there is no literary evidence in the Neo-Babylonian records for a destruction of Lachish by Nebuchadrezzar. See now also, Na'aman, "Sennacherib's Campaign to Judah and the Date of the *LMLK* Stamps," *VT* 29 (1979), 61-86, for a summary of the evidence which points to a date prior to 701 for the stamps.

23. The purpose of the storage jars has been discussed extensively. The proposal here is similar to the view expressed by Aharoni, *Land of the Bible*, pp. 344-346.

24. J. A. Brinkman, "Merodach-Baladan II," in *Studies Presented to A. Leo Oppenheim* (ed. R. D. Biggs and J. A. Brinkman; Chicago: Oriental Institute of the University of Chicago, 1964), 6-53.

25. *Ibid.*, p. 33. For a more recent interpretation of the various strategies used by Sennacherib to resolve the problem of the rulership of Babylonia, see J. A. Brinkman, "Sennacherib's Babylonian Problem: An Interpretation," *JCS* 25 (1973), 89-95.

26. The narrative sequence in 2 Kgs 18:13-20:21, Isa 36:1-39:8, and 2 Chr 32:1-31 is uniformly: a) Sennacherib's campaign against Judah; b) Hezekiah's illness; and c) the Babylonian embassy to Judah.

27. Cf. Brinkman, "Merodach-Baladan II," 32-33.

28. W. W. Hallo, "The Royal Correspondence of Larsa: A Sumerian Prototype for the Prayer of Hezekiah?" in *Kramer Anniversary Volume* (=AOAT 25, ed. B. L. Eichler; Neukirchen-Vluyn: Neukirchener Verlag, 1976), 209-224.

29. Hallo, "Royal Correspondence," p. 210.

30. Hallo's article also refers to a second letter-prayer of Sin-iddinam which, according to Hallo's comments in a private conversation, also exists in a seventh century B.C.E. bilingual duplicate. The publication of this bilingual text by Hallo is forthcoming. The existence of this letter-prayer of Sin-iddinam in a seventh century duplicate makes the association with Hezekiah's prayer much more feasible on chronological grounds.

31. For a recent defense of the two-campaign theory, see S. H. Horn, "Did Sennacherib Campaign Once or Twice Against Hezekiah?" *AUSS* 4 (1966), 1-28.

32. A. K. Jenkins, "Hezekiah's Fourteenth Year," *VT* 26 (1976), 284-298.

33. Jenkins interprets Hezekiah's fourteenth year (which in Isa 36:1 is the date given in the account of Jerusalem's deliverance from Assyria) as a reference to an event which took place circa 714, viz., the outbreak of the Ashdod revolt. This particular date has been included in the biblical accounts (cf. also 2 Kgs 18:13) because of the letter that Hezekiah received from the Assyrian king (cf. 2 Kgs 19:14). "It is quite possible that when Sargon heard of the outbreak of the revolt, he sent a letter warning Hezekiah not to join it. Such a letter, received in 714 B.C. and subsequently deposited in the archives, could have provided a date 'the fourteenth year'" (*ibid.*, 294-295).

34. K. A. Kitchen, "Late-Egyptian Chronology and the Hebrew Monarchy," *JANES* 5 (1973), 225-233.

35. A. F. Rainey, "Tarhaqa and Syntax," *Tel Aviv* 3 (1976).

36. Kitchen, "Late-Egyptian Chronology," p. 231.

37. J. Pritchard, ed., *ANET*[3], p. 288.

38. *Ibid.*, p. 291.

39. *Ibid.*, p. 294.

40. The so-called Rassam Cylinder (*ibid.*).

41. R. Borger, *Die Inschriften Asarhaddons Königs von Assyrien* (=AfO Beiheft 9, 1956), 67: 30-35.

42. Cf. Cogan, *Imperialism and Religion*, p. 69.

43. In this same campaign, Ba'lu king of Tyre, who had also joined in the rebellion, was a target of Assyrian reprisals, but his life and position were spared (Pritchard, ed., *ANET*[3], p. 292).

44. Cogan, *Imperialism and Religion*, p. 69. The more common view concerning the Chronicler's testimony is that, if it is based on any historical situation at all, it belongs in the aftermath of the strife that marked the years between 652 and 648 (cf. Bright, *History*, p. 313).

45. Bright, *History*, p. 313. Bright attributes the fortification of Jerusalem and the Judahite towns, reported in 2 Chr 33:14, to the circumstances mentioned in the previous note. However, he places the return of the captured territory in the period following the conjectured second campaign of Sennacherib.

46. The solution offered here, unlike Bright's, has the advantage of associating both the fortifications and the return of territory to the same set of circumstances, as might be inferred from the Chronicler's report.

47. D. J. Wiseman, "The Vassal Treaties of Esarhaddon," *Iraq* 20 (1958), 1-99, plus 53 plates.

48. R. Frankena, "The Vassal Treaties of Esarhaddon and the Dating of Deuteronomy," *OTS* 14 (1965), 122-154.

49. M. Weinfeld, "Traces of Assyrian Treaty Formulae in Deuteronomy," *Bib* 46 (1965), 417-427.

50. Borger, *Die Inschriften Asarhaddons*, pp. 91-92.

51. Frankena, "Vassal Treaties," p. 150.

52. M. Streck, *Assurbanipal und die letzten Assyrischen Könige bis zum Untergange Ninevehs* (=Vorderasiatische Bibliothek 7; Leipzig: J. C. Hinrichs, 1916), IX. 115-128.

53. A. Malamat, "The Historical Background of the Assassination of Amon, King of Judah," *IEJ* 3 (1953), 26-29. The correlation of Amon's assassination with the more general revolt has been made uncertain, however, by the proposed redating of the Rassam cylinder edition of Ashurbanipal's annals to 643 (cf. Cogan, *Imperialism and Religion*, p. 70, n. 31).

54. Malamat, "Historical Background," p. 27.

55. Cf. S. Talmon, "The Judean ʿAm Haʾares in Historical Perspective," in *Fourth World Congress of Jewish Studies*
I (Jerusalem: World Union of Jewish Studies, 1967), 71-76,
who discusses the relation of the "people of the land" to
the house of David. Talmon acknowledges the variety of con-
notations which are associated with the "people of the land"
(cf. E. W. Nicholson, "The Meaning of the Expression עַם הָאָרֶץ
in the Old Testament," *JSS* 10 [1965], 59-66) but proposes
to explain this state of affairs by "assuming a semantic
division of the term which resulted in its synchronic employ-
ment: a. as a general noun which refers to a variety of human groups; b. as a technical term which can be applied only
to a specific entity in the Judean body politic" (p. 73).
The technical term, according to Talmon, refers to the group
that safeguarded the Davidic dynasty.

56. F. M. Cross and D. N. Freedman, "Josiah's Revolt
Against Assyria," *JNES* 12 (1953), 56-58.

57. J. Reade, "The Accession of Sinharishkun," *JCS* 23
(1970), 1-9.

58. A. Malamat, "Josiah's Bid for Armageddon," *JANES*
5 (1973), 267-279.

59. A. Malamat, "The Twilight of Judah: in the Egyptian-
Babylonian Maelstrom," in *Congress Volume, Edinburgh 1974* (VT
Sup 28; Leiden: E. J. Brill, 1975), 123-145.

# UNIVERSALIZATION OF HISTORY IN DEUTERO-ISAIAH

John B. White
DePauw University

## I.  The Comparative Method and Deutero-Isaiah

Important directions have recently been charted by scholars who believe the careful analysis of certain Mesopotamian materials can add significantly to the understanding of OT literature. J. J. M. Roberts, for example, has called our attention to the importance of a comparative approach which "with caution" seeks to examine theological interpretation of historical events both in Israel and Mesopotamia.[1] Likewise, Peter Machinist has directed our attention to the subtle political use of epic literature, illustrating from both the Epic of Tukulti-Ninurta I as well as the pentateuch and Israelite historical writings.[2] The so-called "divine exaltation" of the deity in cuneiform literature where historical events have been given universal significance in myth which depicts a god's mighty acts and awesome power has provided T. W. Mann with a host of interesting insights into Israelite traditions about the exodus.[3] And Roberts himself has discussed the possible background of Psalm 47 as a celebration of Yahweh's political dominion mirrored in the political consolidation of the Davidic age:  on analogy with similar divine accessions to power (Ishtar with Akkad's, Marduk with Babylon's, and Assur with Assyria's).[4]

In part, these recent applications of a comparative methodology come in response to an inordinate emphasis some scholars have placed on the *disjunction* between Israel's literature (and thus her worldview) and that of her neighbors in the ancient Near East.  Scholars arguing this point of view have held that Israelite historiography was distinctive, if not even sui generis.  Myth and history, moreover, were seen to be divergent modes of self-presentation--the former characterizing Mesopotamian culture in a timeless, cosmic framework and the latter

depicting Israel's unique possession of historical revelation.[5]
As early as 1958, however, J. J. Finkelstein warned of the dangers inherent in such a radical polarity between Hebrew and Assyro-Babylonian culture, social institutions, and literary heritage.[6] Other scholars added their voices and views to those
of Finkelstein until presently a comparative methodology which
seeks to "examine the theological interpretations of historical
events across the whole spectrum of literary genres native to
the cultures being compared" is shedding important light on the
interpretation of OT literature within the *context* of its Near
Eastern environment.[7]

Among recent literature on Deutero-Isaiah, S. M. Paul's
article comparing the language of the prophet's call to similar
language in Mesopotamian royal inscriptions stands as an important example of comparative method.[8] Cuneiform literature supplies numerous examples of epithets in royal titles which exhibit a motif of divine predestination and selection. Paul
singles out several of these titles for consideration--espe-
cially those inscriptions which refer to the king's destiny
being established *prior* to birth. Šamaššumukin, for example,
remarks " ... in the place of forming (=womb) of the mother
who bore me, Erua, the queen of the gods, favorably called my
name for lordship over mankind."[9] Such phraseology is reminiscent of several passages in Deutero-Isaiah. In 49:1, Yahweh
calls the prophet while he was still unborn (*mibbeten qěrā'ānî*)
and there (in the womb) "determined my name" (*hizkîr šěmî*).
Likewise, in other passages, Paul notes that Deutero-Isaiah
employs similar language to speak of the mission of the *entire
nation:* "He who created me in the womb ... (said) 'I will
make you a light to the nations'" (49:5-6).[10] By using the
comparative method, then, Paul illustrates an important theological dimension of Deutero-Isaiah's prophetic ministry:
that Israel herself (the *nation,* not just the prophet) was
called to be a "prophet nation" with a universal message and
role to play in history.

In surveying the recent commentaries on Deutero-Isaiah,
one is astonished by the absence of significant references to
the Mesopotamian literary corpus--peculiar indeed when one
considers the historical background and provenance of the
prophet's message! Claus Westermann does, however, underscore
Assyro-Babylonian echoes in the so-called "self-predication"
formulae of Yahweh, characteristic of several units in Deutero-
Isaiah (see, e.g., 41:10 ["for I am with you"]; 43:25 ["I
alone, I am he"]; 44:24 ["I, Yahweh, make all things"]; and
51:12 ["I, I myself am he"]). According to Westermann, the
prophet's use of this technique of Yahweh's self-description
is quite intentional: to counter dramatically (and "mono-

theistically") a similar use of the divine self-predication
found frequently in the Babylonian cult where the first person self-description/exaltation was common.[11] In Isa 40:3,
Westermann notes that the prophet's allusion to *mĕsillâh*
("highway") is reminiscent of Babylonian hymns which allude
to the triumphant procession of the gods or king into the city.
Just as in the case of the self-predication, Westermann asserts
that Deutero-Isaiah transforms a well-known pagan motif into a
unique Israelite affirmation of faith:  now Israel would have
her own *mĕsillâh* upon which she would make her triumphant journey homeward.[12]  In both instances, then, Israel *transforms*
allusions from the Near Eastern world, and the new Israelite
context provides the prophet with a novel way of communicating
his message as well as serves as a polemic against Assyro-
Babylonian culture and religion.

That Israel borrowed ideas, literary allusions, and
mythology from the ancient Near East is well known and acknowledged by many scholars.  Likewise, that she also transformed borrowed motifs in light of her unique, historical
faith is well-nigh orthodoxy.  J. Hempel's work on Israel's
adaptation of Near Eastern myth illustrates the process of
retooling myth into the Hebrew *Geist*.  According to Hempel,
it is the monotheistic character of Yahweh which controlled
the formation of the literature of the OT and which, in terms
of myth, either "obliterated" or adapted it.[13]  F. M. Cross,
Jr. has argued, moreover, that Israel frequently utilized
*already* existing language and thought forms of the ancient
world "to help to invest events and circumstances in Israel's
history with some abiding significance."[14]  This insight of
Cross should be directed to the message of Deutero-Isaiah:
the prophet utilized thought forms or styles of argumentation already extant in the ancient Near East in the presentation of his message of salvation for the exiles?  The crucial nature of this question is related to a second which
also must receive consideration in light of the comparative
method:    the prophet utilized Israel's own unique mythological presentation in the context of his message and how
may comparative material from the Near East illumine our
understanding of the prophet's presentation of Yahweh's
salvation for the broken nation?[15]

Two articles have recently appeared which attempt to
argue that Deutero-Isaiah did mythologize events such as the
Egyptian deliverance by employing images of the cosmic victory of Yahweh over the chaotic elements of the universe.
T. M. Ludwig has focused his attention on the so-called
"establishing of the earth" formulae (e.g., *yōsēd 'ereṣ*, "who
establishes the earth," [Isa 51:13; cf. 48:13; 51:16]) and

notes that the idea appears to stem, in part, "from a creation tradition that involves conflict with chaotic forces
and victory over them by Yahweh, with the subsequent ordering
of the cosmos."[16] Following Cross and others, Ludwig sees
this mythologizing of events as part of cultic tradition which
celebrates Yahweh as the orderer of the creation (see Pss 104:
1-9; 24:1-2; 89:6-13) as a result of his cosmic victory over
Rahab--the powerful sea monster--and his ordering of the těhôm
(e.g., Isa 51:9-16).[17] This struggle with the forces of chaos
and the ordering of creation, then, becomes paradigmatic for a
"continuing struggle" which is taking place during the exilic
period and the subsequent assurance that once again Yahweh
will reign supreme.[18]

In a second article, D. M. Gunn has argued that Deutero-
Isaiah's poetry exhibits what he terms "multiple allusion,"
that is references of the prophet to past, saving events are
not confined to one, single allusion. For example, in Deutero-
Isaiah's depiction of the "drying up of the waters" (Isa 44:27;
50:2; 51:10), Gunn argues that the poetic references cannot be
confined merely to the exodus tradition or even the cosmic
creation battle but also might well include the flood motif--
an aspect of Deutero-Isaiah's thought rarely considered by
scholars.[19] Although Gunn's article does not deal with comparative Near Eastern material regarding flood imagery, his
is a forceful statement concerning the prophet's use of mythological allusion from earlier tradition to reflect on the contemporary theological situation of the exile and to underscore
Yahweh's intent to restore the nation. By allusions to the
flood motif, the kerygmatic message is clear: the nation
will soon experience a mighty deliverance comparable to that
of Noah during the nation's prehistory.[20]


## II. Salvation Prophecy: A Comparative View


Westermann has noted that "the unique feature" of Deutero-
Isaiah's prophecy is its character of proclaiming salvation--
and salvation only--to the people of Israel.[21] As one might
expect, the forms of speech used by the prophet are equally
unique insofar as his prophetic counterparts are concerned.
Prominent in his proclamation of salvation is the so-called
"assurance of salvation"--that even though the nation is still
in Babylonian hands "her term of sentence has been completed"
and "her bond has been paid" (Isa 40:2). The essence of salvation for Israel, then, is at hand "for Yahweh has redeemed
Jacob" (Isa 44:23). There is, therefore, a crucial element

to Deutero-Isaiah's message: the same Yahweh who destroyed
the nation for her sinfulness and who had previously announced
the defeat of his own chosen people, now accomplishes restoration (see Isa 42:24-25).

Y. Kaufmann cautions us against a commonly held view in
the ancient world that a nation's victory was a victory of its
god over the gods of a rival nation, and likewise, defeat was
a significant defeat for the deity; hence, the exile should
*not* be interpreted as the defeat of Yahweh at the hands of
Marduk.[22] Both Ezekiel and Deutero-Isaiah make it clear that
Israel's defeat is not due to Marduk, but to Yahweh's own
punishment of his people (see Ezek 8:18 and Deutero-Isaiah's
affirmation that Yahweh himself showed his anger to the nation
for her sinfulness [Isa 42:25]). Kaufmann, moreover, goes on
to point out that the "commonly held notion" concerning national disaster's being related to the defeat of a nation's
deity may not always be the case even in the non-Israelite
world. He notes that even in the Near East "the conquered
nation was likely to view the enemy as the rod of the wrath
of its god."[23]

One cuneiform text edited and translated by W. G. Lambert
seeks to explain the reasons for the destruction of Babylon at
the hands of the Elamites and the subsequent removal of the
Marduk statue from Babylon to Elam.[24] The text, probably originating from the time of Nebuchadnezzar I who was responsible
for the statue's return to Babylon from Elamite captivity,
notes that Marduk "became angry and got furious" over the evil
deeds which were going on in Babylon.[25] As a result, Marduk
uses the Elamites to punish his own nation--Elamites, inciden-
tally, whom the document itself does not hold in high regard.
Note the following:

> The wicked Elamite, who did not hold (the
> land's) treasures in esteem, [...] his battle,
> his attack was swift. He devastated the habi-
> tations and made them into a ruin, he carried
> off the gods, he ruined the shrine.[26]

This important cuneiform text indicates, as does the prophetic
reflection of the Israelite exile, that the deity could indeed
be responsible for the destruction of his own nation--destruc-
tion as punishment for national shortcomings.

If the deity could be responsible for the *destruction* of
the nation, could he, then, also be responsible for restoration? Recently another cuneiform text, now known as "The
Prophetic Speech of Marduk," has been edited and translated

and serves as an interesting example of the deity's bringing
about the defeat of his own people and then announcing their
subsequent salvation and rebuilding.[27]

This text also would appear to have Nebuchadnezzar I's
campaign against the Elamites and the subsequent return of
the Marduk statue to Babylon as a focal point.  There are two
thematic divisions of the document, the first part of which
forms a recital of past historical events as Marduk explains
in an autobiographical manner how and why he made many trips
throughout the Near East—culminating in his journey to Elam.
One of the major reasons for his "travels" appears to be
"business trips" taken in the establishment of Babylonian
caravan routes throughout the world (no mention is made of
Babylon's defeat at the hands of Mursilis I or Tukulti-Ninurta
I and the removal of the statue!).[28]

J. J. M. Roberts has noted that this first section of
the text strongly emphasizes Marduk's control over history,
for the deity is clearly in charge of all situations:

> I am Marduk the great lord.  I alone am
> lord of destinies and decisions.  Who has
> taken this road?  Wherever I went, from
> there I have returned.[29]

It would seem that the Elamite conquest of Babylon would be
somewhat difficult to pass off, however, as a simple "business
trip" over to Elam to check out economic affairs.  Yet, what
the text makes clear is that it is Marduk himself who brings
about Babylon's disaster.  Note the following:

> I myself gave the command.  I went to the
> land of Elam, and all the gods went with
> me—I alone gave the command.  The food
> offerings of the temples I alone cut off.[30]

Our document which we are considering now turns from an
autobiographical recital of *past* history to a second thematic
section which appears to be prophecy of restoration (what
Borger calls *Heilsprophetie*).[31]  Marduk announces the mission
of a king to arise in Babylon (we may assume Nebuchadnezzar
I) who will restore the temple and return Marduk to his proper
place in Babylon.  Elam is to be completely destroyed by this
appointed king and by the deities which are in league with
him.[32]  It is natural that both Borger and Roberts raise the
issue that this salvation prophecy which speaks of the defeat
of the Elamites and the restoration of Babylon's cult with
Marduk might, in fact, be *vaticinium ex eventu*, an appealing

idea when one considers that the extant text is a late copy.
While Borger seems to leave the issue open, Roberts concludes
the following:  "... the tone of the document argues for dating the original prior to Nebuchadnezzar I's Elamite victories."[33]

If we are dealing with a genuine salvation prophecy in
a document which may have its genesis in the period *prior* to
the accession of Nebuchadnezzar I (ca. 1127 B.C.E.) and which
places salvation prophecy in a context of the recital of "past
history" (i.e., for our text, the autobiographical explanations of the prior "trips" of the Marduk statue), then I believe we have an intriguing comparative text to consider along
side of Deutero-Isaiah's prophecy of salvation.[34]

The interweaving of past history--what has happened--to
salvation prophecy--what is now or about to happen--is characteristic of the message of Deutero-Isaiah.  As with both cuneiform texts we have considered, the Israelite prophet clearly
articulates that the present state of political affairs, the
nation in exile, was the work of Yahweh's judgment (Isa 42:24-
25).  Yet, this understanding of recent history is followed
by a  concomitant understanding that judgment is not the final
word of Yahweh on the nation's plight.  Immediately following
Isa 42:24-25 and its assertion that Yahweh brought about the
punishment is the salvation oracle Isa 43:1-7.  "But now,"
that is in the present, significant moment of history, the
nation is being reclaimed, called by name, and ransomed by
Yahweh.[35]

Deutero-Isaiah's use of historical recital is under-
scored by the prophet's direct allusions to the sacred history.  He appears to be well-versed in the so-called Zion
tradition--for Israel is frequently called by that name (Isa
40:9; 41:27; 49:14; etc.)--and the prophecies about Jerusalem
(see 54:11-17).  Specific figures, moreover, are mentioned
from the sacred history:  David (55:3); Abraham (e.g., 41:8);
Sarah (51:2); the fathers of the faith in general (43:27);
and Noah (54:9).

In the allusion to Noah and the flood traditions, the
interconnection between the recital of past events and the
assurance of future salvation can be clearly noted.  The
exilic community might well view the trauma of deportation
comparably with the events of the primeval flood; yet Deutero-
Isaiah argues that the new community of those returning home
will be like the remnant of Noah to carry on God's purposes
in history (Isa 54:7-10).[36]  Restoration, then, involves
Yahweh's action to re-establish the community:  grace in response to national disaster.

In the unit Isa 46:9-13, the prophet calls upon the nation to be open to future salvation *because* they have a sense of historical memory. In "remembering former things" (*ri' šōnôt,* 46:9), the people will begin to discern the continuity of God's saving plan.[37] Yahweh's purpose, then, involves the commissioning of "one from the east" (Isa 41:2) or, in another place, "a bird of prey from the east" (46:11). These are obviously references to Cyrus, the divinely appointed savior of the nation, whose very call affirms Yahweh's control of history: "I have spoken; I will bring it to pass. I have planned; I will accomplish it" (Isa 46:11). Likewise, the unit 52:4-12 begins with the historical recital of Egyptian and Assyrian oppression and once again illustrates the interweaving of historical memory and the promise of salvation.[38] According to this pericope, it is against the background of this past oppression that Yahweh now heralds salvation:

> Break forth together into singing, you ruins
>     of Jerusalem;
> for Yahweh has comforted his people,
> and ransomed Jerusalem (Isa 52:9).

### III.  Divine Exaltation
### as Harbinger of Israel's Return

The exploration of "exodus typology" in Deutero-Isaiah has been an important emphasis of scholarship, bringing to light the prophet's use of earlier tradition in the presentation of his message of salvation.[39] Deutero-Isaiah employs the earlier exodus traditions to convey a "new exodus"--the eschatological rule of God to be inaugurated along the lines of the historical event so crucial to Israel's formative past.[40] Recently, however, the exodus traditions in the pentateuch have been studied in the light of the so-called "exaltation typology" in Near Eastern literature.[41] The re-presentation of these exodus traditions and the continuing process of literary reflection on this pivotal event in the message of Deutero-Isaiah yields another important area of study in light of the comparative method, for the themes of exaltation of the deity and other accompanying motifs can be found in the prophet's speech.

The typology of divine exaltation is a rich and complex literary motif which mythologically reflects an awesome, terrifying picture of a deity often set against the background of battle and victory over the enemy. In the "Exaltation of Inanna," the goddess is vividly pictured as she rains terror upon the city of Uruk and the mountain Ebih (a prototypical enemy):

43  In the mountain where homage is withheld from you vegetation is accursed.

44  Its grand entrance you have reduced to ashes.

45  Blood rises in its rivers for you, its people have nought to drink.

46  It leads its army captive before you of its own accord.

47  It disbands its regiments before you of its own accord.

48  It makes its able-bodied young men parade before you of their own accord.

49  A tempest has filled the dancing of its city.

50  It drives its young adults before you as captives.[42]

It is striking to note that Yahweh of the exodus is portrayed as an awesome figure of might in his exaltation in such passages as Ex 15:1-11 where Yahweh vanquishes the Egyptian foe, casting the chariots of Pharaoh's army into the sea.[43] Hence, the typology of divine exaltation celebrates the victorious deity who by sheer force overwhelms the enemy--often using the powers of nature and the storm to subdue the foe (see Ps 77:17-20; Ex 15:10).

Scholars who have worked extensively with texts such as "The Exaltation of Inanna" and other pieces of literature reflecting the exaltation typology have pointed out a crucial *connection* between myth and history. W. W. Hallo, for example, has noted that the typology of divine exaltation is connected to specific *historical* antecedents, so that myth has a specific historical, political horizon universalizing specific historical events.[44] In this light, myth, aside from generally dealing with supernatural beings, actors, and events, has another crucial dimension: it presents a legendary occurrence as a paradigm for continuing human experience. Hallo puts it succinctly: "Myth uses the punctual to explain the durative."[45] Similarly, C. Wilcke affirms the historical

origin of myth in the Near East and follows Hallo in noting
that "The Exaltation of Inanna" is not merely a mythological
battle, but a myth which universalizes a specific historical
episode.[46]  In short, this Near Eastern poem describes the
solidification of the political position of Akkad and Sargon
(Inanna subdues her foes).  We may note, likewise, that the
exaltation of Yahweh in the exodus traditions confirms Israel's political independence from immediate Egyptian political power so that now Yahweh achieves unchallenged supremacy
in the life of the nation.  The exodus, then, becomes Israel's
attempt to mythologize, i.e., universalize her religio-political, historical rise to power.

In discussing the exodus traditions in light of the exaltation typology of the Near East, T. W. Mann has observed the
presence of the so-called divine vanguard motif, i.e., the
deity's "going before" his people, leading them into battle.[47]
This image is integrated with divine exaltation.  It is our
contention that Deutero-Isaiah in representing the exodus
motif in his salvation prophecy announces to the broken nation
Yahweh's exaltation.  The proclamation is that Yahweh is indeed still supreme over the nation and that he will be their
vanguard as they return to rebuild and restore Jerusalem.

The awesome character of Yahweh to accomplish this goal
is expressed by the prophet using language reminiscent of the
divine exaltation:

> I will lay waste mountains and hills,
>     and wither all their herbage;
> I will turn rivers into dry land
>     and I will dry up swamps (Isa 42:15).

But the use of the vanguard motif by the prophet makes it
clear that these potentially destructive powers are to be put
to use for Israel's restoration:

> And I will *lead (wĕhôlāktî)* the blind in a
>     way they do not know,
>   and *guide* them in paths they do not know;
> I will turn darkness into light *before them,*
>     and the rough places into level ground
>                                         (Isa 42:16).

From the wilderness traditions, according to Mann, the
phrase *hlk lpny* ("to go before") has exclusive use (see Ex
13:21; 14:19; 23:23; Num 14:14; etc.).[49]  The phrase and its
occurrences are prime examples of the vanguard motif:  the
"going before" God's people.  Deutero-Isaiah's prophecy has

richly represented this vanguard motif as a theological con-
fession of Israel's assurance of salvation. "I will go before
you," ('ănî lĕpānekā 'ēlēk) Yahweh says to the community,
"and will level the swellings" (Isa 45:2). Likewise, in Isa
52:12, it is Yahweh who will secure the nation's orderly return: "for Yahweh will go before you (kî-hōlēk lipnêkem yhwh)
and the God of Israel will be your rearguard" (see also 58:8,
and cf. Ex 13:21; 14:19-20; and Deut 1:30-33).

Crucial for understanding the message of Deutero-Isaiah
is that Yahweh's exaltation is announced *in spite of* the nation's current plight. In the ideology of the age in which
cosmic events were linked with particular historical events,
the prophet was proclaiming something totally new, using the
language, however, of Israel's own past (see Isa 43:19). The
joy of the prophet's message is to be found in its announcement that once again Yahweh would attain an unchallenged supremacy in the eyes of his people:

> I have given a promise of victory,
> a promise that will not be broken,
> that to me every knee shall bend
> and by me every tongue shall swear (Isa 45:23, NEB)[50]

In Deutero-Isaiah's re-presentation of the exodus traditions,
then, the image of divine exaltation is cast into an eschatological framework which celebrates Yahweh's future intervention based upon the continuity of his past grace (see Isa 43:
1-4).


## IV. Universalization of History


The salvation prophecy of Deutero-Isaiah has drawn upon
Israel's own mythological heritage in order to speak words of
*durative* significance to his own people.[51] Through the comparative method we have noted that the prophet's words stand
in the context of Near Eastern materials which exhibit themes
of the recital of past events, the deity's punishment, and
his subsequent announcement of restoration through salvation
prophecy. Moreover, Deutero-Isaiah utilizes Israel's own
mythologizing of the crucial exodus event to express dramatically both a new eschatological hope for Yahweh's people and,
in the language of myth, the restoration of the nation and
Yahweh's sovereign role.

The announcement of Yahweh's exaltation and his vanguard

image in the return of the exiles *over against* the contemporary, historical situation underscores the prophet's attempt to portray the universal significance of imminent events. His use of the exodus mythology by which to cast his message suggests that Deutero-Isaiah saw deliverance in the moment of military-political distress coming on a grand scale indeed. By tapping Israel's earlier universalizing of historical events--the exodus tradition--the prophet has re-presented the historical on an even grander stage and in a more powerful scenario.

## NOTES

1. J. J. M. Roberts, "Myth *Versus* History," *CBQ* 38 (1976), 13. Roberts provides examples of this comparative analysis in several other recent articles, among them the following: "The Religio-Political Setting of Psalm 47," *BASOR* 22 (1976), 129-132, and "Nebuchadnezzar I's Elamite Crisis in Theological Perspective," *Essays on the Ancient Near East in Memory of Jacob Joel Finkelstein* (ed. M. de Jong Ellis; Hamden, Conn.: Archon Books, 1977), 183-187.

2. Peter Machinist, "Literature as Politics," *CBQ* 38 (1976), 455-482.

3. T. W. Mann, *Divine Presence and Guidance in Israelite Traditions* (Baltimore: Johns Hopkins University, 1977).

4. Roberts, "Psalm 47," p. 132.

5. Brevard Childs has seen this radical disjunction between "history" and "myth" as part of the demise of the so-called "biblical theology movement" which had exalted history as the chief medium of revelation for the Hebrews. See Childs, *Biblical Theology in Crisis* (Philadelphia: Westminster, 1970), chaps. 1-4.

6. J. J. Finkelstein, "Bible and Babel: A Comparative Study of the Hebrew and Babylonian Religious Spirit," *Commentary* 26 (1958), 444.

7. Roberts, "Myth *Versus* History," p. 13. The literature suggesting a greater rapprochement between Israelite and Mesopotamian historiography, use of myth, and development

of religious and social institutions is massive. Initially, however, one might wish to consult the following: J. J. Finkelstein, "Mesopotamian Historiography," *Proceedings of the American Philosophical Society* 107 (1963), 461-472; H. Gese, "The Idea of History in the Ancient Near East," *Journal for Theology and the Church* 1 (1965), 65-102; B. Albrektson, *History and the Gods* (Lund: CWK Gleerup, 1967); J. Barr, *Old and New in Interpretation* (London: SCM, 1966), 65-102; and J. J. M. Roberts, "Divine Freedom and Cultic Manipulation in Israel and Mesopotamia," *Unity and Diversity* (ed. Hans Goedicke and J. J. M. Roberts; Baltimore: Johns Hopkins University, 1975), 181-187. By way of contrast, one might wish to consult the following by W. G. Lambert who cautions against oversimplifying the distinctive character of Mesopotamian literature and its worldview: his review of Albrektson's work in *Or* 39 (1970), 170-177, and "Destiny and Divine Intervention in Babylon and Israel," *OTS* 17 (1972), 65-72.

8. S. M. Paul, "Deutero-Isaiah and Cuneiform Royal Inscriptions," *JAOS* 88 (1968), 180-186.

9. *Ibid.*, p. 185.

10. *Ibid.*, p. 186.

11. Claus Westermann, *Isaiah 40-66* (Philadelphia: Westminster, 1969), 72 and 156.

12. *Ibid.*, pp. 38-39.

13. J. Hempel, "Glaube, Mythos, und Geschichte im Alten Testament," *ZAW* 65 (1953), 109-111. It is interesting that Hempel terms this process of adaptation "demythologizing."

14. See F. M. Cross, Jr., "The Divine Warrior in Israel's Early Cult," *Biblical Motifs* (ed. A. Altman; Cambridge: Harvard University, 1966), 19.

15. Concerning the question of Israel's creation of myth, we note that G. H. Davies concluded that Israel, like her Near Eastern neighbors, "developed her own peculiar mythology within the orbit of Yahweh's personality, and in particular in reference to the Presence theme now discoverable in the pages of the OT" ("An Approach to the Problem of Old Testament Mythology," *PEQ* 88 [1956], 91). Likewise, William Johnstone ("The Mythologizing of History in the Old Testament," *SJT* 24 [1971], 211) has proposed that Israel does create her own myths when an event is "interpreted in a way in which it transcends itself and in the light of Israel's own origins

and goals." For a recent discussion of the problem of myth in relation to Hebrew scriptures and a survey of recent scholarship, see J. L. Rogerson, *Myth in Old Testament Interpretation* (BZAW 134; Berlin:  de Gruyter, 1974), esp. chap. 10.

16.  T. M. Ludwig, "The Tradition of the Establishing of the Earth in Deutero-Isaiah," *JBL* 92 (1973), 350-351.

17.  See, e.g., Cross, "Divine Warrior in Cult," pp. 16-18, or his "The Song of the Sea and Canaanite Myth," *Canaanite Myth and Hebrew Epic* (Cambridge:  Harvard University, 1973), 143, where he notes the following:  "The reenactment of primordial events of cosmogonic myth gave way to festivals reenacting epic events in Israel's past, thus renewing her life as a historical community."

18.  Ludwig, "Establishing the Earth," p. 357.  Ludwig sees the creation images of Yahweh's ordering of chaos as an independent tradition *not* subordinated to the exodus tradition.  Cf., however, G. von Rad's assessment of creation and exodus traditions in Deutero-Isaiah in his "The Theological Problem of the Old Testament Doctrine of Creation," *The Problem of the Hexateuch and Other Essays* (New York:  McGraw-Hill, 1966), 134.

19.  D. M. Gunn, "Deutero-Isaiah and the Flood," *JBL* 94 (1975), 495-496.

20.  *Ibid.*, p. 508.

21.  Westermann, *Isaiah*, p. 9.

22.  Yehezkel Kaufmann, *The Babylonian Captivity and Deutero-Isaiah* (New York:  Union of American Hebrew Congregations, 1970), 19.  Ezek 8:12 and 9:9 allude to one rationale for Israel's plight:  Yahweh has simply forsaken the country.  Ezekiel, of course, does not agree with such a notion!

23.  Kaufmann, *Babylonian Captivity*, p. 20.  The so-called Moabite Stone is a prime example.  Omri was able to "humble" Moab for many years "for Chemosh was angry at his land."  See *ANET*[2], 320.

24.  W. G. Lambert, "Enmeduranki and Related Matters," *JCS* 21 (1967), 126-138.

25.  *Ibid.*, p. 130.  The translations are those of Lambert.

26. *Ibid.* See Roberts, "Elamite Crisis," p. 186, n. 37, for another fragmentary allusion to the destruction of Babylon by the Elamites at Marduk's instigation.

27. Rykle Borger, "Gott Marduk and Gott-König Šulgi als Propheten: Zwei prophetische Texte," *BO* 28 (1971), 3-24. See also A. K. Grayson and W. G. Lambert, "Akkadian Prophecies," *JCS* 18 (1964), 7-23, esp. p. 8.

28. Borger, "Gott Marduk," p. 16. For an historical overview including the various captures of the Marduk statue see the following: J. A. Brinkman, *A Political History of Post-Kassite Babylon* (AnOr 43; Rome: Pontifical Biblical Institute, 1968), 104-110; W. W. Hallo and W. K. Simpson, *The Ancient Near East: A History* (New York: Harcourt Brace Jovanovich, 1971), 105-106 and 117; and Machinist, "Literature as Politics," 470-474.

29. Roberts, "Elamite Crisis," p. 184. Roberts' translation is used here. See also Borger, "Gott Marduk," p. 16.

30. Roberts' translation, "Elamite Crisis," p. 184.

31. See Borger, "Gott Marduk," p. 21.

32. Note Borger's translation of the text at this point, *ibid.*, pp. 16-17.

33. Roberts, "Elamite Crisis," p. 185. Roberts notes that there are "genuine" prophecies which allude to future victories by kings from both Mari and later Assyrian documents (p. 185, n. 29).

34. *Ibid.* Roberts affirms here that our text "would appear to be a genuine 'prophecy of salvation' seeking credence by an appeal to past history."

35. Karl Elliger comments on the significant particle *wĕ'ātâh* ("but now") as a point of transition, introducing the radically new word of salvation in the oracle Isa 43:1-7. See his *Jesaja II* (BKAT XI/4; Neukirchen-Vluyn: Neukirchener, 1973), 292.

36. So argues James D. Smart, *History and Theology in Second Isaiah* (Philadelphia: Westminster, 1965), 219; see also Gunn, "Deutero-Isaiah," p. 508, and Westermann, *Isaiah*, p. 275.

37. N. C. Habel, in a recent article, notes that the prophet is placing his emphasis upon "the priority of the divine word that initiated ... events" by his allusion to historical tradition. See his "Appeal to Ancient Tradition as a Literary Form," *ZAW* 88 (1976), 265.

38. In the unit 52:4-12, vv. 4-6 may, in fact, be a gloss. See Westermann, *Isaiah,* p. 248. If these verses are not directly from the prophet, they still capture the substance of his argument about past history's relation to future salvation. See also J. L. McKenzie, *Second Isaiah* (AB 20; Garden City: Doubleday, 1968), 127.

39. The exodus typology has been worked out in detail by Bernhard Anderson, "Exodus Typology in Second Isaiah," *Israel's Prophetic Heritage: Essays in Honor of James Muilenburg* (ed. B. Anderson and W. Harrelson; New York: Harper, 1962), 177-195, esp. 181-185.

40. See James Muilenburg's comments on the "new exodus" imagery of Deutero-Isaiah in *The Interpreter's Bible* (ed. G. A. Buttrick; Nashville: Abingdon, 1956), V, 602.

41. See above, n. 3. Mann's study is indebted to the work of W. W. Hallo in Near Eastern literature who has, in a recent study on the Sumerian literary work *nin-me-šar-ra,* defined the characteristics of this motif. See W. W. Hallo and J. J. A. van Dijk, *The Exaltation of Inanna* (New Haven: Yale University, 1968), esp. 64-68.

42. Hallo and van Dijk, *Exaltation,* p. 21 (Hallo's translation).

43. See Mann, *Divine Presence,* pp. 123-125.

44. Hallo and van Dijk, *Exaltation,* p. 60.

45. W. W. Hallo, "The Cultic Setting of Sumerian Poetry," *Recontre assyriologique internationale* 17 (1969), 117, n. 1. Hallo has developed the idea of the universalization of historical events into a mythological framework into a criterion of "canonization" for ancient literature; thus, some literary works may have disappeared from the "canon" because they failed "to sublimate their historical particulars sufficiently to qualify for enduring and universal interest in the cuneiform curriculum." See Hallo, "Toward a History of Sumerian Literature," *Assyriological Studies* 20 (1974), 187.

46. C. Wilcke, "Politische Opposition nach sumerischen Quellen: der Konflikt zwischen Königtum und Ratsversammlung. Literaturwerke als politische Tendenzschriften," *La voix de l'opposition en Mésopotamie* (ed. A. Finet; Brussels: Palais des Akademies, 1973), 55-56. Wilcke terms this myth a "pro-Akkadian Inanna myth." There are many other Near Eastern texts which embody the typology of divine exaltation, the above mentioned "Exaltation of Inanna" being among the earliest. For other texts, see Hallo and van Dijk, *Exaltation*, pp. 65-67; Wilcke, "Politische Opposition," pp. 57-65; and Mann, *Divine Presence*, pp. 33-51.

47. Mann, *Divine Presence*, pp. 27, 51, 132-133. The vanguard motif is linked with the on-going presence of the deity in a community. Mann's volume includes representations of Assyrian standards which were carried into battle, planted in newly acquired territory, and became symbols of rule. In the OT, one might wish to see the images of the ark or the cloud of Yahweh against the background of such symbols (see *ibid.*, 265-268).

48. Hebrew *hlk*, with Yahweh as subject, is frequently found in the vanguard "terminology" as discerned by Mann, *ibid.*, p. 253. See also Isa 48:21.

49. *Ibid.*

50. The christological hymn of Phil 2:6-11 appears to reflect a similar exaltation of the figure Jesus Christ. Its form is certainly pre-Pauline and it may reflect an early Christian exegesis of Isa 52:13 where the "servant of Yahweh" is humiliated as well as exalted.

51. One can justifiably argue that other mythological elements have been reactualized by the prophet including creation and flood images. These too should be seen against the background of Deutero-Isaiah's universalizing of the temporal into the mythological.

THE OIKOUMENE IN FERMENT:

A CROSS-CULTURAL STUDY OF THE SIXTH CENTURY*

Jean M. Davison
University of Vermont

During the sixth century the ancient world experienced
political and cultural changes which were to have a decisive
effect upon the later course of history, both ancient and
modern. This is the time of the Hebrew prophets of the Exile,
of the Ionian philosophers and the mystery cults of the Greek
world, of Zoroaster in Iran, of Buddhism and Jainism in India,
and of Confucius (and possibly Taoism) in China. While the
exact dates of the actual or presumed founders of some of the
religious movements of the Farther East may be in doubt, the
effect of the intellectual activity ascribed to them seems
well enough attested for us to accept the general view of the
sixth century as a pivotal one in speculative and religious
thought.[1]

The metaphor offered by the use of the term 'ferment'
to describe the situation in the sixth century may be extended
to aid our understanding of the period. The *process* of fermentation can be fairly readily observed, for the various ingredients involved in the historical situation are well documented. The *nature* of the fermentation also is not difficult
to recover, for either through the monuments and literature
of the period itself or from later references we are very well
informed as to its intellectual and artistic output. Important questions remain, however, concerning both the beginning
and the end of the process: To what extent is the output to
be considered a 'blend' resulting from outside influences

---

*Because of the synoptic nature of this paper, depth must
necessarily be sacrificed to breadth; also, the farther east
the discussion moves, the more obvious will be the weakness in
the scholarly control of the evidence. For this reason, an
attempt has been made to give more ample documentation in the
footnotes for peripheral areas.

rather than native to its own district, and is there any
common denominator which may be recognized as the responsible agent--the 'yeast' which started the whole process?

This paper, then, will begin with a brief description
of the process of fermentation and the nature of its final
result and then will consider how and why it came to be.


## I.   Process of Fermentation:   The Ingredients


At first sight the political history of the Near East
during the sixth century is merely a re-run of a familiar
scenario:  A new Semitic power has usurped control of Mesopotamia from a previous one; the area of Syria-Palestine is
included in its inheritance or grasp; and Egypt, enfeebled
but ambitious, paces in the wings, eager to snatch a share
of her former holdings.

But Egypt, although still enjoying the revival of prosperity introduced by the 26th (Saïte) Dynasty early in the
seventh century, must depend upon mercenary troops for protection against both external and internal dangers and has
no strength left to force her way into any permanent position
in Palestine.  Psammetichus II, with the aid of Ionian Greek
mercenaries and the Jewish military garrison at Elephantine,
carries on a punitive expedition against Nubia in the late
590's.  His successor, Apries (the biblical Hophra), abandons
the former policy of peace with Babylon and attacks Phoenicia;
he even comes to the relief of Jerusalem during its siege by
Nebuchadnezzar in 587.  But it is a brief challenge; when the
Egyptians withdraw the city falls, captives are taken to Babylon and many refugees flee to Egypt.  A successful retaliatory
attack against the Delta by Nebuchadnezzar in 570 results in
the paying of tribute by the new pharaoh, Amasis, but no real
Babylonian control is exercised and no further hostilities
occur.  Amasis, a notable diplomat, wins the favor of the
Greek city-states by gifts and alliances, while at the same
time calming nationalist xenophobia by confining the Greek
mercenary forces to quarters in Memphis and the Greek merchants to the single trade depot of Naucratis.[2]

The first half of the century, then, does appear to follow the script:  Nebuchadnezzar is in firm control of the Neo-
Babylonian empire and has scotched the ambitions of Egypt; to
the east the Medes, former allies in the destruction of the
Assyrian Empire, are constructing a kingdom of their own under

the leadership of Cyaxares and Astyages. To the west the
kingdom of Lydia under the Mermnadae has recognized the
Halys River as the boundary between Lydia and Media, and
intermarriage has taken place between the two ruling families. Alyattes, the Lydian king, has succeeded in imposing
his rule upon the Greek city-states along the coast, and
his son Croesus has consolidated his control over these
East Greeks as well as developing diplomatic connections
with the Greeks of the mainland, where he is renowned for
his wealth and generosity. The Near East state system
during the first half of the sixth century is thus composed
of familiar faces; the Chaldaean kingdom is new but rooted
in traditional Mesopotamian culture; Judah has been removed
into captivity in Babylon and the Phoenician monopoly of Mediterranean trade has been seriously infringed by Greek interests, but in general the period is one of flourishing trade,
building activity, and prosperity--and if it is not politically stable, it is at least politically predictable.

But these familiar features were radically rearranged
during the course of the second half of the sixth century.
Soon after the accession of Croesus to the throne of Lydia
in 560 B.C.E., the Median power of Astyages succumbed to
the restless ambition of his Persian grandson, Cyrus (ca.
549 B.C.E.). In quick succession Cyrus overthrew the three
major Near Eastern powers, despite their attempts to ally
against him: Lydia fell in 546, when Croesus crossed the
Halys in reaction to the deposing of his Median brother-in-
law; Babylon in 539,3 when the priesthood of Marduk could no
longer abide the apostasy of Nabonidus; and Egypt in 525 to
Cyrus' son, Cambyses, soon after the death of Amasis. By
the end of the century, therefore, all the previously independent states of the Near East, Semitic and non-Semitic
alike, have fallen into the hands of Persia. Aside from some
intermittently successful rebellions, the rule of native pharaohs in Egypt is over, although the dynastic sequence will
continue, according to Manetho's systematization, into the
fourth century through Dynasty 30. Lydia and her East Greek
subjects are now controlled by Persia, which under the leadership of Darius will encompass a European as well as an
Asian empire and will threaten to absorb mainland Greece.

Beyond the confines of the Near East, the Greek world
has been steadily forcing itself upon the attention of the
older civilizations. Since its emergence from the 'Dark Ages'
around the middle of the eighth century, mainland Greece, as
well as the East Greeks of the Aegean islands and the coast
of Asia Minor, has been experiencing two centuries of political and cultural turbulence. The exuberantly decorated

'Orientalizing' pottery of the seventh century has already attested renewed contacts with Egypt and Syria-Palestine; by the sixth century there are Greek colonies established the length and breadth of the Mediterranean Sea, and the hundreds of Greek city-states are in the midst of experimentation with a variety of forms of government, including monarchy, tyranny, oligarchy, and incipient democracy. There is no national state; aside from the East Greeks of Asia Minor, who are first under the control of Lydia and then of Persia, the Greek city-states are all independent and are constantly involved in internal factional disputes or in attempts to infringe upon the independence of their neighbors. The major states of the period are Athens, under the leadership first of Solon and later of the tyrant Peisistratos; Sparta, which under its dual kingship is developing into a military power and exerting its control over the Peloponnesus; Syracuse, the most powerful of the colonies in the western Mediterranean; and the Ionian cities of Ephesus and Miletus, under local tyrants within the Persian satrapy of Lydia.

Farther to the east, India is in the late stages of the Vedic period (ca. 1000-500 B.C.E.) and has just emerged into its historic period, the early part of which is named the Śaiśunāga Period (642-413) from the ruling dynasty at Magadha. Urbanization of the Ganges Valley has begun, and the tribes are settling down into either monarchies (Ganges plain) or republics (foothills of the Himalayas and the Punjab). By 519 Gandhāra on the Indus has been included as one of the 22 satrapies of the Persian Empire. By the middle of the first millennium iron technology is attested throughout most areas of India.[4]

China is now in the second ('Eastern') half of the Chou dynasty (1122/1027-221) which had been established in the Yellow River basin by chariot warriors over the defeated Shang dynasty. After the transfer of the capital to Lo-yang in 771, the earlier subdivision of this Eastern Chou period is known as the Ch'un-ch'iu, or Spring and Autumn Period (722-481). A feudal society has been established with hundreds of tiny city-states ruled by an elite tyranny, nominally bound to the service of the emperor.[5]

## II. Nature of Fermentation: The Vintages

What has excited admiration and curiosity about the sixth century is not merely the fact of its intellectual activity, but its variety: Thought is rampant from east to west, but it is not the same thought.

> The Ionians had emerged from the age of
> myth and tradition and were speculating
> on the causes of cosmic order, the Buddha
> was in search of the permanent truths of
> life, and Zoroaster was concerned with
> the revelation of a god of life and good-
> ness. But, inheriting the revealed truths
> of earlier Hebrew prophecy and stimulated
> by the intellectual ferment of his age,
> Deutero-Isaiah declared that the world
> was created by One God, eternal in His
> Being, universal in His sovereignty ....[6]

This variety of course is an expression of the differing frames of reference specific to each area and people. None-theless, amid the diversity can be discerned a common theme: the search for a single principle to explain all phenomena.

### A. The Near East

The concentration on the nature and purpose of God and the question of restoration and redemption is unique to Israel, for the disastrous fall of Jerusalem at the hands of Nebuchad-nezzar forced the prophets of the exilic age to re-think some of the basic assumptions and assertions of their faith. The original geographical limitation of the covenant and the im-position of collective guilt was replaced by the concept of universal deity and individual responsibility. The loss of independence brought about a consideration of past and future in spiritual as well as political terms.

Within the Persian Empire Zoroaster makes an appearance, traditionally by the middle of the century, as the prophet of a religion which is essentially ethical monotheism. In reac-tion to the animal sacrifice and lack of moral content in the rituals surrounding the Indo-European deities of eastern Iran, Zoroaster seems to have created a totally new concept based on the duality of good and evil. Ahura-Mazda, representing a

sole primary deity, is conceived as involved in a constant
struggle with a demonic force of evil; and it is the responsibility of every individual to participate in this contest
for his soul.  Animal sacrifice is condemned, and fire, as
the symbol of truth, takes a prominent place in the ritual.
It is uncertain when and to what extent the Achaemenid rulers
considered themselves followers of Zoroaster.  In the Behistun
inscription Darius emphasizes that he has received control of
the empire through the aid of Ahura-Mazda, and he mentions no
other god in his inscriptions.[7]  The high moral tone of many
of his pronouncements also implies an adherence to the teachings of Zoroaster:  "Says Darius the King:  By the favor of
Ahura-Mazda I am of such a sort that I am a friend to right,
I am not a friend to wrong; it is not my desire that the weak
man should have wrong done to him by the mighty; nor is that
my desire, that the mighty man should have wrong done to him
by the weak."[8]

     As far as the former 'great powers' of the Near East
are concerned, during the height of Neo-Babylonian hegemony
there is evidence of active trade and prosperity and an ambitious building program, especially during the reign of
Nebuchadnezzar.  A strong antiquarian flavor pervades the
cultural activities of all the Chaldaean kings, however; and
Nabonidus is merely the last and most devout representative
in the search for monumental and literary authentication of
religious foundations.  A similar antiquarian emphasis had
been evident in Egypt from the very beginning of the Saïte
Dynasty.  At the same time that the pharaohs of the Twenty-
Sixth Dynasty were promoting commercial enterprises in the
Delta, the cultural output was being modeled after the preferred prototypes of the Old and Middle Kingdoms, a millennium
and more in the past.[9]

### B.  The Farther East

     In India the great epics Mahābhārata and Rāmāyana may
be dated to this period, but the literature remains an oral
mixture of history and legend which will be constantly edited
and re-worked into the early centuries C.E.  The earliest
Upanishads may have been composed during the eighth to the
sixth centuries; they represent the first formulation of an
attempt (already noticeable in the Brahmana commentaries on
the Vedic texts) to find some unifying principle within the
polytheistic cosmos.  Not worship or sacrifice but a pathway
of meditation is recommended as the only means to true knowledge and salvation.[10]  This new concept is more fully enunciated by the two important thinkers of the era, Siddhattha

Gautama, the founder of Buddhism (ca. 560), and Mahavira (ca. 540), the founder of Jainism. Gautama rejected his life as a minor Bengal prince for that of an ascetic, and then in his 36th year received a vision of what he would teach for the next 40 years of his life. In reaction to the many gods and the complicated and socially restrictive rituals of Brahmanism, he formulated a 'Gospel of Deliverance from life' which was open to all and was to prove a serious challenge to the caste system of Brahmanism. Future existence, or rather the final bliss of future non-existence, was determined by conduct: "All life is evil, dominated as it is by Desire, and the completest victory is the casting out of all desire for life. When this has been achieved the nightmare of existence is broken."[11] Jainism is similar to Buddhism in its renunciation of the world and its pleasures (and pains) but is regulated by more ascetic practices. Both preached a new ethical doctrine of *ahiṃsa,* or non-violence to living creatures, and both used local dialects in place of the Brahmanic language of Sanskrit.[12]

A far more practical view of the world is represented in China during the Ch'un-ch'iu Period in the person of Confucius, whose teachings are in many ways reminiscent of the moral maxims common to Middle Kingdom Egypt. Confucius was active in public service and held several administrative appointments. "His major attention was devoted to the problem of the organization of society in accordance with ethical principles"; therefore, he was not primarily a religious leader.[13] He did not think of himself as an originator but as a transmitter of principles which were 'the biddings of Heaven,' as he is quoted in the *Analects.*[14] Both God and King were considered as representing benevolent and paternal authority, with more intimate and personal worship reserved for the spirits of the dead.[15] Knowing man was regarded as more important than knowing nature, but *"traditionalism,* not democracy, was Confucius' master theme."[16]

### C. The Greek World

The Greek world during the sixth century shows the greatest diversity in cultural development, in both the monumental and intellectual sense. This is the high point for archaic sculpture and architecture, for black-figure and beginning red-figure pottery. This period also marks the development of law and the experimentation with various political systems. In literature lyric poetry has made its appearance, dealing with subjects as varied as love, nature, and politics; drama has begun, and attempts at geographical and historical works

in prose.  It is possible that the *Iliad* and *Odyssey* of
Homer have now been written down for the first time.  But
it is in the field of speculative thought that Greece makes
its mark in this century, with the Ionian school of natural
philosophers: Thales, Anaximander, and Anaximenes of Miletus, Heraclitus of Ephesus, Pythagoras of Samos, and Xenophanes of Colophon.  Quite aside from the quality of their
thought, they introduced into the vocabulary the abstractions
which were essential for thinking and classifying in terms
of general concepts.[17]

Aside from Pythagoras, who developed a religious brother-
hood along with his mathematical concepts, these thinkers are
basically secular in their outlook and monistic in their philosophy.  In their concern with the nature of the universe,
they seek the single, ultimate principle of physical (and,
in the case of Heraclitus, intellectual) causation.  The concept of a universal god had long been familiar to the Greeks
in the person of Zeus, but merely as the chief deity of the
Olympian pantheon.  Xenophanes scoffs at the anthropomorphic
nature of the Greek gods, while Pythagoras expounds the trans-
migration of souls.  It is only within the Orphic, Eleusinian,
and Dionysian mystery cults that a concern is shown for man's
relationship to god and the possibility of personal salvation;
but the sense of sin and redemption so prominent in Hebrew
thought is scarcely felt.  Prophecy finds a place in the Del-
phic oracle, but it is more of a political than a moral force;
revelation in the Hebrew sense does not exist.


### III.  Process of Distilling and Blending: 'Bottling' and Distribution


In general terms it might be said that the Greeks are
the great tasters and distillers of the age and serve as the
western distributors, while Persia serves as the great inland
watershed between the Near and Farther East.  The question
remains to what extent the influence of foreign contacts,
so visible in the art and architecture of Greece and Persia,
is reflected in the thought as well.  Some scholars do not
recognize any significant influence at all:  "The period
before 500 B.C. is predominantly one of preparation in comparative isolation.  The fundamental ideas in religion and
philosophy had been formulated and had developed into considerable systems.  In very few cases, however, had there
been any interaction."[18]  Astour, on the other hand, sees a
Semitic penetration of the Aegean so much earlier as to have

exercised a decisive effect on all that came later: "Long
before Hellenism imposed itself over the ancient civilizations of the East, Semitism had exercised no less an impact
upon the young civilization of Greece. Hellenism became
the epilogue of the Oriental civilizations, but Semitism
was the prologue of Greek civilization."[19]

The means for borrowing and exchange of ideas were
surely at hand, and while the product remains distinct, in
many cases the process of selection and rejection (digestion
and elimination) can be clearly discerned. It is unlikely
that the Greeks of the sixth century could or would have
sustained the prolonged fierce and relentless gaze directed
toward their God by the Hebrew prophets, for the Greeks
tended toward peripheral vision. In terms of our metaphor
of ferment, the Hebrews would drink only one brew, and that
preferably straight from the bottle; the Greeks would drink
anything once but from this experience developed a very dis-
criminating taste as to what they would keep in the house.

The clearest effects of foreign contact could be expected
to appear among the Greeks, for they are the ones who have
been most actively involved in trade, colonization and travel
during the seventh and sixth centuries. Their new trading
centers of Naucratis and Cyrene in Egypt and Libya and the
continuation of the older foundations of Al-Mina and Tell-
Sukas in Syria;[20] the indications of an active trade with
Attica in sixth-century Palestine;[21] the constant use of
Greek mercenary or conscripted soldiers by Lydia, Neo-Baby-
lonia, Egypt, and Persia, and the use of Ionian craftsmen in
the building projects of the various rulers[22]--all establish
an opportunity for cultural interchange. The more visible
effects of this mixture of influences have already occurred
in the seventh century, with the appearance of such decora-
tive motifs as the lotus and palmette and winged composite
creatures on the 'Orientalizing' pottery, the *kouros* figure
based on the Egyptian canon in sculpture, and the development
of the Doric and Ionic orders in architecture.[23] In literature too, earlier influences from the Near East are apparent
in the Homeric epics and in the works of Hesiod.[24]

West has discerned Babylonian, Egyptian, and Iranian
influence in the thought of the earliest Ionian philosophers.
The idea of metempsychosis, for example, was at home in
Greece, India, and Egypt. Anaximander's arrangement of the
world in concentric rings of sun, moon, stars, and earth
finds a close counterpart in the Persian conception of astro-
nomical order; and this wheel-theory is also reminiscent of
Ezekiel's vision of the throne of God with its wheeled

Cherubim.[25]  Thales himself, the father of geometry, is said
by Herodotus to be of Phoenician ancestry (I. 170).  West
suggests, however, that the early Greek philosophers were
most directly affected by Iranian thought, which he describes
as literally 'the gift of the Magi'.  He sees a strong probability that with Cyrus' annexation of Media in the middle of
the sixth century, the Median priestly group of the Magi may
have taken refuge abroad, both in India and in the West.[26]
The seaboard of Asia Minor, though nominally under the control of Persia, could offer the friendly Greek cities of
Miletus and Ephesus, with an independent Samos only 20 miles
offshore.

Iranian contact with India has long been assumed on
archaeological, linguistic, and documentary grounds.  Gandhāra on the Indus has already been mentioned as being included within the administrative organization of Darius and
probably played a major role as the channel of communication
between Iran and Central Asia.  Also, around 515 B.C.E.,
Darius authorized a voyage of discovery which established a
sea route between Persia and India.[27]  In the case of China,
too, a trade route from Asia to the cities of the Near East
is assumed to have been in use from very early times (the
later 'Silk Route').[28]  While technological innovations may
be thought to have originated from Western Asiatic societies
(metallurgical techniques, the introduction of the horse;
pottery techniques in the case of China),[29] there is no immediate evidence of influence in either direction as far as
concerns the religious and philosophical thought of the
sixth century.

In the case of Israel, Ackroyd points out the dangers
of too facile an assumption of Persian influence on Old Testament thought.[30]  "Old Testament language and literature,
religion and daily life, belong in [the] context [of the
rich life of the Near East], and the problem is often to
distinguish what is the special character of Old Testament
thought and material in the context of all that it shares
with the ancient world of the Near East."[31]  Ackroyd recognizes the possibility of external influence in the two areas
of dualism and angelology, as well as assured linguistic
influence in the later borrowing of Persian words.[32]  Literary references to the Greeks themselves (assuming the name
*Yawan* to be the equivalent of *Ionian*) appear in several
books of the Old Testament whose subject matter or actual
composition may be assigned to the sixth century,[33] but
there is otherwise no hint of Greek influence.

## IV.  Impulse of Fermentation:  The Yeast

While it is clear that the Greeks were particularly
open to influences from all quarters, and that trade connections made cultural exchange possible even as far east
as China, there is no real indication of any constant flow
and interchange, either of artifacts or of ideas, which
actively involved the Farther East.  There is no *one* visible
agent which can be held responsible for the inspiration,
imposition, or dissemination of cultural development even
in the West; still less, then, can a single agent be suggested for the stimulation of West and East together.  Yet
there is no doubt that 'original and unprecedented movements
of thought' were operating more or less simultaneously during
the sixth century in widely separated areas.[34]  Is it possible to find some common denominator, some political, economic,
or social factor not necessarily dependent upon an outside
agency, which can account for the ferment of the age?

The political and economic impulses may be considered
together, for as Burns says, "In all these regions ... it was
in a time of stress, violence and injustice, though also in
a society full of economic vitality, that the new movements
arose."[35]  The variety of political expression is represented
by the city-states of Greece, the imperial organization of
Persia, monarchies and republics in India, and in China a
feudal system of many small tyrannies under the nominal control of an emperor.  There is no one political system, then,
which can be considered peculiarly conducive to cultural
activity; to put it more accurately, the various states were
not in fact operating under a form of government common to
them all.

The economic factor offers a more promising field of
investigation, for trade is flourishing everywhere and there
is widespread urbanization and technological innovation.
Trade, however, has been an important element in other centuries beside the sixth and in itself does not deserve undue
emphasis.  Toynbee has combined geography and trade to serve
as an all-purpose explanation for the development of the
higher religions (including those of later periods as well):
The two areas of Syria and the Oxus-Jaxartes Basin serve as
potential traffic centers, a kind of 'round-about' where
traffic from all directions can be switched to any other
point.  "As a result of these [frequent and varied] encounters, each of these two peculiarly 'numeniferous' (religion-

bearing) regions had been included in the universal states of a number of different civilizations, and the exceptionally active intercourse between civilizations in these two areas explains the extraordinary concentration, within their limits, of the birthplaces of higher religions."[36] This helps to explain the generation and dissemination of individual religions but not contemporaneous gestation. Urbanization, so often associated with the development of trade, is not, however, a necessary condition or result of it. The cities of Greece, the Semitic Near East, and India, where the trade is apparently in the hands of independent merchants, may be contrasted to non-urban Persia and the feudal fortress towns of China, where the trade is under the control of the imperial ruler.

The decisive impulse may at first sight seem to reside in the introduction of some technological innovation, such as iron, coinage, or writing. But while iron technology had been introduced into northern India between 700 and 600 B.C.E.,[37] iron objects in China date only from the fourth, or (at the earliest) mid-fifth, century.[38] Fine Attic and Corinthian silver staters were in circulation throughout the Greek and Near Eastern world alongside the handsome gold darics introduced by Darius; but a regional silver coinage was in use in India no earlier than the fifth century, while the use of a regional copper currency did not become common in China until after 500 B.C.E.[39] Writing (alphabetic), like coinage, was a fairly recent development for the Greeks, Hebrews, and Persians; India for centuries seems to have depended upon an oral literature, for no script is attested until the third century. Chinese pictograms are known from the time of the Shang dynasty; they appear on bones for the purpose of divination and on bronze ritual vessels, but the script was not standardized until 213 B.C.E. upon the formation of the first empire.[40]

The movement of peoples for other than purposes of invasion may provide a clue to the activity of the sixth century, for this is a period of considerable shifting of populations, both voluntary and under duress. The Babylonian Captivity provides a unique example, but the Greek world too was filled with individuals and groups who had suffered temporary exile as a result of the interminable political squabbling within the city-states. Colonization, trade, and mercenary service provided more voluntary opportunities for travel and contact with other cultures; but while these varieties of experience were a constant of the Eastern Mediterranean world, there is no evidence that such similar movements as may have existed within India and China ever passed beyond their own boundaries.

There remain two social phenomena and one political peculiarity which are common to all the areas under discussion and which, separately or together, may be held responsible for the axial position of the sixth century in ancient history:

1. The rise of a middle class as represented by the merchant and the civil servant (and presuming with it the rise of the individual).

2. Reaction against a previous religious, social, or political system which has proved unsatisfactory.

3. A noticeable break or discontinuity between one phase and the next of the same or a related civilization or culture.

One of the ramifications of the trading activities of the sixth century was the rise of a merchant class no longer solely in the service of the state and no longer dependent upon land or birth for social and political recognition. The greater freedom of action afforded the merchant, and the greater risks entailed both in travel and in commercial transactions, as well as the opportunities for seeing and hearing new things, may have spawned greater independence of thought. Certainly some of the leading thinkers of the day were themselves merchants, such as Solon and Thales, while Confucius was a notable civil servant and administrator.[41] The practical aspects of Greek and Chinese philosophy were also strikingly similar; Solon and Thales were both numbered among the Seven Wise Men, whose advice tended to be political and utilitarian rather than moral.[42]

There were many aspects of the political and social conditions of the sixth century which invited reaction and reform; and while the conditions and the nature of the reaction might vary from one area to another, reaction there certainly was. The Buddha was reacting to the rigid strictures of Brahmanism,[43] Zoroaster to what he considered debasing features of earlier Iranian cults, the prophets of the exile to the disaster of the fall of Jerusalem and the loss of their spiritual and political center. The Ionian philosophers and the devotees of the mystery cults were reacting in very different ways to the sterility of the Olympian pantheon, while Solon and Confucius were reacting to social inequity and social disorder.[44]

    The final point is the one which I think is both a necessary and sufficient cause to account for the cultural developments of the sixth century:  a previous break in the continuity of those civilizations presently showing the most energetic intellectual activity.  Here I have been somewhat anticipated by Burn, who phrases it this way:  "... in all these areas it took about the same time for the first human civilizations to work themselves out, for the precocious bronze-age cultures to decline and fall, and for cultures of a new 'second generation' to arise from their ruins."[45] The sixth-century 'grand revision' is as amazingly widespread as the twelfth-century eclipse.  The clearest break is that of the Greek Dark Ages between the Mycenaean Age and the Hellenic Age, but similar hiatuses exist between the Vedic and Saiśunāga periods in India, between the Shang and Chou dynasties in China,[46] and between the arrival of the Medes in Iran and their eventual freedom from vassalage to Assyria and the formation of Media.  Two points should be emphasized: None of these new cultures or states is really new in the sense of developing out of a cultural void; and all are in some way a continuation of or are related to the culture they later emerge from or usurp--there is some sense of in-herited traditions.

    The older continuous civilizations of the Near East can serve as a control to test the thesis that the cultures of the sixth century which demonstrate the greatest intellec-tual activity are those which have experienced a break in their continuity.  Egypt during the Saïte Dynasty and Babylon under the Chaldaean kings were trying to recover the purity of their archaic beginnings and thus there was no room for innovation or speculation.[47]  While Confucius and the Buddha were also looking to the past, their intent was not quite so fossilized:  The Buddha was seeking a way of transcending both present and future, and Confucius was attempting to adapt traditional ways to serve (or counteract) the problems of the present.  The Hebrew prophets were also seeking a re-turn to a purer past.  But unlike that of Babylon and Egypt, the Hebrew past had no real existence in any monumental or documentary sense; Israel's quest for its purer beginnings resulted in the creation of a spiritual past which ensured itself a future even without the recovery of political in-dependence.

# NOTES

1. Jack Finegan, *The Archeology of World Religions.*
*The Background of Primitivism, Zoroastrianism, Hinduism,
Jainism, Buddhism, Confucianism, Taoism, Shinto, Islam,
and Sikhism* (Princeton University, 1952); *Zoroaster* (hypo-
thetical date) ca. 570-493 B.C.E. (pp. 77-83); *Buddha* ca.
567-487 (p. 248); *Confucius* ca. 551-478 (pp. 343-347);
*Lao Tzu* (Taoism) traditionally a sixth-century contemporary
of Confucius, arguably ca. 300 or 240 B.C.E. on the basis
of the grammar and style of the *Tao Te Ching* (p. 382).
The dates vary somewhat from scholar to scholar, but there
is no serious disagreement about the sixth-century milieu
except in the case of Zoroaster as a historical figure.

2. Mary F. Gyles, *Pharaonic Policies and Administration,
663-323 B.C.* (University of North Carolina, 1959 [The James
Sprunt Studies in History and Political Science, Vol. 41]),
35-36. Anthony Spalinger ("Egypt and Babylonia: A Survey
[c. 620 B.C.-550 B.C.]," *Studien zur altägyptischen Kultur*
5 [1977], 221-244) gives the most recent review of this
intercourse, which he characterizes in a laconic comment
(p. 222): "... from the latter half of the seventh century
B.C. to the first quarter of the sixth, Egypt's policy in
the Levant was commercial in intent, benevolent in application, laissez-faire in nature, and short in duration."

3. Richard N. Frye, *The Heritage of Persia* (London:
Weidenfeld and Nicolson, 1962), 78: "... an important date
in world history for in a sense it marked the end of a long
tradition in the land of Sumer and Akkad and the beginning
of a new union of the Mesopotamian lowlands with the plateau
which would continue for centuries."

4. Finegan, *Archeology of World Religions*, p. 234;
Luigi Pareti, assisted by Paolo Brezzi and Luciano Petech,
*History of Mankind: Cultural and Scientific Development.*
Volume II. *The Ancient World 1200 BC to AD 500* (in two
volumes; London: Allen and Unwin, 1965), Vol. II, Part I,
pp. 40-42; Bridget Allchin, "The Iron Age and the Beginnings
of History," in *The Birth of Indian Civilization: India and
Pakistan Before 500 B.C.* (Baltimore: Penguin Books, 1968),
207-232, esp. pp. 212-213:

But by the end of the Painted Grey ware
period a more or less uniform culture,
whose hallmark is the black lustrous
pottery known as N.B.P. or Northern
Black Polished ware, extended from the
lower Ganges to the Punjab. This culture provided the milieu for the life
of Gautama the Buddha, and Mahāvīra,
the founder of the Jain sect, no less
than for such dynasties as the Śaiśunāgas,
the Nandas and the Mauryas; and for the
development of the characteristic Indian
script, the *Brāhmi lipi*, and of Indian
coinage. [Script and coinage appear *after*
500 B.C.E.: see p. 215.]

5.  Richard L. Walker, *The Multi-State System of Ancient
China* (Hamden, CT:  Shoe String, 1953), 5-7; Kwang-chih Chang,
"Relative Chronologies of China to the End of Chou," in *Chro-
nologies in Old World Archeology* (2nd ed.; ed. Robert W.
Ehrich; University of Chicago, 1965), 503-526, esp. pp. 505-
506; Chang, *The Archaeology of Ancient China* (3rd ed.; Yale
University, 1977), 384:  *Table 15*, "Some Aspects of Inter-
related Changes of Chinese Civilization in its Formative
Stages"; D. Howard Smith, *Confucius* (New York:  Charles
Scribner's Sons, 1973), 11:  Map showing China at the time
of Confucius, with the absorption of the smaller feudal
states by the larger--only 15 such entities existed by Confucius' day (p. 36); Yu-lan Fung, *A History of Chinese Philosophy*.  Vol. I.  *The Period of the Philosophers (from the
Beginnings to circa 100 B.C.)* (trans. Derk Bodde; Princeton
University, 1952 [Chinese original, 1931; first Eng. ed.
1937]), xvii (historical introduction by translator):

It was an age of uncertainty and of expansion, both geographically and intellectually
.... In this age of unrest there began toward
the end of the Ch'un Ch'iu period, the Period
of the Philosophers, as it is called in this
book, a period inaugurated by *Confucius (551-
479)*, and largely coincident in time with
what in political history is known as the
period of Warring States.

6.  C. F. Whitley, *The Exilic Age* (Westport, CT:  Green-
wood, 1975 [reprint of 1958 ed.]), 152; cf. D. Winton Thomas,
"The Sixth Century B.C.:  A Creative Epoch in the History of
Israel," *JSS* 6 (1961), 33-46.

7.  Frye, *Heritage of Persia,* p. 90:

> One cannot say that Zoroaster himself
> 'invented' Ahura Mazda .... Just as with
> Old Persian cuneiform writing, so with the
> god Ahura Mazda, it is under Darius that
> both appear in abundance. Ahura Mazda,
> however, is the god of the Aryans, as the
> Elamite version of the Behistun inscrip-
> tion (IV. 62) says.

8.  On Darius' Tomb at Naqsh-i-Rustam (Finegan, *Archeology of World Religions,* p. 95). See now the authoritative German edition by Walther Hinz, "Die dreisprachige untere Grabin-
schrift des Darius" (akkadische Fassung von Rykle Borger) in
*Altiranische Funde und Forschungen* (Berlin: Walter de Gruyter,
1969), 53-62 and Taf. 18a. This is the first publication of
all three versions (Old Persian, Elamitic, and Akkadian) of
the lower inscription (DNb) on Darius' Tomb, on both sides of
the entrance. The German translation reads (Sect. 8, p. 57):

> Kündet Darius der König: Nach dem Willen
> des Allweisen Herrn bin ich so geartet, dass
> ich das Recht liebe, das Unrecht hasse. Ich
> will nicht haben, dass der Schwache des Star-
> ken wegen Unrecht erleide; aber will ich auch
> nicht haben, dass der Starke des Schwachen
> wegen Unrecht erleide.

*Ahura-Mazda* appears in all three texts as the original
of what the German translates as 'Allweiser Herr'. The reference to the protection of the weak from the strong seems
to go back ultimately to the prologue of the Laws of Hammurabi
(*ANET*, 164, lines 37-39 of col. i):

> to destroy the wicked and the evil,
> that the strong might not oppress the weak

--but the suggestion that the strong have a similar right to
protection from the weak is a unique pronouncement.

9.  John A. Wilson, *The Culture of Ancient Egypt* (University of Chicago, 1951 [orig. *The Burden of Egypt*]), 293-
296, esp. pp. 294-295:

> A marked reaction appeared in the age
> following 720 B.C., with a deliberate
> archaism manifesting itself chiefly in
> art. The spiritual emptiness of the

day sought compensation by seeking out
ancient models and copying them faithfully. For the most part, the artists
avoided the Empire and went back to the
Old and Middle Kingdoms for their inspiration, back to the ages when the
Egyptian spirit had been most vigorous
and most native.

and p. 296:

This attempt to escape an inglorious
present was not confined to ·Egypt. Over
in Babylonia, Nabonidus, a contemporary
of the Twenty-Sixth Dynasty, was deeply
and reverently absorbed in the antiquity
of his country, studying ancient records
and attempting to restore temples with
fidelity to the old plan.

See also G. Goossens, "Les recherches historiques à
l'époque néo-babylonienne," *RA* 42 (1948), 153:

... la recherche des documents anciens,
loin d'être propre au règne de Nabonide,
est générale à l'époque néo-babylonienne,
et ... ce n'est pas la passion de l'arché-
ologie qui pousse les souverains à l'entre-
prendre, c'est une nécessité religieuse.

10.  Finegan, *Archeology of World Religions*, p. 136.

11.  O. E. Burton, *A Study in Creative History. The
Interaction of the Eastern and Western Peoples to 500 B.C.*
(London:  Allen & Unwin, 1932), 230.

12.  Finegan, *Archeology of World Religions*, pp. 202-213;
W. Norman Brown, "Mythology of India," in *Mythologies of the
Ancient World* (ed. Samuel N. Kramer; Doubleday Anchor [A229]
1961), 317: Pāli for Buddhism, Ardhamagadhi for Jainism.

13.  Finegan, p. 349.

14.  Finegan, p. 350; Fung, *History of Chinese Philosophy* I, p. 7, quoting from *Lun Yü* [*Analects*], III. 14:  "Chou
had the advantage of surveying the two preceding dynasties.
How replete is its culture!  I follow Chou."  See also p. 48,
quoting from *Lun Yü* VII. 1:  "A transmitter and not a creator,
a believer in and lover of antiquity."

15. Derk Bodde, "Myths of Ancient China" (Kramer, *Mythologies*), 369-408.

16. John M. Koller, *Oriental Philosophies* (New York: Charles Scribner's, 1970), 203; Joseph R. Levenson and Franz Schurmann, *China: An Interpretive History from the Beginnings to the Fall of Han* (University of California, 1969), 46.

17. A. R. Burn, *The Lyric Age of Greece* (London: Edward Arnold, 1960), 337.

18. Burton, *Study in Creative History*, pp. 312-313.

19. Michael C. Astour, *Hellenosemitica: An Ethnic and Cultural Study in West Semitic Impact on Mycenaean Greece* (2nd ed.; Leiden: E. J. Brill, 1967), 361. The same idea is expressed in a different way by Cyrus H. Gordon ("Homer and Bible: The Origin and Character of East Mediterranean Literature," *HUCA* 26 [1955], 43-108; p. 47): "... the literatures (and for that matter the entire civilizations) of the Greeks and Hebrews are parallel structures built upon the same East Mediterranean foundation."

20. John Boardman, *The Greeks Overseas: The Archaeology of their Early Colonies and Trade* (2nd ed.; Penguin Books, 1973): Naucratis (pp. 114-140); Cyrene (pp. 151-157); Al-Mina (pp. 37-55); Tell-Sukas (pp. 52-53); P. J. Riis, *Sūkās I: The North-east Sanctuary and the First Settling of the Greeks in Syria and Palestine* (Publications of the Carlsberg Expedition to Phoenicia 1; Copenhagen: Munksgaard, 1970), 126-175.

21. Dominique Auscher, "Les relations entre la Grèce et la Palestine avant la conquête d'Alexandre," *VT* 17 (1967), 8-30, esp. chart on pp. 12-13.

22. J. Naveh, "The Excavations at Meṣad Ḥashavyahu: Preliminary Report," *IEJ* 12 (1962), 89-113; C. Nylander, *Ionians in Pasargadae. Studies in Old Persian Architecture* (2 vols.; Stockholm: Almquist & Wiksell, 1970): H. W. Parke, *Greek Mercenary Soldiers from the Earliest Times to the Battle of Ipsus* (Oxford, 1933).

23. Ekrem Akurgal, "Early Greek Art and its Connections with the Near East," in *The Art of Greece: Its Origins in the Mediterranean and the Near East* (trans. Wayne Dynes from orig. Ger. ed. 1966; New York: Crown, 1968), Ch. VI, 162-222; J. N. Coldstream, "Oriental Influences," in *Geometric Greece* (London: Ernest Benn Limited, 1977), Ch. 15, 358-366.

24. W. F. Albright, "Some Oriental Glosses on the Homeric Problem," *AJA* 54 (1950), 162-176; Gordon, "Homer and Bible"; Peter Walcot, *Hesiod and the Near East* (Cardiff: University of Wales, 1966), and "The Comparative Study of Ugaritic and Greek Literatures I-III," *UF* 1 (1969), 111-118; 2 (1970), 273-275; 4 (1972), 129-130. James D. Muhly ("Homer and the Phoenicians: The Relations between Greece and the Near East in the Late Bronze and Early Iron Ages," *Berytus* 19 [1970], 19-64, esp. pp. 58-59) refuses to recognize Semitic precursors [cf. note 19 above) or Ugaritic influence on the Homeric epics; he does, however, accept the "existence of oriental influence upon Greek civilization from the time of Hesiod on."

25. M. L. West, *Early Greek Philosophy and the Orient* (Oxford, 1971), 88-89, 96. Contrast W. T. Stace, *A Critical History of Greek Philosophy* (London: Macmillan, 1920), 17: "The whole character of Greek philosophy is European and un-oriental to the backbone"; and John Burnet, *Early Greek Philosophy* (4th ed.; London: Adam and Charles Black, 1930), 24: "... the Greeks did not borrow either their philosophy or their science from the East."

26. West, p. 241.

27. Frye, *Heritage of Persia,* p. 117; Hdt. IV. 44.

28. Grahame Clark, *World Prehistory: A New Outline* (2nd ed.; Cambridge at the University Press, 1969), 222.

29. Henry Hodges, *Technology in the Ancient World* (London: Allen Lane, 1970), 218.

30. Peter R. Ackroyd, *Exile and Restoration* (Philadelphia: Westminster, 1968), 7-12; *Israel under Babylon and Persia* (Oxford University, 1970), 340-344.

31. *Israel,* pp. 341-342.

32. *Ibid.,* pp. 342, 344.

33. Gen 10 :2; Isa 66:19; Ezek 27:13, 19; Dan 8:21, 10:20, 11:2. Riis, *Sūkās I,* pp. 133-137; Albright, "Oriental Glosses," pp. 171-172; Edouard Dhorme, "Les peuples issus de Japhet," in *Recueil Édouard Dhorme* (Paris, 1951), 167-189.

34. Burn, *Lyric Age of Greece,* p. 327.

35. *Ibid.,* p. 329.

36. Arnold J. Toynbee, *A Study of History* (orig. ed. Oxford University, 1947; abridgement of Volumes VII-X by D. C. Somervell, Oxford University, 1957), Vol. IX (Somervell abr.), 144-145.

37. See note 4 above; R. J. Forbes, "The Early Story of Iron," in *Studies in Ancient Technology*, Vol. IX (2nd ed.; Leiden: E. J. Brill, 1972), Ch. III, 187-288; p. 248.

38. *Fourth century:* Forbes, p. 252; Hodges, *Technology,* pp. 224, 226. *Fifth century:* Chang, *Archaeology,*[3] p. 352, concerning the first occurrence of iron implements in graves of the Warring States period. He goes on to postulate a still earlier date, however:

> It seems very likely that the emergence
> of iron metallurgy as a major industry
> for toolmaking should be placed in the
> sixth century B.C. at the latest, although
> the techniques probably were not perfected
> and widely used until the fifth century,
> as far as archaeological evidence is con-
> cerned.

In any case, the production is limited to implements and does not include weapons.

39. Allchin, *Birth of Indian Civilization,* p. 215; Pareti, *History of Mankind* II, Part II, pp. 401-403.

40. Pareti, pp. 375-376; Chang, *Archaeology,*[3] pp. 211-214.

41. Fung (*History of Philosophy* I, pp. 8-15) outlines the steps in the gradual emancipation from the elaborately graded hierarchy of the feudal aristocracy that is taking place during the Chou period; see esp. pp. 12-13, where he emphasizes the changing status of the serfs and the merchant class:

> ... it is evident that the collapse of
> feudalism was brought about through this
> continual increase of economic power of
> the former agricultural serfs and of the
> merchants .... the breakdown of the sys-
> tem of the hereditary revenues [and of
> the system of the land division]; the
> emancipation of the common people; and
> the amassing of private fortunes, were

the outstanding changes in the economic
structure during the ancient period.

42.  Bruno Snell, *Die Entdeckung des Geistes: Studien
zur Entstehung des europäischen Denkens bei den Griechen*
(4th ed.; Göttingen:  Vandenhoeck & Ruprecht, 1975), 154;
277:

> Die Sieben Weisen ... appellieren denn
> auch mehr an den gesunden Sinn für das
> Nützliche, als dass sie Moral predigten
> .... sie waren in der Hauptsache noch
> praktisch Wirkende, die meisten im Staat,
> als Gesetzgeber, Herrscher oder Ratgeber ...

43.  That the reaction is in fact to the problems of
urbanization is suggested by Walter A. Fairservis, Jr., *The
Roots of Ancient India:  The Archaeology of Early Indian
Civilization* (New York:  Macmillan, 1971), 379:  "For basically early Buddhism seems to be both a protest against
and a direction out of a complex way of life in which ambition, social inequality, civil strife, hunger, disease,
temptation, superstition, riches, poverty, and the like
are prevalent."  It is the nobility and the upper classes
(including the merchants) who actually become Buddhists,
for "Buddhism is a reaction to an order outside the seasonal
harmonies of rural life."

A similar anti-urban polemic has been postulated by
William W. Hallo (NEH Summar Seminar 1978) as being one
root of the story of the Tower of Babel in Gen 11.

44.  Fung (*History of Philosophy* I, p. 14) presents
Confucius as a reactionary in every sense--as a conservative
who tries to supply reasons for upholding the ancient institutions that are being threatened by the new political and
economic developments.

45.  Burn, *Lyric Age of Greece*, p. 3.

46.  Chang, *Archaeology*,[3] pp. 383-386 and *Table 15* on
p. 384:

> ... the 'conquest' in 1122 B.C., whereby
> the Chou replaced the Shang as China's
> masters, cannot be called a conquest by
> an alien people having an alien culture.
> It was, in fact, from all evidence, no
> more than an internal struggle for power

(p. 383) .... The latter part of the
Western Chou and the beginning of the
Eastern Chou [=Spring-Autumn], the
period covered by the Middle Chou style,
was between the classical 'Archaic' Yin
[=late Shang] and Chou civilization and
the youthful, spirited Eastern Chou ren-
aissance in style and revolution in
technology and economy. The Middle Chou
period thus represents a transitional
stage wherein the classical styles began
to give way to the innovations in all
Chinese territory (p. 385) .... at the
beginning of the Eastern Chou, Chinese
society underwent fundamental changes
in every archaeologically pertinent
respect, and this must mark a trans-
formational process of the first magnitude, whatever label we come to use to
capture the spirit of that process
(p. 386).

47. See note 9 above.

# THE POLITICAL TENSIONS REFLECTED
# IN EZRA-NEHEMIAH

Carl Schultz
Houghton College

The internal situation within Judaea, following the return in 539 B.C.E. from the Babylonian captivity, can only be understood as the details surrounding the deportation and the exile itself are considered. While the destruction of Jerusalem in 587 B.C.E. was tragic, it was a watershed, a significant turning point in the history of Israel. The destruction of the temple[1] and the termination of the Davidic dynasty had a profound influence on the peoples' thinking, since they had subscribed to the continuity of the Davidic dynasty[2] and the invulnerability of Jerusalem.[3] The religious faith that emerged from the exilic period and continued to be developed in post-exilic time was determined to a great extent by the collapse of the city, the temple, and the Davidic dynasty.

## I.  Comparative Assessments of the Fall

That Jerusalem was captured by Nebuchadnezzar in March 597 B.C.E. is now established on the basis of both biblical[4] and Babylonian[5] evidence. Another ten years, however, transpired before the Babylonians returned and destroyed the city. Zedekiah, appointed king of Judah by Nebuchadnezzar, is portrayed by Jeremiah as being unable to cope during these ten intervening years with the internal struggles between the pro-Babylonian and the pro-Egyptian factions within Jerusalem.[6] Encouraged by the Egyptians and disregarding Jeremiah's requested advice, Zedekiah rebelled against Babylon.[7] Nebuchadnezzar responded quickly, returned with his army, and besieged the city. Jerusalem resisted for some eighteen months, but then capitulated and was destroyed in 587 B.C.E.[8]

The extent of the devastation associated with this fall of Jerusalem is uncertain. Under debate are both the matters of the geographic extent of the destruction and the numerical proportions of the deportations.

The Chronicler seems to picture this catastrophe of 587 B.C.E as complete, resulting in either the destruction or the exile of the people so that the land was left empty and desolate for seventy years to "enjoy its sabbaths."[9] This, as we shall see later, is to locate the hope and future of the nation with the exiles.

Torrey reacted negatively to this assessment of the Chronicler, maintaining that "the Babylonian exile of the Judaean Hebrews ... was in reality a small and relatively insignificant affair...."[10] Such an extreme position can now be dismissed quickly. In addition to the biblical claims,[11] the archaeological evidence seems to indicate devastation of such a magnitude that Albright refers to it as a complete destruction of Judah. Not only was Jerusalem destroyed, but many other Judaean cities and important centers were leveled.[12]

The number of people deported is difficult to determine. Using the regnal years of Nebuchadnezzar, Jeremiah indicates a three-fold deportation totaling 4,600 persons,[13] while the Book of Kings gives two sets of figures for the first (597 B.C.E.) deportation (10,000[14] and 8,000[15] persons) but simply makes a very general statement about the second deportation (587 B.C.E)--"rest of the people ... the captain of the guard carried into exile,"[16] while allowing some of the poorest in the land to remain.[17]

Ackroyd, while acknowledging the above data, concludes that the devastation and depopulation were by no means complete. He contends that there is biblical and archaeological evidence for continuity of existence. Not only were the "poor of the land" left but even the alleged removal of the landed citizens and leaders was at best only partial. Further, those who had fled and hid themselves, returned as indicated by Jeremiah.[18] Even though many if not most of the cities had been destroyed this did not prevent a certain measure of reoccupation which would have left little archaeological evidence.[19] In short, there was a continuity of existence; there was a community of people left in Judaea which engaged in a great deal of activity.[20]

If so, however, our information about those who remained is extremely limited.[21] Why? The answer seems to be that

these people have been totally rejected by God and are of
no further historical significance. The issue confronting
us then in the Chronicler's account is not simply a matter
of historical reconstruction, i.e., how many people remained
in the land in contrast to those who were deported and where
did these survivors live?--but it is rather a matter of the
theological implications of the data, i.e., the importance
of the exiles to the post-exilic community and the insignifi-
cance, if not the liability, of the survivors who remained
in the land. Thus the Chronicler can state that the land was
depopulated and left veritably empty.

Not only the Chronicler but also the Deuteronomist is
apparently unconcerned with the group who remained behind.
He declares that some of the poor of the land were left to
be vinedressers and plowmen but Judah (!) was taken into
exile out of its land.[22] This statement can be taken to
convey the impression which the destruction of the state
made rather than to give an accurate description of it.[23]
It is equally possible, however, to regard it as having its
basis in the position that those who were deported were the
true remnant of Judah while those who remained in the land
were of little or no significance.[24]

It would seem that the *dallat hā'āreṣ* did not impress
the Deuteronomist relative to their piety or religious knowledge. According to Jeremiah, the *dallîm* "have no sense for
they do not know the way of the Lord, the law of their God."[25]
The future of the nation then was not to be found in those
people who remained.

This fact is confirmed in the continuing Deuteronomistic
narrative of 2 Kings 25. In five verses (22-26) it gives us
the brief history of the community under Gedaliah, his assassination and the flight of the community to Egypt. Our attention is then diverted to the release of Jehoiachin (27-30)
and by the same token, to the Babylonian exile.[26]

In addition to the Chronicler and the Deuteronomist the
Prophets also share this negative evaluation of the remnant
remaining in the land. In Jeremiah it finds expression in the
vision of the two baskets of figs. The bad figs, so bad they
could not be eaten, represent those who remain in the land or
fled to Egypt. The good figs, very good, are those who are
already exiles in Babylon but will be brought back and established. The future of Judah lay with the exiles.[27]

The presumption of those who remained in the land, that
it would be through them that renewal would result, predicating

their claim on the promise given to Abraham, was emphatically rejected by Ezekiel.[28] He denounces such a claim and warns of judgment:

> Say this to them, Thus says the Lord God:
> As I live, surely those who are in the
> waste places shall fall by the sword; and
> him that is in the open field, I will give
> to the beasts to be devoured; and those who
> are in the strongholds and in caves shall
> die by pestilence. And I will make their
> land a desolation and a waste; and her
> proud might shall come to an end, and the
> mountains of Israel shall be so desolate
> that none will pass through.[29]

This sharp contrast between the exiles and those who remained in the land is also discernible in Isaiah. It is the community in exile that is the personification of Zion and Jerusalem[30] with whom is the hope of restoration.[31] By contrast the land of Judaea is desolate and waste, perhaps an allusion also to the inhabitants who remained.[32]

It would appear then that this evaluation of the two groups--the exiles receiving a positive assessment while those remaining in the land receive a negative one--is a common biblical assessment. The Chronicler does not stand alone here. Such an appraisal was predicated upon a belief that renewal and restoration would come by the way of the exiles.

As the book of Ezra opens, the description given by the Chronicler remains--Judaea is a desolate land and she must be repeopled and restored by the returning exiles. It is they who have experienced God's judgment and as such are now open to God's grace upon which a new beginning can be made.[33]

A tension develops between those who have returned and those who have remained. It is this fact which will concern us in the balance of this paper. We will endeavor to show that this tension was not primarily religious but rather essentially political.

## II. The Returnees

An important feature of Ezra-Nehemiah is the lists it contains.[34] These lists seem to have both cultic and political purposes. Of particular significance to this paper is the Golah list of Ezra 2 and Neh 7.[35]

*Composition*

This list includes laymen, priests, levites, singers, gate keepers, temple servants,[36] Solomon's servants, and those without proof of ancestry. It also records various contributions to the temple.

The simple introductory statement of this list is that these were the persons who accompanied Zerubbabel back to Jerusalem. However, it appears to be an amalgamation of lists since some names are oriented by families, other names by localities, and still others by class.[37] Galling organizes the list as follows: 2b-20 are family names, 21-33 are place names; 34-35, another family list; 36-37, place names; and 38, the family of Senaah. The lack of order in this arrangement perhaps indicates successive supplements to the list.[38] However, the arrangement should not be viewed as haphazard or proof that the sections existed independently.[39]

*Purpose*

While several explanations have been given for the purpose of this list, none have been completely satisfactory. Among these explanations are the following:

1. C. C. Torrey: The list is fictitious, a creation of the Chronicler.[40]

2. W. Rudolph: A genuine list of returnees, composed of different registers covering the period from 539-515 B.C.E.[41]

3. W. F. Albright: A list compiled by Nehemiah (ca. 440 B.C.E.), hence the revised form of the census of Judah begun at the Restoration. It represents natural increase and the continuing influx of immigrants.[42]

4.  A. Alt:  A list compiled by Zerubbabel for the purpose
    of determining land rights.  With some 40,000 people to
    be repatriated, this question of land rights would be
    acute.[43]

5.  G. Hölscher:  A tax list drawn up by the Persians.[44]  The
    emphasis upon geographic locations and upon numbers would
    give some support to this position.[45]

6.  K. Galling:  A legitimation list furnished to Tattenai
    in connection with the investigation of the temple build-
    ing activities.  Behind it looms the controversy between
    Samaria and Jerusalem.  The list made clear the ecclesi-
    astical and legal structure of the golah community, being
    a register of the religious community.  The people named
    therein are the members of the amphictyonical *qāhāl*, led
    by the twelve men heading the list.[46]

This position gains some support from Talmon's research
relative to the word *yaḥad* which appears in Zerubbabel's answer to those neighboring tribes who had volunteered their
service for the building of the temple.[47]  Talmon shows that
this word as used here (and elsewhere) is a noun and is a
synonym for *qāhāl*.  Reading it accordingly, Zerubbabel would
have said:  "We, the *congregation*, will build...."  Talmon
insists that this answer clearly reflects a religious or
communal delineation.  Only the members of the *qāhāl* can
assist in the building of the temple.[48]

While recognizing the religious significance of this
list, it seems to me that the political aspect should not be
overlooked.  In the Hebrew version of the edict to Cyrus,[49]
the responsibility to build the temple is delegated to a
specific group--the exiles.[50]  In the passage cited above,
Zerubbabel so understands the edict for he declares that it
is the exiles who will do the building.[51]

It is clear that there was tension between the Samarian
leadership and the returning exiles.  Tattenai in his investigation did demand the names of the men involved in the temple building.[52]  Then in his letter to Darius he stated that
the names had been requested for the king's information.[53]
Further to indicate the care that had been used, some dubious
cases were referred to the Persian-appointed governor who
made disposition of them.[54]  These builders were then legitimate.

Comparing this proclamation of Cyrus with the authorization permitting the rebuilding of the Eanna sanctuary, some

interesting parallels become apparent. Weisberg calls this
Neo-Babylonian text "A Craftsmen's Charter," seeing in it a
guarantee of the positive rights of the builders of that
sanctuary.[55] These builders, while maintaining independence,
do so within the framework of the state and have taken a
loyalty oath to Cyrus. They are restricted to work only on
the sanctuary of Eanna. Weisberg sees this as a means of
speeding the work but also as a protection of their rights,
giving them a monopoly in the building. Further it would
also be a means of preventing the imitation of design.[56]

Applying this data to the building of the temple in
Jerusalem, Zerubbabel's actions become more intelligible as
do the inquiries of Tattenai. Only those who have been granted the right to build, may do so. The list of names is provided to give the legitimate builders. Further it assures
that there are sufficient means and personnel to complete the
temple. While independent, the temple builders are nevertheless responsible to the Persian government. Every effort was
made then to maintain political legitimacy in building.

Actually the proclamation of Cyrus to the Jews, made in
539 B.C.E., was promulgated four years before his agreement
with the artisans of Eanna. Weisberg suggests that the earlier attention to the Jerusalem temple may have been due to
Cyrus' policy of securing his outlying defenses. He wished
to gain the allegiance of his subjects in those areas first.
Only then did he turn his attention to sanctuaries in Mesopotamia.[57] Thus we read concerning Cyrus that in: "the
·region from ... as far as Ashur and Susa, Agade, Eshnunna,
the towns Zamban, Me-Turnu, Der as well as the regions of
the Gutians, I ... established for them permanent sanctuaries."[58]

While the Golah list deserves more attention relative
to an analysis of persons and places, the above limited treatment relative to its purpose will suffice for this paper.
Clearly the builders of a temple had a monopoly, and in the
case of the Jerusalem temple it was composed of the returning
exiles. No outside assistance was allowed or wanted. Even
as in the Craftsmen's Charter, so in the Golah list ancestry
is traced, frequently in terms of skill.[59] However, it is
possible that the trades are not being designated *per se*, but
simply family connections. As Weisberg observes, it is possible for people to bear names that do not necessarily indicate their skills.

## III.  The Opposition

To understand the internal situation within Judaea
following 539 B.C.E., attention must not only be given to
those who returned but to the antagonists already in the
land.  This is true not only of the rebuilding of the temple
but also of the rebuilding of the walls by Nehemiah a century
later.  In Ezra 4 the Chronicler combines these events.  It
seems to me that the Chronicler is not confused here as some
would indicate, but is rather deliberately telescoping the
material to emphasize the hostility and the opposition.  The
events are not the points of significance but the common opposition.

Relative to the rebuilding of the temple, the Chronicler
uses the opposition to explain the long interval between its
beginning (second month of the second year after the return)[60]
and its completion some twenty years later (third day of the
month of Adar in the sixth year of the reign of Darius the
king).[61]  This picture is exceedingly more complex than that
presented in Haggai and Zechariah where the delay in the temple completion is attributed to the lethargy of the people.

According to the Chronicler, the identity of the opponents to the rebuilding of the temple is as follows:

1.  Adversaries of Judah and Benjamin who are equated
with the returning exiles.[62]

2.  Descendants of those whom Esarhaddon had settled in
Palestine.[63]  Nothing is directly known of such a settlement
Ackroyd contends that the Chronicler has confused the king
of Assyria of the time of Samaria's fall with the later Esarhaddon (681-669 B.C.E.).[64]  However, such a resettlement may
be referred to in Isaiah.[65]  Further, the inscriptions of
Esarhaddon indicate that he invaded the west where he cam-
paigned vigorously, even conquering Egypt.  After he had taken
Sidon, he apparently settled people there from the east.[66]
Assuming such a resettlement of people in Palestine, Myers
suggests that they came south to fill the vacuum left by the
Neo-Babylonian conquest of Judah.[67]  Reference is also made
in this chapter to the resettlements of Osnappar.[68]  Even
though the context of this resettlement reference has to do
with the rebuilding of the walls rather than the rebuilding
of the temple, it should be considered here.  Osnappar is

perhaps Ashurbanipal (669-627/6 B.C.E.).[69]  We know that
he received the formal submission of twenty-two kings of
the west.  While there is no reference to the resettlement
of people, he seems to have continued the Assyrian practice
as reflected from his exile of captives from Kirbit to
Egypt.[70]  Malamat associates this resettlement with the
suppression of an Elamite revolt around 642 B.C.E.[71]

3. *'am hā'āreṣ.*[72] This term, used some 70 times in
the Old Testament, has been variously interpreted.[73]  The
inclination has been to give it a fixed, a technical meaning,
but Nicholson has shown that it is a very general term varying in meaning from context to context.[74]  For instance, as
used by Haggai it is parallel to *šě'ērît hā'ām*[75] and as such
could refer to both those who returned from captivity as well
as those who initially escaped the captivity.  These groups
are urged to persevere in the building of the temple.  Hence
the term in the Haggai context seems to mean land-owning
citizens with full rights.

By contrast, the Chronicler in the Ezra passage uses
this term either ethnically to refer to the people of the
neighboring country, Samaria, or contemptuously to designate
the religious illiterate.  These cannot assist in the building
of the temple.

Another possibility needs to be considered.  If the term
designates the rural population[76] then we may have here a kind
of tension between the urban and rural centers of power.[77]

Finally, following Ackroyd, the Chronicler may be using
this term to designate the ruling groups in Samaria who claim
to have accepted the worship of Yahweh but who are in fact
engaged in intrigue to prevent the redevelopment of Jerusalem
as Sanballat and his associates will be in the following century.[78]

4. Samarians.  Reference here to Samaria necessitates
a consideration of the Chronicler's attitude toward Samaria
and its inhabitants.  That the Chronicler's intention was
polemical is most apparent but the identification of those
against whom this polemic was addressed is not clear.[79]

Up to recent times Torrey's conclusion was basically
accepted, i.e., that the Chronicler had a twofold purpose
to establish beyond all question the supremacy of the mother
church and to reject the Samaritan claim that they were true
Israel.[80]  Even Rowley, normally critical of Torrey, concludes
that the Chronicler betrays an anti-Samaritan bias which

cannot be mistaken.[81]

Ackroyd warns, however, that:

> At no point is there any reference in
> these events to the opposition of a
> religious party later to be equated
> with the Samaritans, perhaps for the
> simple reason that whatever different
> elements may ultimately have made up
> the Samaritan religious community, the
> core of it must be regarded as having
> come from the very centre of the Jewish
> community with whom it shared the Pen-
> tateuch ...[82]

While acknowledging friction between the returnees and
their Samaritan neighbors, Cogan observes that the foreign
cult of 2 Kgs 17 never became an issue for rejection in the
Ezra-Nehemiah documents.[83] The Chronicler concedes that the
Samaritans looked to Yahweh as their God. Further the Samaritans did not present themselves as descendants of the old
indigenous Israelite population but rather as foreigners!

Kaufmann maintains that even though a kind of paganism
had developed in the north, it had disappeared because of the
Judaization of the Assyrian deportees' formal cultic practices. They were rejected then not on a religious basis but
on an ethnic basis: they were non-Israelites.[84]

This position seems to be more in keeping with the
Ezra context. If as we suggested above, the Golah list of
Ezra 2 and Neh 7 was to give a political as well as a religious legitimation to the temple builders, then the strong
emphasis upon the foreign background of the opponents would
be sufficient to exclude them from assisting in the temple
construction which had been made a monopoly of the returning
exiles. Hence the issue was not primarily religious but
political.

5. Neighboring governors. In this same context, the
tension between Nehemiah and the surrounding governors needs
to be considered.

Nehemiah came to Jerusalem as governor.[85] It is not
certain whether he is one of a series of Persian-appointed
governors, a line reaching back to Sheshbazzar and Zerubbabel or, whether, as Alt claims, there was no final establishment of a governorship in Jerusalem before Nehemiah,

Judaea being a part of the province of Samaria.[86] (The
reference in Malachi to "the governor" is ambiguous and may
refer either to the governor in Jerusalem or in Samaria.[87])
Whether Nehemiah is the first Persian-appointed governor of
Judaea or an *ad hoc* official[88] on a special assignment, the
tension which developed between him and Sanballat[89] is most
understandable.

As governor of Samaria, Sanballat is joined by three
other provincial governors (Tobiah[90] of Ammon, Gašmu of the
Qedarite Arabs and perhaps ʿAbd of Dedan)[91] to oppose the
rebuilding of the walls of Jerusalem. The reason for their
opposition is clearly political. While these governors protest their allegiance to the Persian king, it is quite obvious that they are selfishly motivated. Nehemiah, with his
enthusiasm and his *poor* (!) example of repudiation of the
allowance allotted to the governor, was a threat to these
surrounding governors.[92]

It should be noted that Sanballat appears to have been
a good Yahwist, giving good Yahwistic names to his sons
Delaiah and Shelemiah.[93] Further, it is significant that
when Nehemiah returns to Jerusalem the second time, he discovers that the son of Joiada the Zadokite high priest and
the daughter of Sanballat had been joined in a diplomatic
marriage[94] uniting the two great families of Judah and Samaria.[95] This matter of marriage between the aristocracy
of Samaria and the theocratic family of Jerusalem is one
indication that the schism which separated the Samaritans
finally and irreversibly from their Jewish coreligionists
came much later, long after the end of the Persian rule.

Nehemiah's conflict with Tobiah, following his return
to Jerusalem, is also pertinent here. Discovering Tobiah
entrenched in the temple, sustained by Eliashib the priest,
Nehemiah reacted in his own inimitable way and threw Tobiah
and his belongings out of the temple.[97] Nehemiah considered
this another effort to subvert the restoration of Jerusalem.
His Persian authorization gave him control over the affairs
of the temple. An interesting parallel to this is found in
an act of Cambyses in Egypt. Upon complaint that foreigners
were settled in the temple of Neith, he gave orders that they
should be driven out. The houses and goods of the Greek mercenaries were destroyed and the temple was purified.[98]

Tobiah, according to Mazar, was a Jew, being the ances-
tor of the prominent Tobiad family of the Ptolemaic period.
This family supported the Jewish Hellenizers, favoring a compromise with the Greek regime. The biblical statements about

Tobiah indicate that he was a relative of the high priest[99] and that he was a leader of the Jews,[100] receiving their support and maintaining their loyalty. He is described as "the Ammonite servant,"[101] a term indicating an official of high standing even though Nehemiah uses it to scorn a political opponent.[102] Mazar suggests that this phrase means "the servant of the king of Persia in residence at Ammon," concluding that there is basis for the assumption that Tobiah was governor of Ammon.[103]

While the "land of Tobiads" seems to have been situated in Gilead and not in Ammon, it must be remembered that this area appears as the heritage of Gad in the Bible. The Ammonites attempted repeatedly to occupy the land of Gad[104] but it was only after the conquest of the Israelite Trans-Jordan by Tiglath-Pileser III that they succeeded in dominating the southern part of Gilead. Jeremiah notes that the Ammonites occupied part of Gad.[105] In the time of Jehoiakim the Ammonites tried to enlarge their territory at the expense of Judah.[106] Finally at the time of the destruction of the First Temple there was a considerable Jewish population in that part of Gad so that Ishmael could flee there after slaying Gedaliah.[107] Thus the citizens of this area remained Judaean even under the Ammonite occupation in the seventh and sixth centuries B.C.E. though this area was officially in the land of Ammon.

The Tobiads were landowners in this area, being local rulers and enjoying an autonomous state.[108] It would seem then that the tension between Nehemiah and Tobiah was not so much ethnic or religious but rather political.

Gašmu was another local governor who opposed Nehemiah.[109] While the Edomites had encroached on the southern lands of Judah during the exile,[110] they drop from view, following the return, to be replaced by a confederation of Arabian tribes led by Gašmu. He seems to have established control over a wide area of North Arabia, displacing Moab and Edom, even perhaps reaching into Egypt. Thus the Qedarite Arabs led by Gašmu replaced Judah's hated southern neighbors. Nehemiah's confrontation by Gašmu should be seen in this light. Gašmu's name has been found on a silver bowl from the temple at Tell al-Maskhûta, twelve miles east of Ismailia in Lower Egypt. The inscription written in the standard Aramaic of the Persian Period reads: "Cain, son of Gašmu, king of Qedar."[111]

It would seem that Gašmu's loyalty to Persia was not always certain. In the later part of the fifth century along with the king of Egypt, he seems to have had plans to take Phoenicia, necessitating Persian intervention.[112]

As with the other surrounding governors, Nehemiah's confrontation with Gašmu was predicated on political reasons.

The above evidence seems to indicate that the tension between the returning exiles and their neighbors was primarily political rather than religious. The Chronicler, while pro-Judaean, is not necessarily anti-Samaritan.[113] He is clearly anti-Samarian, but this is due to political rather than religious reasons. The religious break between the Judaeans and the Samarians came at a later time. It does not figure in the tensions of Ezra and Nehemiah.

## IV.  The Leadership

One other dimension which will contribute to our understanding of the political situation is the appointment of governors.

It is not necessary for us to deal with the Sheshbazzar/ Zerubbabel issue here. It now seems clear that they are two distinct individuals with Sheshbazzar laying the foundation of the temple,[114] to be succeeded by Zerubbabel who will resume the delayed building and complete it. We have already noted Weisberg's calculation that the proclamation of Cyrus to the Jews was promulgated four years before his agreement with the artisans of Eanna. The rebuilding of the far-off Judaean temple received immediate attention because Cyrus wished to gain the allegiance of his subjects in those regions first.[115] He wished to secure his outlying defenses.

Darius I came to the throne in 522 B.C.E., following an insurrection. Rebellion was rampant in Babylon, Media, Armenia, Sardis, Egypt, and elsewhere.[116] In Judaea, messianic hopes were high but there was apparently no political unrest. Nevertheless, an investigation of the temple construction was ordered by the satrap Tattenai.[117] After reviewing the records, Darius ordered the continuation of the temple project.[118] Again, political self-interest seems to have prevailed. A loyal Judaea is needed.

Following this episode, we have a long period of silence in Ezra-Nehemiah. Whether Ezra is the next figure to arrive on the scene is a much debated point and is beyond the scope of this paper. However, the acceptance of the traditional date (458 B.C.E.)[119] gains some support from the political situation. The early years of Artaxerxes I (465-424 B.C.E.)

are filled with unrest.  In addition to a revolt by his
brother Hystaspes,[120] a more serious problem had developed
in Palestine and Egypt.  It appears that Athens under the
leadership of Pericles had established a base at Dor, a
coastal city of Palestine below Mt. Carmel, shortly after
460 B.C.E. with the intention of assisting rebellious Egypt
against the Persians.[121]  The biblical text reflects the
dangerous situation by having Ezra, who had promised Artaxerxes I divine help, hesitant to request an army to protect
him and the exiles enroute to Jerusalem.[122]  Ezra's appointment can then be viewed as an effort to provide greater
allegiance and security in Jerusalem and to prevent defection
to the Athenians.

Nehemiah's appointment in 445 B.C.E. followed this period
of unrest.  Further, in 448 B.C.E., Megabyzus, the satrap of
the province Beyond the River, had rebelled.[123]  He was quickly reconciled but obviously there was need for loyalty in
Jerusalem.

Clearly the Persians needed a loyal province and a reliable governor in the territory bordering Egypt.

## V.  Conclusion

Crucial to an understanding of the Chronicler's account
of the events and circumstances in Achaemenid Judaea is the
recognition of the loyalty agreement between the returning
exiles and the Persian government.  Recorded actions and
events of Ezra-Nehemiah which had been said to reflect the
religious bias of the Chronicler can be better understood as
reflecting the political situation.

The edict of Cyrus which permitted the rebuilding of the
Jerusalem temple gave a kind of independence to the returning
exiles, granting them a monopoly in that particular construction.  They exercised that monopoly, rejecting the proffered
assistance.  While such a refusal reflects a selfish attitude
and a kind of religious separation, it also was in keeping
with the terms of the contract.  This political dimension
must not be overlooked.  While the builders had a kind of independence they were nevertheless bound by the loyalty agreement, which precluded working in another sanctuary.

The Chronicler's selection of the exiles as the hope of
the nation need not simply be a bias but may well have its

basis in the agreement between Cyrus and the exiles. To them comes the responsibility of restoring Jerusalem.

It seems quite clear that Cyrus and his successors were not simply magnanimous in their agreements and appointments, but also protective of their own self-interests. They sought to ingratiate themselves with the people of Judaea. As shown above, their gracious acts were frequently exercised in a time of empire crisis. A loyal Judaea, bordering on Egypt, was essential to the Achaemenid Empire.

## NOTES

1. Ackroyd observes that the condition of the temple site remains uncertain. He notes that there is no explicit statement that the altar was destroyed, that worship continued there in the time of Gedaliah, and that the stress of 1 Kings 8 is upon the temple as a place of prayer rather than as a place of sacrifice. He concludes that the temple could not have been thought to have lost its sanctitiy entirely, and that some attempts must have been made at re-use. Peter R. Ackroyd, *Exile and Restoration* (London: SCM, 1968), 25-29.

2. Cf. Nathan's promise to David in 2 Sam 7:4-17.

3. The people's violent reaction to Jeremiah's great temple sermon (chapters 7 and 26) reflects their belief in the invulnerability of the city and its temple.

4. 2 Kgs 24:8-17; 2 Chr 36:9-10.

5. BM 21946 Reverse Lines 11-13: "In the seventh year, the month of Kislev, the king of Akkad mustered his troops, marched to the Hatti-land, and encamped against (i.e., besieged) the city of Judah and on the second day of the month Adar he seized the city and captured the king. He appointed there a king of his own choice (lit. heart), received its heavy tribute and sent (them) to Babylon." D. J. Wiseman, *Chronicles of the Chaldean Kings (626-556 B.C.) in the British Museum* (London: The Trustees of the British Museum, 1956), 73.

6. Cf. Jer 27:1-22. Zedekiah stands in direct contrast to Hezekiah who managed to control similar tensions during the earlier Assyrian crisis.

7. Lachish Ostracon III seems to suggest Egyptian complicity. "It was reported to your servant that the commander of the host, Coniah son of Elnathan, has come down in order to go to Egypt" (*ANET*, 322).

8. A gap exists here in the *Chronicles of the Chaldean Kings* so only biblical evidence is available--2 Kings 25:8-12.

9. 2 Chr 36:17-21.

10. Charles Cutler Torrey, *Ezra Studies* (Chicago: University of Chicago, 1910), 285-287.

11. 2 Kgs 25:9-11; 2 Chr 36:18-19; Jer 52:13-14; Lam 1:4, 5:18.

12. W. F. Albright, "The Seal of Eliakim and the Latest Pre-Exilic History of Judah," *JBL* 51 (1936), 102-105. Albright disagrees with R. Kittel who contends that the cities of the Negeb and Shephelah were spared since the list of exiles in Ezra 2 and Nehemiah 7 does not include any names of towns in these areas. The fact that Lachish and Azekah fell to the Babylonians would indicate otherwise. Cf. S. S. Weinberg, "Post Exilic Palestine, An Archaeological Report," *Israel Academy of Sciences and Humanities* 4 (1971), 78-97.

13. Jer 52:28-30. The date and size of the three deportations are as follows:

| | |
|---|---|
| 7th year | 3,023 |
| 18th year | 832 |
| 23rd year | 745 |
| TOTAL | 4,600 |

Perhaps these figures reflect males only, necessitating an enlargement to include women and children.

14. 2 Kgs 24:14.

15. 2 Kgs 24:16.

16. 2 Kgs 25:11. There is no reference in 2 Kings to a third deportation in Nebuchadnezzar's 23rd year as found in Jeremiah 52:30. Josephus (*ANT.* X, 6:3-7:1) also maintains that there were two deportations of 3,000 and more than 10,000.

17. W. F. Albright, *The Biblical Period from Abraham to Ezra* (New York: Harper and Row, 1965), 87, 110. Here Albright estimates the population remaining in Judea as less than 20,000 people.

18. Jer 40:7-12.

19. Ackroyd, *Exile*, 20-31. Cf. K. M. Kenyon, "Excavations in Jerusalem, 1961," *PEQ* 94 (1962), 85.

20. Noth maintains that the Babylonian group represented a mere outpost, whereas Palestine was and remained the central arena of Israel's history. Martin Noth, *The History of Israel* (New York: Harper and Row, 1960), 296.

21. There are only limited sources in the Old Testament concerning these who remained in the land and apparently no sources at all outside the Bible. This stands in contrast to available information (at best limited) about the exiles in Babylon and Elephantine.

22. 2 Kgs 25:12, 21.

23. Ackroyd, *Exile*, 29.

24. E. W. Nicholson, *Preaching to the Exiles* (New York: Schocken, 1971), 132.

25. Jer 5:4. This verse has led to the equating of the *'am hā'āreṣ* by rabbinic writers as the religious illiterates. The identity of the *'am hā'āreṣ* will be discussed below.

26. Cf. Jer 40:7-44:30. The community which remained in the land was written off as the possible bearers of the hope of a renewed state.

27. Jer 24:1-10.

28. Ezek 33:23-24.

29. Ezek 33:27-28.

30. Isa 52:2.

31. Isa 49:6.

32. Isa 43:28; 51:3; 52:9.

33. Nicholson, *Preaching*, 130.

238

34. The following personnel and topographical lists are also found in Ezra-Nehemiah:

| | |
|---|---|
| Golah List | Ezra 2 and Neh 7 |
| Returnees with Ezra | Ezra 8:1-19 |
| Those Guilty of Marriage Infraction | Ezra 10:18-44 |
| Builder's List | Neh 3:1-32 |
| Interpreters | Neh 8:4-7; 9:4-5 |
| Signatories on the Reform Document | Neh 10:1-28 |
| Census List | Neh 11:3-24 |
| Occupied Towns in Judah and Benjamin | Neh 11:25-36 |
| Clerical Genealogies | Neh 12:1-26 |
| Participants in Wall-Dedication | Neh 12:31-43 |

For an excellent alignment of these lists, see Jacob M. Myers, *Ezra, Nehemiah* (AB 14; Garden City: Doubleday, 1965), 223-245.

35. Cf. 1 Esdr 5:7-46. This list differs from that in Ezra at many points, both as to name and numbers. The totals are almost identical. The importance of the priestly and levitical genealogies can be seen in the great harmony which exists among Ezra 2, Neh 7, and 1 Esdr 5:7-46.

36. Cf. Baruch Levine, "The $N^e t\hat{i}n\hat{i}m$," *JBL* 82 (1963), 207-212.

37. Myers, *Ezra, Nehemiah*, 16.

38. Kurt Galling, "The Gola-List According to Ezra 2/Nehemiah 7," *JBL* 70 (1951), 152.

39. Myers, *Ezra, Nehemiah*, 16.

40. Torrey, *Ezra Studies*, 250.

41. Wilhelm Rudolph, *Esra and Nehemiah* (Tübingen: Mohr, 1949), 17.

42. W. F. Albright, *The Biblical Period from Abraham to Ezra* (New York: Harper and Row, 1965), 110.

43. Albrecht Alt, "Die Rolle Samarias bei der Entstehung des Judentums," *Kleine Schriften zur Geschichte des Volkes Israel* (Munich:  C. H. Beck, 1953), II, 316-318.

44. G. Hölscher, *Die Bücher Esra und Nehemia* (Tübingen: Mohr, 1923), 504.

45. For a discussion of the numbers of this list, see H. L. Allrik, "The Lists of Zerubbabel (Nehemiah 7 and Ezra 2) and The Hebrew Numerical Notation," *BASOR* 136 (1954), 21-27.

46. Galling, "Gola-List," 153-154.

47. Ezra 4:3.

48. S. Talmon, "The Sectarian יחד --A Biblical Noun," *VT* 3 (1953), 133-140.

49. For a discussion of the two accounts of Cyrus' edict, one in Hebrew and the other in Aramaic, see E. Bickerman, "The Edict of Cyrus in Ezra I," *JBL* 65 (1946), 247-275.

50. Ezra 1:2-4.

51. Ezra 4:3.

52. Ezra 5:3--Tattenai seems to be referred to in a Babylonian document dated June 5, 502 B.C.E.:  "Ta-at-t[anni] governor (paḫat) of Ebirnari."  A. T. Olmstead, "Tattenai, Governor of Across the River," *JNES* 3 (1944), 46.  [vs 4:152.]

53. Ezra 5:10.

54. Ezra 2:63.

55. David B. Weisberg, *Guild Structure and Political Allegiance in Early Achaemenid Mesopotamia* (New Haven:  Yale University, 1967), 1-4.

56. *Ibid.*, 37-38.

57. *Ibid.*, 48.

58. *ANET*, 316.

59. Weisberg, *Guild Structure*, 103.

60. Ezra 3:8.

61. Ezra 6:15.

62. Ezra 4:1; cf. Ezra 1:5.

63. Ezra 4:2.

64. Ackroyd, *Exile*, 150-151.

65. Isa 7:8b.

66. *ANET*, 290, and D. J. Wiseman, "An Esarhaddon Cylinder from Nimrud," *Iraq* 14 (1952), 54-60.

67. Myers, *Ezra, Nehemiah*, 35.

68. Ezra 4:10.

69. Josephus (*ANT*. XI, 19) has Shalmaneser here.

70. D. D. Luckenbill, ed., *Ancient Records of Babylonia and Assyria* (Chicago:  University of Chicago, 1927), Vol. II, 326, 340, 346, 351.

71. A. Malamat, "The Historical Background of the Assassination of Amon, King of Judah," *IEJ* 3 (1953), 26-29.

72. Ezra 4:4.

73. Several definitions of the ʿam hāʾāreṣ have been given:

   A. Representatives of the people in government, a kind of Parliament.  Cf. M. Sulzberger, "The Polity of the Ancient Hebrews," *JQR* 3 (1912-1913), 1-81;  N. Slousch, "Representative Government Among the Hebrews and Phoenicians," *JQR* 4 (1913-1914), 303-310;  C. U. Wolf, "Traces of Primitive Democracy in Ancient Israel," *JNES* 6 (1947), 98-108.

   B. Country inhabitant in contrast to the city folk with an emphasis upon the cultural, social, and economic differences.  Cf. R. Gordis, "Sectional Rivalry in the Kingdom of Judah," *JQR* 25 (1934-1935), 237-259;  S. Zeitlin, "The Am Haarez," *JQR* 23 (1932-1933), 45-61.

   C. The landed gentry, the landowners, the landed aristocracy, the lords of the land.  S. Daiches,

"The Meaning of עַם הָאָרֶץ in the Old Testament,"
*JTS* 30 (1929), 245-249; P. Lemaire, "Crises
et Effondrement de la Monarchie Davidique,"
*RB* 15 (1936), 161-183; E. Würthwein, "Der 'amm
ha'arez im Alten Testament," *BWANT* IV:17 (1936).

D. A body of free men, enjoying civil rights in a
given territory; the whole body of citizens.
Cf. R. de Vaux, *Ancient Israel* (New York: McGraw-
Hill, 1965), I, 70-72; M. H. Pope, "'Am Ha'arez,"
*The Interpreter's Dictionary of the Bible*, ed. by
G. A. Buttrick (New York: Abingdon, 1962), I,
106-107.

74. E. W. Nicholson, "The Meaning of the Expression
עַם הָאָרֶץ in the Old Testament," *JSS* 10 (1965), 59-66.

75. Hag 2:2.

76. R. Gordis, "Sectional Rivalry," 237-259.

77. Cf. *City Invincible*, eds. Carl H. Kraeling and
Robert M. Adams (Chicago: University of Chicago, 1960), 79-
83; and Lewis Mumford, *The City in History* (New York: Harcourt, Brace, and World, 1961), 64-70.

78. Ackroyd, *Exile*, 150-151.

79. R. J. Coggins, *Samaritans and Jews* (Atlanta: John
Knox, 1975), 68-69.

80. Torrey, *Ezra Studies*, 153.

81. H. H. Rowley, "The Samaritan Schism in Legend and
History," in *Israel's Prophetic Heritage*, eds. B. W. Anderson
and Walter Harrelson (New York: Harper and Row, 1962), 219.

82. Ackroyd, *Exile*, 152.

83. Morton Cogan, *Imperialism and Religion* (Missoula:
Scholars Press, 1974), 108.

84. Yehezkel Kaufmann, *The Babylonian Captivity and
Deutero-Isaiah* (New York: Union of American Hebrew Congregations, 1970), 57-58.

85. Neh 5:14. The term *pehāh* is applied to Sheshbazzar (Ezra 5:14), Zerubbabel (Hag 1:1, 14, 2:2, 21), and the Persian officials (Ezra 5:3, 6, 6:6, 7, 13, 8:36; Neh 2:7, 9, 3:7).

86. Alt, *Rolle Samarias*, 331.

87. Mal 1:8.

88. Coggins, *Samaritans and Jews*, 53.

89. Neh 3:33-4:17.

90. Cf. B. Mazar, "The Tobiads," *IEJ* 7 (1957), 137-145, 229-238.

91. Frank M. Cross, "A Reconstruction of the Judean Restoration," *JBL* 94 (1975), 16-17.

92. Neh 5:14-19.

93. A. Cowley, *Aramaic Papyri of the Fifth Century B.C.* (Oxford: Clarendon, 1925), Texts 30:29 and 31:28, pp. 114, 121. Similar names also appear in Neh 6:10 and 13:13.

94. Neh 13:28-29.

95. Frank M. Cross, "Aspects of Samaritan and Jewish History in Late Persian and Hellenistic Times," *HTR* 59 (1966), 202. On the basis of fourth-century papyri from Daliyeh where a Sanballat (II) appears, Cross concludes that the Sanballatids held the governorship of Samaria for several generations and that it is possible that the marriage mentioned by Josephus of a daughter of Sanballat (III) to the son of the high priest is distinct from the similar marriage in Nehemiah. However, he feels that Josephus confuses the biblical Sanballat with Sanballat III, jumping from the fifth to the late fourth century.

96. Cross, *ibid.*, 205.

97. Neh 13:7-9.

98. A. T. Olmstead, *History of the Persian Empire* (Chicago: University of Chicago, 1948), 91.

99. Neh 6:18.

100. Neh 6:17, 19.

101. Neh 2:10, 19.

102. Neh 13:1-13.

103. Mazar, "The Tobiads," 144.

104. Amos 1:13; Zeph 2:8.

105. Jer 49:1-2.

106. 2 Kgs 24:2. Cf. Ezek 25:1-5.

107. Jer 41:1-15.

108. Mazar, "The Tobiads," 144-145.

109. Neh 2:19.

110. Obad 12-14. Alt also notes that Idumea, the Judean hill region south of Beth-zur, was part of Gašmu's realm (*Kleine Schriften* II, 343-345). Cf. F. M. Cross, "Geshem, the Arabian, Enemy of Nehemiah," *BA* 18 (1955), 46-47.

111. I. Rabinowith, "Aramaic Inscriptions of the Fifth Century B.C.E. from a North Arab Shrine in Egypt," *JNES* 15 (1956), 2.

112. A. F. Rainey, "The Satrapy 'Beyond the River,'" *Australian Journal of Biblical Archaeology* 1 (1969), 64-65.

113. As Coggins indicates, terminology is difficult here. See *Samaritans and Jews*, 8-9.

114. Ezra 5:14-16.

115. Weisberg, *Guild Structure*, 48.

116. Olmstead, *Persian Empire*, 107-113.

117. Ezra 5:3.

118. Ezra 6:1-12.

119. Ezra 7:7.

120. Olmstead, *Persian Empire*, 290.

121. Olmstead, *Persian Empire*, 302-304; and Fritz M. Heichelheim, "Ezra's Palestine and Periclean Athens," *ZRGG* 3 (1951), 251-253. Cf. J. B. Bury, *A History of Greece* (London, 1955), 354-355, 357-358.

122. Ezra 8:22.

123. Olmstead, *Persian Empire*, 312-313. Cf. Rainey, "Satrapy," 64, and Ctesias, *Pers.* xiii, *Epit.* 68-70.

# JEWISH APOCALPYTIC AND THE
# COMPARATIVE METHOD


J. Douglas Thomas
Missouri Baptist College


Apocalyptic literature undergoes periodic revivals of
both popularity and scholarly study.  Until recent decades,
two features characterized most academic studies of apocalyptic, one being a common rootage in Iranian religious ideas
and the other long lists of characteristic features.  The
history of religions school attributed apocalyptic to the
Jewish importation of Persian, especially Zoroastrian, ideas
during the exile and frequently concluded that it was of little significance compared to prophecy.[1]  The *Interpreter's
Dictionary of the Bible* typically identifies apocalypticism
as an ancient Zorastrian religious idea taken over by Judaism
in the exilic and postexilic periods.[2]  The characteristic
features of apocalyptic identified by various scholars include dualism, determinism, esoteric knowledge, angelology,
cosmic imagery and myth, pseudonymity, visions, messianism,
resurrection, predictions *ex eventu*, individualism, numerolo-
gy, cataclysmic judgment, and a future golden age for the
righteous.[3]  Recent discussions have proposed, however, to
place apocalyptic literature and its ideas in a more definite
Israelite context.  Three of the most influential theories
are surveyed below, followed by a brief critique and preliminary suggestions for future study.


I


Proposals for a specifically Israelite matrix for apocalyptic literature and ideas generally focus on one aspect of
Israelite tradition as the major contributor and suggest that
other elements in the Israelite experience provided additional
features.  H. H. Rowley described apocalyptic as a readapta-
tion of earlier ideas and aspirations to a new situation.

Although seeing prophecy as the primary ingredient in this process, he contended that apocalyptic was different from prophecy.[4] Even though both delivered God's message to his people, combined political and religious dimensions in the presentation, and looked toward deliverance for God's faithful, followed by a golden age,[5] Rowley acknowledged that many apocalyptic ideas had roots far back in a non-Israelite past. Zoroastrian eschatological ideas such as a highly developed hierarchy of angels and a dualistic antithesis between God and evil found a place in apocalyptic.[6]

Nevertheless, Rowley contended that circumstances of the Maccabean age contributed more to the rise of apocalyptic than even prophecy or foreign ideas. The Hellenization program initiated by Alexander and furthered by both Ptolemies and Seleucids attracted many influential Jewish leaders but alienated others, producing tension within the Jewish community. In the conquest of Palestine by the Seleucids, the heavy taxation to finance Seleucid military campaigns, and the usurpation of the Seleucid throne by Antiochus IV, Rowley saw a series of events resulting in increased tension and hostility between king and vassal. In addition, according to Rowley, Greek interference in the high-priestly succession followed by the attempt of Antiochus IV to replace Jewish religion by a syncretistic Hellenistic-Baal faith set the stage for the birth of apocalyptic. In the stories about Daniel and the visions of the end-time victory of God, the first apocalyptic author attempted to guide and encourage his beleaguered comrades. Men living in that difficult period easily understood Daniel as a source of strength. Later apocalypticists repeated that message of hope to their own distressed communities even though they misunderstood Daniel as primarily a prediction.[7]

D. S. Russell similarly interpreted apocalyptic as deriving primarily from Hebrew prophecy, with some distinctive ideas developing from contact with Persian religious concepts and Babylonian mythic imagery. Hellenistic culture also encouraged a syncretism to which Jewish people, both in Palestine and the diaspora, were subject.[8] Using the analogy of the roots of a tree, Russell said that apocalyptic drew from "many sources, prophetic and mythological, native and foreign, esoteric and exotic," but that its "taproot" sank deep into the thought and language of the prophets, especially the postexilic prophets.[9]

Russell traced prophetic roots for both the form and content of apocalyptic to Ezekiel, particularly chapters 38-39. Postexilic prophets like I and II Zechariah, Zephaniah (Sic),

Joel, and the Isaiah Apocalypse (Isa 24-27) then elaborated
on the imagery, visions, and auditions in order to emphasize
such themes as divine transcendence and God's victory over
the forces of evil. Russell seemed to favor a fourth or
third century B.C.E. date for these postexilic prophecies.
He did not call them apocalyptic but contended that they
constituted the "stuff" which would go into apocalyptic when
historical conditions became suitable.[10] These prophetic
seeds subsequently received elaboration and specificity from
Persian influences, providing apocalyptic literature with
more detailed concepts of angelology and demonology, life
after death, and the division of history into two ages. Regardless of the source of the elaborations, however, Russell
repeatedly emphasized that the apocalyptic idea of the day of
judgment and the dawn of a new age grew out of the new needs
of the prophetic day of the Lord. The apocalyptic writer developed and universalized embryonic prophetic ideas by drawing
on new mythological metaphors, resulting at times in a very
different end result from prophecy. Even then, Russell said,
apocalypticists spoke what they believed the prophets would
have said in the changed circumstances of a later day.[11]
Apocalypticists especially studied unfulfilled prophecy, reading it in view of the last days, their own days. They reinterpreted and applied the unrealized promises by drawing on
non-biblical, even foreign, ideas and by sprinkling their
works with reflections of Babylonian mythology.[12] When the
apocalyptic reinterpretation remained unfulfilled, for example, Daniel's fourth beast (7:11), it was subject to further
reinterpretation, as in 2 Esdr 11:1-12:12.[13]

Rowley and Russell approached the origin of apocalyptic
primarily by describing it and then locating parallels to its
form and ideas.[14] Otto Plöger, while sharing a common view
of apocalyptic as a development from OT prophecy combined with
other elements, sought to analyze the nature of the community
reflected in the literature.[15] From a study of Daniel, Plöger
concluded that the second century Jewish resistance movement
included a coalition of groups who entered the movement with
different presuppositions and motives. He found, for example, divergent interpretations of the Antiochene persecution
in Daniel and 1 Maccabees. Daniel interpreted it as unparal-
leled since the beginning of time and concluded that the eschaton was rapidly approaching. 1 Maccabees, although admit-
ting the severity of the period, seemed to regard it as another difficult period which could result in recovery through
faithfulness and courage. Plöger designated the activism of
1 Maccabees, in contrast to Daniel, as non-eschatological.[16]
On the basis of this disagreement within the Hasmonean community, he investigated the formative period of apocalyptic

to ascertain whether similar differences existed in the Jewish community in the earlier period.

Plöger identified the periods of the overthrow of Judah, the exile, and the restoration as decisive in the development of apocalyptic. He contended that the radical alteration from political nationhood to religious community attendant upon the fall of Judah produced eschatological expectations of a markedly different nature than those held by the prophets.[17] In the priestly redaction and the work of the Chronicler, Plöger found Israelite history depicted in terms of religious community rather than national identity. In fact, this community interpreted prophetic concerns as largely accomplished with the establishment of the postexilic community, the New Israel. For Plöger, Daniel's eschatological views rose as a protest against a priestly establishment which had excluded eschatology as a proper concern for Jewish people.[18] Contemporaneous with the establishment of the Torah as absolutely binding in Jerusalem, often referred to as the theocracy, Plöger saw the prophetic canon taking shape in certain underground conventicles which maintained belief in the relevance of the prophetic word. As their eschatological theology dropped from view in official circles, these underground groups increasingly viewed themselves as the true Israel. Both the majority and minority groups existed and developed in the same community until historical circumstances brought their divergent perspectives into the open. Plöger pictured a development extending from the founding of the postexilic community to the persecution by the Seleucids.[19]

Plöger found an opening for foreign ideas precisely in the estrangement of the eschatological groups. They continued to frequent the Temple and participate in the cult, but drew community support from each other as they isolated themselves from the official theocratic theology. Against this experience of alienation they found the dualistic outlook emanating from Persia as expressive of the distinctions existing within their own community. As a result, by the time of Daniel, *two* resurrections were necessary, one for those recognizing eschatological realities, the other for those indifferent to them.[20] Because no authoritative leadership existed within the apocalyptic conventicles, what Plöger called "rampant speculation" characterized later apocalyptic.[21]

Plöger pointed to the Isaiah Apocalypse, Trito-Zechariah (12-14) and Joel (especially chapter 3) as evidence of the deepening division within the postexilic community[22] and dated those passages in the period between the restoration and the Greek conquest under Alexander. The conflict between the official and the eschatological theologies surfaced during the Antiochene persecution and was formulated in the two resurrections of Daniel.[23] Plöger's analysis established an important model which has significantly influenced the most recent phase of research into apocalyptic beginnings.

II

The differences between preexilic prophecy and full-blown apocalyptic called forth interpretations which looked beyond the prophetic phase of Jewish tradition as sources for apocalyptic. Gerhard von Rad ruled prophecy "completely out of the question" as the matrix of apocalyptic,[24] basing his conclusion on the totally different views of history found in the two genres. Prophecy was rooted in the election traditions of Israel, while apocalyptic saw all of history moving according to God's immutable and eternal decree toward the salvation of its "now" generation.[25]

Instead of prophecy, von Rad identified wisdom as the thought world which gave birth to apocalyptic. Ancient wisdom was the world of scholarship, and apocalyptic exhibited familiarity with and interest in astrology, geography, and history, all scholarly subjects. Wise men in the ancient world interpreted dreams at least as much as prophets. Von Rad argued that one aspect of wisdom's effort to understand and apply the laws governing the world resulted in the apocalyptic focus on specially revealed knowledge of the end of time.[26] In a later work, he began with the wisdom premise that everything has its own time and season (Eccl 3:1-9), contending that wisdom books like the Wisdom of Sirach and Judith developed the idea that God unalterably determined the times, a key idea in apocalyptic. Von Rad said that he was not "trying to understand Sirach as an apocalypticist, but, rather, the apocalypticist as a wise man."[27] Because the wisdom concept of determinism did not originally include eschatological ideas, von Rad attributed them to a syncretism which caused Iranian doctrines such as the two ages to adhere to Jewish deterministic teachings. He also explained the contrast between the transparent divine activity in wisdom proper and the inscrutable ways of God which must be especially revealed in apocalyptic as resulting from Iranian influences.[28]

Recent scholarship has not followed von Rad's theory of a unilinear derivation from wisdom,[29] but wisdom connections still receive attention. John J. Collins has called for recognition of a distinction between the content of apocalyptic and the carriers of apocalyptic. Through a form-critical analysis of Daniel 1-6 he concluded that these tales originated in circles of Jewish "wise men" active in or aspiring to court service in the diaspora, and that they reflected an understanding of "revelation" as given miraculously by God to his faithful servants. Collins suggested that some of these diaspora wise men returned to Palestine in the second century and, under pressure of persecution, used this understanding of revelation mediated through dreams and visions as the basis for their eschatological mysteries. The content of their visions came primarily from OT prophecy, but the emphasis on special wisdom, a major characteristic of apocalyptic, distinguished apocalyptic from prophecy.[30] In a recent study Collins noted that, in spite of differences regarding their modes of presentation and their perspectives on whether salvation occurs within the natural order or beyond the present age, both wisdom and apocalyptic shared the conviction that the cosmos mediates salvation. For both, the experience of salvation came through alignment with cosmological powers rather than through the obedience required by prophetic oracles. Collins concluded that this unique emphasis on the cosmos shared by wisdom and apocalyptic "must be sought in their common environment in the Hellenistic age" rather than in direct interaction between the two traditions.[31]

In a comparative study of apocalyptic in Hellenistic Mesopotamia and Egypt, Jonathan Z. Smith concluded that apocalyptic elements resulted from the application of scribal wisdom to historiographic materials. Apocalyptic situations, created by loss of kingship and domination by a foreign power, broke into literary expression during times of religious persecution. Smith believed that the widespread existence of apocalyptic indicated that it grew out of the inner history of its tradition rather than of syncretism with Iranian ideas.[32]

III

The most recent efforts to reconstruct the origins of apocalyptic come from Paul D. Hanson. Rejecting Iranian influences and Hellenistic elements as additions after the essentials of apocalyptic were fully developed and designating wisdom as a secondary, though important, source in apocalyptic, he contended that "Jewish apocalyptic literature emerged in an unbroken, inner-Israelite development out of pre-Exilic and Exilic prophecy, though greatly expanding upon several archaic mythic motifs which had been held in check by the prophets."[33]

Hanson felt that the nature of the literature prohibited dating and interpretation on the basis of supposed historical allusions and, therefore, proposed a new "contextual-typological" method for tracing the origins of apocalyptic. Using this method, he interpreted the development of apocalyptic in the context of the community struggle within which the various oracles developed, and, by analyzing the material, he developed typologies of poetic structure and meter, prophetic genres, and the history of ideas.[34]

Using II Isaiah (40-55) as the basic poetic type, Hanson arranged the various oracles around their similarity or dissimilarity to the meter and structure of II Isaiah and established this order as a relative chronology of the material.[35] Comparing the classic prophetic oracles of judgment and salvation with III Isaiah and II Zechariah convinced Hanson that apocalyptic literature gradually developed a new salvation-judgment oracle in which the salvation promise went only to the apocalyptic community, while the established power group received a pronouncement of judgment. This salvation-judgment oracle increasingly used the divine warrior hymn for cosmic mythological imagery.[36]

Definitions become central in Hanson's analysis of themes. He defined "prophetic eschatology" as a religious perspective which allowed the prophets to look into the divine council and translate the divine plans discovered there into "the terms of plain history, real politics, and human instrumentality."[37] "Apocalyptic eschatology," on the other hand, was a perspective which disclosed a cosmic vision of Yahweh's sovereignty and coming redemption for the faithful without translating the cosmic imagery, that is, myth, into the terms of plain history, real politics, and human instrumentality. This failure to translate their visions into mundane historical categories occurred because of increasing pessimism that the historical realm was a suitable context for the restoration of Yahweh's people.[38] Hanson established prophetic eschatology and apocalyptic eschatology as the extremes of a thematic typology and related various late prophetic oracles to the two extremes based on the purity or mixture of the themes. Thus, in Hanson's methodology, apocalyptic may be characterized and identified by the breakdown of II Isaiah's regular poetic structure and meter into longer, more baroque units which finally resolve into prose by the use of a salvation-judgment oracle, frequently combined with a divine warrior motif and structure, and by the failure to translate mythological language into real nations, rulers, and groups on the contemporary scene.

The final phase of the contextual-typological method involved studying the texts for evidence of the conditions of the community which gave birth to apocalyptic ideas and literature. Based largely on the polemic found in III Isaiah, Hanson described a community divided over the nature of the sixth century restoration program. On one side was a priestly element, dominated by Zadokites, who purposed to establish a theocratic community in Judah on the basis of Ezekiel 40-48. In a rebuilt Temple and reestablished cult made holy by their distance from the people, the Zadokites believed conditions would be realized in which the prophetic promise of God's return to Zion would be realized. When work on rebuilding the Temple proceeded slowly, Haggai and Proto-Zechariah motivated the people to complete the task. Once the eschatological promises were fulfilled, the theocratic hierarchy no longer needed or tolerated eschatological ideas. The Zadokites gradually took over exclusive control of the cult to the exclusion of all other elements.

On the other side of the divided community, Hanson found visionary disciples of II Isaiah allied with a group of Levites who had been ousted from participation in the cult by the restoration Zadokites. The postexilic prophecies of III Isaiah and II Zechariah reflected the polemic of this visionary group against the theocratic majority. Hanson arranged the oracles in an order progressing from mild protest to acrimonious attack as the visionary group found themselves and their eschatological ideas more and more repressed by the theocratic majority and vented their steadily growing hostility. Before 450 B.C.E. they viewed themselves alone as Yahweh's faithful and the Zadokite-led majority as enemies of the faith awaiting the doom of eschatological judgment. During the period of Ezra and Nehemiah, the priestly party took a more conciliatory attitude because, Hanson contended, they had won their point and could afford to be generous. By the time of the Chronicler (about 400 by Hanson's dating), calm had returned, but the cosmic vision of Yahweh's victory and deliverance of his faithful espoused in apocalyptic eschatology remained to flash up again in the second century during the Seleucid persecution.[39]

Several important points made by Hanson about the origin of apocalyptic deserve emphasis. First, his work with genre, themes, and motifs has shown that authors of early apocalyptic were certainly at home in the Israelite tradition, especially in the thought world of the prophets. Second, his attention to the polemic within the early apocalyptic writings produced a sociological model which sheds light on the type of situation which gave rise to the literature.[40]  Finally, Hanson reduced the essential characteristics of apocalyptic to a manageable number--only one, that being apocalyptic eschatology.  Whether the announcement of cosmic intervention by Yahweh to deliver his faithful and judge the unfaithful adequately covers the field of apocalyptic deserves further attention.

Hanson, then, interpreted fully developed apocalyptic as the mid-fifth century result of a completely inner-Israelite development, stemming primarily from prophecy using tribal league traditions which combined historical election with mythic imagery.  The royal cult which rose with kingship in tenth century Israel retained a more thoroughgoing mythic perspective which reflected the stability and order so important to the monarchy.  In opposition to this royal theology, prophecy emphasized Yahweh's movement in history to bring the covenant promise to fulfillment, translating cosmic activities into political-historical terms.  Hanson said that Isaiah's long career best exemplified this balancing of vision and reality, of myth and history.  The Deuteronomic history demythologized that tension, but its theology of transparent divine activity based on obedience to the central cult proved untenable after the death of Josiah and the fall of Jerusalem.

The exilic prophets Jeremiah and Ezekiel resisted the effort to historicize Yahwism, but Hanson saw Jeremiah's pessimism and hope for a radically changed new age and Ezekiel's extensive use of cosmic imagery as first moves toward apocalyptic.  II Isaiah drew on the divine warrior hymn of the defunct royal cult and boldly maintained and heightened the tension between myth and history, although with him the strain began to show.  In the tensions of the restoration community the scale tipped toward the mythic as the early apocalypticists increasingly left their visions on the cosmic plain.

In Hanson's view, apocalyptic developed in stages in the postexilic community.  He called II Isaiah "proto-apocalyptic" because later apocalypticists drew on him for their mythic images.  "Early apocalyptic," including III Isaiah, Zechariah 9-13, and the Isaiah Apocalypse, originated in a community of disciples of II Isaiah which increasingly lost a historical perspective and developed the salvation-judgment oracle.  Zechariah 14 represented the first example of full-blown apocalyptic eschatology, with an almost total absence of historical references, a fully developed salvation-judgment oracle, and a totally divided community upon which the eschaton would soon fall.[41]

IV

One of the most impressive points of the scholarly discussions surveyed is the evidence for rivalries within the postexilic Jewish community as reflected in the literature. The intensive studies of Plöger and Hanson have demonstrated the ideological and political struggles underlying early apocalyptic literature. The two men, in spite of approaching the material from similar sociological perspectives, have reached different conclusions as to the dates of many oracles. Plöger dated the material from the fourth century to the early decades of the Greek period,[42] while Hanson limited the same basic material between 550-450 B.C.E.[43]

This distinction raises a question regarding Hanson's method of dating and the exclusion of virtually all nonprophetic influences on apocalyptic. Drawing an analogy with an archaeological typology of lamps in which intermediate forms indicate the connection between the oldest and the newest, he developed a typology of poetry, themes, and genres and dated each oracle along a continuum based on its similarity or lack of similarity with II Isaiah. But other factors bear on archaeological dating, such as stratification, inscriptions, and other datable material, which are not analogous to the study of late prophetic oracles. An essential question is whether a typology showing the range of poetic form and theological motif within a body of literature *ipso facto* establishes the straight line chronological development of the literature which Hanson seemed to assume.[44]

One possible approach in testing the adequacy of Hanson's dating of III Isaiah and II Zechariah is to inquire whether any other period in the postexilic community fits the model of division and hostility centered on events in the Temple which Hanson has so plausibly drawn out of the material. If Morton Smith's reconstruction of the conflicts and upheavals of the Jewish community between 400 and 200 B.C.E. has validity, that period deserves to be tested against the textual evidence. Smith pictured a vacillating control of the Temple cult between a strictly separatist religious party, descendants of Nehemiah, and an assimilationist party, including most of the priests and leaders, who were less strict both religiously and politically.[45] Klaus Koch's thesis regarding Ezra's return gives this suggestion even more plausibility. Koch studied the Ezra source (Ezra 7-10; Neh 8-9) and concluded that Ezra understood his return from Babylonia as preparation for the fulfillment of prophetic promises rather than as the establishment of a theocracy. His goal was to rebuild Israel as a nation of twelve tribes, including the later Samaritans, centered in a Temple made and kept holy by application of the Torah. Only at a later time did the community replace cult with Torah. According to Koch, Ezra's motives were prophetic rather than legal.[46] On the basis of Koch's study, the return under Ezra-Nehemiah appears somewhat more flexible and fluid theologically than is sometimes proposed, raising the possibility that community tensions reached advanced stages only at a later time.

Most historical developments are marked by ebb and flow, by advance and retreat, by initiation and revision. Such processes take time to reach maturity. In Hanson's typology-chronology, hardly a generation passes from the first early apocalyptic oracle (Isa 60-62) to the presence of all the essential elements of apocalyptic in Isaiah 66 and 56-57. In slightly over another generation Zechariah 14 ushered in "full-blown apocalyptic."[47] But the community conditions described by Hanson, a group in control of the Temple which was considered corrupt by the visionary community, loss of power by the Levites, and lack of interest in eschatology by the priestly group, also existed in the fourth century. Smith argued that early in the fourth century the assimilationists regained control of the Temple.[48] Afterwards, the Levites began to be fused with Temple singers and doorkeepers, and the final redaction of the Pentateuch allowed the Samaritans to accept the law and continue their cult under its umbrella. This rapprochement was formalized through intermarriage between Jews and Samaritans. Proselyte laws developed to legitimate aliens, an especially helpful move for aliens married to Jews. The assimilationists formed alliances with Egypt and possibly with Sparta.[49] On all of these points the separatist priests and their followers took opposite positions. Many of the acrimonious charges of paganism and ungodly alliances in the apocalyptic passages become much more understandable if they represent protests of the separatist group against the assimilationists rather than prophetic groups in opposition to the theocratic leaders reestablishing the cult on the basis of the Torah.

One result of an early dating of apocalyptic oracles with their attendant community division is Hanson's labeling of Ezekiel, Haggai, and Zechariah as basic literature of the theocratic element,[50] even though later apocalyptic communities recognized apocalyptic elements in both Ezekiel and Zechariah.[51] A longer period of development allows the vision of these prophets to nourish both visionary and realist in a genuine way.

Further, as great a gap seems to separate Zechariah 14 from Daniel as separates II Isaiah from Zechariah 14. Non-prophetic elements cannot be ignored in the final form of apocalyptic. John J. Collins surveyed the Hellenistic Near East from the fifth through the second century B.C.E. and found a number of Egyptian and Mesopotamian parallels to char-acteristic features of Jewish apocalyptic literature, includ-ing messianism, divine intervention following a four kingdom survey of history, and the revival of ancient myths.[52] Scholars of the ancient Near East have identified cuneiform tablets which date between 1000 and 700 B.C.E. and exemplify the prophecy *ex eventu* characterizing Daniel and later apoca-lypses.[53] A "prophecy" of events through the reign of Nebu-chadnezzar apparently functioned to support and legitimate his son and successor, Amel-Marduk, thus bringing the *ex eventu* form to about 562 B.C.E.[54] A. K. Grayson published another exemplar of this Mesopotamian genre which "prophesied" down to Seleucid times and apparently concluded with a genuine prediction of the fall of the Seleucid dynasty similar to Daniel, though less visionary.[55] The parallels between these texts and later apocalyptic must receive consideration in the rise of apocalyptic.[56] Likewise, recent studies emphasizing one or another aspect of the wisdom tradition within apocalyp-tic cannot be dismissed lightly, especially in view of paral-lels in the wider geographical area.[57] A longer period of development takes seriously these later influences. Hanson's limitation of the visionary perspective to apocalyptic escha-tology will also likely require revision to take account of the very complex nature of mature apocalyptic literature.

As Hanson has correctly pointed out, apocalyptic writers sought to universalize their message, especially through the use of myth. The longer gestation period allows more time, not only for the historical realm to become less significant as the scene of God's activity, but also for the apocalyptic writers to transform myth into new forms and make it useful in communicating new levels of meaning to their beleaguered community. The difficult judgments regarding the unity of some oracles may be partially explained on the hypothesis that portions of them have been used at different times in different contexts,[58] and that in the process oracles have been universalized through the loss of historical references and through various combinations with other myths and materi-al.[59]

One final word regarding classifications of apocalyptic may be helpful to the scholarly discussion. Since II Isaiah, Ezekiel, Haggai, and I Zechariah exhibit both the historical and mythical elements to a significant degree, they should be designated as "late prophetic." Materials which demonstrate initial signs of the breakdown of history into pure myth, such as the Isaiah Apocalypse and portions of III Isaiah and II Zechariah, should receive the designation "proto-apocalyptic." Those materials in which myth predominates significantly over history but which lack the more elaborate developments of later apocalyptic, for example Zechariah 14, should then be designated "early apocalyptic." All of these designations refer to typology, with chronology being determined, where possible, on other grounds.

## NOTES

1. See D. W. Bousset, *Die Religion des Judentums im Neutestamentlichen Zeitalter* (2d ed.; Berlin: Reuther und Reichard, 1906), 242-245; M. Buber, *Mamre: Essays in Religion* (Westport, CN: Greenwood, 1946), 27-28; and W. R. Murdock, "History and Revelation in Jewish Apocalypticism," *Int* 21 (1967), 173-174.

2. S.v., *IDB.*

3. For a typical list of literary characteristics, see D. S. Russell, *The Method and Message of Jewish Apocalyptic, 200 B.C.-A.D. 100* (Philadelphia: Westminster, 1964), 105-139, and for the characteristic ideas, 205-390. See also W. Schmithals, *The Apocalyptic Movement: Introduction and Interpretation* (Nashville: Abingdon, 1975), 13-28; and K. Koch, *The Rediscovery of Apocalyptic* (Naperville, ILL: Alex R. Allenson, 1972), 23-34.

4. H. H. Rowley, *The Relevance of Apocalyptic: A Study of Jewish and Christian Apocalypses from Daniel to the Revelation* (3d ed.; London: Lutterworth, 1963), 15.

5. *Ibid.,* 16-42.

6. *Ibid.,* 43.

7. *Ibid.,* 43-53.

8. Russell, *Method and Message,* 18-20.

9. *Ibid.,* 88.

258

10. Russell, *Method and Message*, 89-91.

11. *Ibid.*, 92-95, 118, 122-126. Russell allowed some Greek influence on the apocalyptic view of the nature of man, e.g., man as constituted of the four primal elements and as dualistic in nature, but concluded that Greek influence was slight compared to that of the Hebrew tradition.

12. *Ibid.*, 184-186.

13. *Ibid.*, 193-194.

14. Rowley (*Relevance*, 54-165) surveyed the literature with primary attention to the common ideas of each book, whereas Russell (*Method and Message*, 205-390) organized the last half of his book thematically and discussed the contribution of various apocalypses to those topics.

15. For a sociological analysis of modern apocalyptic movements, see R. R. Wilson, "This World--and the World to Come: Apocalyptic Religion and the Counterculture," *Encounter* 38 (1977), 117-124.

16. O. Plöger, *Theology and Eschatology* (Oxford: Basil Blackwell, 1968), 17-18.

17. *Ibid.*, 28-29.

18. *Ibid.*, 29-43.

19. *Ibid.*, 45-46, also 26-27.

20. *Ibid.*, 46-49.

21. *Ibid.*, 51.

22. *Ibid.*, 53-105.

23. *Ibid.*, 108-114.

24. G. von Rad, *Old Testament Theology* (2 vols.; New York: Harper & Row, 1965), 2, 303.

25. *Ibid.*, 303-305.

26. *Ibid.*, 306-308.

27. G. von Rad, *Wisdom in Israel* (London: SCM, 1972), 263-270, 277.

28. Von Rad, *Wisdom,* 279-282.

29. For criticism of von Rad's unilinear derivation of apocalyptic from wisdom, see Koch, *Rediscovery,* 45-47; and P. L. Redditt, "Postexilic Eschatological Prophecy and the Rise of Apocalyptic Literature," *Ohio Journal of Religious Studies* 2 (1974), 28.

30. J. J. Collins, "The Court-Tales in Daniel and the Development of Apocalyptic," *JBL* 94 (1975), 218-234. See also G. W. E. Nickelsburg, "The Apocalyptic Message of I Enoch 92-105," *CBQ* 39 (1977), 309-328.

31. J. J. Collins, "Cosmos and Salvation: Jewish Wisdom and Apocalyptic in the Hellenistic Age," *HR* 17 (1977), 121-142, esp. 123, 134-142.

32. J. Z. Smith, "Wisdom and Apocalyptic," in *Religious Syncretism in Antiquity: Essays in Conversation with Geo Widengren* (ed. B. A. Pearson; Missoula: Scholars, 1975), 131-156. For a discussion of apocalyptic situations in non-biblical settings, see J. Z. Smith, "A Pearl of Great Price and a Cargo of Yams: A Study in Situational Incongruity," *HR* 16 (1976), 1-19.

33. P. D. Hanson, "Jewish Apocalyptic Against its Near Eastern Environment," *RB* 78 (1971), 33-34. For a similar thesis at approximately the same time, see W. S. McCullough, "Israel's Eschatology from Amos to Daniel," in *Studies on the Ancient Palestinian World* (ed. J. W. Wevers and D. B. Redford; Toronto: University of Toronto, 1972), 86-101. McCullough concluded that "all the really important features in [Israel's] eschatology, at least down to Daniel, can be most satisfactorily accounted for by carefully scrutinizing Israel's own traditions."

34. Hanson, "Jewish Apocalyptic," 33; "Zechariah 9 and the Recapitulation of an Ancient Ritual Pattern," *JBL* 92 (1973), 37-40; and *The Dawn of Apocalyptic* (Philadelphia: Fortress, 1975), 29.

35. As examples, see Hanson, *Dawn,* 59-60, 87-88, 299; however, in "Zechariah 9," Hanson assigned poetic structure and meter to a relatively minor position in favor of analysis of the genre of the divine warrior hymn.

36. Hanson, *Dawn,* 106-108, 328-333, 404; and "Zechariah 9," 40-59.

37. Hanson, *Dawn*, 11; and "Jewish Apocalyptic," 35.

38. Hanson, *Dawn*, 12; and "Jewish Apocalyptic," 35.

39. Hanson, *Dawn*, *passim.*; and "Jewish Apocalyptic," 50-53.

40. In depicting this divided community, Hanson echoed the sociological insights of Plöger's *Theology and Eschatology* but without attribution.

41. P. D. Hanson, "Old Testament Apocalyptic Reexamined," *Int* 25 (1971), 454-479; "Jewish Apocalyptic," 40-50, 56; and *Dawn*, *passim*.

42. Plöger, *Theology and Eschatology*, 77-78, 80-82, 94.

43. Hanson, *Dawn*, 207-208, 314, 323-324, 400-401; and "Jewish Apocalyptic," 56.

44. Several reviewers have questioned Hanson's use of meter and structure (with emendations based on same) to date prophetic oracles. See J. R. Lundbom, in *Andover Newton Quarterly* 16 (1976), 282-283; P. L. Redditt, in *RevExp* 73 (1976), 80; P. R. Ackroyd, in *Int* 30 (1976), 413; and S. B. Frost, in *SR* 6 (1976), 310.

45. M. Smith, *Palestinian Parties and Politics that Helped Shape the Old Testament* (New York: Columbia University, 1971), 148-192.

46. K. Koch, "Ezra and the Origins of Judaism," *JSS* 19 (1974), 173-197. See also W. J. Dumbrell, "Malachi and the Ezra-Nehemiah Reforms," *Reformed Theological Review* 35 (1976), 42-52.

47. Hanson, *Dawn*, 168-173, 194-195, 369.

48. M. Smith, *Palestinian Parties*, 172. H. G. M. Williamson ("The Historical Value of Josephus' *Jewish Antiquities* XI.297-301," *JTS*, n.s., 28 [1977], 49-66) concluded that the sharp divisions in the postexilic community, especially in the priesthood, were not restricted to the fifth century B.C.E. but continued much longer.

49. M. Smith, *Palestinian Parties*, 172-186. For a similar dating of the Pentateuch and its reception by the Samaritans, see W. S. McCullough, *The History and Literature of the Palestinian Jews from Cyrus to Herod, 550 B.C. to 4 B.C.*

(Toronto: University of Toronto, 1975), 51, 78-79.

50. Hanson, *Dawn*, 225-228, 234-238, 240-259.

51. The later apocalyptic community thought Zechariah echoed apocalyptic ideas to such an extent that it attached Zechariah 9-14 to it. Rex A. Mason ("The Relation of Zech 9-14 to Proto-Zechariah," *ZAW* 88 [1976], 227-238) has concluded that II Zechariah is the product of a community of disciples or at least a circle of tradition deriving from I Zechariah. He traced five themes in both sections and noted that the later material expressed increasing disillusionment with the theocratic leadership, looking instead for direct divine intervention to bring the new age into existence. Regarding the role of Ezekiel in the later apocalyptic community, see Redditt, *RevExp* 73:80; and R. G. Hamerton-Kelley, "The Temple and the Origins of Jewish Apocalyptic," *VT* 20 (1970), 1-15.

52. J. J. Collins, "Jewish Apocalyptic Against Its Hellenistic Near Eastern Environment," *BASOR* 220 (1975), 27-36.

53. See A. K. Grayson and W. G. Lambert, "Akkadian Prophecies," *JCS* 18 (1964), 7-30; W. W. Hallo, "Akkadian Apocalypses," *IEJ* 16 (1966), 231-242; and R. Borger, "Gott Marduk und Gott-König Šulgi als Propheten," *BO* 28 (1971), 3-24. For a study of Daniel from a similar perspective, see R. J. Clifford, "History and Myth in Daniel 10-12," *BASOR* 220 (1975), 23-26.

54. H. Hunger and S. A. Kaufman, "A New Akkadian Prophecy Text," *JAOS* 95 (1975), 371-375.

55. A. K. Grayson, *Babylonian Historical-Literary Texts* (Toronto Semitic Texts and Studies 3; Toronto: University of Toronto, 1975), 3-37.

56. For a discussion of these parallels, see S. A. Kaufman, "Predictions, Prophecy, and Apocalypse in the Light of New Akkadian Texts," *Proceedings of the Sixth World Congress of Jewish Studies* 1 (1977), 221-228.

57. See Collins, "Cosmos and Salvation," 121-142; and J. Smith, "Wisdom and Apocalyptic," 131-156.

58. Peter Ackroyd suggested that lamentations, psalms, and prophetic oracles experienced use in many historical situations with each setting contributing something to the form. See P. R. Ackroyd, *Exile and Restoration: A Study of*

*Hebrew Thought of the Sixth Century B.C.* (Philadelphia:
Westminster, 1968), 45-46, 172-173.

59.  Hanson (*Dawn*, 134-135, 161-163, 292-295) and
Plöger (*Theology and Eschatology*, 54-55, 62-63) already
allow that some of the oracles have been combined secondarily
in their final form.  William Millar (*Isaiah 24-27 and the
Origin of Apocalyptic* [Missoula:  Scholars, 1976], 117-120)
reached the same conclusion in his study of the Isaiah Apocalypse.  See also Redditt, "Postexilic Prophecy," 38-39; and
S. B. Frost, "Apocalyptic and History," in *The Bible in
Modern Scholarship* (ed. J. P. Hyatt; Nashville:  Abingdon,
1965), 98-113.

# ANTIOCHUS EPIPHANES
## AND THE PERSECUTION OF THE JEWS

Bruce William Jones
California State College, Bakersfield

The purpose of this paper is to discuss the causes of the persecution of the Jews by Antiochus IV. A long series of scholars, going back at least to Elias Bickermann in 1937,[1] has contributed to our understanding of this persecution by suggesting some very insightful interpretations. However, no single interpretation is sufficient to explain the complex series of events. I shall offer some corrections to previous interpretations and shall attempt to combine their insights into a more multi-faceted explanation.

The persecution is traditionally explained as the result of Antiochus' madness or his wickedness. The tradition of his madness goes back to his contemporary, Polybius, who reports that Antiochus was called *epimanes* (mad) as well as *epiphanes* (*The Histories*, 26.1). The most recent commentary on Daniel uses such an explanation when it speaks of Antiochus as "a despot of the worst sort, eccentric and unpredictable, ferocious and tyrannical," and speaks of "the tyrant's untiring Hellenistic policy."[2] The new revision of Schürer's *History* by Vermes and Millar also accepts this traditional evaluation of Antiochus.[3] We ought not to consider Polybius a reliable reporter, however. In his own career as a statesman, he was invariably on the side of Antiochus' nephew, Demetrius I, whose throne was usurped by Antiochus.[4] Polybius did not approve of some of Antiochus' behavior, which he considered erratic and too undignified for a king, so he reports it in the worst possible light, but Polybius probably did not understand what lay behind all the gossip reports.[5]

When Otto Mørkholm examined Antiochus' actual accomplishments, even after his humiliation by the Romans in 168, which is supposed to have driven the king to the edge of insanity, he concludes that "Antiochus ... quickly regained his firm grasp of the political realities. His behaviour down to his death does not reveal a broken or unsettled mind."[6] Mørkholm concludes that Antiochus IV was "well above average" in comparison to the other Seleucid kings.[7] Mørkholm also points out that Antiochus was remembered very favorably by his subjects after his death. His son and successor, Antiochus V, was called "Eupator" because of his father's reputation for virtue. Later, the memory of Antiochus IV was used in political propaganda by Alexander Balas when he claimed the throne by pretending to be the son of Antiochus IV and when he appealed to the latter's memory by calling himself "Theopator." Antiochus Epiphanes was "cherished with affection by at least a substantial portion of the Syrian population."[8]

The idea that Antiochus IV was so wicked stems primarily from the Jews. They suffered greatly under his rule, and their very legitimate complaints produced the historiographical record upon which we have depended for our evaluations.

Let us compare that historiographical record with the other information available to us, including some clues--often overlooked--which have been preserved as part of that record. First, we will look at the statement in 1 Macc 1:41-43 that Antiochus initiated a kingdom-wide program of religious unification whereby all peoples would give up their own customs, adopt the king's religion and become one people. This agrees with the charge in Dan 11:36-39 that the king of the north (Antiochus IV) will honor a new god whom his fathers did not know and will exalt himself at the expense of all other gods, not just the God of the Jews. "To no god will he pay heed but will exalt himself above them all" (11:37, NEB). On the other hand, other evidence from the Hellenistic period makes us doubt that there was ever a general imposition of religion. The indications are, rather, that all religions were tolerated, including, usually, Judaism.

For example, Rostovtzeff has pointed out that documents from "Babylon and Uruk show that in the official terminology the Seleucids were represented there as the legitimate successors of the Babylonian kings, as rulers who, like Alexander, had received their power from the hands of Bel and Marduk .... In Syria, the kernel of their empire, Seleucus and his descendants adopted a similar attitude in regard to the local gods and traditions."[9] The same seems to be true for Asia Minor as well.[10]

As nearly as we can tell, Jews, too, enjoyed this same toleration of local traditions. Martin Hengel describes in detail the very positive attitude that Greeks had toward Jewish ethical monotheism. Judaism fit well into Greek ideas of

universalism, but at the same time, the Greeks were never
able to understand its particularism. For example, Hengel
says that in spite of the praise of Greek writers they were
not interested in Jewish history or Jewish religious practice.[11] As we shall see below, this basic inability to grasp
the uniqueness of Judaism led to tragic consequences.

When Palestine passed from the hands of the Ptolemies
to the Seleucids, Antiochus III confirmed the autonomy of the
Jews. Josephus quotes a letter of Antiochus III:

> Inasmuch as the Jews, from the very moment
> when we entered their country, showed their
> eagerness to serve us, ... and furnished an
> abundance of provision to our soldiers and
> elephants, and also helped us to expel the
> Egyptian garrison in the citadel, we have
> seen fit on our part to requite them for
> these acts and to restore their city which
> has been destroyed by the hazards of war,
> and to repeople it by bringing back to it
> those who have been dispersed abroad. In the
> first place we have decided, on account of
> their piety, to furnish them for their sacri-
> fices an allowance of sacrificial animals,
> wine, oil and frankincense to the value of
> twenty thousand pieces of silver, and sacred
> *artabae* [an Egyptian measure] of fine flour,
> in accordance with their native law .... And
> all the members of the nation shall have a
> form of government in accordance with the laws
> of their country, and the senate, the priests,
> the scribes of the temple and the temple sing-
> ers shall be relieved from the poll-tax and
> the crown-tax and the salt-tax which they pay.[12]

Then he grants a further exemption of taxes to the inhabitants
and those who return before a specified period "in order that
the city may the more quickly be inhabited" (*Ant.*, 12.143).
His political and economic motivations are clear. Josephus
also reports Antiochus III's decision to resettle Jews in
Asia Minor. Even if the language has been embellished somewhat, the fact of the resettlement clearly points to the trust
and confidence that Antiochus III had in the loyalty of the
Jews in Babylonia. He writes to his governor in Babylonia,

> Learning that the people in Lydia and Phrygia
> are revolting, ... I determined to transport two
> thousand Jewish families with their effects from

Mesopotamia and Babylonia to the fortresses
and most important places. For I am convinced that they will be loyal guardians of
our interests because of their piety to God
(*Ant.*, 12.149,150).

He then goes on to specify the grants of land and the exemptions from taxation to be made as compensation to the colonists for resettlement.

Jews were apparently so open to Greek ideas that some of
them were departing from the religion of their fathers. Well
before the accession of Antiochus IV, Ben Sirach warns his
fellow Jews not to be ashamed of their law and covenant (Sir
42:1-2). In the mid-third century, Tobias, who was married
to the sister of the high priest, can write to a Greek, "If
all goes well with you, ... many thanks be to the *gods*."[13]

These general observations about the Hellenistic toleration of minorities and their religions do not tell us whether
or not Antiochus IV changed his ancestors' policies.[14] We do
know that he encouraged the worship of various forms of Zeus
throughout his kingdom, but the evidence suggests (1) that
this encouragement was not new with Antiochus IV, as formerly
believed,[15] (2) that Antiochus did not identify himself with
Zeus, as formerly believed,[16] (3) that his kingdom-wide worship
of Zeus and the king was motivated by political reasons,
rather than religious (see below), and (4) that neither the
royal cult nor the cult of Zeus involved the suppression of
the cults of other gods. Rather, Zeus was identified with
them wherever possible, and that was the intention in Judea
as well. This last point merits some explanation.

Antiochus Epiphanes did promote the cult of Zeus and of
himself, but there is no evidence outside our Jewish sources
to indicate that there was ever any intention to suppress the
worship of other gods as a result. In fact, when Antiochus
held his famous festal assembly (*panēgyris*) in Daphne in 166--
right in the middle of the period of Jewish persecution--with
its athletic games and sacred procession (*pompeia*), Polybius
reported that there were too many images of different gods in
the procession to be able to count them. Every god or spirit
was there whether worshipped or even mentioned by mankind
(*Histories*, 30.25.13).

It also seems to be the case that Antiochus IV confirmed
the gifts of his predecessors to Babylonian temples,[17] so
there was no suppression of local cults there. He continued
to show reverence for Apollo at Delos and extended the temple

of that god at Daphne.[18]

Much has been made of the fact that Zeus replaced the traditional Seleucid Apollo on Antiochus' coins after 173/2, but coins continued to be minted with traditional representations of Apollo even after the appearance of Zeus Olympius.[19] Also, the copper coins which Antiochus IV authorized for local mints for the first time show a wide variety of local deities.[20] Poseidon, the Dioscuri, Europa on a bull, and a six-winged Kronos of "a decidedly un-Greek character" appear on other coins.[21] This shows clearly that Antiochus was not trying to make "one religion" or stamp out other cults.

The whole purpose of Antiochus' encouragement of the Zeus cult seems to have been motivated by a desire to unify his kingdom by identifying the various local gods with Zeus. Since 1884 biblical scholars have known that the Zeus Olympius mentioned in 2 Macc 6:2 is really a Greek name for the Syrian Baal Shamen, "lord of heaven," and that is the basis for the pun in Daniel on šōmēm, "desolating."[22] We know from Philo of Byblos that the Phoenicians identified Zeus and Beelsamēn.[23] Presumably, Anu of Uruk was identified with this "lord of heaven," and the gentiles and even some of the Jews also understood the God of Israel to be so identified.

We know that many Jews seemed comfortable with such identifications. Already in Ezra 1:2, 5:11, 12; 6:9 and Neh 1:4, 5; 2:4, 20, God is called "God of heaven," sometimes when the speaker is a gentile but sometimes when Nehemiah is addressing God. The Septuagint used "lord," "the God" or "the Almighty" for various Hebrew proper names. First Maccabees frequently refers to God simply as "Heaven." In Josephus' paraphrase of the Letter of Aristeas, Aristeas can tell Ptolemy Philadelphus that both of them worship the same God, called Zeus (*Ant.*, 12.22).[24] Not all Jews may have liked using that Greek divine name, but it seemed to be no problem for the Samaritans, who took the initiative themselves, according to our sources, for renaming their temple either for Zeus Xenios (2 Macc 6:2) or for Zeus Hellenios (*Ant.*, 12.257-264). There is every reason to think that Antiochus did not expect it to be a problem for Jews either.[25]

The Book of Daniel must be part of the evidence cited on behalf of Jewish ideas of assimilation. The authors betray no criticism that Daniel and his companions take non-Jewish names, even one based--by a false etymology--on the name of the god Bel.[26] B. A. Mastin has also pointed out that the monotheistic authors seem undisturbed that Nebuchadnezzar should express his gratitude to Daniel by giving him cultic honors that befit a god, using the common Greek pattern of the cult of the "benefactor."[27]

The Book of Daniel is, of course, the best contemporary example of opposition to Antiochus' religious policies, but it continues to tell tales about pagan kings who can be persuaded to worship the God of Israel under some universalist name such as "God of gods" (2:47), "Most High God" (3:26, 32 = Eng. 4:2), "the Most High" (4:21, 22, 29, 31 = Eng. 4:24, 25, 32, 34), "King of heaven" (4:34 = Eng. 4:37), or "the living God" (6:21, 27 = Eng. 6:20, 26). These tales are usually considered to be pre-Maccabean in date, but the fact that they are preserved and included in the book suggests that the Maccabean author-editor was not totally hostile to their content.

He is, however, very hostile to the idea that the God of gods could be properly worshipped by the mixed and unclean practices then being used at the temple. Dan 11:39 says that the king (Antiochus IV) will garrison his strongest fortresses with the help of "a foreign god." The verse undoubtedly refers to the troops stationed in the various garrisons, such as the Acra at Jerusalem, and to the hybrid god worshipped there. Antiochus and the Hellenizers may have thought that they could identify the God of Israel with "a foreign god," but the authors of Daniel reject that identification.

In spite of Antiochus' toleration for the religious practices of most of his subjects and regardless of his original intentions toward the Jews, it is clear that he did move to stamp out Judaism in Jerusalem and the surrounding area. There is no hard evidence, however, that Jews in other parts of his kingdom were affected. If, in fact, his persecution were limited geographically, we ought to doubt that he was motivated by religious fanaticism. He did not display the thoroughness of a Hitler. Bickermann argued that the persecution had no impact at all beyond Palestine.[28] Not everyone has been convinced by him,[29] but it is significant that even 1 and 2 Maccabees make no mention of Jews in Syria or Babylonia participating in the revolt. It seems likely that Diaspora Jews had not experienced the same pressure that was felt in Jerusalem. We have some support for this conjecture in our sources. When 2 Macc 12:29-30 reports on Judas Maccabeus' travels north of Jerusalem, it says,

> They advanced to Scythopolis, some seventy-five miles from Jerusalem. The Jews who lived there testified to the goodwill shown them by the people of Scythopolis and the

kindness with which they treated them in
their bad times (NEB).

Also, *Ant.* (12.257-264) reports a petition from the Samaritans to Antiochus IV, asking that they be excused from the
king's proscription of religion, since they are not Jews.
It is a strange letter, in which they claim to be "Sidonians."
They ask that their temple be rededicated to Zeus Hellenios.
Their requests were granted. It is difficult to sort out the
truth from Josephus' anti-Samaritan biases, but at least it
seems clear--if there is any kernel of truth to the story at
all, and I think there is[30]--that Samaria was involved in the
Hellenization process. According to Josephus, the Samaritans
*thought* that the persecution would apply to them, but in the
end it did not. They were allowed to worship their own God,
presumably the same God worshipped at Jerusalem, as long as
they called him by a Greek name. So far as we know, they
continued to read Torah and to practice circumcision and the
other rites forbidden to Jews. Josephus would have been de-
lighted if he could report that the Samaritans had surrendered
Torah or circumcision, but he does not.

If it is the case that it was not the general policy of
the Seleucids or even of Antiochus IV to discourage the worship of local gods, why did he prohibit the practice of Judaism with such bloody violence? Many scholars have adopted
the suggestion of Bickermann, that the initiative came not
from Antiochus IV, but from Hellenizing Jews.[31] One of the
more recent defenders of this view has been Martin Hengel.[32]
According to this position, events moved in a series of
stages. Both 1 and 2 Maccabees and Josephus say that lawless
Jews took the initiative to make a "covenant" with the gentiles: "There appeared in Israel a group of renegade Jews,
who incited the people. 'Let us enter into a covenant with
the Gentiles round about,' they said" (1 Macc 1:11). As soon
as Antiochus IV became king, Jason, the brother of the high
priest Onias III, bribed the king to make him high priest in
place of his brother.[33] At the same time he petitioned Antiochus for permission to establish a gymnasium and an *ephebion* or school for young men, "and to enroll in Jerusalem a
group to be known as the 'Antiochenes'" (2 Macc 4:9). It is
almost universally agreed now that these were the three steps
necessary to transform Jerusalem into a Greek *polis*.[34] The
change in the status of Jerusalem was a constitutional transformation from the status of *ethnos* to that of *polis*. The
former implied legal exemptions. The latter carried with it
the privilege of being in the political and social mainstream.[35]
As Hengel points out, there is no report of any Jewish opposition at this stage.[36] Also, the sources do not suggest any

religious motivation on the part of Antiochus. He was motivated by Jason's bribe and by political realities (see below).
Religious attraction *may* have motivated Jason, but the Hellenizers were probably much more interested in gaining prestige and perhaps economic power as citizens of the *polis*.
They are depicted as being embarrassed at being Jews (1 Macc
1:15) or indifferent (2 Macc 4:14-15), but they show no
particular enthusiasm for any other religion either. Thus,
when a group of them takes money to the Tyrian games for a
sacrifice to Hercules, they donate it for outfitting ships
instead. "The bearers thought it improper that this money
should be used for a sacrifice" (2 Macc 4:19). The change
did have religious implications, however. The temple now
belonged to the *polis*.[37] The transformation would give the
king the right to appoint the high priest, since the *ethnos*
would no longer be self-governing as it had been. Interestingly, as 2 Macc 4:7-10 reports the events, the usurpation
of the office and the change in status of the city occur
simultaneously. The association is quite logical, and we
have no reason to doubt it.

The change in the status of Jerusalem would also make
the king think that he had a more legitimate right to the
treasury of the temple. Additionally, Antiochus IV would
now be considered the *ktistes*, the founder of the new *polis*,
which usually involved a local cult with divine honors paid
regularly to the founder.[38]

The next stage, after the initiative of the Hellenizers,
was a more direct involvement of Antiochus IV. Again he de-
posed the high priest and appointed a new one for a bribe,
this time Menelaus, a non-Zadokite and a member of the aris-
tocratic Tobiad family. Now that the temple was an institution of the *polis* and not the *ethnos*, Antiochus undoubtedly
no longer felt bound by the Jewish rules of succession.

Menelaus and his brother soon became involved in looting
the temple treasury. Both these acts, as well as the murder
of Onias III, the rightful high priest, which probably happened about this time, angered pious Jews, who started rioting
(2 Macc 4:23-50).

While Antiochus was engaged in his second battle in
Egypt, there was a rumor of his death, and Jason made an attempt to regain the high priesthood by force of arms. Antiochus, very much alive and very angry at the revolt, came back
to Jerusalem, killed thousands, and looted the temple in person (1 Macc 5). Then, convinced that the peculiar religion
of the Jews lay at the heart of their rebellion, Antiochus

took steps against its practice. "King Antiochus sent an elderly Athenian to force the Jews to abandon their ancestral customs and no longer regulate their lives according to the laws of God. He was also commissioned to pollute the temple at Jerusalem and dedicate it to Olympian Zeus" (2 Macc 6:1-2). Antiochus' fury was not directed only to Jason and his thousand supporters, but against all the Jews.

My reconstruction of these events depends upon Tcheri-kover,[39] and it agrees to a great extent with the sequence reported in 2 Maccabees, although the author of 2 Maccabees has played down the extent of the popular revolt prior to the involvement of Judas Maccabeus.[40] Tcherikover is right to point out that Antiochus' decree was a response to rebellion and not its cause. However, I do not accept his conclusion that there was "a people's revolt" against both Jason *and* Menelaus. The dispute between the two of them over the high priesthood involved only a minority of the population. There is reason for confusion, however, as follows: According to 2 Maccabees, Jason took control of Jerusalem with great brutality, and Menelaus fled to the citadel (5:5). What happened next is less clear. Jason did not "gain control of the government; he gained only dishonour as the result of his plot, and returned again as a fugitive to Ammonite territory" (5:7). When Antiochus came to Jerusalem, "Judaea was in a state of rebellion" (5:11), which he put down vigorously. Tcherikover takes this to mean that first Jason drove out Menelaus and that there was then "a people's revolt against Jason," which drove him out. Tcherikover argues that if Menelaus had already regained control of the city, there would have been no need for Antiochus' intervention. Rather, the common people had wrested control from both the Hellenizing high priests, and Antiochus needed to make a show of strength against them in order to reassert his authority.[41]

I maintain, rather, that Jason was in control of Jerusalem until Antiochus' soldiers came and restored Menelaus. When Apollonius was sent to Jerusalem later, he did not come because the popular "rebellion blazed up afresh"[42] or to restore Menelaus once more. The city was already pacified and Apollonius came to raze the walls of Jerusalem and build an Acra. He could not have come into the city peacefully, as 2 Macc 5:25 says he did, if it were still in open rebellion. Tcherikover depends too much upon the order of events as reported by 2 Maccabees, where Jason's flight is described before the sending of Antiochus' troops. Thus, Tcherikover gives credit to the people of Jerusalem, not to Menelaus and Antiochus, for expelling Jason. But 2 Maccabees does not intend us to take this report as the actual order of events.

Rather, it tells the story in an organized fashion by giving us a complete history of the rebel Jason, down to his igno- minious death. Then, the author/summarizer picks up the story by returning to the rebellion proper: "When news of this reached the king, it became clear to him that Judaea was in a state of rebellion" (5:11). The "news of this" (*peri tōn gegonotōn*) is obviously not the news of Jason's unmourned death en route to Sparta, much later, just men- tioned in the previous verses, but the original news of Jason's attack on Jerusalem.

It is correct that the Hellenizers played an important role in the events that led up to the persecution. However, (1) we must not describe that role in a way that neglects the responsibility of Antiochus or the significance of the political realities he was facing (see below). (2) We must be cautious about accepting at face value the statements in 2 Maccabees and Josephus that Menelaus or the Hellenizers were the only cause of trouble. (3) Bickermann and Hengel overstate their case in such a way that we are left without an adequate explanation of the motives of the Hellenizers. They depict the Hellenizers as intolerant promoters of toleration.

In 2 Maccabees 13 and in *Ant.*, 12.384, Lysias informs Antiochus V Eupator that Menelaus was the cause of all the trouble. I have no doubt that Menelaus played a decisive role, but in these two reports, Lysias is looking for a scapegoat so that he need not blame the king's father. Also, those who are familiar with Josephus' account of the First Jewish Revolt (*J.W.*, 2-7) against Rome know that he is only too willing to attribute problems to intra-Jewish con- flict rather than to gentile rulers. Neither Josephus nor 2 Maccabees is prone to whitewash Antiochus IV, but their biases make them emphasize other factors. In the case of 2 Maccabees, either Jason of Cyrene or his summarizer believe in a strict theology of divine retribution (4:16, 26, 38; 5:6-10; 8:34-36; 9:4-12, 28; 13:3-8), so that if the Jews suffer, it must be because they have deserved to do so. Thus, the "sins of the people of Jerusalem had angered the Lord for a short time, and that was why he left the temple to its fate. If they had not already been guilty of many sinful acts, Antiochus would have fared like Heliodorus" (5:17-18). Suffering and even martyrdom are forms of discipline to ex- piate their sin so that they may be forgiven and not destroyed (6:12-16). Because of this theological understanding of his- tory, 2 Maccabees must emphasize the role of sinful Jews in bringing about their own suffering, and we need to take that bias into account.

In Hengel's case, religious biases have influenced his interpretations. This is most obvious in his last eleven pages of "summary," which are much more than summary. The implications drawn there go beyond the evidence he has brought to bear in the body of the book, and his discussion ranges considerably past the chronological period which is the subject of his book. His book begins by explaining that the study of Hellenistic Judaism is "one of the indispensable foundations of a true understanding of the New Testament."[43] In my opinion, his interest in the New Testament and in the origins of Christianity has influenced his interpretations of the events from Alexander through the Maccabean revolt. There is a tension throughout that period between those Jews who are attracted to assimilation and those more conservative ones who stress their separation from the gentiles. The conflict is a "struggle over the law."[44] According to Hengel, the victory of the separationists, represented by the triumph of the Maccabees and the rejection of the Hellenizing priesthood, led to an emphasis on the law and an "extreme sensitivity ... towards even an apparent usurpation of power over the law and the sanctuary" which "made it extremely difficult for the Jews to be governed by their own or foreign rulers."[45] The tendency to "segregation from non-Jews" and the "connection between nation and religion" were strengthened.[46] The attitude toward Torah became fixed so that "any fundamental theological criticism of the cult and law could no longer develop freely within Judaism." All of this meant that mainstream Judaism "inevitably misunderstood" the Christian gospel "as an attack on the supreme articles of Israelite faith or even as apostasy to paganism." "Creative, self-critical transformation" was impossible now because of the "strongly national and political colouring" of Judaism.[47] "Paul's struggle against circumcision and the law" was seen by Jews as a "betrayal of Judaism,"[48] whereas for Hengel it is absolutely necessary if the "eschatological and revolutionary" Christian movement is to fulfill its universalistic mission to the nations.[49] He says,

> In the Hellenistic period, say from the
> second half of the second century B.C.,
> Judaism was well on the way towards be-
> coming a *world religion* .... The anxious
> and zealous fixation on the letter of the
> Torah which we meet in Pharisaism was, of
> course, in manifest opposition to this ....
> A universal missionary consciousness could
> not freely develop in the face of this
> elemental impulse towards national self-
> preservation.[50]

Hengel attributes greater importance to the Hellenizers than they deserve, because as he describes them they espouse a position very similar to that of Paul over two centuries later.

It is wiser to regard the Hellenizers as only one faction in a religious conflict over assimilation, in a socio-economic conflict, and in a political conflict that involved not only the Seleucid and Ptolemaic kingdoms but a total shift in power toward Rome. They were only one group caught up in an interplay of forces that led to an outcome they did not intend. As Tcherikover says,

> The theologians (who have arrogated to
> themselves a monopoly of the study of
> Jewish history) entirely dismiss this
> whole long and complicated process in-
> volving ... the social antagonism be-
> tween the wealthy aristocratic Hellen-
> izers and the common people ... [and]
> the whole complex of political affairs.[51]

Tcherikover has supplemented our picture of the persecution by pointing out the extent to which it was a response to the Jewish rebellion rather than its cause (see above) and by calling our attention to the way social classes were related to the conflicts of the period. He has a Marxist interpretation of the struggle which emphasizes the conflict of interest between the "wealthy bourgeoisie"[52] and the poor people from the cities and rural areas. The former constituted the Hellenizers. Antiochus IV wanted their support in his struggle against Egypt, so the creation of the Jerusalem *polis* in 175 was to their mutual benefit. "From the day of its birth to its demise the Hellenizing party was bound up with the restricted group of Jerusalem capitalists."[53] Hellenization was a way for them to increase their wealth by giving them greater entree to the Greek world. When Jason received permission to register certain people in Jerusalem as "Antiochenes" (2 Macc 4:9), that gave Jason the right to decide who were worthy to be enrolled as citizens in the new *polis*. Surely this honor was limited to the wealthy aristocracy. The *ephebion* which is mentioned in the same verse was an expensive school, so the new institutions would have been dominated by the upper classes.[54] These changes fanned the flames of the class struggle because they gathered power more closely into the hands of the rich and widened the gap between them and the poor, who were excluded from the *polis*. He also says that the urban poor and the village population were "doubtless also linked ... for both classes had a common enemy."

Together they formed a "revolutionary movement."[55]

I would add that Dan 11:39 confirms the socio-economic dimensions of the Hellenization controversy. It says, "Those whom he (Antiochus IV) favours he will load with honour, putting them in office over the common people and distributing land at a price."

Reservations about some of Tcherikover's conclusions should be registered. He considers that the Hasidim had been "the chief scribes and authoritative interpreters of the regulations and commandments of the Torah." Then,

> The abolition of the "ancestral laws" by
> Jason made their entire class superfluous;
> if the Law of Moses was no longer to be the
> prevailing law in Israel, what point would
> there be in interpreting it? ... Hence the
> struggle of the Hasidim against the Hellen-
> izers was not merely an ideological struggle
> for the maintenance of the commandments of
> the Law, but also the struggle of an entire
> class for its existence.[56]

Tcherikover errs here in attributing an authority to the Hasidim which they could not have enjoyed this early. Also, it is wrong to tie their "existence" to their supposed authority in interpreting the law. Even in much later periods, when the rabbis had the power to give authoritative interpretations of the law, they did not depend on their positions and authority as means of livelihood. They had other means of support. Thus, even if there had been no one to consult the interpreter, the interpreter's existence was not at stake.

Also, the concept of a class struggle should not obscure the fact that the aristocrats were divided among themselves. The irregular turnover in the office of high priest, from Onias III to Jason to Menelaus, is an example of such a division. Those groups who initiated Hellenization were not unified.

When 2 Maccabees describes the personal rivalry in terms of religious differences, it oversimplifies because of its tendency to paint events and persons in stark black and white contrasts. Onias III is praised as "this benefactor of the holy city, this protector of his fellow-Jews, this zealot for the laws" (4:2), in contrast to Jason who "made the Jews conform to the Greek way of life" (4:10). Onias may or may not have been so zealous. When he fled for his life

he took refuge in the temple of Apollo and Artemis at
Daphne.[57]  Later his son built a schismatic Jewish temple
at Leontopolis in Egypt.[58]

The element of class struggle has also been overempha-
sized in the case of the Hasmoneans.[59]  The war can be portrayed as an uprising of the village peasants against the
urban aristocracy, but it is very likely that the Hasmonean
family itself was part of that urban aristocracy.  Even though
Modein seems to be their ancestral home (2 Macc 13:25), they
were a priestly family with connections in Jerusalem.  Thus,
after Apollonius' slaughter in Jerusalem, Judas Maccabeus fled
*from* there into the wilderness where he and his companions
survived on stray vegetation (2 Macc 5:27).  In this context
Modein is not even mentioned.

More important is Eddy's observation that they were a
wealthy, ambitious family, competing with Menelaus and the
Oniads for the high priesthood.[60]  In Modein, they were recognized as a family of substance.  Mattathias is "a leader, ...
a man of mark and influence," a candidate worthy of becoming
a friend of the King (1 Macc 2:17-18).  Their religious motivation was sincere, but Eddy points out that the Maccabees
kept fighting after Antiochus V rescinded the decrees against
Judaism, after Judas had recaptured the temple, and after a
high priest initially acceptable to the Hasidim (1 Macc 7:12-
14) had been appointed.  This indicates, he says, that the
Maccabees "must therefore have fought for more than religious
freedom."[61]  The Hasidim must have thought so, too, for they
soon separated from the Hasmoneans.

We may also note that the Maccabees were not supported
by all the rural population.  They needed to use force in the
countryside to tear down pagan altars and to force Jews to
circumcise their children.  Many of these unwilling Jews escaped  the Maccabees by taking refuge with gentiles (1 Macc
2:44-48), perhaps fleeing from the country to the cities.

The Hasmonean war is described for us in religious terms
because of the nature of our sources, but the army included
soldiers who carried "amulets sacred to the idols of Jamnia"
(2 Macc 12:40).

Several times I have referred to the military and political context of the Jewish persecution, and now I want to focus
on it in more detail.  No explanation of the multiplicity of
causes for the persecution can avoid this context.  Neither
Daniel nor 1 and 2 Maccabees take particular account of the
effect of Ptolemaic-Seleucid tension on the partisan divisions

among Jews, but the effects must have been considerable.
When Antiochus IV came to the throne, Palestine had been
part of his family's kingdom for only a quarter century.
The Ptolemies had not given up their claim that Palestine
belonged to them. During the period of Ptolemaic control,
some prominent members of the Tobiad family had been closely
associated with the Ptolemies, and the military colony in
trans-Jordan controlled by the Tobiads was presumably still
loyal to the Ptolemies. On the other hand, at least some of
the high-priestly Oniad family supported the Seleucids as
early as their annexation of Palestine in 198 B.C.E and
probably earlier.[62] Josephus says that the Jews welcomed
Antiochus III to Jerusalem and joined him in eliminating
the remnant of soldiers left in the citadel (*Ant.*, 12.133).
The Oniad high priest must have been involved in the negotiations with Antiochus III that led to the latter's very favorable grant of self-government and remission of taxes for the
Jews, already mentioned (*Ant.*, 12.138-146). This brief account oversimplifies the situation in the two families. Each
had divisions within itself so that brother opposed brother.
Clearly the Oniads had family members both opposed to and in
support of Hellenization, and both families had members who
differed among themselves in their sympathies toward the Ptolemies and Seleucids. Even this brief account, however, is
enough to show that Antiochus IV would have been very concerned about the political sympathies of his Jewish subjects.
This criterion would obviously have been much more important
to him than their religious leanings, and yet the sources upon
which we primarily depend do not mention this factor at all.
Hengel even suggests that Antiochus IV was so willing to depose Onias III in favor of his brother Jason because he sus-
pected Onias of Ptolemaic sympathies.[63] We have already noted
that it was in Egypt that his son built the schismatic temple,
which suggests Ptolemaic leanings. By contrast, 2 Maccabees
describes the difference between the two brothers solely in
religious terms.

When Josephus describes Antiochus' attack on Jerusalem
after Jason's rebellion in *J.W.*, 1.32, he says that the king
killed a large number of Ptolemy's supporters. Whether or
not Hengel is correct that Josephus is using a pro-Seleucid
source here,[64] surely it represents that perception of the
struggle that would have been uppermost in the mind of Antiochus. He had little or no interest in the religious differences between Jason and Menelaus.

Each in his own way, Mørkholm, Bunge, and Goldstein stress
the importance of Rome as the proper background for understanding the actions of Antiochus. Mørkholm describes in

convincing detail the close relationships between Antiochus
IV and the rest of the Greek world.  These relationships can
best be explained as a consequence of his need for allies
against the growing power of Rome on the one hand and, on
the other, the feelings of nationalism that were threatening
the unity of his kingdom.[65]  These nationalistic impulses
were already described a generation ago by J. W. Swain.[66]
In other words, the revolt of the Jews was not an isolated
phenomenon.  As John J. Collins points out, the Seleucids had
to contend with various nationalistic uprisings from at least
250 B.C.E., beginning with the Parthians.  It is likely that
the Elamite priests had fostered a religious revolt against
Antiochus III, because he accused them of being at war with
him.  He lost his life, in fact, while attacking an Elamite
temple.  A similar uprising took place during the reign of
Antiochus IV in 168 in Babylon.  Gold from the Esagila treasury had been appropriated for statues of Hellenized gods, and
"thieves"--probably nationalists with patriotic and religious
motivations--attacked the temple and removed the gold.[67]  Antiochus Epiphanes was engaged in a losing struggle to preserve
his prestige on his eastern and southern frontiers.  Arsacid
power in Babylonia began to emerge simultaneously with that
of the Hasmoneans.  The king must have hoped that the worship
of Zeus would allow the unification of local cults and serve
to counteract the centrifugal force of emerging nationalism.

Bunge adds to our understanding by identifying the
turning-point in Antiochus' royal career.  It was the Roman
victory over the Macedonians at Pydna in 168 which allowed
Rome to concentrate its attention eastward.  The "day of
Eleusis" took place right afterward, when the Romans forced
Antiochus to return from Egypt.[68]  Without the Roman interference, he would probably have seized the whole Ptolemaic
kingdom.

Bunge says that when Antiochus left Egypt, his security
was uppermost in his mind, so that he ordered Apollonius to
fortify an Acra for him in Jerusalem.  He also laid plans at
that time for a grand festival in Daphne, mentioned above, to
show that the Seleucids were not beaten.[69]  He could not afford, particularly now, to have a rebellion at his Egyptian
border.  He would be very prone to perceive any unrest in
Jerusalem as a danger to his own authority--even though the
rebellion may have begun as an internal civil war between
Jason and Menelaus over the high priesthood.

Bunge is less convincing when he suggests that 1 Macc
1:41 and 2 Macc 6:1 are specific reports of the king's invitation to the Jews to participate in his festival at Daphne.

"Besser und kürzer kann man die spätere Vereinigung aller
Götter in Daphne, die in gewisser Weise eine Vereinigung
aller Völker des Reiches darstellte, nicht beschreiben."[70]
Bunge says that we are in the dark about how the invitation
was received at Jerusalem, since the reports in both books
of Maccabees are colored by the later persecution. Thus
they maintain that the messengers urged the Jews to aposta-
size. We don't know what happened, "doch hat es den Anschein,
als ob dort eine Art totale 'Machtergreifung' erfolgte."[71]

The visit of the messengers became the occasion for the
Hellenizers to take possession of the temple under the protection of the Acra. Thus, he says, on the 25th of Kislev, they
brought an offering for the king's birthday.[72] This is the
profanation of the temple.

Bunge's explanation of the profanation is quite flimsy.
He has the king asking for one thing, which the Hellenizers
could easily have granted without much opposition, but instead
they do another thing, unrelated, which predictably causes revolt. That is, the king wanted sacred embassies (*theōriai*,
Polybius, *Histories*, 30.25,12) for his procession at Daphne,
including one from Jerusalem, presumably. The Hellenizers
could easily have complied. If 1 Macc 1:41 is related to the
invitation to the festival, then surely we ought to.note 1:
42-43, which says that many from Israel did, in fact, comply
with the king's order.[73] Antiochus would have been quite
satisfied, and would have had the show of political unity
that he wanted.

Instead, according to Bunge, the Hellenizers used the
arrival of the king's messengers as an excuse to seize the
temple, to build a new altar there, and to make an offering
in honor of the king's birthday. However, the Hellenizers
needed no excuse "von dem Tempel Besitz zu ergreifen."[74]
They already held it, and Menelaus was its high priest.
Secondly, Bunge has no reason to think that Antiochus' birthday fell on the 25th of the month; we do not even know the
year of his birth. It does seem to be true that a monthly
celebration of the king's birthday was held in Jerusalem
(2 Macc 6:7), which suggests that the new cult there was
connected personally to Antiochus IV as a cult of the founder
of the *polis*. Such cults of the founder were celebrated at
other *poleis* in the kingdom, and it is possible that the
events of 25 Kislev were connected to that cult. However,
birthday or not, the king could have been honored with a
traditional Jewish sacrifice as his father[75] and brother
(2 Macc 3:3) were and Darius before them (Ezra 6:10). The
suppression of Judaism is more complicated than that.

Lastly, if there were a connection between the festival at Daphne and the king's letter in 1 Macc 1:41, both 1 Maccabees and Bunge have misunderstood the nature of the festival. It was aimed to bolster Antiochus' prestige after his humiliation by Rome and to demonstrate the unity of his kingdom, but it did not involve a unity of religion. Polybius stresses the variety and quantity of images in the procession, as already noted. Also, most of the king's letter, as reported in 1 Macc 1:41-50, deals with local events having no relation to Daphne.

Goldstein's contribution is to point out that Antiochus copied the methods of Rome in dealing with his subject peoples. Both his political and his religious policies were based on what he had learned during his thirteen years as a hostage in Rome, according to Goldstein. Just as Roman citizenship was being granted about this time to non-Romans in order to win their loyalty, so Antiochus was copying them by creating communities of "Antiochene citizens" throughout his kingdom, including Jerusalem.[76] Thus, all we have said about the initiative of the Jewish Hellenizers, above, needs to be balanced by an awareness of the initiatives coming from Antiochus. Goldstein says that the conflict between the conservative Jews and the "Antiochenes" has similarities to conflicts in Babylon between "Antiochenes" and "natives"[77] and similarities to the experience of Roman citizens a few years later who found it "hazardous" to live among non-citizens.[78] Also, to confiscate Jewish property and to redistribute it to citizens, as Antiochus did (Dan 11:39; cf. 1 Macc 1:33-40), is comparable to Scipio Nasica's treatment of the Boii in 191. It was a deliberate policy in both cases, displacing troublemakers to provide room for supporters of the government.[79]

Thus, "Antiochus' policy toward the Jews down through the establishment of the Akra in 167 can be explained as an effort to use the patterns of Roman civic institutions to cope with the problems of the Seleucid empire."[80]

Goldstein notes that there is even some evidence of religious differences between the Antiochene and the non-Antiochene cities. At least nineteen cities were suddenly allowed to mint their own bronze coinage during the reign of Epiphanes. Some of those cities call their citizens "Antiochenes," and coins from those cities show only Zeus on their obverse sides, but coins from the non-Antiochene cities have local motifs.[81]

Goldstein goes on to compare Antiochus' suppression of Judaism to the suppression of the Bacchanalia that occurred while he was in Rome.[82] Goldstein has overstated this part

of his case, I believe. I am not at all persuaded that
Antiochus would confuse the worship of the God of Israel and
the worship of Bacchus.[83] The evidence is too strong that
the LORD was being associated with Baal Shamen and Zeus.
Antiochus thought that Judaism was a "subversive cult," but
it is less clear that the Romans attacked the Bacchanalia because it had "the earmarks of a revolutionary conspiracy."[84]
The account in Livy (*History of Rome*, 39.8-16), which is his
evidence, suggests that the Romans were motivated more by the
cult's immorality and the fear that Romans would be attracted
to it. The parallel breaks down at this point. It is true,
however, that both Jews and Bacchii were accused of ritual
murder and had similar propaganda directed against them, as
Goldstein has shown.[85]

He thinks he has found evidence that Antiochus tried to
suppress "philosophers," which Jews were considered to be,[86]
but the connections are not firm.

He also wants to connect Antiochus' cult at Jerusalem
with worship of a divine triad, such as Baal Shamen, the
father; Asherah or Anath, the "queen of heaven"; and Adonis-
Tammuz-Dionysius, the dying-rising son.[87] Unfortunately,
Bacchus is also identified with the latter god, and Goldstein
is not consistent in arguing that Antiochus also suppressed
his cult in Jerusalem and Babylon.[88]

He even suggests that the lapse of time between the
15th and 25th of Kislev in 1 Macc 1:54-59 may be related to
the Roman Senate's decree against the Bacchanalia, which allowed ten days for destroying places of worship, after the
decree was received.[89] This similarity of detail is probably
a coincidence. The events of the 15th and 25th of Kislev are
not analogous to receiving the Roman decree and acting upon
it.

It is true that in suppressing the Bacchanalia, the
Roman Senate allowed the old, "legitimate" cult of Bacchus
to be practiced. Goldstein believes that in favoring the
Hellenizers, Antiochus may have either intended or claimed
to be restoring the old, legitimate, and rational religion
of Moses, as it existed before it was corrupted by the introduction of circumcision, dietary laws, and "intolerance."[90]
This is possible, since the worship of Baal Shamen and the
practice of cultic prostitution were ancient, but the argument presupposes a great deal of sophisticated higher criticism on the part of Antiochus and his advisors.

In spite of my criticisms of Goldstein, he has given

the best explanation of Antiochus' motivation.[91] To the king, Jewish particularism was subversive and represented a threat to his political security.

It is ironic that Antiochus tried to use religion to unite his kingdom and to win the support of his subjects, but in the case of the Jews at least he only succeeded in alienating them, because he never understood the importance of the temple to Jews or the importance of their customs. What seemed to him to be a broadening of the worship in the temple was seen as desecration by observant Jews, and they were willing to risk their lives to restore the true worship of their God. Their loyalty enabled them to survive as a distinct, identifiable community. The worshippers of Zeus Olympius and Anath-Yahu have been absorbed long since and their deities are relics of history. During the Hellenistic period, Jewish syncretistic cults existed in the trans-Jordan, Asia Minor, Egypt, and the Bosporus,[92] but these groups have disappeared. Those who maintained their particularity survived.

## NOTES

1. Elias Bickermann, *Der Gott der Makkabäer: Untersuchungen über Sinn and Ursprung der makkabäischen Erhebung* (Berlin: Schocken, 1937).

2. Louis F. Hartman and Alexander A. Di Lella, *The Book of Daniel: A New Translation with Notes and Commentary* (AB 23; Garden City: Doubleday, 1978), 39, 40.

3. Emil Schürer, *The History of the Jewish People in the Age of Jesus Christ*, revised and edited by Geza Vermes and Fergus Millar, with Pamela Vermes, vol. I (Edinburgh: T. & T. Clark, 1973), 146.

4. Otto Mørkholm, *Antiochus IV of Syria* (Classica et Mediaevalia: Dissertationes, 8; Copenhagen: Gyldendalske Boghandel--Nordisk Forlag, 1966), 184. Polybius reports himself to be pro-Ptolemaic when the Egyptians ask for help in 169 against Antiochus IV (*Histories*, 29.23).

5. Antiochus is reported to have worn a Roman toga in his capital, and asked citizens to vote for him in city elections. Polybius (*Histories*, 26.1) considers this erratic,

but Mørkholm suggests that Antiochus may have been trying to create interest in public life, such as he had seen in Rome (*Antiochus IV*, 39, 40).

See also Joseph Ward Swain, "Antiochus Epiphanes and Egypt," *Classical Philology* 39 (1944), 73, n. 2.

6. Mørkholm, *Antiochus IV*, 96.

7. *Ibid.*, 187-191.

8. *Ibid.*, 184, 185.

9. M. Rostovtzeff, *The Social and Economic History of the Hellenistic World* (Oxford: Clarendon, 1941), vol. I, 437. See also 436, 502.

10. *Ibid.*, I, 439.

11. Martin Hengel, *Judaism and Hellenism: Studies in Their Encounter in Palestine During the Early Hellenistic Period*, trans. John Bowden (Philadelphia: Fortress Press, 1974), vol. I, 255-261.

12. Josephus, *Ant.*, 12. 143. Translations are from LCL (Ralph Marcus, Cambridge, Massachusetts: Harvard University, 1943). Horst R. Moehring has reminded us that Josephus is an apologist, trying to prove that his "nation" has been accepted by gentile emperors. He is not above forging "documents," so that he is not always a reliable source of information ("The Acta pro Judaeis in the Antiquities of Flavius Josephus: A Study in Hellenistic and Modern Apologetic Historiography," *Christianity, Judaism and Other Greco-Roman Cults: Studies for Morton Smith at Sixty*, ed. Jacob Neusner [Studies in Judaism in Late Antiquity, 12; Leiden: E. J. Brill, 1975], vol. III, 124-158). At the same time, these letters agree with our other information about Antiochus III. For example, 2 Macc 4:11 speaks of the "royal privileges" which Jews enjoyed in the generation prior to the Jewish alliance with Rome, undoubtedly referring to agreements made with Antiochus III. Marcus discusses the authenticity in detail (Appendix D of LCL 7) and concludes that the decree is genuine.

13. Hengel, *Judaism and Hellenism*, I, 268.

14. Mørkholm surveys the evidence and concludes that Antiochus IV made no significant changes in the central administration of his kingdom and its provincial organization

(*Antiochus IV*, 114).  If this is correct for his political
administration, it suggests that Antiochus would probably
not be likely to make religious changes either, unless, as
we shall see, he did so in response to particular circumstances.

15.  Hengel points out that there is evidence for the
worship of Zeus in Syria from the very beginning of the
Seleucid dynasty, and specifically worship of Zeus Olympius
from Seleucus IV.  Nor is the cult of the king new.  There
are priestly lists of that cult from the reign of Seleucus IV,
and Seleucus I called himself "Zeus Nicator," just as Antiochus I was called "Apollo Soter," (I, 286).  Mørkholm says
that "a state cult for the ruling king and his queen is attested from the reign of Antiochus III" (*Antiochus IV*, 74,
see also 122).  See also Victor A. Tcherikover, *Hellenistic
Civilization and the Jews*, trans. S. Applebaum (Philadelphia:
Jewish Publication Society, 1961), 180-182, 184.

16.  The new "Anchor Bible" on Daniel still accepts
this identification (Hartman and Di Lella, AB, 301), but there
seems to be no evidence for it, as Mørkholm has shown.  He
says, "The hypothesis that Antiochus IV identified himself
with Zeus Olympius was first advanced by E. R. Bevan in 1900
and has won a wide acceptance."  This identification was
based on Daniel 11 and some of Antiochus' coins.  "Contrary
to the opinion of Bevan, we do in fact not possess any coin
portraits of Antiochus IV impersonating Zeus Olympius.  The
coin type in question represents the Olympian god; any resem-
blance between the god and the king is purely accidental and
can be explained by the easy assumption that the same die
cutters were responsible for both portraits.  Moreover, the
epithet 'Nicephorus,' appearing on a number of coins, was
thought to apply to Zeus/Antiochus because the common reverse
type of the coins is a seated Zeus carrying a small Nike on
his extended right hand.  However, as the title 'Nicephorus'
is also found on coins with an Apollo reverse, it is better
taken in its common meaning 'victorious' and applied to Antiochus IV as victor in the war against Egypt.  Thus the
numismatic evidence for Antiochus IV's identification with
Zeus is seen to be non-existent, and once this is realized
the whole theory is ruined" (*Antiochus IV*, 130, 131).

Mørkholm has discussed the coins in more detail in his
older *Studies in the Coinage of Antiochus IV of Syria* (His-
torisk-filosofiske Meddelelser, 40:3; Copenhagen:  Det Konge-
lige Danske Videnskabernes Selskab, 1963), esp. 59-61, 68-74.

17.  Mørkholm, *Antiochus IV*, 132.

18. Hengel, *Judaism and Hellenism*, I, 286.

19. *Ibid.*, I, 285; II, 189, nn. 171-174. Mørkholm, *Antiochus IV*, 113, and *Studies*, passim.

20. Hengel, *Judaism and Hellenism*, I, 285. However, see the observation made about these coins by Jonathan A. Goldstein, *I Maccabees: A New Translation with Introduction and Commentary* (AB 41; Garden City: Doubleday, 1976), 115, discussed below.

21. Mørkholm, *Antiochus IV*, 127. Also see Bickermann, *Gott der Makkabäer*, 90.

22. E. Nestle, "Zu Daniel," *ZAW* 4 (1884), 247, 248.

23. Hengel, *Judaism and Hellenism*, I, 297.

24. In *Ep. Arist.* itself (16), all men are said to worship Zeus, but Jews address him by another name. See also M. Simon, "Jupiter-Yahvé," *Numen* 23 (1976), 40-66.

25. Tcherikover (*Hellenistic Civilization*, 200) is one of the many writers who says that Antiochus' decrees were not intended to end worship of YHWH. "The innovation consisted entirely in that the god was henceforth called by his Greek name Zeus Olympius .... Clearly Antiochus saw no profanation in this action, for the local god, Yahweh, could easily be identified with the Greek deity."

Mørkholm reminds us that when Antiochus acceded to Jason's request to make Jerusalem into a *polis*, he had just become king after living in Rome for thirteen years. "His knowledge of the state of affairs in Judaea must have been rather limited. More especially, he can hardly have had any deep understanding of the peculiarities of the Jewish religion. And why should he mistrust Jason, who was a Jew of the best family?" (*Antiochus IV*, 138).

26. B. A. Mastin, "Daniel 2:46 and the Hellenistic World," *ZAW* 85 (1973), 84.

27. *Ibid.*, 85-90.

28. Bickermann, *Gott der Makkabäer*, 120-127.

29. Mørkholm, *Antiochus IV*, 147, n. 41.

30. 2 Macc 6:2 is different enough from Josephus to indicate that the two versions of the story must come from

independent sources. Thus, their contradictions tend to
corroborate that something happened. The reference to "the
practice of the local inhabitants" in 2 Maccabees confirms
that the Samaritans took some sort of initiative in the renaming of the temple.

31. E.g., Bickermann, *Gott der Makkabäer*, 126.

32. E.g., Hengel, *Judaism and Hellenism*, I, 287.

33. 2 Macc 4:7-8. Josephus (*Ant.*, 12.240) gives
Menelaus, not Jason, credit for being the first to want to
abandon the Jewish law and "adopt the Greek way of life" (LCL),
but like both books of Maccabees, he assigns the initiative to
a Jewish high priest, not to Antiochus. Taking all the evidence into account, Jason is more likely than Menelaus to be
correct.

34. For example, Hengel, *Judaism and Hellenism*, I, 278;
Tcherikover, *Hellenistic Civilization*, 161, 180, 404-409; Mørkholm, *Antiochus IV*, 138, 116-118. Goldstein considers Antiochus
to be copying Rome, which had begun to extend Roman citizenship
through Italy (AB, 112-116). Most of his case is convincing,
as we shall see below, but Antiochus is also reviving a pattern
of founding Greek cities (or refounding old cities as *poleis*)
which had been established by Seleucus I and Antiochus I.

35. Tcherikover, *Hellenistic Civilization*, 168.

36. Hengel, *Judaism and Hellenism*, I, 73.

37. Tcherikover, *Hellenistic Civilization*, 165.

38. *Ibid.*, 164.

39. *Ibid.*, 186-191.

40. *Ibid.*, 191.

41. *Ibid.*, 187, 188.

42. *Ibid.*, 188.

43. Hengel, *Judaism and Hellenism*, I, 1.

44. *Ibid.*, I, 305. See also Morton Smith, *Palestinian
Parties and Politics That Shaped the Old Testament* (New York:
Columbia University, 1971), esp. 148-192.

45. Hengel, *Judaism and Hellenism*, I, 306.

46. *Ibid.*, I, 306, 307.

47. *Ibid.*, I, 309.

48. *Ibid.*, I, 307, 308.

49. *Ibid.*, I, 314.

50. *Ibid.*, I, 313.

51. Tcherikover, *Hellenistic Civilization*, 206.

52. *Ibid.*, 169.

53. *Ibid.*, 202.

54. *Ibid.*, 161, 162.

55. *Ibid.*, 192, 193.

56. *Ibid.*, 197; see also 125, 126.

57. 2 Macc 4:33. See also Hengel, *Judaism and Hellenism*, I, 277.

58. Josephus, *Ant.*, 13.62-79. See discussion in Tcherikover, 275-281, and Jochen Gabriel Bunge, *Untersuchungen zum zweiten Makkabäerbuch: Quellenkritische, literarische, chronologische und historische Untersuchungen zum zweiten Makkabäerbuch als Quelle syrisch-palästinensischer Geschichte im 2. Jh. v. Chr.* (Dissertation; Bonn: Rheinische Friedrich-Wilhelms-Universität, 1971), 555-595. The temple is sometimes attributed to the father because of an apparent confusion in the sources.

59. Tcherikover speaks of the Hasmonean family being derived from the "priestly democracy resident in the provincial towns." Even if their victory did not yet reach the proportions of "a social revolution," it was "an important democratization" of public life. "Members of humbler families took the places of the previous communal elders," *Hellenistic Civilization*, p. 221.

Despite my reservations about this characterization, I agree with Tcherikover's judgment that the uprising had been going on before the incident in Modein, and that the role of Mattathias was insignificant. He points out that 1 Maccabees plays down the role of Judas, who died childless, in order to underline the importance of Simon. The writer was court historian under John Hyrcanus, and he emphasizes John's father

Simon and his grandfather Mattathias, the founder of the dynasty, *Hellenistic Civilization,* pp. 204, 205.

60. Eddy says that the sons of Mattathias "undoubtedly risked their lives for the law of Moses, and this does show a measure of religious motivation; at the same time, I think, they wanted very badly to improve their position in respect to the other priestly families of Judah, or, in other words, to become high priests. This is what actually happened, and there is no reason for thinking that it was not a motive from the beginning. Their piety was tempered with ambition"-- Samuel K. Eddy, *The King is Dead: Studies in the Near Eastern Resistance to Hellenism, 334-31 B.C.* (Lincoln: University of Nebraska, 1961), 215.

61. *Ibid.,* 218.

62. Hengel, *Judaism and Hellenism,* I, 271-276. Josephus reports that Onias III withheld the tribute which was due Egypt, which may mean that he had Seleucid sympathies. As a consequence of his action, Joseph, a Tobiad, was given the right to collect the taxes in place of the high priest. See *Ant.,* 12.158-179.

63. Hengel, *Judaism and Hellenism,* I, 277.

64. *Ibid.,* I, 281.

65. Mørkholm, *Antiochus IV,* 51-63.

66. Swain, *Classical Philology,* 39 (1944), 75, 76, 79, 82. See also Eddy, *passim.*

67. John J. Collins, "Jewish Apocalyptic Against Its Hellenistic Near Eastern Environment," *BASOR* 220 (December 1975), 28.

68. Bunge, *Untersuchungen,* 470.

69. *Ibid.,* 471. See also his "Die Feiern Antiochus IV. Epiphanes in Daphne im Herbst 166 v. Chr.," *Chiron* 6 (1976), 53-71.

70. Bunge, *Untersuchungen,* 473.

71. *Ibid.,* 474.

72. *Ibid.,* 474, 475.

73. The Jewish delegation would have been hard-pressed

to find an image to bring to Antiochus' parade, but surely
that would not have been an issue. Hengel has shown that
the Greeks respected the Jewish avoidance of idols, I, 256-
259.

74. Bunge, *Untersuchungen*, 475.

75. Josephus, *Ant.*, 12.140. I am assuming here that
the provision by Antiochus III of "sacrificial animals, wine,
oil and frankincense," and grain and salt would have given
him the right to have prayers and sacrifices made on his behalf.

76. Jonathan A. Goldstein, "The Persecution of the Jews
by Antiochus IV," *Proceedings of the Sixth World Congress of
Jewish Studies*, ed. Avigdor Shinan (Jerusalem: World Union
of Jewish Studies, 1977), vol. I, 135, and AB, 112-116.

77. Goldstein, AB, 114, 122.

78. *Ibid.*, 121.

79. *Ibid.*, 123.

80. *Ibid.*, 125. See also *Sixth World Congress*, I, 135.

81. Goldstein, AB, 115.

82. *Ibid.*, 125-132.

83. *Ibid.*, 129-135.

84. *Ibid.*, 132.

85. *Ibid.*, 133, 134.

86. *Ibid.*, 126-129.

87. *Sixth World Congress*, I, 144-147; AB, 152-156.

88. *Ibid.*, 128, 131.

89. *Ibid.*, 139.

90. *Sixth World Congress*, I, 136, 137, 147; AB, 138-142,
156, 261, 262.

91. See also Bunge, *Untersuchungen*, 479, and Tcherikover, *Hellenistic Civilization*, 199.

92. See Hengel, *Judaism and Hellenism*, I, 308, and references.

# INDEX OF SUBJECTS

mystery cults, 197, 204
myth, mythology: literary function of, 33; in Canaanite
religion, 128-135, 144; in the ancient Near East, 142,
143, 147, 148; in relation to history, 179, 181, 187,
188, 189, 190, 194 (n. 45), 195 (nn. 46, 51), 253;
Israel's use of, 181, 182, 188, 189, 190, 191 (n. 15),
192 (nn. 17, 18), 246, 247, 256; use in apocalyptic,
246, 247, 251, 253, 256

Nabonidus, 199, 202, 214 (nn. 9, 10)
Naram-Sin of Akkad, 142
Nebuchadnezzar I, 183, 184, 185
Nebuchadnezzar II, 198, 201, 221, 236 (n. 16), 256
neo-Babylonian politics: and the exaltation of Marduk, 183,
184, 185; and Assyrian decline, 171; in the 6th century,
198, 199, 201, 202, 205; and the fall of Jerusalem, 221,
228
new criticism, 83, 84
New Year Festival, 109, 110
Ninurta, 109, 118 (n. 61), 119 (n. 66)
Nippur, 111, 142
Noah, 185; and the Israelite flood, 181, 182, 185
Nuzi texts, 11

*Odyssey*, 204
Onias III, 269, 270, 275, 276, 277, 278 (n. 62)
oral poetry: Sumerian, 28, 29, 34, 37; contemporary studies
in, 29, 55 (n. 27), 81; formulae in, 38, 39, 40, 42, 51;
Hebrew, 36, 37, 56 (nn. 34, 35, 36), 126
Osnappar, 228, 229

postexilic community, 224; politics in, 224, 225, 226, 227,
230, 233, 234, 260 (n. 48); Seleucid persecution of,
246, 248, 252; relation to apocalyptic eschatology, 248,
253, 254
pre-Socratics, 204, 205, 209
primitive democracy, 141, 142
Prophetic Speech of Marduk, 183, 184
prophets: visions of, 141, 148, 149, 151; lawsuits of, 141,
148, 149, 150, 151; messenger formulae of, 148, 149, 150,
151; conflicts of, 125, 130, 131, 134; at Mari, 149; of
salvation, 182, 184, 189, 193 (n. 34); of the exile,
180-190, 197, 201, 210, 250; at Delphi, 204; in the
postexilic period, 246, 247, 248, 252, 253, 255, 256,
259

# INDEX OF AUTHORS

Auscher, D., 215 (n. 21)

Avi-Yonah, M., 20 (n. 19)

Avigad, N., 20 (n. 18), 119 (n. 64)


Barr, J., 191 (n. 7)

Barthes, R., 84, 85, 88, 98 (n. 16), 99 (n. 23)

Beitzel, B. J., 76 (n. 72)

Bell, R., 21 (n. 28)

Ben-Sasson, H. H., 19 (n. 10)

Benveniste, E., 86

Bevan, E. R., 284 (n. 16)

Bickerman, E., 239 (n. 49), 263, 268, 269, 272, 282 (n. 1),
    285 (nn. 21, 28), 286 (n. 31)

Biggs, R. D., 175 (n. 24)

Birot, M., 75 (n. 57)

Björkman, G., 20 (n. 26), 23 (n. 54)

Blackmur, R. P., 98 (n. 13)

Boardman, J., 215 (n. 20)

Bodde, D., 212 (n. 5), 215 (n. 15)

Boehl, Fr., 119 (n. 65)

Böhl, F. M. Th., 70 (n. 15)

Boling, R. G., 114 (n. 20)

Booth, W., 84

Borger, R., 176 (n. 41), 177 (n. 50), 184, 185, 193 (nn. 27,
    28, 29, 31, 32), 213 (n. 8), 261 (n. 53)

Borges, J. L., 83

Bottero, J., 72 (n. 31)

Bousset, D. W., 257 (n. 1)

Bowra, C. M., 55 (n. 27)

Brewer, E., 1

Brezzi, P., 211 (n. 4)

Bright, J., 19 (n. 13), 21 (n. 32), 70 (n. 9), 111, 120
    (n. 82), 172 (n. 3), 177 (nn. 44, 45, 46)

Gadd, C. J., 54 (n. 19)

Galling, K., 225, 226, 238 (n. 38), 239 (n. 46)

Gaster, T. H., 145, 154 (n. 23)

Gese, H., 191 (n. 7)

Gevirtz, S., 22 (n. 40), 37, 56 (n. 36), 73 (n. 47), 115 (nn. 37, 38)

Ginsberg, H. L., 145, 153 (n. 16), 154 (n. 23)

Glueck, N., 61, 69 (n. 5), 71 (nn. 26, 28)

Goedicke, H., 115 (n. 35), 191 (n. 7)

Goetze, A., 75 (n. 67)

Goldstein, J. A., 277, 280, 281, 285 (n. 20), 286 (n. 34), 289 (nn. 76, 77, 78, 79, 80, 81, 82, 83, 84, 85, 86, 87, 88, 89, 90)

Gomes, P. J., 18 (n. 2)

Goossens, G., 214 (n. 9)

Gordis, R., 240 (n. 73), 241 (n. 76)

Gordon, C. H., 11, 127, 137 (n. 23), 215 (n. 19), 216 (n. 24)

Grant, F. C., 154 (n. 26)

Gray, J., 115 (n. 29), 116 (n. 40), 124, 125, 129, 131, 136 (n. 8), 137 (n. 11), 138 (nn. 27, 39), 154 (n. 26)

Grayson, A. K., 23 (n. 51), 73 (n. 48), 193 (n. 27), 256, 261 (nn. 53, 55)

Grelot, P., 70 (n. 15)

Gunkel, H., 82, 98 (n. 11)

Gunn, D. M., 182, 192 (nn. 19, 20), 193 (n. 36)

Gurney, O. R., 54 (n. 19), 55 (n. 21)

Gyles, M. F., 211 (n. 2)


Habel, N., 124, 137 (n. 10), 194 (n. 37)

Hallo, W. W., 18 (n. 5), 19 (nn. 15, 16), 20 (nn. 24, 25), 22 (nn. 36, 40), 23 (nn. 54, 56, 58, 59, 61), 24 (nn. 63, 64, 67), 26 (nn. 86, 88), 54 (n. 19), 57 (n. 48), 67, 74 (n. 50), 75 (nn. 58, 64, 68), 76 (nn. 69, 70, 72, 73, 74, 75, 77, 81), 116 (n. 45), 117 (n. 51), 119 (n. 63), 120 (nn. 76, 82), 152 (n. 7), 164, 173 (n. 9), 175 (n. 28), 176 (nn. 29, 30), 187, 188, 193 (n. 28), 194 (nn. 41, 42, 44, 45), 195 (n. 46), 218 (n. 43), 261 (n. 53)

Hamerton-Kelley, R. G., 261 (n. 51)

Hanson, P. D., 2, 18 (n. 6), 24 (nn. 68, 69, 70, 71, 72),
    25 (n. 78), 250, 251, 252, 253, 254, 255, 256, 259
    (nn. 33, 34, 35, 36), 260 (nn. 37, 38, 39, 40, 41, 43,
    44, 47), 261 (n. 50), 262 (n. 59)

Harland, J. P., 71 (n. 22)

Harrelson, W., 155 (n. 33), 194 (n. 39), 241 (n. 81)

Hartman, L. F., 282 (n. 2), 284 (n. 16)

Hauer, C., 118 (n. 53)

Hayes, J. H., 19 (nn. 9, 14), 22 (n. 43), 23 (n. 57), 71
    (n. 28), 72 (nn. 29, 34), 76 (n. 78), 114 (n. 19)

Heichelheim, F. M., 244 (n. 121)

Held, M., 56 (n. 36)

Hempel, J., 19 (n. 13), 181, 191 (n. 13)

Hengel, M., 264, 265, 269, 272, 273, 274, 277, 283 (nn. 11,
    13), 284 (n. 15), 285 (nn. 18, 19, 20, 23), 286 (nn.
    32, 34, 36, 43, 44), 287 (nn. 45, 46, 47, 48, 49, 50,
    57), 288 (nn. 62, 63, 64), 289 (n. 73), 290 (n. 92)

Herrmann, S., 69 (n. 1), 70 (n. 11), 172 (n. 3)

Hinz, W., 213 (n. 8)

Hodges, H., 216 (n. 29), 217 (n. 38)

Hoftijzer, J., 156 (n. 44)

Holladay, J. S., 156 (n. 39)

Hölscher, G., 226, 239 (n. 44)

Hooke, S. H., 119 (n. 67)

Horn, S. H., 176 (n. 31)

Huffmon, H. B., 118 (n. 52), 150, 156 (n. 41)

Huizinga, J., 6, 7, 20 (n. 27)

Humphreys, W. L., 26 (n. 84)

Hunger, H., 261 (n. 54)

Hyatt, J. P., 262 (n. 59)

Jackson, B. S., 22 (n. 35)

Jacobsen, T., 31, 32, 33, 39, 54 (n. 18), 55 (nn. 20, 22),
    56 (nn. 38, 39), 141, 142, 151 (n. 4), 152 (nn. 5, 6,
    8, 9, 11)

Kraus, H.-J., 120 (n. 74)
Kupper, J.-R., 70 (n. 15)

LaDriere, J. C., 87, 99 (n. 30)
Laessøe, J., 53 (n. 8), 152 (n. 12)
Lambert, W. G., 28, 53 (n. 10), 152 (n. 12), 183, 191 (n. 7), 192 (nn. 24, 25), 193 (nn. 26, 27), 261 (n. 53)
Lance, H. D., 163, 174 (n. 20), 175 (n. 21)
Landsberger, B., 27, 75 (n. 58)
Lapp, P. W., 174 (n. 20)
Larsen, M. T., 74 (n. 53)
Leach, E., 85, 99 (n. 22)
Leemans, W. F., 74 (n. 54), 76 (n. 69)
Lehman, R. P., 21 (n. 31)
Leiman, S. Z., 24 (n. 75)
Lemaire, A., 20 (n. 21)
Lemaire, P., 241 (n. 73)
Levenson, J. R., 215 (n. 16)
Lévi-Strauss, C., 33, 84, 85,
Levine, B. A., 19 (n. 17), 238 (n. 36)
Lewis, C. S., 79, 97 (n. 1)
Lewy, J., 109, 118 (nn. 57, 61)
Lieberman, S. J., 24 (n. 63)
Long, B. O., 56 (n. 34)
Lord, A. B., 35, 36, 38, 55 (nn. 27, 29, 30, 31, 32)
Lubbock, P., 82, 98 (n. 13)
Luckenbill, D. D., 240 (n. 70)
Ludwig, T. M., 181, 182, 192 (nn. 16, 18)
Lundbom, J. R., 260 (n. 44)
Lutz, H.-M., 120 (n. 74)

Maass, F., 72 (n. 35)
Machinist, P., 114 (n. 17), 179, 190 (n. 2), 193 (n. 28)

Malamat, A., 3, 16, 24 (nn. 73, 74), 67, 71 (n. 25), 74 (n. 55), 75 (nn. 64, 65), 76 (n. 76), 116 (n. 44), 152 (n. 11), 154 (n. 28), 170, 177 (n. 53), 178 (nn. 54, 58, 59), 240 (n. 71)

Mallon, A., 117 (n. 48)

Malten, L., 21 (n. 30)

Mann, T. W., 179, 188, 190 (n. 3), 194 (n. 43), 195 (nn. 46, 47, 48, 49)

Marcus, R., 283 (n. 12)

Mason, R. A., 261 (n. 51)

Mastin, B. A., 267, 285 (nn. 26, 27)

Mays, J. L., 155 (n. 32)

Mazar, B., 77 (nn. 86, 87), 107, 112 (n. 2), 115 (n. 31), 116 (n. 43), 117 (n. 48), 119 (n. 65), 231, 232, 242 (n. 90), 243 (nn. 103, 108)

Meinhold, A., 25 (n. 84)

Millar, F., 263, 282 (n. 3)

Millar, W., 81, 262 (n. 59)

Millard, A. R., 28, 53 (n. 10), 152 (n. 12)

Miller, G., 24 (n. 75)

Miller, J. M., 19 (nn. 9, 14), 22 (n. 43), 23 (n. 57), 71 (n. 28), 72 (nn. 29, 34), 76 (n. 78), 113 (n. 15), 114 (n. 19)

Moe, H. A., 1, 18 (n. 1)

Moehring, H. R., 283 (n. 12)

Moran, W., 55 (n. 20), 56 (nn. 38, 39), 106, 115 (nn. 35, 36, 40), 151 (n. 4), 155 (nn. 35, 36)

Morenz, S., 26 (n. 85)

Morgenstern, J., 146, 154 (n. 24)

Mørkholm, O., 263, 264, 277, 282 (n. 4), 283 (nn. 5, 6, 7, 8, 14), 284 (nn. 15, 16, 17), 285 (nn. 19, 21, 25, 29), 286 (n. 34), 288 (n. 65)

Mowinckel, S., 25 (n. 76)

Muhly, J. D., 23 (n. 60), 74 (n. 56), 216 (n. 24)

Muilenburg, J., 29, 54 (n. 13), 86, 99 (n. 27), 155 (n. 30), 194 (n. 40)

Zeitlin, S., 240 (n. 73)

Zimmerli, W., 72 (n. 35)

Zimmern, H., 119 (nn. 65, 66)

# INDEX OF BIBLICAL REFERENCES

## I. TANAK

II. APOCRYPHA

## III. NEW TESTAMENT